# Entangling Relations

PRINCETON STUDIES IN INTERNATIONAL HISTORY AND POLITICS

*Series Editors*
*Jack L. Syder and Richard H. Ullman*

RECENT TITLES

# Entangling Relations

AMERICAN FOREIGN POLICY
IN ITS CENTURY

*David A. Lake*

PRINCETON UNIVERSITY PRESS

PRINCETON, NEW JERSEY

Copyright © 1999 by Princeton University Press
Published by Princeton University Press, 41 William Street,
Princeton, New Jersey 08540
In the United Kingdom: Princeton University Press, Chichester, West Sussex

*Library of Congress Cataloging-in-Publication Data*

Lake, David A., 1956–
Entangling relations : American foreign policy in its century /
David A. Lake.
p.   cm. — (Princeton studies in international history and politics)
Includes bibliographical references (p.    ) and index.
1. United States—Foreign relations—20th century.   2. National
security—United States—History—20th century.   I. Title.
II. Series.
E744.L27   1999   327.73—dc21   98-37330   CIP

ISBN 0-691-05990-X (cloth : alk. paper). — ISBN 0-691-05991-8
(pbk. : alk. paper)

This book has been composed in Berkeley

The paper used in this publication meets the minimum requirements of
ANSI/NISO Z39.48-1992 (R1997) (*Permanence of Paper*)

http://pup.princeton.edu

Printed in the United States of America

1   3   5   7   9   10   8   6   4   2
1   3   5   7   9   10   8   6   4   2
(Pbk.)

*To my parents*

# CONTENTS

# FIGURES AND TABLES

# PREFACE

THIS BOOK has had a long gestation. Stimulated by postmodern and, later, constructivist criticisms of the statist nature of international relations theory, I began to reconsider the patterns and determinants of political authority within the international system. The longer I thought about these issues, the more convinced I became that the critics were right—and wrong. The organization of political authority into separate, sovereign states could not be taken for granted, and the structure of political authority within the international system was an important topic for inquiry. Indeed, once I began to look for it, I saw not a world of homogenous states but a world of rich, complex, and variegated patterns of political authority. I also found that how political authority was organized mattered deeply for foreign policy choices, even in the contemporary era. At the same time, I concluded that explaining these patterns did not require abandoning rationalist, positivist theory.

I wrote the first paper on the ideas that would become this book in 1987. In the years since I have incurred an enormous number of professional and personal debts. I was first introduced to theories of relational contracting at the Tuesday Political Economy lunch at UCLA. This remarkable institution, and the people who composed it between its founding and 1992, did much to shape this book through what we read and argued about and by subjecting several early chapters to the usual thrashing. Jeff Frieden, as always, was both my hardest and most patient critic. At UCSD, Peter Gourevitch has offered insightful guidance.

I am grateful for the constructive advice and even the harsh criticisms I have received from friends, colleagues, and sometimes anonymous participants in seminars around the globe. Richard Betts, Joseph Grieco, Peter Katzenstein, Robert Keohane, Paul Papayoanou, Robert Powell, Jack Snyder, and Stephen Walt read the penultimate draft of the manuscript. Although too many colleagues provided comments and assistance to thank each individually, I want to acknowledge Michael Hiscox, Jeffrey Legro, Andrew Moravcsik, Ronald Rogowski, Richard Rosecrance, Arthur Stein, Michael Tierney, Celeste Wallander, and Beth Yarbrough for especially helpful comments on various chapters. I had many outstanding research assistants on this project, including Risa Brooks, Scott Bruckner, Kathleen Hancock, Steven Lobell, and Adam Stulberg; I am especially grateful to Matt Baum for his assistance on the statistical portion of Chapter 7.

I am pleased to acknowledge the financial assistance of the academic senates at UCLA and UCSD, as well as the Center on International Relations at

UCLA. The University of California's Institute on Global Conflict and Cooperation provided substantial support before, during, and after my tenure as research director. None of these individuals or institutions is responsible for the errors remaining in this book.

Portions of this book appeared in an earlier form as "Anarchy, Hierarchy, and the Variety of International Relations," *International Organization* 50, 1 (Winter 1996): 1–33; published here with the permission of MIT Press, Cambridge, MA. I am also grateful to Malcolm Litchfield at Princeton University Press for seeing the value in this book, and to Margaret Case for her outstanding copyediting.

I am very grateful to my family for their encouragement over the years. My children, Brenden and Dylan, deserve special thanks. They have lived with this book their entire lives, and have suffered the response "I'm sorry, I have to work" to many requests. I hope one day they experience the joy that comes from the passionate pursuit of ideas. As ever, I am profoundly indebted to my wife, Wendy, for her love and support.

# Entangling Relations

## Chapter 1

# INTRODUCTION

IN HIS FAREWELL ADDRESS to the country he had led through war and its first years of independence, President George Washington warned his fellow citizens against permanent alliances in the conduct of foreign affairs. "Why," he asked, "by interweaving our destiny with that of any part of Europe, entangle our peace and prosperity in the toils of European ambition, Rivalship, Interest, Humour, or Caprice?"[1] In his inaugural address five years later, President Thomas Jefferson echoed Washington's warning and declared the principles of America's foreign policy to be "peace, commerce and honest friendship with all nations, entangling alliances with none."[2] The vision outlined by Washington, Jefferson, and other statesmen of the time was emphatically not a policy of isolationism, of withdrawal from international affairs. Reacting against the Franco-American alliance, necessary during the struggle for independence but now threatening to entrap the United States into the revolutionary wars then unfolding in Europe, the founding fathers argued only for a policy of strict unilateralism in world politics.[3]

This injunction against foreign entanglements was elevated, over time, into an almost sacred principle of American policy. Repeated in subsequent pronouncements, including the famous Monroe Doctrine, it became the standard against which nearly all foreign policy initiatives were measured. Although it did not stop the United States from expanding across the continent and incorporating new territories into the union, and it did not prevent the country's hesitant steps toward an overseas empire at the turn of the century, the principle of nonentanglement remained the guiding light of America's relations with other sovereign powers. Even in World War I, President Woodrow Wilson insisted that the United States fight only as an "associated" and not an allied power.

Over the course of what publisher Henry Luce dubbed the "American century," the United States has been forced time and again to reassess its relationship with the world. Since World War I, there have been three defining moments in American foreign policy. In each, the United States has had to decide whether to cooperate with others in the pursuit of security and, if so, how to craft relationships to safeguard its interests. First, in 1919 and

---

[1] Reprinted in Gilbert 1961, 145.
[2] Quoted in LaFeber 1994, 54.
[3] On the diplomacy of this period, see Perkins 1993, 81–110.

1920, after a long, thoughtful, and occasionally bitter debate, the United States rejected membership in the League of Nations and reaffirmed its historic policy of unilateralism. This "lone hand" foreign policy lasted for over two more decades, eventually dissolving only in the heat of war. Second, between 1947 and 1949, the country turned decisively toward international security cooperation. Breaking with tradition, the United States entered into permanent alliances in both Europe and the Pacific; and while granting the Philippines independence, it simultaneously forged a new empire in Micronesia. These unprecedented security relationships endured throughout the Cold War, and became almost as deeply ingrained in America's philosophy of foreign affairs as Washington's original maxim. Finally, today, a new form of security cooperation based on ad hoc, American-led coalitions is emerging. As revealed in the Persian Gulf War and the humanitarian intervention in Somalia, the United States has demonstrated an unprecedented willingness to work with other states and, more importantly, to work within the international consensus on the proper goals and means of foreign policy. Nonetheless, this new form of security cooperation is still being contested. The future of American security cooperation remains cloudy.

In these defining moments, the issues have not been who or what threatened the United States—on this, there was actually fairly widespread agreement. Rather, in each, the United States has wrestled with the problem of how best to manage security cooperation and build effective relationships with foreign partners. Two specific questions have loomed large. Should the United States pursue its security unilaterally or in cooperation with others? And if the latter, how can its interests be best protected against opportunism by untrustworthy partners? Instead of seeing foreign policy as simply the product of threats in the international system or domestic politics, I argue that policy was shaped in important ways by the benefits and costs for the United States of alternative security relationships with its partners. Central to the choice of cooperation and the form it was to take are the gains from pooling resources and efforts with others, the expected costs of opportunistic behavior by partners, and the costs of monitoring, safeguarding, and enforcing alternative security relationships.

In this study, I attempt to interpret these defining moments of American foreign policy and to understand the choices made. I develop a general theory of security relationships, summarized below and developed in detail in Chapters Two and Three. Seen through the lens of this theory, American foreign policy looks different: for instance, the United States broke with its historic policy of unilateralism after World War II, I argue, not simply because of the Soviet threat but because of the then larger gains and lower risks of security cooperation. Old debates are brought into clearer focus, including the mysterious failure of the United States to ratify the League of Nations covenant. Finally, certain features of the foreign policy terrain are defined more sharply; the geographically small but analytically important anomaly of the American empire in Micronesia is explained, as is the current willingness of the United States, despite its nearly unprecedented power and status, to form international coalitions and work within international institutions.

This study of American foreign policy and the theory that guides it also have broader implications for our understanding of international relations. Security relationships take a variety of forms, some relatively hierarchic, like the Trust Territory of the Pacific, others relatively anarchic, like NATO. Yet, most analysts typically concentrate on an extremely attenuated range of international relationships, studying alliances or empires, for instance, but rarely both together. In order to offer a complete explanation of policy, the full range of alternatives must be specified and their costs and benefits compared. Even when concerned with only a single type of security relationship—say, an alliance—analysts must place that relationship into a spectrum of other possibilities. By artificially truncating the range of variation, scholars significantly—if unwittingly—bias their assessments of international cooperation. Not only does disciplinary specialization blind scholars to other parts of international relations but it also causes them to misinterpret what they see.

## Understanding International Security Relationships

To explain the choice of security relationships, I draw upon a central metaphor in which polities are understood as firms producing security.[4] In choosing how to produce, polities may act alone, as in unilateralism, or cooperate with others. If they choose to cooperate, polities may enter into "arms-length" relationships, as in alliances between two sovereign states, integrate their production in some hierarchy, as in empires, or construct some intermediate relationship between the two. In this way, unilateralism is akin to production within a single firm, alliances are analogous to joint production by separate and independent firms, and empires are similar to integration within firms—with the modern, multidivisional corporation being the closest analog. This metaphor has been employed with great effect in economic history and, especially, the study of property rights and institutions.[5] It allows us to tap directly into theories of relational contracting, most developed in economics, to understand broader forms of political organization. I extend the key insights to international security relations.

Cooperation is defined here as the pooling of resources and efforts in pursuit of some joint goal by two (or more) polities. International security

---

[4] For reasons developed in Chapter 2, polities not states are the basic units of analysis in this study.

[5] Lane 1979; North 1981.

affairs are commonly perceived as the realm of struggle and conflict, not cooperation. This may be true between antagonists.[6] It is certainly not true between polities brought together by common opposition to the expansionist aims of others, the starting point for the analysis here. When polities cooperate, in turn, they must choose some relationship to govern or regulate their interactions. Security relationships have actually been quite prevalent historically, suggesting that the range of security cooperation may be broader than is often recognized.

Security relationships can take many forms, and vary along a continuum from anarchy to hierarchy. In anarchic relationships, such as alliances, the parties are formally equal. As Kenneth Waltz writes about international relations in general, under anarchy "none is entitled to command; none is required to obey."[7] Even though the polities may agree to perform certain joint actions, including commitments to come to the other's aid in event of an attack, they remain free to make all other political decisions, including how to interpret the terms of their agreement. Formal equality does not imply that the polities possess equal capabilities, power, or influence over one another or world affairs. Rather, alliances are simply authority relationships in which each party recognizes the other as possessing full and autonomous rights to make political decisions. This is defined more formally in Chapter 2 as full residual rights of control.

In hierarchic security relationships, such as empires, one party is formally subordinate to the other; in hierarchic relationships, to reverse Waltz's aphorism, one party is entitled to command, the other is required to obey. In an empire, for instance, the subordinate polity is not free to make its own political decisions; rather, the dominant state decides policy for both and interprets the terms of the cooperative undertaking according to its own designs. Like alliances, empires are authority relationships. In such hierarchic relations, however, the parties recognize, even if they do not necessarily accept, that the subordinate member possesses only a highly abridged ability to decide its own political fate. In other words, the subordinate polity has only highly constrained or, perhaps, no residual rights of control.

In between these two extremes is a variety of intermediate security relationships characterized by increasing restrictions on the subordinate members' ability to reach independent decisions. In spheres of influence, even when they remain aloof from the dominant state, subordinate polities lack the ability to enter into security relationships with other, third parties. The Monroe Doctrine, proclaimed by the United States in 1823 to limit European ties with the newly independent states of Latin America, is a classic example

---

[6] Even in intense struggles, however, there may be mutual restraints that constitute a weak form of international cooperation; see Legro 1995.

[7] Waltz 1979, 88.

of a sphere of influence. In protectorates, subordinate polities cede their ability to conduct foreign policy to dominant states. During much of Britain's imperial reign in South Asia, the so-called Native or princely states of India actually remained independent but, as protectorates, gave control over their foreign and defense policies to London. And in informal empires, dominant states exercise substantial but incomplete decision-making authority over both domestic and foreign affairs in their subordinate polities. The Soviet Union maintained an informal empire over much of Eastern Europe during the Cold War.

As the examples suggest, all of these security relationships have been employed at one time or another. International politics is a rich tapestry of relationships. The choices before polities are between unilateralism and cooperation, and within the latter, between more anarchic and more hierarchic security relationships. The appropriate question for both analysts and practitioners alike is not "Why do countries ally?" but rather, "Why do countries ally rather than act unilaterally, build an empire, or form, say, a protectorate?"

The choice between unilateralism and cooperation, and among alternative forms of security cooperation, I argue, is determined by three primary factors: joint production economies, the expected costs of opportunism, and governance costs. Each of these variables is discussed in detail in Chapter 3. All three are necessary components of any complete explanation.

When joint production economies exist, the pooling of resources by two polities produces more security than the sum of their individual efforts; the two polities can thereby enjoy more security for the same cost or the prior level of security at less cost to themselves. Joint production economies are necessary for polities to cooperate at all: as cooperation is costly, for reasons to be outlined shortly, there must be some benefit that is not available through unilateralism. The greater the gains from joint production, in turn, the more likely polities are to cooperate.

Gains from joint production arise in three ways, all illustrated here with examples from the Cold War (discussed in Chapter 5). First, technology influences the costs of projecting force over distance. For instance, the technological innovations that occurred during World War II—such as the long-range bomber and atomic weapons—substantially reduced the costs of projecting force but nonetheless required forward bases for their effective use. As a result of these innovations, the gains from cooperation increased substantially. Second, the production of security for one polity often produces benefits for other polities as well, much as American efforts after 1945 to deter possible Soviet expansionism created benefits for both the United States and potential targets in Europe and Asia. By coordinating their efforts—or, in economic parlance, "internalizing" their positive externalities—polities may be able to reduce redundant efforts and share costs, lowering joint defense burdens from their unilateral levels. "Burden sharing" was a key feature in many of America's security relationships after World War II. Third, pooling resources and efforts opens up the possibility of a division of labor between polities. As in other areas of activity, security cooperation can produce mutual rewards through specialization and exchange. The Cold War witnessed a limited division of labor between the United States and its European allies, with the former taking responsibility for the nuclear deterrent and naval forces and the latter for land forces and tactical air power. As the examples here suggest, the increase in joint production economies during and after World War II was an important force behind the switch in American policy from unilateralism to cooperation. Some gains from joint production must exist for cooperation to emerge.

In all cooperative undertakings, polities face a risk that their partners will act opportunistically, behavior that Oliver Williamson defines as "self-interest seeking with guile."[8] In international relations, opportunism can take the form of abandonment, where the partner shirks or fails to live up to an agreement; entrapment, where the polity is drawn by its partner into actions and conflicts it would otherwise avoid; and exploitation, where the partner alters the terms of a relationship to extract a better deal. In any of these forms, opportunism by one's partner imposes costs upon a polity. The greater the costs likely to be imposed by such behavior, the less likely polities are to cooperate, in general, and when they do cooperate, the more likely polities are to insist upon more hierarchical relationships to control better the behavior of their partners.

The actual cost of opportunism, when it occurs, is determined by the degree to which assets are relationally specific—that is, the extent to which they possess more value in one relationship than another. Ports in strategic locations are a prime example. The forward-based defense strategy employed by the United States after 1945, for instance, depended upon a seamless web of naval bases in the western Pacific (see Chapter 5). Any gap might allow foreign forces to slip through the perimeter, and thus vitiate the entire strategy. If there had been a large number of first-class sites, no specific assets would have been created by this strategy; if the United States was denied a base on one island, it might, under these favorable circumstances, simply move next door. In actuality, however, there was only a limited number of sites, principally Okinawa, the Philippines, and Guam. Each was essential to the forward defense, as the absence of any one would open up consequential gaps in the perimeter. Since each partner was thus necessary to the overall success of the strategy, each could "hold up" the United States and potentially expropriate all of the benefits from cooperation. Thus, here as elsewhere, the costs of opportunism threatened to be substantial precisely because of the specific nature of the assets in question.

[8] Williamson 1985, 30.

The ability of a partner to act opportunistically, in turn, is determined by the type of security relationship, or "governance structure," the parties choose to construct. In relatively anarchic security relationships, such as alliances, both parties retain substantial decision-making capabilities, and thus can act opportunistically if they choose. Despite promises, say, to come to one another's aid, states within an alliance are the ultimate judges of their obligations. In more hierarchic security relationships, on the other hand, one party exerts substantial control over the other, and the subordinate polity, at the extreme, lacks the ability to decide to act in ways that contravene the interests of the dominant member. When England declared war in 1914 and again in 1939, for instance, Britain's colonies were automatically placed at war with Germany.

For any given level of asset specificity, then, the expected costs of opportunism, after the fact, decline with greater hierarchy (but at different rates). It is precisely to constrain the decision-making capabilities of partners and to reduce the probability that they will act opportunistically that leads polities, beforehand, to prefer and attempt to construct hierarchic security relationships. When few specific assets are at risk, alliances and other relatively anarchic security relationships may be adequate to safeguard the interests of the parties. When more specific assets are at risk, however, more hierarchic relationships may be necessary for cooperation to proceed.

Polities may also choose to invest in more specific assets as relational hierarchy increases, if such assets also expand the joint production economies. Joint production economies are partly determined by the environment. Yet polities choose whether to invest in a division of labor, internalize positive externalities, or use particular technologies, each of which nearly always creates specific assets between partners. As the probability that their partner will act opportunistically declines with greater hierarchy, polities may increase their asset-specific investments. In this case, even though the probability of opportunism declines with relational hierarchy, the expected costs of opportunism may remain constant. The net benefits of cooperation, however, will increase as polities benefit from greater joint production economies. In this way, the joint production economies are partially endogenous to the choice of security relationships.

Governance costs are incurred in creating and maintaining all security relationships. Crafting an agreement, monitoring the behavior of one's partner, and enforcing the security relationship all consume resources that could be put to other uses. Although the expected costs of opportunism generally decline with relational hierarchy, governance costs for the dominant party increase with greater hierarchy. It is the expanded control acquired by the dominant state over the subordinate polity that makes hierarchy attractive, but this greater control only comes at an increasing price.

Governance costs arise in three ways. First, in ceding decision-making authority to the dominant state, the subordinate party gives up its valued freedom. To gain voluntary compliance, dominant states must not only expend resources to monitor and enforce their writs in their subordinate partners, but they must also compensate them for their lost autonomy. Ironically, in a purely voluntary relationship, the costs of subjugation are borne not by the subordinate polity but by the dominant state. The greater the subordination, the higher the costs to the dominant partner. Although combined with a measure of coercion, the resource transfers from the Soviet Union to the members of its informal empire in Eastern Europe provide a particularly clear example of these governance costs. In 1988, just as Moscow was reevaluating its imperial relationships, the Soviet subsidy to Eastern Europe was estimated—by the Russians themselves—to be $17 billion per year.[9] Yet even this was not enough to keep the East Europeans from fleeing the informal empire at the first opportunity.

Second, by ceding decision-making authority to the dominant state, the subordinate polity opens itself to even greater opportunism by its partner. To gain the voluntary compliance of the subordinate polity, then, the dominant state must impose costly constraints on its own freedom of action to signal its benign intent and limit its potential for opportunism. Again, in a purely voluntary relationship, the costs of subjugation fall on the dominant state. It must convince the subordinate polity that, despite its now greater decision-making authority, it will not take advantage of the latter's vulnerable and exposed position. The more authority it wields over the subordinate polity, the greater and more costly are the constraints it must impose upon itself. During the Persian Gulf War, for instance, the entry of the United States into the region transformed Saudi Arabia and other local states into American protectorates. To tie the hands of the Americans, the Gulf states desired a broader coalition, and to demonstrate its commitment not to exploit them, the United States not only acquiesced in but eagerly expanded upon this desire. The coalition, in turn, strongly constrained the conduct and goals of the United States in the eventual war, especially in the hasty termination of the ground war (see Chapter 6).

Finally, coercion is a substitute for voluntary relationships between polities. Coercion allows states to sidestep the kinds of concessions and compromises that would otherwise be required in voluntary negotiations between two parties. Nonetheless, using coercion to govern relationships is costly. The more hierarchic the relationship, the greater are the sidepayments and constraints that would otherwise be necessary; it follows that coercion, when used as a substitute for voluntary negotiations, must also escalate with hierarchy. As this implies, violence has historically been an important instrument in the process of empire building. Empires have extended furthest when one side possessed disproportionate power capabilities, as in the European ex-

---

[9] Stone 1995, 45. See also Bunce 1985 and Lake 1997.

pansion into the developing regions of the world, or when the costs of coercion were already paid for other valued reasons, as in the Soviet Union's informal empire in Eastern Europe, acquired in the process of defeating Germany.[10]

Together, joint production economies, the expected costs of opportunism, and governance costs interact to determine the optimal security relationship and, in turn, the relative benefits of unilateralism and cooperation. Unilateralism is the default policy, adopted whenever the expected costs of opportunism and governance costs of the optimal security relationship exceed the joint production economies. Alliances and other relatively anarchic security relationships are most likely when there are substantial gains from joint production, little risk from pooling resources with others, and only slight costs to monitoring and enforcing relationships. When there is little benefit to be gained from greater hierarchy, the escalating governance costs are likely to deter consideration of such alternatives. Empires and other relatively hierarchic security relationships, on the other hand, are most likely when joint production economies are large, the expected costs of opportunism are high and fall significantly with greater hierarchy, and governance costs are low and increase slowly with hierarchy. Under these conditions, there are, again, substantial gains from joint production, but there are now substantial risks to cooperation. As long as these risks can be successfully mitigated through greater hierarchy at acceptable cost, there are strong incentives for the emergence of empire or some similar security relationship.

As this discussion implies, it is the combined effect of the variables that determines the choice of policy. Even large joint production economies, for instance, may not produce cooperation if the expected costs of opportunism and governance costs are larger still. Situations like this will appear almost paradoxical to outside analysts, with possibly "obvious" gains from cooperation given up by polities who cannot "trust" one another sufficiently. This merely emphasizes the importance of considering all factors, as polities themselves are likely to do. Likewise, if governance costs are sufficiently low, empires may emerge even when there are few gains from joint production and only minor expected costs of opportunism. As often claimed about Britain's nearly global expansion in the nineteenth century, such empires would appear to have been acquired in "a fit of absentmindedness," but they are quite reasonable products of nearly costless rule. As a final example, unilateralism may be chosen even when governance costs are low if the joint production economies are sufficiently small and expected costs of opportunism are sufficiently high. In this case, even though cooperation may impose few constraints on the state itself, even moderate fears of cheating by partners may block international cooperation. This condition may be all too

---

[10] See Lake 1996 and 1997.

common in international relations. In sum, the effects of any one factor are contingent upon the others, but together they shape policy in fundamental and often quite unexpected ways.

The theory outlined above implies that three concerns should have been central in each of the defining moments of American foreign policy. How large are the gains from cooperation? Are partners reliable, and how effective are alternative institutional arrangements likely to be in reducing opportunism? How costly are the possible security relationships? Issues of research design are quite complex, and are discussed in Chapter 3. In each case, however, a plausible reading of the three primary variables identified above—joint production economies, expected costs of opportunism, and governance costs—appears to be consistent with the policy choices made by the United States. Moreover, the domestic policy debate in each period focused precisely on the questions raised by the theory. Following World War I, the key issue was whether to engage in international security cooperation with other states. The ratification of the League of Nations covenant was the focal point of this debate. After World War II, the central policy problems were whether to cooperate with Europe and Asia and, if so, whether effective but still relatively anarchic security relationships could be designed and implemented. At present, the same central questions present themselves: whether to cooperate with others in security affairs and, if so, through what kind of relationship? Both the policy choices and the policy debates offer tentative support for the approach advanced here. The three periods, discussed at length in Chapters 4 through 6, are briefly summarized in Table 1.1.

American foreign policy during the interwar period is a case of aborted cooperation or, more positively, reaffirmed unilateralism. Noteworthy in this instance is how close the United States came to cooperating with others, indicating that the forces that would later overturn the historic policy of unilateralism were already having an effect. In this "failed" case, more so than in those that follow, I focus on the domestic policy debate in which politicians and analysts alike sought to reconcile their competing visions of the future and to estimate the likely costs and benefits of alternative security relationships.

I pose a new interpretation of the debate over the League of Nations in Chapter 4. At the end of World War I, the United States faced only moderate expected costs of opportunism, driven largely by fears of entrapment into future European wars. At the same time, the governance costs faced by the United States were relatively high and rose rapidly with greater hierarchy; to safeguard the nation's interests, even partially, against the risk of European

TABLE 1.1
Summary of Cases and Findings

| Observed Policy | Joint Production Economies (JPE) | Expected Costs of Opportunism (ECO) | Governance Costs (GC) |
|---|---|---|---|
| **I. Interwar Period (1919–1939)** | | | |
| Unilateralism | Modest. Technological scale limited, no division of labor contemplated, and the U.S. could free ride on Europe effectively in unilateralism. No significant gains from pooling resources and efforts with others | Moderate. High probability of opportunism inhibited investment in specific assets and cooperation. Anarchic relationships unlikely to be effective in reducing probability of European opportunism | High; escalated rapidly with hierarchy. To safeguard interests against risk of European opportunism required significant constraints on America's freedom of action. Limited U.S. to relatively anarchic security relationships |
| **II. Cold War (1945–1989)** | | | |
| Relatively anarchic cooperation in many dyads. Initial hierarchy in Germany and Japan, protectorate in the Philippines, and formal empire in Micronesia | Large. Technological scale greatly expanded but still required forward bases. Large positive externalities could be internalized by burden-sharing among allies. Modest division of labor in NATO | Moderate; fell slowly with hierarchy. Low probability of opportunism facilitated investment in greater JPE and cooperation. Greater American control over others would have created disaffection rather than support. In Micronesia, absence of effective indigenous government and unique site created large ECO | Low; escalated rapidly with hierarchy. Direct costs of modifying incentives of partners not large; few constraints on U.S. As suggested by occupations of Germany and Japan, costs of empire were prohibitive, except in the case of Micronesia |
| **III. New World Order (1989–present)** | | | |
| In Persian Gulf War (PG), protectorates in Gulf states, anarchic relationships elsewhere. In Somalia, anarchic | In PG, large; technological need for a forward base in Gulf and large positive externalities. In Somalia, small; | In PG, high in Gulf dyads with need for forward bases, moderate-to-low elsewhere. In Somalia, negligible; | In PG, high; escalated rapidly with hierarchy. Other states feared opportunistic behavior by U.S.; America con- |

TABLE 1.1 *cont.*

| Observed Policy | Joint Production Economies (JPE) | Expected Costs of Opportunism (ECO) | Governance Costs (GC) |
|---|---|---|---|
| cooperation. In both, ad hoc, American-led coalitions | forward bases not necessary, but some burden-sharing | no specific assets at risk | strained by coalition. In Somalia, low; escalated rapidly with hierarchy. U.S. not constrained by partners; coalition served as a signal of humanitarian intent |

opportunism required significant and costly constraints on its own freedom of action. In the League, then, the United States faced a difficult contractual problem: a bargain that was difficult to enforce and that could be made effective only at substantial cost to itself.

Central to the failure of the League, however, were the relatively modest joint production economies then available in cooperation. The small joint economies limited the benefits of cooperation and greatly constrained the expected costs of opportunism and governance costs the United States could bear. Moreover, the high probability of opportunism inhibited the United States from investing in greater joint economies. In short, the United States ultimately rejected the League of Nations and reaffirmed its traditional unilateralism because the benefits of cooperation were too small relative to the likely costs.

In contrast to the interwar period, American foreign policy after 1945 is a case of successful security cooperation. Equally important is the variation in security relationships created by the United States, which range from an alliance with Britain to an empire in all but name in Micronesia. The shift to cooperation and the within-case variation in relationships allows for a more direct assessment of the theory.

In Chapter 5, I argue that after 1945 the joint production economies were substantially larger than earlier. Technological innovations that either matured before or were initiated during the war greatly lowered the costs of projecting force and enlarged America's security frontiers. The containment of the Soviet Union created large benefits for others, and a burden that could be shared profitably among partners. And at least in Europe, the United States developed a modest division of labor that further increased the gains from cooperation.

Although the United States feared entrapment and exploitation during the Cold War, the probability that its partners would act opportunistically fell substantially from the interwar period, permitting it to invest in greater joint production economies despite the more specific assets entailed. A low probability combined with more specific and therefore "costly" assets suggests that the expected costs of opportunism remained moderate, or at least did not rise significantly from interwar levels. Moreover, the probability that its partners would act opportunistically did not decline significantly with greater hierarchy; as revealed in the occupations of Germany and Japan, the United States believed that greater control over its partners would produce not more unified effort, ex post, but greater disaffection and conflict.

Finally, the governance costs of America's anarchic relationships were relatively low but increased rapidly with hierarchy. Unlike the case of the League, the direct costs of governing the alliance were not large and the allies did not greatly constrain the United States. As the occupations of Germany and Japan again suggest, however, the governance costs of hierarchic relationships were virtually prohibitive.

These factors combined to suggest that the United States, if it cooperated with others, would choose relatively anarchic security relationships. All three variables and their interactions are necessary to explain why the United States abandoned a century and a half of unilateralism in favor of largely anarchic forms of international security cooperation. Micronesia is the principle exception to this rule. In this instance, large joint economies, high expected costs of opportunism and relatively low governance costs combined to produce the only new imperial relationship formed by the United States after 1945.

American foreign policy since the end of the Cold War is also a case of successful cooperation. In every military intervention it has undertaken since 1989, the United States has chosen to construct and lead an ad hoc coalition of states.

In the Persian Gulf War, America's technological need for a forward base in Saudi Arabia and the large generalized benefits produced by expelling Iraq from Kuwait created large joint production economies. This formed a solid foundation on which to build cooperation; as always, however, joint economies, however large, are insufficient to explain the emergence of cooperation.

The expected costs of opportunism differed across the coalition. The need for land bases in the Persian Gulf, necessary for a war designed to expel Iraq from Kuwait, created highly specific assets for the United States in Saudi Arabia and the other states of the region. In the broader coalition, there were far fewer specific assets, and thus less cause for concern. As a result of the significant assets at risk in the Gulf, the United States determined that it must deploy sufficient forces not only to expel Iraq, should that become necessary, but to dominate and thereby "lead" the coalition. In doing so, it established de facto protectorates over the Gulf states.

As expected, other states, especially those in the Gulf, feared opportunistic behavior by the United States. To assuage these fears, the United States had to commit itself to operating within the limits of the prevailing international consensus, both as it developed in the United Nations and in the coalition of states lined up against Iraq. Building the coalition, in other words, was a costly signal of its commitment not to exploit others. The coalition did indeed constrain the United States, particularly regarding the conduct and goals of the war; the governance costs of the Persian Gulf coalition were substantial. Even so, the United States was willing to bear these costs to reap the great benefits of cooperation.

In Somalia, by contrast, the joint production economies were small, suggesting again that this factor alone cannot account for the new form of cooperation found in the new world order. The expected costs of opportunism and governance costs in Somalia, however, were even smaller, permitting cooperation to proceed in this otherwise unfavorable setting. In this case, the coalition in Somalia did not constrain the United States, but served more as a signal of America's own strictly humanitarian and limited objectives. Cooperation succeeded in this case only because the governance costs were negligible. The United States was willing to tie its own hands through the coalition only because it—not others—determined how loose or tight the knot would be.

The political battle today is not between isolationists and internationalists, as sometimes portrayed, but between unilateralists and internationalists. Debate remains vigorous, as in the interwar years, because there is no "obvious" foreign policy choice for the United States. Contradictions within current policy serve to limit the gains and raise the costs of cooperation (see Chapter 8). Although cooperation remains attractive, unilateralism is now a more viable alternative than at any time since World War II. The questions remain those that began this section and that have featured in each of the defining moments of the American century. Only the answers change.

# Chapter 2

## SECURITY RELATIONSHIPS

INTERNATIONAL RELATIONISTS routinely ignore, both empirically and analytically, much of world politics. It is a central tenet of the academic discipline of international relations that world politics are anarchic. As there is no authority higher than the state, the international system is presumed to be comprised of fully sovereign, formally equal actors. According to Kenneth Waltz, international politics imply relations of coordination, not domination and subordination. In his words, "Formally, each is the equal of all the others. . . . International systems are decentralized and anarchic."[1] This axiom holds for both political realists, of whatever stripe, and neoliberal institutionalists, who focus on international regimes and institutions as sources of cooperation but recognize that these are merely instruments of "self-help" in an anarchic world.[2]

Although the precise meaning of anarchy may differ between analysts, it is a near truism that the international system lacks any political authority higher than that of the state.[3] Nothing within this study challenges this description at the level of the system as a whole. Yet it is incorrect to infer from this axiom that all analytically interesting or politically important relations within the international system are anarchic. Historically, a wide range of relations of varying degrees of hierarchy have existed between polities within the international system, even in the area of security affairs, where realism is believed to hold most fully and accurately. Alliances are but one form of security cooperation between states. Throughout modern history, polities have also entered into more hierarchic security relationships, including spheres of influence, protectorates, informal empires, and empires. Moreover, even if alliances have become more common in the twentieth century relative to other possible relationships—a suspect claim—this development cannot be fully understood without a theory of the feasible alternatives.

This chapter begins with a discussion of the polity as the basic actor in international relations, proceeds to an examination of the concept of security, and culminates in a typology of the possible security relationships between

---

[1] Waltz 1979, 88.

[2] Keohane 1984; see also the essays in Baldwin 1993.

[3] Compare the increasing degrees of "sociality" in the discussions of anarchy in Waltz 1979; Bull 1977; and Wendt 1992. None of these authors, however, disputes the claim that the current international system is anarchic.

two polities. The following chapter seeks to explain the choice of security relations.

## The Polity as Actor

In this book, I assume that polities are the basic actors in world politics. A polity is defined as any organized political community that has or could have a history of self-rule.[4] Polities differ from acephalous political communities, which lack any central organization, and from political communities that are below the minimum efficient size to survive.[5] Actual polities, then, are contingent, and may vary with changes in internal organization and minimum scale. At any moment in time, however, the universe of polities is defined by those organized political communities that could, at least in the abstract, survive as independent actors in world politics.[6]

This assumption differs from most other theories of international relations, which assume that states (sometimes, nation-states) are the primary actors in international relations.[7] This is certainly true for "third image" or systemic theories, which focus on the strategic interactions of states.[8] It is also true for unit-level theories. Although such theories look to individuals, groups, and political institutions to understand better the domestic causes of foreign policy, they still take the state to be the primary actor on the world stage. Even theories of transnational relations, which allow for multinational corporations, international organizations, nongovernmental organizations, and other actors to have some autonomous standing in world politics, nonetheless continue to give pride of place to states and, indeed, are often interested in nonstate actors only for the constraints they exert on state behavior.[9] Like any other assumption, the primacy of the state is a simplification of a more complex reality that is unlikely to hold universally or without qualification. It also takes as given and unproblematic that which is itself the product of deep social and political interactions. Nonetheless, state primacy is a useful fiction for many purposes in international relations.[10]

---

[4] For an interesting attempt to code, identify, and describe transitions of various polities, see Strang 1991.

[5] On the optimal size of states, see Bean 1973; Friedman 1977; Wittman 1991; Dudley 1990 and 1992; Yarbrough and Yarbrough 1994; and Findlay 1994.

[6] In this book, I do not offer a precise enumeration of the set of polities. This is likely to vary depending upon the analytic and empirical purposes of particular authors. For an example of how I use the concept of polity, rather than state, see the discussion of Micronesia in Chapter 5.

[7] For alternative views of the problematic nature of the state, see Ashley 1984; Wendt 1987; and Spruyt 1994.

[8] Waltz 1979; Keohane 1984.

[9] Keohane and Nye 1972 and 1977; Risse-Kappen 1995.

[10] For a defense of state centrism and "problem solving theory," see Waltz 1986, 338–39. On the pragmatic nature of theory building in international relations, see Lake and Powell forthcoming.

Since the hierarchical security relationships discussed below may alter who or what constitutes the state over time, however, the analysis here cannot take "stateness" as unproblematic or given. The analysis must start with a more basic unit of analysis, which I define here as the polity. The United States today and throughout the period covered in this book, of course, has lived in a world of states, and thus the distinction between states and polities is not of central empirical importance to the cases below. Analytically, however, the distinction is vital both to the concept of security relationship discussed later in this chapter and the theory developed in the next. Moreover, once used as a lens through which to view international relations, the analytic shift made here brings even recent relationships between the United States and other polities into sharper focus and allows us to see previously unobserved textures and variations.

Polities often coincide with states, especially when, as in the modern age, the state provides a highly salient form of political community. Yet the universe of polities is broader than the universe of states, and includes regions, ethnic groups, clans, and other communities within current states that could potentially survive as autonomous political entities. The set of polities also includes organized political communities that stood for centuries outside the Eurocentric world of sovereign, mutually recognized states, including the Ottoman, Mogul, and Chinese empires and their constituent parts.[11] In short, all states are polities, but not all polities are states. Throughout this study, I use the term *polity* to refer to the broad, abstract set of potential actors in world politics. I use the concept of *state* only when referring to actual states or to the dominant members of hierarchic relationships, who are not inappropriately referred to by this label.

States are, of course, more concrete entities than polities. They are defined by widely accepted norms and practices of recognition by other similarly constituted actors.[12] Even so, the concept is not entirely unambiguous. Today, membership in the United Nations is often used as an indicator of statehood, yet Byelorussia and the Ukraine were members of that international organization from its founding even though they were part of the Soviet Union. The point is not that "stateness" is entirely amorphous but that even this seemingly clear concept is fuzzy at the margins.

Polities are defined, in turn, by the admittedly ambiguous criterion of an actual or potential history of self-rule. Potential self-rule is important for excluding from the universe of polities small municipalities, ethnic enclaves, and other communities that could not survive as independent actors. From this perspective, the primary anomalies are today's micro-states, such as

[11] On the world outside Europe, see Bull and Watson 1984.

[12] In this way, states are socially constructed entities that exist in the realm of "social facts" rather than physical facts. On social facts, see Searle 1995. To recognize the social nature of states, however, is not necessarily to adopt a constructivist approach to the study of international relations. This point is discussed more fully in Chapter 7.

Liechtenstein or Monaco, whose territories and populations are far smaller than many North American cities. On closer examination, however, these polities are not states in the full sense of the term, and typically fall into one of the intermediate relationships defined below. Even when such entities are sovereign, however, I would argue against dismissing the definition of polities advanced here and for seeking to identify the circumstances that allowed these actors to emerge and survive as states while other similar entities have not.

Including as polities all political communities that have enjoyed a period of self-rule even though they might not be viable under present or future circumstances does, of course, privilege analytically some entities at the expense of others. The justification is both theoretical and practical. A history of self-rule is an important foundation upon which political entrepreneurs and other activists often seek to build movements for independence from some larger state or empire. In this way, past self-rule appears to make future self-rule more likely, and therefore more analytically and politically interesting. A history of self-rule, within some long but not infinite time period, is also the single best indicator of a polity's existence and can be used as a "first cut" in identifying the relevant universe of actors.

Despite these not insignificant problems of definition and operationalization, shifting our focus from states to polities is important and, I hope to show, progressive. There is no reason to limit our units of analysis to states if doing so unduly constrains the questions we ask and the answers we find.

## SECURITY

Security, a concept central to all international relations, is too often undefined, and when it is, it is usually tailored either to the specifics of time and place or the idiosyncratic preferences of the author.[13] Walter Lippmann offers one of the few general definitions. "A nation is secure," he writes, "to the extent to which it is not in danger of having to sacrifice core values if it wishes to avoid war, and is able, if challenged, to maintain them by victory in such a war."[14] Arnold Wolfers seconds this theme. "Security, in an objective sense," he states, "measures the absence of threats to acquired values, in a subjective sense, the absence of fear that such values will be attacked."[15] Although according with common usage and now widely cited, these definitions are ambiguous, as Wolfers recognizes, for values are difficult and perhaps impossible to define. Building on these and other attempts, Barry Buzan writes that "security is about the ability of states and societies to maintain

---

[13] See Baldwin 1997 for a conceptual treatment of this contested concept.
[14] Cited in Wolfers 1952, 484.
[15] Wolfers 1952, 485.

their independent identity and their functional integrity."[16] Although substituting identity and integrity for values, this definition does not go far in resolving the fundamental ambiguity of what we mean by security. Because of their ambiguity, as Wolfers warned, all of these definitions can be used and misused toward a variety of ends in the realm of practical politics; they provide an equally tenuous footing for theories of international relations.

In this study, I begin with a materialist conception of security, from which I then deduce the importance of core values, independence, and integrity. I do not disagree with the spirit of these earlier definitions. Rather, I attempt only to pose a more pragmatic but nonetheless general approach to this central concept.[17]

In my view, security has two faces. The first is defined by the risk of death or impairment from violence intentionally employed by others. For a polity, this individual-level condition can be generalized as the risk of death or impairment to its members acting as a collectivity. The lower the risk from intentional violence, the more secure—or the less threatened—is the individual or polity.

The second face is defined by the ability to accumulate and allocate wealth free from external coercion. Again, this individual-level condition can be generalized to a polity acting as a collectivity. In this way, an individual or polity is more secure—or again, less threatened—to the extent that its wealth cannot be coerced or otherwise extorted from it by some outside party.[18] Security is not a guarantee of accumulation. An individual or polity may invest poorly, dissipate its resources, or give its wealth away. The concept refers only to the ability to consume, invest, or dispose of wealth absent external coercion. Wealth, in turn, is defined in the standard fashion as either the goods and services that are available for consumption or the total stock of factors of production—land, labor, capital, and human capital—that can be used to produce future goods and services.

It follows from this definition of security that polities will be especially concerned with the pursuit of three essential freedoms. The first is the ability to engage in politics without the threat of violence. This freedom is always

---

[16] Buzan 1991, 18–19.

[17] Because of the fundamental similarity in the definitions, most of the arguments in the remainder of this book apply both to the materialist conception of security offered here as well as the more traditional expositions based on core values.

[18] More fully, security is the ability to possess wealth and the future income streams it generates. The value of this second face of security, then, is the present discounted value of current and future wealth. The definition developed here excludes constraints on national wealth generated by foreign-produced externalities, such as pollution and other forms of environmental degradation. As the world becomes more densely populated and industrialized, these externalities appear to be increasing; an analysis similar to the one developed here could be applied to such questions. In this study, however, I restrict the analysis, and the definition of security, to coercive threats to wealth.

problematic. Even within highly institutionalized democracies like the United States, for instance, presidents have been assassinated for their political views,[19] communities have erupted into mass violence over unpopular policies and judicial rulings, and the fear of escalating urban violence colors much of the contemporary debate over social reform. Violence casts a long shadow. Nonetheless, even in international relations there appear to be areas, such as relations between the United States and Canada and economic relations among the developed states, where violence is not seriously considered as a political option.[20]

The second essential freedom is the ability to possess wealth. Historically, this has been associated with the territorial integrity of the polity, as wealth has been produced by land (nonmobile by definition), labor (potentially mobile, but typically faced with state restrictions and high transactions costs), and geographically fixed capital assets (that is, "physical plant"). Even today, the loss of territory reduces national wealth by the value of the assets seized, whether they be farms, factories, freeways, or other factors of production. The freedom to possess wealth, however, has always been broader than territory alone. Simple destruction of property, such as frequently occurs in terrorist activity or wars designed to diminish military capacity, also reduces a polity's wealth. Expropriations of moveable assets without territorial claims also infringe upon this freedom, leading in the nineteenth century to "gunboat diplomacy" through which the European powers sought to ensure the prompt repayment of loans and bonds issued by the new states of the developing world. As assets have become more mobile internationally over the last century—and over the last decades in particular—foreign threats of expropriation have challenged the security of various polities.[21] The growth in assets owned by a polity's citizens but held in other locales has led to a breakdown in the historic relationship between wealth and territory. This has complicated the pursuit of security, but it has not fundamentally altered the meaning or nature of the concept, at least as defined here.

The third essential freedom is the ability to choose one's own form of rule. Embodied in constitutional independence, the freedom to choose one's own form of rule is often cited as the defining characteristic of national sovereignty.[22] Central here is the ability of a polity to decide autonomously how to

---

[19] Barring the conspiracy theories surrounding the death of John F. Kennedy, the last president assassinated for his political views was William McKinley, killed by an anarchist in 1901.

[20] Keohane and Nye 1977. On the concept of pluralistic security communities, see Deutsch et al., 1957; and Adler 1992.

[21] With the shift from raw materials and primary extraction to manufacturing, expropriations of foreign direct investments have generally declined. See Jodice 1980 and Kobrin 1980. Nonetheless, the quantity of foreign owned assets continues to grow throughout the world, suggesting that the threat noted here has not gone away.

[22] James 1986.

accumulate and use its wealth. This requires, in turn, that the collective choice mechanism, whether it be democracy, autocracy, or some other form of rule, be free from foreign control.

A polity's freedom to choose its form of rule captures, in turn, much of the concern with core values central to other definitions of security. Core values include wealth, of course; but Lippmann, Wolfers, and others at least implicitly prefer the term *values* because it highlights other important political attributes and principles, such as democracy, private property, and freedom of speech in the United States or economic equality and a leadership role for the Communist Party in the former Soviet Union. Such values, as the qualifier suggests, lie at the core of a polity's system of rule. The protection of the polity's right to choose a particular form of rule implies the defense of such core values. Without denying that core values may also be politically meaningful on their own terms, however, it is important to recognize that they are instrumentally important for a society in choosing how to accumulate and allocate its wealth, and hence can be expected to follow from the definition of security offered here. In this sense, core values are derived from the larger goal of protecting wealth.[23]

As this discussion implies, security is more often aspired to than realized. Polities are not secure or insecure, they are only more or less safe and more or less free to manage their wealth autonomously. Security is a probabilistic, not an absolute, condition. Indeed, conceived in this way, the pursuit of security poses two paradoxes. First, when polities invest resources to protect themselves from others, they are compromising their ability to accumulate and allocate wealth. Threats from others automatically reduce a polity's security by either exposing it to greater risk or forcing it to allocate more resources to defense. Even when polities respond to threats by increasing defense efforts, and therefore maintain a constant level of risk, they become less "secure." Second, as explained below, hierarchic security relationships constrain a polity's autonomous decision-making ability. To cooperate with others in the joint production of security against third parties may require ceding some policy autonomy to partners. Indeed, as discussed in Chapter 3, compromising one's independence is a central (but variable) cost of cooperation. Security is not a "free good."

Like food, shelter, and clothing, security is a primary or necessary good for all humans. Just as individuals cannot survive without food, they cannot survive if they are subject to violence and their other primary goods are subject to seizure or infringement by others. Security is a primary good because it is necessary for the creation, possession, and future enjoyment of

---

[23] The emphasis here on material motivations, of course, is open to the criticism of elevating "things" over "people" and "values." My definition of security is not intended as a normative statement but as a conceptual building block that should be evaluated on its ability to help us understand the behavior of actors in the world as we know it.

other goods. Nonetheless, it is not superior to other primary goods: an individual or group that is not adequately fed, clothed, and sheltered will be unable to defend itself against violence or encroachments by others.

As a primary good, the demand for security is likely to be relatively inelastic, or comparatively insensitive to price, at least until some basic level is satisfied. As it is one of several primary goods, however, individuals and polities never desire security to the exclusion of all other goods. This implies that a greater or lesser tradeoff always exists between security and other valued goods—a "guns/butter" tradeoff in common parlance. This tradeoff is central to the implication, developed more fully in Chapter 3, that polities will seek to minimize the costs of producing their desired level of security.

## THE VARIETY OF SECURITY RELATIONS

Security does not exist naturally or of its own accord. Like any good, it must be produced or manufactured. In this process, polities choose the means of production, sometimes relying upon their own resources—a strategy of unilateralism—and at other times pooling their resources and efforts with others—a strategy of cooperation.

Unilateral strategies are independent efforts in which polities choose to rely only upon their own resources and abilities. In this category are programs to create and maintain military forces, build fortifications, gather intelligence, stockpile raw materials, and invest in research and development. In short, unilateral strategies comprise all of the actions normally taken to deter an adversary, defend against invasion, project force abroad, and attack a foreign power. The distinguishing feature of unilateralism, however, is that polities produce security without attempting to coordinate actions with potential partners. They neither seek to exercise influence over possible collaborators nor accept influence over themselves. America's "isolationism" in the interwar period and Britain's "splendid isolation" in the mid-nineteenth century are commonly cited examples of unilateral strategies. In actuality, however, most dyads, most of the time, are characterized by unilateralism. Most polities do not attempt to pool their security efforts with one another. Unilateralism is the default or reservation strategy for all polities.

As the examples just cited imply, isolationism is often used as a synonym for unilateralism. This is only partially correct. Isolationism is one form of unilateralism.[24] In addition to an emphasis on independent action or nonentanglement, in the more colorful language of America's founding fathers, isolationist polities attempt to minimize interactions with the rest of the world, to pursue what Eric Nordlinger recently termed a "national strategy" of "stra-

---

[24] In a similar way, multilateralism is often used as an antonym for unilateralism. This too is only partially correct. Multilateralism is a particular form of cooperation (see below) involving joint efforts between three or more polities within the same governing structure.

tegic nonengagement."[25] Unilateralist polities, on the other hand, can be quite active, mobilizing to counter threats or even acting aggressively to pre-empt threats from others. America's war with the Barbary states in the early 1800s, its first overseas military conflict after independence, and its war with Spain in 1898 were unilateral but, nonetheless, active efforts.[26] All that uni-lateralism entails is foreign-policy independence. This is the relevant concept for this study. I use the term isolationism only when referring to policies of withdrawal or when quoting others.

Alternatively, polities can choose to cooperate and pool, to a greater or lesser extent, their security efforts.[27] Following Robert Keohane, cooperation is defined as mutual adjustment in policy that improves the welfare of at least one party.[28] To produce security through cooperation, then, the resources and efforts of two or more polities must be brought together in some organized or coordinated fashion. Each polity must adjust its security efforts to reflect the efforts of the other, and at least one party—and typically both—must be made better off as a result.[29] As interdependent action, coop-eration is the antithesis of unilateralism.

Cooperation is inherently relational in character, defined not by individual actors but by the dyad comprising two polities. The dyadic nature of cooper-ation is important to emphasize. Each polity has many potential partners, and there are many different forms of cooperation possible within each pair-ing. In most dyads, unilateralism prevails. Even within the universe of con-temporary states, for instance, the United States cooperates with only a small set of partners. Countries do not adopt universal policies of cooperation in

---

[25] Nordlinger 1995, 3, 29, and 34, distinguishes nonengagement, with a low level of activism, from adversarial engagement and conciliatory engagement, both with a high level of activism but differing in their degree of firmness. In Chapter 4, I show that isolationism can also be understood as a willingness to accept greater risks to one's security, and that this is likely to occur during periods of economic recession.

[26] Even these two "unilateral" actions had elements of cooperation. In the struggle with the Barbary "pirates," the United States navy eventually leased a port on the island of Majorca in order to respond more quickly and effectively to attacks on American shipping. In the Spanish-American War, of course, the United States acquired an overseas empire, including the islands of Cuba, the Philippines, and Puerto Rico. Although most of the other possessions seized by the United States in the war eventually gained their independence, the last is still a formal part of the American empire; see Martínez 1997.

[27] In this study, I do not focus on the level of security produced, defined as the level of resources and effort employed, or on the "quantity" of cooperation in a relationship, defined as the extent to which efforts are pooled. Rather, I examine the political form of the relationship. In the theory in Chapter 3, the extent of pooling is partly derived from the optimal relationships of the polities.

[28] Keohane 1984, 51–52; see also Milner 1992, 467–70.

[29] Simple free riding by one party on the positive externalities unilaterally provided by an-other, however much it might benefit the first, does not constitute cooperation. If the second were to adjust its policy to provide greater externalities for the first, this would be understood as cooperation.

which all partners are treated the same. Rather, their policies are differentiated by partner and may differ across dyads within the same system at any moment in time.

All cooperative undertakings require a security relationship to govern or regulate their joint efforts. Security relationships vary along a continuum defined by the degree of hierarchy between the two parties. The degree of hierarchy, in turn, is defined by the locus of rights of residual control or, less formally, by the decision-making authority possessed by each polity.[30]

Agreements between polities, the rough equivalent of "contracts" between firms and other actors within a domestic legal system, can be completely or incompletely specified.[31] Complete agreements detail numerous contingencies and set forth appropriate responses by the parties. Incomplete agreements contain holes that are filled in by the parties as necessary. In other words, the parties may either "contemplate all conceivable bridge crossings in advance, which is a very ambitious undertaking," or address actual bridge crossings as events unfold.[32] With costly information (see Chapter 3), no agreement can address all contingencies in all possible states of the world. In practice, all agreements are imperfectly specified and thus possess a varying "residual" of unspecified rights, obligations, and expected actions. Which party has the ability de jure or de facto to make decisions in this residual—to cause the parties to act in desired ways under conditions and contingencies that are not clearly specified in the agreement—defines the rights of control.

The terms "right" and "authority" do not necessarily imply that both parties recognize as legitimate the control exercised over the residual areas of decision making; the concepts may simply reflect a de facto ability by one party to control the behavior of the other in some areas.[33] Rights and authorities differ from mere influence, however, by constituting an enduring pattern within an ongoing relationship. This focus on rights and authorities emphasizes the inherently social nature of security relationships. For any relationship to endure, the parties must understand the terms governing their cooperation and participate in the reproduction of these terms through

[30] This definition follows closely from Grossman and Hart 1986.

[31] Even implicit agreements between polities can be understood as "contracts," at least as the term is used in the literature on relational contracting. Even within highly codified domestic legal systems, contracts remain substantially incomplete (such as the marriage contract between two individuals). Nonetheless, the term contract is often misunderstood by international relationists to imply that a formal, written document exists specifying the agreement between the parties. For my purposes here, the broader and less controversial term "agreement" can be used with no loss in meaning. On contracting in international relations, see Chapter 7.

[32] Williamson 1985, 20.

[33] This can also work in reverse. Some Russians today do not recognize or accept as legitimate the increased rights of residual control possessed by the so-called newly independent states or, more graphically, the "near abroad."

Figure 2.1. A Continuum of Security Relationships

conforming behavior, even if they do not fully accept or welcome the potential inequalities in authority.

In anarchy, each party to the relationship possesses full authority to make its own decisions under all circumstances—formally, it possesses full residual rights of control.[34] Although constrained by its environment, each polity is master of its own fate in those areas not specifically ceded in the agreement. In hierarchy, one party—the dominant member—possesses full authority to make all residual decisions, whereas the other party—the subordinate member—lacks this authority. Thus the dominant polity possesses control over all resources and assets of the subordinate actor that have not been specifically delegated to the latter. Hierarchy shifts authority from the subordinate to the dominant polity. As Figure 2.1 illustrates, the range of relations is continuous in principle. As relations move from anarchy to hierarchy, the decision-making authority possessed by the subordinate party declines and that possessed by the dominant state increases. Nonetheless, certain salient forms have been observed historically. The placement of the historic forms along the continuum is only approximate. Table 2.1 summarizes the principal characteristics of these historically salient forms.

In an alliance, which lies at the anarchic end of the continuum, polities pool resources in pursuit of some common security objective while retaining complete authority over all areas of decision making. As noted above, anarchic relations are often assumed to represent all international relations; alliances, in turn, are assumed to be the dominant form of security cooperation. Most modern alliances, including the Rio and Australia-New Zealand-United States pacts formed after World War II, do vest all residual rights in the member states. In an alliance, then, both parties remain fully sovereign. Although allies may commit themselves to perform certain more or less well specified actions, each polity is free to interpret the agreement according to its own designs and pursue its own, self-defined interests in all other areas of policy.

In an empire, which lies at the hierarchic end of the continuum, the poli-

[34] Following now-standard usage, by "anarchy" I do not mean either anomie or chaos. Indeed, as noted above, all relationships require a measure of sociality and patterned behavior and thus constitute a form of order in international affairs. See Bull 1977.

TABLE 2.1
Summary Characteristics of Security Relationships

| Relationship | Defining Characteristic |
|---|---|
| Alliance | Both parties retain full decision-making authority |
| Sphere of influence | Subordinate polity restrained from entering into security relationships, of whatever form, with third parties |
| Protectorate | Subordinate polity cedes decision-making authority over foreign policy to the dominant state |
| Informal empire | Subordinate polity cedes decision-making authority over foreign policy and areas of domestic policy to the dominant state. Subordinate polity conducts relations with others on basis of sovereignty |
| Empire | Subordinate polity cedes decision-making authority over both foreign and domestic policy to dominant state. Subordinate polity does not conduct relations with others on basis of sovereignty |

ties still pool their resources and efforts but one party cedes nearly complete decision-making authority directly to the other. Through empire, two polities are melded together in a hierarchic relationship in which one party controls the other. The European colonial empires remain classic examples.[35] Hierarchies are seldom complete. Even in empires, local officials are usually given some independence in responding to local conditions. The locus of decision making need not reside entirely in the dominant unit for us to regard that entity as hierarchic.[36]

Between these extremes lies a range of intermediate security relationships.[37] Three relationships are historically and analytically salient. In a sphere of

[35] Empires and other relatively hierarchic relationships are generally not formed voluntarily, at least by the subordinate member. Given the transfer of residual rights entailed, and the reduced freedom of decision making this implies, coercion may be central to the process of building empires and other, less hierarchic relationships. Power disparities allow coercion to be effective in shaping relationships, but such relationships cannot be equated with power. See Chapter 3.

[36] Compare the discussion of the United States in Waltz 1967 with that of hierarchy in Waltz 1979.

[37] A study by two international legal scholars prepared for the American negotiators at Versailles after World War I—Willoughby and Fenwick 1974—identified ten types of polities with restricted sovereignty or colonial autonomy, including neutralized states, vassal states, and autonomous dependencies. This is the most complete discussion of different relational forms I have found. Although some distinctions between relationships appear arbitrary or antiquated—for instance, even though they might be similarly subordinate, developed and developing countries are classified differently—nearly all of their categories can be mapped onto the continuum here and grouped within the ideal types specified.

influence, the dominant polity constrains the authority possessed by the sub-ordinate polity in the area of foreign policy, most often limiting the latter's right to cooperate in security affairs with third parties. Proclaimed by the United States in 1823 and addressed to the Europeans, the Monroe Doctrine asserted a sphere of influence over Latin America by prohibiting polities within the hemisphere from entering into new relationships with non-hemispheric powers.[38] This definition of a sphere of influence is more restric-tive than others, which tend to blur together the intermediate types of rela-tionships identified here.[39] Nonetheless, it captures the common notion of an exclusive area of action while distinguishing this security relationship from its close cousins, alliances and protectorates.

In a protectorate, one polity cedes control to another over its foreign af-fairs, abridging in large part its decision-making authority in this area of policy. Although the terms vary, such grants of control are typically made for extended periods of time and are not revocable. Such delegations transfer authority from the "protected" polity to the "protector" and severely con-strain the former's ability to influence the policy choices the latter makes for it. Afghanistan after 1879 is the classic example of a protectorate. Following the Peace of Gandamak, the Amir of Afghanistan "agreed to leave the control of his foreign relations to the British Government, who, on their part, under-took not to interfere with the internal government of Afghanistan, and, in the case of unprovoked foreign aggression on Afghan dominions, to aid the Amir in such manner as to them might seem necessary, provided he unreservedly followed their advice in regard to his external relations." This relationship was confirmed in 1893 and codified in a formal treaty in 1905. Afghanistan's status as a protectorate was recognized in the Anglo-Russian agreement of 1907.[40] Britain's "Trucial System" in the Persian Gulf is a another well-known example.[41] Within the general form of a protectorate, the range of delegated control can be quite narrow or broad. "Neutralized" polities such as Switzer-land, for instance, simply forego the "sovereign right to resort to the pro-cedure of war," typically in exchange for a guarantee of independence and territorial integrity, but they remain "in other respects sovereign and their position within the family of nations is in no way impaired."[42] Alternatively, foreign control can blend into the category of informal empire discussed

[38] LaFeber 1994, 83–88.
[39] See Triska 1986, 6–7.
[40] Willoughby and Fenwick 1974, 14–15.
[41] Kuniholm 1993.
[42] Willoughby and Fenwick 1974, 8. As the other examples in this paragraph make clear, protectorates are not necessarily "neutral," as the example of Switzerland alone might imply; indeed, by transferring control over their foreign policies to another, protectorates are quite likely to become pawns in the strategies of the dominant state. Likewise, although Switzerland gave up the sovereign right of war, it did not give up the right of self-defense, and it remains one of the most militarized societies in Europe.

immediately below. Protected dependent polities, such as the so-called Native States of India or the Federated Malay States under the control of Britain,
"do not hold political intercourse with other powers" and even "admit a
certain amount of interference . . . in their domestic affairs."[43] More recently,
the United States has transformed parts of its Trust Territory of the Pacific
Islands, established as an American empire under United Nations auspices in
1947, into protectorates; under "free association" agreements adopted in
1986, the United States now recognizes the Federated States of Micronesia
and the Republic of the Marshall Islands as sovereign states but continues to
accept responsibility for their defense. Relations between Russia and several
of the Soviet successor states also appear to be evolving into protectorates.[44]

Informal empire exists when one polity controls substantial decision-making authority in the other, including rights over otherwise "domestic" or
internal affairs, but the subordinate polity nonetheless interacts with other
states on the basis of sovereignty. The greater scope of the authority transferred to the dominant polity distinguishes an informal empire from a protectorate, while the retention of sovereignty in relations with others separates
informal and formal empires. The Soviet Union controlled an informal empire in Eastern Europe from the end of World War II.[45] As codified in the
so-called Brezhnev Doctrine, the Soviet Union reserved the right to intervene
to support fraternal socialist regimes under threat from internal foes.[46] Although originally claiming only a sphere of influence in Latin America, the
United States later asserted broad police powers over the internal affairs of
polities in the region, especially in the Caribbean and Central America. In
the so-called Roosevelt Corollary to the Monroe Doctrine, proclaimed in
1904, the United States expanded its limited sphere into an informal empire.[47]
Recent United States interventions in Grenada and Haiti suggest that countries in the Caribbean basin, at least, still do not wholly control their own
domestic politics. In each of these cases, the subordinate member was recognized as sovereign by the international community but was ultimately dependent upon and substantially under the control of the dominant polity not
only in its foreign relations but in its internal policies and politics, as well.

Informal empire is often defined by one possible mechanism of control,
rather than the fact of control. It is the latter that ultimately matters. Accord-

[43] Ibid., 9. In between these two types of protectorates are "protected independent states,"
such as Cuba under the United States while the Platt Amendment was in effect; unlike protected
dependent states, these polities retain their international personality and can represent themselves at international conferences; ibid., 6–7. On the Federated Malay States and Native States
of India, see ibid., 40–41 and 50–53, respectively.

[44] Roeder 1997.

[45] On the Soviet's informal empire, see Lake 1996 and 1997. See also Brzezinski 1967; Ulam
1974; Mastny 1979; Bunce 1985; Holden 1989; and Stone 1996.

[46] Jones 1990.

[47] LaFeber 1994, 245–50.

ing to Michael Doyle, for instance, "informal imperialism achieves [control] through the collaboration of a legally independent (but actually subordinate) government in the periphery." Through a functionally dependent and therefore controllable agent in the subordinate polity, the dominant polity creates the reality of empire without the form.[48] This is, no doubt, a central mechanism for control, perhaps the dominant one. Nonetheless, rule by proxy, with authority delegated from one polity to a dependent elite in the second, is but one of several forms of oversight and control. Dominant polities can also use coercion or threats of coercion to maintain limited control—as the Soviet Union did with Finland. They can also assume directly certain critical functions within the subordinate polity, and because of their importance acquire substantial rights in other areas: foreigners not only achieved extraterritorial jurisdiction in China in the late nineteenth century, but also administered the salt tax and customs revenues;[49] Russia today continues to station troops in and provide for the external defense of several successor states, just as it did in Eastern Europe during the Cold War.[50] Even in the absence of local collaborators, sovereign relations with third parties can and do coexist with the transfer of substantial residual rights to the dominant polity.

In conclusion, not all relevant relations are anarchic, and even despite their nominal sovereignty not all polities have the same freedom of decision making. International relationists have been overly focused on the fact of *systemic* anarchy and insufficiently attentive to variations in hierarchy between polities. With the current movement toward political union in Europe, the ongoing dissolution of the Russian empire, and new efforts to navigate the perilous shoals of the post-Cold War world, it is time that hierarchy was reclaimed as an interesting and variable characteristic of international relations.

## STUDYING SECURITY RELATIONSHIPS

"Pure" cases of anarchy or hierarchy seldom exist. Even in what are mostly consultative relations between allies, some degree of control may be exercised over residual choices. Conversely, no empire is ruled entirely from the center; local authorities nearly always possess some discretion in interpreting and implementing imperial edicts. Nearly all relationships are matters of gray, rather than black and white. Throughout this book, the terms alliance, sphere of influence, protectorate, informal empire, and empire are used simply as shorthand for relationships that have the general forms described above.

[48] Doyle 1986, 38 and 42.
[49] Willoughby and Fenwick 1974, 7.
[50] Roeder 1997.

Discerning the degree of hierarchy within any dyadic relationship is difficult and imperfect. It necessarily requires a measure of subjective judgment
and interpretation. This should not prevent us from studying variations in
hierarchy, but it should make readers skeptical and cautious about the cod-
ing of specific cases.

Care must be taken in applying the definition of hierarchy developed here.
Readers may be tempted to draw conclusions about the nature of the relationship from the process through which it was created. This may be helpful
under some circumstances, but by itself the process of creation does not
define the alternative relationships. Hierarchy, for instance, can be freely negotiated—as in the merger of the German Democratic Republic into the
Federal Republic of Germany—or coerced, as in the late-nineteenth-century
scramble for Africa and Germany's quest in the first half of this century for a
continental empire. Whether entered into voluntarily or through the pain of
battle, it is the shift in decision-making authority from the subordinate to the
dominant polity that defines the degree of hierarchy.

Likewise, it is easy to mistake as anarchy the compliance of a subordinate
polity with the wishes of a dominant polity because no overt governance is
occurring. When the terms of a relationship are well understood and anticipated by both parties, for instance, no resistance occurs, no overt coercion is
necessary, and the subordinate polity complies with the wishes of the dominant state *as if* in a purely anarchic relationship. The absence of any overt
resistance by the subordinate polity does not necessarily indicate that it
possesses complete authority over its own behavior. Only if the partner tests
its subordination will the extent of the hierarchy become manifest. For example, the hierarchical nature of the Soviet bloc established in Eastern Europe
following World War II was revealed only by recurring challenges to Russian
authority. The subordinate peoples periodically tested the limits of informal
Soviet rule by seeking to expand their domestic policy autonomy, sparking suppressions of local dissent in East Germany in 1953, Hungary in 1956,
Czechoslovakia in 1968, and (indirectly) Poland in 1981. In the end, relationships can only be distinguished by observing interactions over some extended period, thereby increasing the chances for encountering anomalous
behavior.[51]

Although difficult, it is not impossible to determine with some degree of
confidence the type of relationship established between two polities. The
terms of the relationship can usually be discerned through careful observation and analysis, especially when they have been institutionalized either in a
formal agreement or by lengthy practice. Although the specific rules and
political practices differ, of course, the process of discerning the degree of
hierarchy in international relations is not different from that in domestic

---

[51] On the problem of identifying informal relationships, see Doyle 1986, 39 and 43.

politics. Many early foreign-policy studies understood the president and bureaucracy to be key decision makers, for instance, but it is now widely accepted that much of their power is delegated by Congress and that the legislature is a more central foreign-policy player than previously realized; indeed, rather than seeing congressional inaction on many policy issues as evidence of legislative weakness, this same behavior is now understood to demonstrate that the president and the bureaucracy, as the legislature's agents, anticipate its wishes and commonly propose what they know it will approve.[52] In international relations, institutional rules and political practices can also be used as guides for inferring the degree of hierarchy. In alliances, for instance, rules for decision typically vary from unit vetoes—where each state can block agreement or, at least, opt out of any action—to some minimal hierarchy. In NATO, while the member states are obligated to respond to any attack on a member state, they are free to determine their appropriate response, making it essentially an anarchic institution. At the same time, the existence of a Supreme Allied Commander, Europe—by informal agreement always an American general and thus ultimately responsible to the American president—creates a degree of hierarchy within the organization. In empires, at the other extreme, the institutional rules lodge ultimate decision-making power in the imperial polity, but to widely varying degrees. Within the British empire, for example, some colonies were ruled directly by British governors, others had local legislatures whose actions could be vetoed by either British governors or Parliament directly, while still others were essentially autonomous, except that their constitutions were written and their basic institutions imposed by Britain. The authority retained by Britain declined across these alternatives, creating variations in the degree of hierarchy within the basic imperial form. In the chapters below, such institutional rules and political practices are a focus of considerable attention. Although inferring the degree of hierarchy between polities may be difficult, it is not inherently more complex than in many domestic political arenas, where substantial theoretical and empirical progress has already been made.

In addition to focusing on rules and practices, the views of key decision makers can be probed to identify the degree of relational hierarchy. Were leaders in subordinate polities aware of restrictions on their decision-making authority? Did leaders in dominant polities self-consciously place limits on the freedom of action granted subordinate polities? The historical record can be mined to see whether the kinds of issues suggested by the different security relationships were, in fact, prominent in people's minds and the policy debate.[53] Such evidence can never prove decisive, of course, but analytic

---

[52] Ripley and Lindsay 1993; Lindsay 1994; O'Halloran 1994.

[53] This is similar to the concept of process tracing; see George and McKeown 1985. King, Keohane, and Verba 1994 define process tracing as a means of making more observations from a

categories that lack any counterpart in policy debates or the calculations of decision makers should be treated even more skeptically than usual. Although words can deceive, the public pronouncements and private musings of key political leaders in both dominant and subordinate polities can prove to be important sources of insight into security relationships.

## CONCLUSION

Relationships lie along a continuum defined by the degree of hierarchy, implying that they are characterized by more or less decision-making authority rather than sharp lines of division and clear thresholds. Alliances, spheres of influence, protectorates, informal empires, and empires are salient historical relationships along this continuum. The lines between these relationships may be difficult to discern, especially in the absence of attempts by subordinate actors to assert their independence. Nonetheless, the distinctions capture important differences in relations—differences that have been, unfortunately, too often ignored in international relations. In the next chapter, I attempt to explain the choice between unilateralism and cooperation and, in the latter, between alternative security relationships.

---

fixed number of cases. In this study, however, I am not breaking the policy process down into stages for separate analysis. Rather, I am using individual understandings as additional observations.

*Chapter 3*

# A Theory of Relational Contracting

AS DISCUSSED in Chapter 2, polities have two general strategies for producing security. They can act unilaterally, relying on their own resources and efforts, or cooperatively, pooling their resources and efforts with others. When cooperating, in turn, polities can form a range of relationships, varying along a continuum from anarchic alliances to hierarchic empires.

This chapter draws upon theories of relational contracting, first developed in economics but now finding increasing application in political science, to explain the choice of security relationships by polities. The choice between these alternatives, I posit, is a function of three main variables. *Joint production economies* determine the gains from pooling resources and efforts with others, and thus shape the incentives of polities to cooperate. *The expected costs of opportunism* specify the risk that partners will abandon, entrap, or exploit the polity; for any given level of asset specificity, these decline with relational hierarchy. *Governance costs*, created by the need to monitor, safeguard, and control partners, are also present in all security relationships. Governance costs rise with relational hierarchy. These three factors determine the optimal security relationship for a polity, the expected benefits of which are then compared to unilateralism.

After a brief review to locate my approach within the broader international relations literature, I develop the theory at some length. The theory is self-consciously general and designed to apply in a variety of circumstances, even though the empirical application in Chapters 4 to 6 is limited to the United States in the twentieth century. The chapter concludes with a discussion of research design.

## THE LOGIC OF SECURITY

International relationists have made substantial progress in understanding the sources and variations of foreign policy and, especially, security policy.[1] Nonetheless, two related problems remain. Although these problems are natural consequences of the magnitude of the subject of "foreign policy," and will not be remedied fully here, they continue to limit further progress. First, despite the attention directed to the many techniques for producing security, scholars typically fail to consider adequately the full range of alternatives

[1] For reviews of research on security policy, see Nye and Lynn-Jones 1988; and Walt 1991.

available to polities.[2] For example, scholars focus on alliances or empires, but fail to ask how, in what ways, and to what extent these relationships are substitutes for one another.[3] When polities choose to seek empire, for instance, they are simultaneously choosing not to form an alliance. The net benefits of imperialism by themselves do not explain action; rather, it is the net benefits of the alternatives relative to one another that drive choice. Any full explanation *must* compare all alternatives.[4]

Second, analysts continue to work within what Benjamin Most and Harvey Starr describe as separate "islands" of theory and fail to appreciate or build upon common political problems and independent variables.[5] This is true even in the comparatively well-developed literatures on alliance formation and imperialism. In the standard texts in international relations, for instance, alliances and empires are nearly always discussed in separate chapters and often in very different theoretical contexts: the first tend to be covered under the headings of Realism, systems-level theories, or the balance of power, the second under Marxism, unit-level theories, or North-South relations. Yet in practice all polities are concerned with problems of aggregating and pooling resources—building power—and coping with opportunism by their partners. These practical problems are also central independent variables in our theories of international politics, even if they are often implicit. Without seeking to minimize differences in the research agendas that have grown up around these and other topics, I want to suggest that a common theoretical core does exist.

The current literature on alliance formation is dominated by a "capability aggregation" model in which states form alliances primarily to counter common threats larger than each individually.[6] Within this model, the primary costs of alliances—and the reasons why states sometimes eschew foreign entanglements—are traditionally understood to arise from opportunistic be-

---

[2] Although several recent studies have made significant headway on this score, the full range of policies remains implicit. Among the best studies, see Friedberg 1988; Snyder 1991; and Morrow 1993. As an exception to the rule, Niou and Ordeshook 1994 ask similar questions but take an approach different from that discussed here. Although not fully distinguishing among alternatives, Gilpin 1981 offers one of the most comprehensive treatments of the costs and benefits of imperialism, broadly defined.

[3] See, respectively, Walt 1987 and Doyle 1986.

[4] Baldwin 1985, 8–18 and 29–40, suggests that international political economists may not be sufficiently attentive to this fundamental tenet of rational choice theory either. Much of the work on trade policy, for instance, has proceeded without sufficient reference to exchange-rate manipulation as an alternative to tariff protection. On this score, I plead guilty; see Lake 1988.

[5] Most and Starr 1984; see also Siverson and Starr 1991.

[6] Morrow 1991. For reviews of the voluminous literature on alliances, see the essays collected in Friedman, Bladen, and Rosen 1970; and Holsti, Hopmann, and Sullivan 1973. Another explanation of alliance formation focuses on national attributes, such as ideology or regime type; see Barnett and Levy 1991; David 1991; and Siverson and Emmons 1991. The historical literature also points to the desire to control partners as a motivation for alliances, but this empirical insight has not been incorporated into the theoretical literature; see Schroeder 1976.

havior by partners. Glenn Snyder has explicated these costs more concretely.[7] In the "alliance dilemma," he writes, states may be "abandoned," defined broadly as free riding or shirking by others, and "entrapped," or embroiled in conflicts the polities themselves might otherwise avoid. More recently, Thomas Christensen and Jack Snyder have termed these costs "buck passing" and "chain ganging," respectively.[8]

The literature on imperialism, on the other hand, has long been rent by three competing perspectives. Metrocentric theory focuses on dispositional features of imperial states, systemic theory highlights competition between the great powers, and pericentric theory emphasizes conditions in peripheral polities and territories. Several recent studies have succeeded in integrating these approaches into a consistent and powerful explanation of imperialism.[9]

With obvious differences, metrocentric and systemic theories of imperialism share with theories of alliance formation an emphasis on capability aggregation. At the most basic level, both hypothesize that states form empires to capture important resources—raw materials, manpower, markets, strategic locations—otherwise unavailable to groups at home or the polity in general. Although many theories of imperialism emphasize the domestic implications of expansion, explanations of alliance formation and imperialism share a common focus on capability aggregation.

More so than the other approaches, pericentric theories attempt to explain the form of imperialism and, in turn, focus on opportunism. Following the pioneering work of John Gallagher and Ronald Robinson, such theories hypothesize that dominant states prefer informal empire, if possible, but create formal empires when local elites are either unwilling or unable to provide acceptable domestic political orders; in other words, formal empires are created when local rulers possess different policy preferences or lack the ability to carry out the interests of dominant states.[10] Whether emphasizing intent or ability, the failure of the peripheral polity to comply with or carry out the desires of the core state is functionally equivalent to abandonment in alliance theories. Within this parallel, however, it is important to note an apparent contradiction, resolved in the theory below: where alliances are thwarted by the potential for opportunism, formal empires are stimulated by this same possibility.

In both alliances and empires, then, our dominant theories understand states as motivated by the desire to aggregate capabilities. Problems of opportunism are also important determinants of behavior in both literatures. This should not be surprising, given the need to build power and manage relations between

---

[7] G. Snyder 1984 and 1990.

[8] Christensen and Snyder 1990.

[9] Smith 1981; Doyle 1986; and Cain and Hopkins 1993. The labels for the three theories are from Doyle 1986, 22–30.

[10] Gallagher and Robinson 1953. In a variant of systemic theory, Gallagher and Robinson also acknowledge that competition between great powers can produce formal empire. On the debate over the "imperialism of free trade," see Louis 1976.

partners in the conduct of international relations. This common theoretical core is central to the approach developed below, which thus builds upon existing approaches in international relations. Yet by failing to appreciate this common theoretical and practical core, extant theories have not made a sufficient effort to explicate the continuum underlying alternative relations, examine when and how there are gains from aggregation, and identify the roots and forms of opportunism or how it varies across these options. While clearly building on and indebted to the existing literature, the theory developed here seeks to explain better the variations in relations across partners and over time.

This common core also ignores the important role of governance costs, which have made a significant contribution to the theory of international regimes and form a necessary part of the analysis below.[11] A second goal of the theory is to incorporate into the core a focus on issues of international governance—a topic often believed to be empirically or theoretically unimportant to security studies.[12] Following Oran Young, we can define governance as "the establishment and operation of social institutions . . . capable of resolving conflicts [and] facilitating cooperation."[13] As a generic problem of politics with a wide variety of possible solutions, governance can be carried out through a range of alternative relationships. As Young continues, "there is nothing in this way of framing the issue that presupposes the need to create material entities or organizations [that is, governments]."[14] As defined in Chapter 2, security relationships are structures or agreements for governing cooperation between partners. Although international organizations and regimes may be of marginal importance for security issues—itself a debatable proposition—governance and the costs associated with it are necessary components in any explanation of security cooperation. Indeed, the failure to include governance costs in the common core described above may have substantially biased the conclusions reached by previous analysts.[15]

## THE LOGIC OF SECURITY RELATIONSHIPS

Theories of relational contracting were first used in economics to explain the institution of the firm and variations in its basic forms.[16] Also known as the

---

[11] Keohane 1984.

[12] Jervis 1983; Mearsheimer 1994/95. For alternative views, see Keohane and Martin 1995; Wallander and Keohane 1995; and Lipson 1994 and 1995.

[13] Young 1994, 15. Young focuses his definition on the alleviation of collective action problems. My definition of cooperation is somewhat broader (see Chapter 2), but his definition of governance fits nonetheless. Implicit in Young's discussion is the need for some intersubjective understanding between the parties. This need is made explicit in Rosenau 1992, 4. Although security relationships are inherently social (see the discussion in Chapter 2), and therefore require some degree of intersubjective understanding, I do not see this as the primary characteristic or cause of "governance."

[14] Young 1994, 15–16. For an extended discussion, see Rosenau and Czempiel 1992.

[15] This is the problem of omitted variables bias. See King, Keohane, and Verba 1994, 168–82.

[16] The approach can be dated from Coase 1937 and 1960; or Williamson 1975. For good

transactions costs economics approach or neoinstitutional economics, the unifying insight of theories of relational contracting is that "transactions must be governed as well as designed and carried out, and that certain institutional arrangements effect this governance better than others."[17] As Oliver Williamson writes, the central working hypothesis of the approach is that economic organizations attempt to "align transactions, which differ in their attributes, with governance structures, which differ in their costs and competencies."[18] In short, actors choose the organization that is most efficient for conducting the transaction in which they are engaged. Theories of relational contracting have received substantial but by no means unequivocal empirical support. They are now sufficiently accepted in economics to be incorporated into mainstream textbooks.[19]

Although first developed in economics, theories of relational contracting actually constitute a more general approach to understanding social organization.[20] This approach was first applied to international relations by Robert Keohane in his theory of international regimes.[21] It has now been extended to explain a range of specific issues, including trade institutions, colonial investments, and the collapse of the Soviet Union.[22] The approach is highly suggestive for the kinds of comparative analyses of policy now lacking in the discipline of international relations.

In this section, I develop a theory of relational contracting tailored to the substance of international security affairs. As we shall see, the optimal relationship is principally a function of joint production economies, the expected costs of opportunism, and governance costs.

### Assumptions and Limitations

In the following theory, I make several assumptions, which I will note here but not defend at length. First, polities are rational and forward-looking. The

---

introductions, see Williamson 1985, 1990, and 1994; Eggertsson 1990; and Furubotn and Richter 1991. Hart 1990 provides a particularly good discussion of the different ways economists have conceived of the firm. For a related approach, see the collected essays of Chandler in McCraw 1988. A second intellectual foundation for the theory developed here is the literature on the economics of crime; for the classic works, see Becker 1968; and Stigler 1970.

[17] Shelanski and Klein 1995, 336.

[18] Williamson 1991, 79.

[19] Shelanski and Klein 1995, esp. 337–38, n.5.

[20] Langlois 1986, esp. 283. There are strong parallels between the theories of the firm developed by Williamson and others, and more general theories of property rights and growth. See North 1981 and 1990. For empirical studies, see Alston, Eggertsson, and North 1996.

[21] Keohane 1983 and 1984.

[22] Yarbrough and Yarbrough 1992; Frieden 1994; Lake 1997; and Hancock 1998. See also Weber 1997a. In American politics, although principal-agent models had already been employed for some time, the first specific application of which I am aware was Weingast and Marshall 1988. For a legal perspective, see Aceves 1996.

"rationality" assumption is common in theories of international politics, but it is also frequently criticized.[23] By rationality, I mean only that polities possess transitive preferences and act purposively to achieve their goals. That polities are forward-looking is less controversial, but no less important. By forward-looking, I mean that polities anticipate the reactions of others to their actions, and base their own choices upon these expectations. This implies that polities choose security relationships on the basis of "rational expectations."

Second, security is a single dimension of policy, the relevant selectorate (whether eligible voters in a democracy or colonels in a military junta) possess single-peaked preferences, and the government is a perfect agent for its selectorate.[24] These are the familiar conditions behind the median voter theorem, applied here more generally to a wider variety of domestic choice mechanisms.[25] This assumption produces a highly stylized view of domestic politics in which policy always reflects the position of the median selector and allows us to treat polities as unitary actors. In making this assumption, I do not intend to imply that domestic politics are unimportant. Rather, I simply want to focus attention on relations between rather than within polities. I have addressed some consequences of relaxing this assumption elsewhere; when the government is not a perfect agent for its society, the primary effect is to create an imperialist bias in its foreign policy, suggesting that it will pursue more hierarchic security relationships than other, more domestically constrained polities.[26] In Chapter 7, in a discussion of several possible directions in which to extend the theory, I suggest how domestic politics might be further integrated in future research. Although I do not build domestic politics into the present theory, the debates between different domestic political actors are relevant in assessing the theory empirically; I develop this point later in this chapter.

Third, polities do not possess preferences over particular security relation-

[23] See Allison 1971; Steinbruner 1974; Jervis 1976. For arguments that polities are more appropriately modeled as boundedly rational, see McKeown 1986. For a review of nonrational models of decision making, see Levy 1994. For a defense of the rational-actor assumption, especially an argument that polities are more likely to be rational than individuals, see Bendor and Hammond 1992. I use the assumption of rationality here because it is the only general assumption of decision making available. Any other assumption requires detailed, actor-specific information to make behavioral predictions (for example, in prospect theory, does the actor see this choice framed more as a gain or a loss?).

[24] Roeder 1993, 24, defines a selectorate as "the body that holds the power to select and remove policymakers." The selectorate can be smaller than the set of political participants, which in turn is smaller than the population. In autocracies, the selectorate may be quite narrow. See also Shirk 1993.

[25] For a good introduction to public choice models, see Schwartz 1987. For a related approach, see Achen 1988.

[26] Lake 1992.

ships. That is, the selectorate does not innately prefer alliances or empires, but values these alternatives only as inputs in the process of producing security. Polities may be expansionary or status-quo powers, risk-averse or risk-acceptant; this assumption merely restricts polities from having preferences for or against particular mechanisms for managing security cooperation. Like the second, this assumption may often be violated in reality, but its effect is to concentrate our attention on the environment of polities rather than their dispositions.[27] Whether environmental theories such as this one or dispositional theories prove more useful is an empirical question.[28]

Together, these first three assumptions imply that polities choose the relationship that minimizes their costs of producing a desired level of security. By so choosing, polities (and their selectorates) maximize their utility by conserving resources that can then be used to obtain other valued ends.[29] In general, this implication—while clearly artificial—is nonetheless plausible. When decision makers are perfect agents for their principals, whether these be shareholders in a firm or voters in a democracy, they have no incentive to conduct relations in ways that intentionally "waste" resources. Yet at this level, the implication is also a virtual truism, as it is relatively easy to concoct stories after the fact about why any observed relationship is "efficient" for the parties involved; indeed, this is perhaps the most common criticism of the relational contracting approach. The real test of a theory of relational contracting comes from specifying more concretely the range of alternatives and the determinants of efficiency, around which there continues to be substantial debate and, thus, multiple theories united by a common approach.

Fourth, I also assume that information is costly and, therefore, limited. Though rational, polities possess only incomplete and imperfect information. Although they may know their own defense effort with certainty, for example, polities can observe features of their environment—including their partner's defense effort—only at some cost. Due to diminishing marginal returns, polities never acquire full information about their partners. Formally, polities are taken to be Bayesian decision makers that choose relations on the basis of *expected* utility calculations.[30]

---

[27] The alternative assumption, that innate preferences do exist, implies that polities, ceteris paribus, should construct relatively similar security relationships across dyads. If polities prefer empire, for example, they should seek imperial relationships across the board. This alternative assumption is clearly problematic, since polities do vary in their security relationships at any moment in time.

[28] For examples of dispositional theories of security from a variety of theoretical perspectives, see Katzenstein 1996b; Maoz 1996; and Snyder 1991. On the problems of studying preferences, see Frieden forthcoming.

[29] In other words, these combined assumptions imply profit maximization for firms, which then allows them to distribute the maximum dividends to their shareholders, and cost minimization for polities, which allows governments to set taxes at their lowest sustainable level.

[30] This is one of many "as if" assumptions in this theory. I do not assume that polities really

This assumption is quite consequential. It underlies the claim, made in Chapter 2, that all agreements between polities are necessarily incomplete. Since information is costly, polities do not attempt to foresee all possible contingencies.[31] This contractual incompleteness, in turn, creates the need for security relationships.[32]

The assumption of costly information also implies that all of the variables below are probability distributions over which polities possess some set of prior beliefs. In other words, the level of any particular variable is not known with certainty, but polities estimate the range and pattern of likely costs and benefits. To take an example, polities do not know exactly how effective an empire will be at reducing opportunistic behavior by their subordinate partners. They estimate the distribution of likely outcomes, but they do not know in any instance whether empire will produce effective, very effective, or very ineffective control. Likewise, polities do not know exactly how costly it will be to govern any particular imperial relationship; based on past experience, they estimate the likely distribution of costs, but they do not know in advance whether the actual costs will be very high, very low, or pretty much what they expected "on average."

As in any model of costly and therefore incomplete information, it is the beliefs of the actors rather than the actual values of the variables that motivate the choice of relationships. In principle, I cannot think of any reason why the beliefs of polities about the variables discussed below would be systematically biased; although polities may possess incorrect beliefs in any instance, there is no reason that they should be consistently wrong or always wrong in the same direction.[33] I therefore further assume that, on average, the actual distribution and the expected distribution are the same. Thus, as a shorthand, it is possible to speak of governance costs, rather than the expected distribution of governance costs. Nonetheless, it remains the case that the variables are probability distributions and it is the beliefs of the polities about the variables rather than the variables themselves that matter. This does not pose a difficulty for the theory, but it does raise significant

---

are Bayesian decision makers, only that they can be usefully modeled as if they are Bayesians. For an introduction to Bayesian decision making in a fully strategic setting, see Morrow 1994, 161–87.

[31] Even if the partners possessed full information, transactions costs might prevent them from writing agreements that specify behavior under all contingencies. If information is costly, however, the parties will never formally consider some range of contingencies in which they will at least occasionally find themselves.

[32] In many theories of relational contracting, this same result is motivated by the assumption of bounded rationality. See Williamson 1985. For reasons outlined in note 23, I find the assumption of bounded rationality incomplete as a general theory of behavior, and thus prefer here to motivate the analysis by assuming costly information.

[33] This is not simply an artifact of assumption three. Beliefs here do not correspond to preferences over outcomes, but to estimates of the distribution of values of the independent variables.

problems in evaluating the theory empirically. Issues of research design and operationalization are discussed in the concluding section of this chapter.

Fifth, the threats faced by polities are assumed to be exogenous. Positing exogenous threats is merely an analytic convenience that produces a "cut" into the ongoing cycle of action and reaction in international politics. Phrased differently, the theory begins with the existence of a security threat from a third party and seeks to explain how the members of a dyad choose a particular response. This assumption allows me to focus on the relationship between two polities rather than the triadic relationship between two partners and a common foe. The threat from others, of course, is a complex phenomenon, driven by the third party's goals and risk propensities, the polity's own goals, the security dilemma, and many other factors. Without explaining where threats come from, it is nonetheless appropriate to ask how others respond.

Analytically, the origin and level of threat cannot by itself determine or explain the nature of the security relationship, if any, constructed between two polities. This is an important but subtle point for the analysis below. Threats from third parties may require responses by the polities, but threats do not mandate a particular response. Polities may choose to produce their desired level of security through unilateralism or cooperation, and within the latter through any of the security relationships discussed in Chapter 2. To the extent that these relationships are true alternatives, however, threats alone cannot explain why one option is chosen over another.

Finally, the present theory is decision theoretic in construction. The reactions of a polity to the actions of its partner are not modeled explicitly. Nonetheless, following the first assumption above, the actions and reactions of polities are assumed to be anticipated by partners and factored into their calculations. The governance costs of empire, for example, include the anticipated resistance of the subordinate polity to the dominant polity's demands and the anticipated costs to the latter of either inducing or coercing the former's compliance. It would, of course, be preferable to have a fully strategic theory, but because of the complexity of the choice problem addressed in this book a game theoretic model remains out of reach, at least for now.[34]

Although one must be cautious in claiming too much for a theory, I am

---

[34] In some areas, it is possible to specify verbally the strategic "game" (or, more accurately, subgame) being played by two polities. In these instances, I use the insights gained while recognizing that they remain only partial because the full game is not articulated. Portions of the theory also overlap with game models developed by others; these models produce very similar results to those below, and can be understood, in some sense, to replicate and validate the decision-theoretic approach taken here. See Papayoanou 1995; Niou and Ordeshook 1994. Powell forthcoming examines within a single unified framework what I refer to here as unilateralism and cooperation within anarchic security relationships (as well as appeasement). He does not, however, consider when states choose one response to threats over another.

reasonably confident in the robust nature of its conclusions. When based on rational expectations, decision theoretic results appear to converge on game theoretic equilibria.[35] Empirically, decision theory is most appropriate when polities are either relationship "makers"—that is, large polities able to set the terms of their relationships with others by declaration—or relationship "takers," small polities that cannot significantly influence the actions of others. In the years after both World War II and the Cold War, the United States clearly falls into the first category; thus, the choice of cases partially offsets the restrictions of decision theory. Regardless, the decision theoretic construction remains an important limitation. Recognizing this, I nonetheless offer the current theory for consideration and, in the spirit of ongoing debate, invite readers to challenge, extend, and possibly refine its logic.

## *Joint Production Economies*

The cost of producing security can be enormous. Polities must bear the expense of staffing an army, navy, and air force, purchasing and maintaining equipment, and investing in military technology and force planning. All of these activities consume scarce resources or factors of production, including capital, human capital, labor, and land. The cost of producing security is properly measured by the rates of return to the factors of production in their next best occupations.

Whether a polity chooses to produce unilaterally or in cooperation with others, it consumes some resources in producing security. When there are joint production economies (or joint economies, for short), however, polities may consume fewer resources by pooling their efforts with others. As polities employ technologies that lower the costs of projecting force over distance, enter into a division of labor, or create positive externalities that are "internalized" in a security relationship, the factors of production that are necessary to produce any given level of security decline. It is the desire to capture these joint economies that motivates all cooperation. Nonetheless, joint production economies vary over time and across dyads, creating greater or lesser incentives to pool resources and efforts. The greater the joint economies, the more likely polities are to cooperate.

### SCALE ECONOMIES

Technological innovations that lower the cost of projecting force over distance increase the economies of scale in producing security. When scale economies are large, one polity may be able to protect the territory of a second more

---

[35] Bueno de Mesquita 1993, 161. This is intuitively plausible but lacks, as far as I know, any formal proof. It is unlikely to hold under *all* circumstances. Nonetheless, it is suggestive to note that all of the decision-theoretic results in Bueno de Mesquita 1981 are subsumed within the game-theoretic models in Bueno de Mesquita and Lalman 1992.

cheaply than the latter can itself. Alternatively, the two polities working together can produce the same aggregate level of security as before, but with
fewer resources than would be required by each individually.[36]

The production of security has been traditionally characterized by increasing returns to scale over some finite distance. Frederic C. Lane asserts this as
a historical truism.[37] Richard Bean finds the source of these increasing returns
in the geographic fact that area increases more rapidly than borders.[38] Technologies that reduce the costs of projecting force over distance also alter scale
economies and, in turn, the optimal area of protection.[39]

As scale economies increase, the optimal area for which security can be
produced expands; when scale economies decrease, the optimal area
contracts. Bean shows how the scale economies produced by well-drilled
infantry led to relatively large political units until the fourth century A.D.;
how the subsequent dominance of the cavalry and, later, castles, both of
which lacked substantial scale economies, led to smaller political units; and
how the rise of the pike phalanx and castle-destroying cannon in the fourteenth century led to a recentralization of authority and the modern state.[40]
Likewise, the steam-powered navy was a contributing factor to the race for
colonies in the late nineteenth century. The offensive advantages of mass
armies, railroads, and, later, armored warfare created similar incentives for
France and Germany to seek continental empires.[41] Technological changes
that produce larger scale economies create incentives for polities to pool their
resources and efforts, since they can be defended more cheaply as a collective
than as individual units.

Technological scale economies produce what is sometimes called offense
dominance, but largely at the strategic rather than tactical level.[42] For instance, railroads greatly increased the strategic mobility of armies from the

---

[36] Scale economies are defined by the relationship between production inputs and outputs.
Constant returns to scale exist when increases in the quantity of factors employed lead to an
equal and proportionate increase in the quantity of output. Under increasing returns, increased
inputs lead to more than proportionate increases in output.

[37] Lane 1958.

[38] Bean 1973.

[39] Although technologies may differ in their scale economies, there may not be a single "best
practice" form of production, especially once the considerations discussed elsewhere in this
chapter are incorporated into the choice; even on technological grounds alone, however, there
may be several alternative modes of production that utilize different methods but prove equally
viable. Just as the textile industry allows small and large firms to compete successfully against
one another by employing different production techniques, so too is the security industry likely
to sustain polities using different strategies for producing security. Nonetheless, as technologies
evolve, strategy should change to reflect alterations in scale economies.

[40] Bean 1973. See also McNeill 1982.

[41] Quester 1977; van Creveld 1989.

[42] On offense versus defense dominance, see Quester 1977; Jervis 1978; Posen 1984; J.
Snyder 1984; and Van Evera 1984 and 1986.

late nineteenth century, allowing countries to move larger numbers of forces more rapidly and cheaply over longer distances; railroads did not, however, increase the mobility of these forces on the battlefield itself, where armies were, around the time of World War I, limited in movement not only by the increased firepower of their adversaries but also by their increasingly heavy supply "tails" and poor logistics.[43] It is at the strategic level that technological scale economies are most evident and, for this study, most important.

Despite scale economies that are often large, the marginal costs of projecting force over distance will eventually begin to rise, limiting the optimal area of production. Increasing returns are constrained at the margin by geographic features, such as mountains or rivers that form natural lines of defense, and logistical difficulties, including command and control problems in larger and more varied forces. The latter were especially important in the Roman empire, when in the second century A.D. it began to convert its mobile legions and forward defense strategy into fixed legions engaged in defense in depth.[44] Both Napoleon's and Hitler's quests for continental hegemony ended in defeat largely because they ignored the limits of the available scale economies and eventually became overextended. Although all are eventually exhausted, some technologies nonetheless possess scale economies that are larger than others. Changes in technological scale economies underlie some of the great political changes of world history.

Security cooperation induced by increased technological scale economies, however, need not take the form of relational hierarchies. Bean and other analysts err by positing that greater scale economies lead straightforwardly to larger unified polities. In principle, alliances between autonomous polities can secure the same scale economies as could protectorates, informal empires and other security relationships. As the most efficient defense perimeter shifts outward, partners are required to host forces on their territory. Likewise, the polity enjoying the increased scale economies receives no benefits directly unless its partner contributes forces to the joint effort, thereby releasing resources in the home polity for other purposes, or pays some form of tribute. For both polities, the benefits from greater scale economies come entirely from releasing factors of production from now unnecessary activities in one, the other, or both. However, neither hosting forces nor burden sharing requires that the partners be integrated into a single relational hierarchy. By themselves, increased scale economies are insufficient to explain the rise of hierarchical security relationships.

Shifting attention from territorial expansion to partnerships allows us to see the more general effect of changes in technological scale economies on security relationships. Greater scale economies always require new partners if

---

[43] van Creveld 1989, 174–77.
[44] See Luttwak 1976.

they are to be effectively exploited. Although steam-powered navies allowed greater firepower to be brought to bear in any particular battle, for instance, they also required extensive networks of overseas coaling stations, some of which were controlled as formal colonies but most of which were not.[45] Likewise, the "long-range" aircraft developed by the allies in World War II required refueling facilities or forward bases to reach their areas of operation, and first-generation missiles developed by the United States had to be deployed in Eurasia to reach their targets in the Soviet Union. These technological innovations dramatically lowered the costs of projecting force and allowed polities to develop a global reach at an acceptable price, but they also required new forms of cooperation if they were to be employed effectively.[46] For the United States, as we shall see in Chapter 5, these increased scale economies did not result, in most cases, in hierarchic relationships.[47] For the Soviet Union, on the other hand, many of these same innovations supported the informal empire in Eastern Europe.[48] Scale economies promote cooperation, but they do not dictate particular security relationships.

Technological change that lowers the costs of projecting force has important implications for international relations. Much of the recent security literature has focused on technology and the propensity for war. Yet, as recognized by economic historians and some political scientists, technological change can also produce incentives for security cooperation.

### THE DIVISION OF LABOR

As with other goods, there are "gains from trade" in security that are potentially available to polities. Polities can improve their welfare, or reduce the factors they must employ in producing security, by specializing in the production of defense and exchanging one form of effort for another. These gains are only available through some form of joint production. The more extensive the division of labor between polities, the greater the benefits from security cooperation.[49]

Defense effort is composed of many distinct activities. Let us assume, for simplicity, that we can think of these efforts as organized into two intermediate products: an army, used to defend territory, and a navy, employed to

[45] Quester 1977, 86–88; van Creveld 1989, 204.

[46] The French attempt to create a forward defense in Belgium in 1940 illustrates the costs of failing to coordinate effectively with one's allies: Quester 1977, 141; Posen 1984, 103.

[47] Some recent developments—such as the ICBM and nuclear-powered ships—have reduced the need for forward bases, confirming that the benefits from cooperation can decrease as well as increase. At the same time, other innovations, particularly "flexible response" and the need for advanced monitoring and early-warning systems, have increased the need for forward bases and thus reinforced past gains from cooperation. Harkavay 1993.

[48] Lake 1996 and 1997.

[49] For a related but broader conception of the division of labor in security affairs, see Boyer 1993.

protect sea lanes and coasts. Each polity can choose to manufacture both products on its own, fielding an independent army and navy; in this sense, unilateralism is equivalent to an autarkic economic strategy. Alternatively, the two polities can choose to specialize according to their respective comparative advantages and exchange the effort of one's army for the other's navy. Even though no goods are actually transferred, no money changes hands, and there is no price announced, the cooperation and the agreement between the two partners can be understood to embody the implicit barter and terms of exchange. By specializing according to their comparative advantages, the polities redeploy their efforts toward their most productive uses, increase the total defense effort obtained, and reap the gains from the other's comparatively less expensive (more efficient) defense efforts. Each polity increases its welfare by either enjoying more security for the same cost or, holding the quantity of security constant, freeing factors for use elsewhere in the economy.

As with other goods, the gains from trade are positively related to differences in factor endowments between the two partners and thus the difference in relative prices for the forms of defense effort in autarky. All other things considered, relatively similar polities have fewer potential gains from a division of labor than relatively dissimilar polities.[50] The technology of production also influences the optimal degree of specialization; specialization between the partners need not be complete for there to be substantial gains from trade.[51] Factor endowments and technology set the outer limits to the gains from specialization and exchange.

The extent to which polities engage in a division of labor in the production of security, however, is also a policy choice. Just as polities may use tariffs to "protect" their industries from foreign competition and thereby forfeit gains from trade, so may polities choose not to specialize in security or in particular areas of security production.[52] Most important, polities may

---

[50] The same logic underlies the proposition in international trade theory that small polities benefit comparatively more from trade than large polities. It is the opportunity to exchange goods at prices different from one's own that makes trade attractive.

[51] Again, there is a parallel in traditional international trade theory. In a Ricardian model of trade with one factor of production and constant returns, polities specialize completely (the production-possibilities frontier is a straight line, and opening to trade causes polities to specialize entirely in that good they produce best). In a Heckscher-Ohlin model with two factors of production and diminishing returns, however, specialization is typically incomplete (the production-possibilities frontier is concave, and the gains from trade are normally exhausted prior to complete specialization).

[52] There are, of course, circumstances under which free trade is not the optimal policy: when polities are large and can shift the terms of trade to their advantage, there are increasing returns to scale and first-mover advantages, there are domestic externalities from production, and so on. If the assumption of wealth maximization central to neoclassical trade theory is relaxed, it is possible to generate even more conditions under which free trade is not optimal. Nonetheless,

forfeit degrees of specialization as a hedge against opportunism (see below). Nonetheless, the greater the degree of specialization, the greater the gains from pooling resources.

For reasons discussed below, polities have been reluctant historically to engage in substantial defense specialization. Nonetheless, there was some exchange between France and Britain in the years before both world wars, with the former focusing its efforts on the territorial defense of the continent and the latter emphasizing its control of the seas. Likewise, after World War II there was a division of labor between the United States and countries of Western Europe, embodied in the North Atlantic Treaty Organization: the United States provided generalized deterrence of the Soviet Union through its strategic arsenal, deep-water navy, and air power; the Europeans concentrated on the conventional labor- and land-intensive defense of the continent.[53] The reluctance of polities to pursue the gains from trade in security does not vitiate the existence of such potential rewards. As these examples suggest, the potential gains from trade have in the past helped motivate security cooperation.

### POSITIVE EXTERNALITIES

Also important in determining the gains from cooperation are the positive externalities polities may receive as a result of the security efforts of others. Positive externalities are benefits created by an activity that are not limited or confined to the party producing the good. Just as security forms a public good within countries, the security produced by a polity may benefit other polities within the international system as well. If a polity blocks another's drive for hegemony, it benefits others within the system. Likewise, if a "front line" polity deters expansion by another, it protects those polities which lie to its rear. By "internalizing" or integrating their separate defense efforts within a single relationship, both parties can potentially improve their welfare.

The magnitude and distribution of positive externalities are shaped by threats within the international system and geography, both of which are exogenous to the choices of polities. The origin and nature of the prevailing threats to any dyad determine whether actions by any one party benefit the other. At the extreme, if only one member of a dyad is threatened by a third party, its actions to defend itself against attack provide no benefits for its

---

over a broad class of reasonable circumstances, free trade does appear to improve the welfare of polities.

[53] The measure of specialization is not whether the United States dedicated a substantial number of troops to Europe or even whether it provided more troops than some of the European states themselves. Rather, the United States devoted more resources to the strategic deterrent, navy, and air force relative to its number of troops than the Europeans devoted to the same activities relative to their troops. See Chapter 5.

potential partner. Similarly, geography influences the nature of threats and, in conjunction with technology, whether actions by one member of a dyad will provide benefits for the second. In the interwar years, for instance, the United States was still relatively insulated from direct attack by its oceanic moats; only when the attack on Pearl Harbor demonstrated that it was, in fact, vulnerable, did the United States feel threatened in the same way as its European and Asian partners. Until that time, geography shielded the United States, and made it less sensitive to both the threats and defense efforts of others. Conversely, France's unilateral defense efforts in this same period, and especially its building of the Maginot Line, provided some measure of protection for itself against Germany, but few benefits for others—and it may even have increased the risk to the Netherlands and Belgium by channeling German forces into the low countries. In many cases, however, there are significant positive externalities produced by one polity that benefit others. The United States, though relatively insulated from continental threats, nonetheless benefited from European efforts to maintain a continental balance of power during the interwar years, despite its own vociferous refusal to coordinate its policies in any way with its potential (and eventual) allies (see Chapter 4). Similarly, United States efforts to deter expansion by the Soviet Union after 1945 provided benefits to other polities in both Europe and Asia (see Chapter 5).

By coordinating and pooling efforts in the presence of positive externalities, polities can reduce the factors of production necessary for maintaining a given level of security. In unilateralism, polities may produce security for themselves that benefits others. They may also gain from the production of others. When producing independently, however, one or both polities may believe it necessary and wise to maintain their efforts to deter (or fight) a potential adversary. If and when brought together, their joint production will then be greater than what is necessary to provide an adequate deterrent, and incurred at a higher marginal cost than marginal benefit. One, the other, or both can then reduce their effort and release factors of production for other valued uses. Through cooperation, in short, one or both parties can improve their welfare by reducing redundant production.

When externalities are present, polities may also be able to improve their welfare by redistributing the burden of producing security. Through cooperation, one polity may be able to free ride more effectively on the other, producing less defense effort itself and relying to a greater extent upon the production of the other. Alternatively, a polity that produces an externality enjoyed by another may be able to reduce its own costs by "taxing" the second for the benefits received. Although plagued by free riding, and the counterfactual cannot be known, it is likely that the postwar cooperation between the United States and its allies in Western Europe, for instance, allowed Washington to extract greater contributions from its partners—particularly in the form of German rearmament—than would have been possible if it had retained its traditional unilateralism; a comparison of allied and nonallied states in Western Europe after 1945 supports this inference (see Chapter 5). Where reducing redundant production can potentially benefit both parties, redistributing the burden is a zero-sum bargain in which one party's gain is the other's loss. Both types of gains can be pursued simultaneously, perhaps accounting for both NATO's resilience during the Cold War and its periodic wrangles over burden sharing.

CHOOSING JOINT PRODUCTION ECONOMIES

Joint production economies are determined, in part, by the environment in which polities find themselves. Only certain technologies exist at any time.[54] Positive externalities are contingent upon the locus of the common threat and geography. Factor differences influence the gains from specialization and exchange. Exogenous changes in technology, threats, and factors of production will affect the magnitude of the joint economies and, in turn, will make cooperation more or less likely.[55]

Through the mutual adjustment of policy, moreover, polities can nearly always create joint production economies. By entering into a division of labor, employing technologies that reply upon forward-based partners, or reducing redundant production and sharing common burdens, polities can create joint gains from cooperation. In this way, joint economies are, in a sense, endogenous to the policy choices made by polities. Lest this suggest only a tautology, however, it is important to clarify that it is the desire to capture joint production economies that motivates all cooperation. It is the intent that explains the action, not the reverse. Polities choose the range of technologies available to them when they choose unilateralism or cooperation, and they make this choice, in turn, to reap the benefits made possible by technological innovation. The same holds for the division of labor and positive externalities. Although joint economies exist, and may exogenously expand or contract over time, the extent of the division of labor, scale economies, and positive externalities that are internalized through cooperation are, in fact, choices made by polities when deciding whether or not to pool their resources and efforts with others. To justify cooperation, there must be some advantage to pooling resources and efforts with others that cannot be obtained unilaterally; otherwise, polities are better off relying upon their own resources or, if these prove insufficient, capitulating to the threatening party.

---

[54] This may also be affected at the margin by incentives for research and development.

[55] These factors are, of course, primary variables in extant theories of security studies; on this point, and others, I do not pose the theory as an alternative to others, but as a complement. See Posen 1984; J. Snyder 1984; and Walt 1987. The theory here, however, sees geography, technology, and threats as mediated by their effects on joint production economies, and interacting with the expected costs of opportunism and governance costs.

Whether polities choose to cooperate depends critically on the magnitude of the joint economies they select.

## Opportunism

Opportunism is ubiquitous in international relations. Polities do not honor commitments out of a sense of obligation, but press for individual advantages whenever possible. According to Williamson, opportunism includes both blatant forms of self-interest seeking, "such as lying, stealing, and cheating," and subtle forms of deceit. "More generally," he writes, "opportunism refers to the incomplete or distorted disclosure of information, especially to calculated efforts to mislead, distort, disguise, obfuscate, or otherwise confuse."[56] With particular reference to conflict, James Fearon has recently called this the problem of "private information with incentives to misrepresent," and has pointed to it as a major cause of interstate war.[57] Such "information failures" are also a major determinant of the security relationships between polities. Whenever they cooperate in a world of costly information, polities must suffer the costs of opportunism by their partners or work out beforehand some security relationship to reduce the risk of opportunism.

Opportunism also arises from sequences of mutually contingent actions, or what is sometimes called the "time-inconsistency" problem or the problem of credible commitment.[58] Immediate or "spot" exchanges seldom carry the potential for opportunism: good A is exchanged for good B or an equivalent amount of money, and the faceless transactors walk away mutually satisfied.[59] Sequenced exchanges that proceed in a series of steps and occur over time create quite a different problem. If good A is exchanged today for the promise of the delivery of good B (or its monetary equivalent) next week, it may not be in the interest of the second actor to carry out its promise to turn over good B at the agreed price. Even if full information is available, and the parties know everything that is to be known about the other, sequential interactions still possess the potential for opportunistic behavior; under some circumstances it may be impossible for the parties to commit not to behave "badly." In the absence of a mechanism to regulate such behavior, mutually beneficial interactions may be forgone or entered into only if the benefits are sufficiently high to offset the expected loses from opportunistic partners.

In international relations, polities face three kinds of opportunistic behav-

---

[56] Williamson 1985, 47.

[57] Fearon 1995. For a general discussion of information and sequence in international relations, see Morrow forthcoming.

[58] Fearon 1995.

[59] This is, of course, the expectation of relational contracting theory. Exchanges that are sequenced or based on highly specific assets will not take place on the spot market. If they occur at all, such exchanges will be internalized in some governance structure.

ior by their partners. Polities may be *abandoned*; that is, partners may shirk by formally or informally abrogating agreements. In ways large and small, partners may fail to fulfill their commitments. More generally, abandonment is a problem of adverse selection, a common problem in insurance markets where insurers cannot differentiate between risks, and actors who are poor risks have no incentive to reveal their true propensities. Polities may be *entrapped* by their partners into undesired conflicts and wars. As such, entrapment is a problem of moral hazard, also a problem in insurance markets, where commitments, once issued, cause the partner to act in a more risky, negligent, or aggressive fashion than before.[60] Finally, polities may be *exploited*. Having settled on an initial division of the benefits and costs of the relationship, partners may subsequently seek to alter the terms of agreements and obtain more favorable distributions of the joint gains. This is the general problem of appropriable quasi rents.[61] In all three circumstances, both incomplete information and sequential actions make cooperation between the parties difficult.[62]

All three forms of opportunism, moreover, can arise from the intentional or unintentional actions of partners. Polities may enter into agreements that they do not intend to honor—indeed, they may only reach agreement because they expect to act opportunistically some portion of the time. They may also negotiate in good faith but find themselves unable to fulfill their commitments due to circumstances that were unanticipated at the time of the agreement. Regardless of the intent of the first party, the net effect on the second is the same: it is either abandoned, entrapped, or exploited.

When it occurs, opportunism is costly to a polity. Its partner contributes less to the joint product than promised, forces the polity to divert its own resources toward undesired ends, or seizes a greater share of the joint gain than agreed. Abandonment, for instance, not only reduces the contribution of the partner but can also reduce the efficacy of the polity's own defense efforts; if the polity has specialized in a land-based army and its partner has agreed to provide the complementary naval defense, for instance, opportunism by the latter may leave the former more vulnerable than if it had produced both an army and navy of its own.

The actual cost to a polity of such behavior is determined by the opportunity cost of the resources used in cooperation. Opportunity costs, in turn, are determined by the degree to which assets are relationally specific, or

---

[60] The terms *abandonment* and *entrapment* are from G. Snyder 1984.

[61] Klein, Crawford, and Alchian 1978.

[62] On adverse selection and moral hazard, see Rasmusen 1989, 133–222, but especially 133–36. Rasmusen distinguishes between moral harzard, which depends upon sequenced and unobservable actions, and adverse selection, which depends upon incomplete information. The three quintessential problems in international relations—abandonment, entrapment, and exploitation—typically combine elements of both.

possess more value in one use and relationship than in others. This relationally specific value is also known as the asset's quasi rent. Assets can be highly flexible and easily transferred from one application to another or highly specialized and difficult to redirect. The more relationally specific the asset, the greater are the quasi rents and, in turn, the costs to the polity if a partner should act opportunistically. In security affairs, relationally specific assets range from military forces requiring large investments in dedicated infrastructure or hardware (such as heavily armored divisions designed for a land war against the former Soviet Union or American intermediate-range missiles developed for overseas deployment) to ports uniquely located in strategic areas (such as Guam; see Chapter 5). Nearly all divisions of labor entail some asset specificity: moving from specialized and integrated forces to an autonomous military necessarily requires retooling, retraining, redeployment, and time. The costs of abandonment in the example just noted, for instance, are determined by the costs of redeploying resources used in land-based defenses to naval defenses, which is likely to require a time-consuming and costly effort. In sum, the more specific its assets, the greater the polity's opportunity costs and, in turn, the greater the costs inflicted by the partner's opportunistic behavior.

The probability that a partner will act opportunistically ex post is a function of the security relationship that the polities choose to construct ex ante. As noted in Chapter 2, agreements vary in both their specificity and the rights of residual control possessed by each member; indeed, the latter is the defining attribute of relational hierarchy. In constructing agreements, polities are defining the terms of their relationship and the potential for cheating, defection, and other forms of opportunism. The ability of a polity to act opportunistically is determined by its rights of residual control. The greater its residual rights, the greater its discretion to act in ways that may undermine the joint security effort. Most important, the polity retains both its private information (and its incentives to misrepresent that information) and its ability to make future decisions. The smaller its residual rights, on the other hand, the less discretion a polity possesses, now and in the future. The dominant partner also has greater latitude to structure incentives to extract private information from its subordinate.[63] Thus, by implication, the probability or "risk" that the partner will engage in opportunistic behavior decreases with relational hierarchy. Under hierarchy, the partner simply does not possess the ability or the incentive to act opportunistically.

In an alliance, for instance, each partner retains complete residual rights and thus wide discretion to act in future contingencies on private preferences that were not disclosed to the other. Even though it may agree to declare war

---

[63] On problems of delegation in economics and politics, see Jensen and Meckling 1976; McCubbins and Schwartz 1984; and Kiewiet and McCubbins 1991.

if a third party attacks its ally, a polity nonetheless retains the right to decide who "attacked" and how many resources it will actually commit to the conflict. In anarchic relations, everything else being equal, the probability that the partner will behave opportunistically is comparatively high. In an empire, at the other extreme, polities merge their formerly autonomous decision making processes, reducing problems of "private" information, and transfer rights of residual control to the dominant member, reducing problems of sequential decision making. The dominant polity now decides—to continue with the same example—who is the "victim" of any attack (presumably itself), who is the "aggressor," and how many resources its subordinate can and must mobilize. In World Wars I and II, for instance, when Britain declared war on Germany, the rest of its empire was automatically at war as well, becoming belligerents in the European conflict whether they wanted to or not. In practice, however, even in imperial relationships there is likely to be some local decision-making authority and thus some potential for opportunism. Moreover, it is difficult to design mechanisms that eliminate the problem of private information; even colonial governors sent from the metropole sometimes saw their career prospects enhanced by serving the local constituency rather than their bosses back home. Nonetheless, the more hierarchical the relationship, the lower the probability that the subordinate partner will act opportunistically. It is precisely this desire to reduce the risk of opportunism by partners that leads polities to form hierarchical relationships.

The expected cost of opportunism is a function of its actual cost, if it occurs, and its probability. These costs can be absorbed directly by the polity; here, the polity simply accepts some opportunism by its partner as a necessary evil. Conversely, the polity can deploy some of its own resources as a hedge against possible opportunism. Even when a partner has agreed to help protect it, for instance, a polity may maintain redundant forces for fear that its partner will not produce the promised benefits. Hedging is a form of insurance against opportunism. Like actual opportunism, it is costly to the polity.

Holding the specificity of the asset (and thus the actual cost of opportunism if it occurs) constant, the expected costs of opportunism decline with relational hierarchy ($\Phi$ in Figure 3.1a). As the ability of the subordinate polity to act opportunistically falls, so do the expected costs. A port in a strategic location illustrates this point. The degree of asset specificity in this instance is fixed. The polities either cooperate, and one grants the other basing rights, or they do not. If they cooperate, one polity cannot invest more or less in the asset, it simply is. In this case, the actual cost of opportunism, if it occurs, remains the same across alternative security relationships, and the expected costs of opportunism are determined solely by the type of security relationship constructed by the parties. If the asset is highly specific,

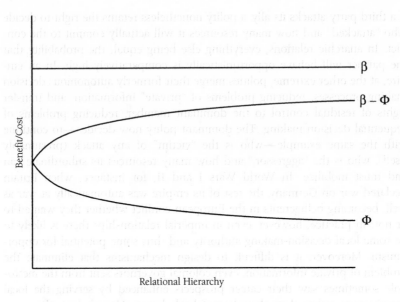

β

β – Φ

Φ

Benefit/Cost

Relational Hierarchy

a. Constant Joint Production Economies, Declining Expected
Costs of Opportunism

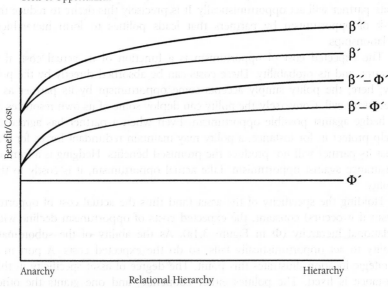

β″

β′

β″– Φ′

β′– Φ′

Benefit/Cost

Φ′

Anarchy

Relational Hierarchy

Hierarchy

b. Constant Expected Costs of Opportunism, Increasing Joint
Production Economies

Figure 3.1. Joint Production Economies and Expected Costs of Opportunism

and the actual costs of opportunism are high, polities may only cooperate if a hierarchical relationship can be formed. In this case, we would normally observe either unilateralism—that is, no cooperation—or an empire (if the governance costs of such a relationship are not too high; see below).

The expected benefits of cooperation, in turn, are defined as the resources saved through the joint economies in cooperation minus the expected costs of opportunism. Joint economies release resources from producing a fixed level of security, whereas opportunism either reduces the effectiveness of the remaining factors of production or, equivalently, requires additional factors to hedge against its effects. Holding joint economies constant, while expected costs of opportunism decline with hierarchy, the expected benefits of cooperation will rise with relational hierarchy. This is illustrated in Figure 3.1a, where $\beta$ represents the joint production economies and $\Phi$ represents the expected costs of opportunism, drawn here to reflect diminishing marginal returns to hierarchy. With joint economies held constant across alternative relationships, the expected benefits of cooperation ($\beta - \Phi$) are simply the inverse of the expected costs of opportunism. Normalizing the returns to unilateralism at the origin, the higher the expected benefits curve, the greater the benefits from cooperation. In other words, the higher the expected benefits curve, the larger the joint economies or the lower the expected costs of opportunism.

Polities may also choose to invest in more relationally specific assets, however, as they enter into more hierarchic security relationships. Knowing that its subordinate partner is less able to act opportunistically, for instance, a polity in a more hierarchic security relationship may choose to incur more relationally specific assets. In this case, although the probability that its partner will act opportunistically falls with greater hierarchy, the expected costs of opportunism may either decline, but more slowly than was the case above, or remain constant, if the lower probability is fully offset by the greater actual cost of opportunism were it to occur.

Polities will choose to invest in greater asset specificity only if such investments simultaneously increase the joint economies in cooperation. If joint economies do not expand, greater asset specificity only decreases the expected benefits of cooperation. On the other hand, utilizing the most efficient technologies or internalizing positive externalities will often require more specific assets; this is almost always the case for a deeper division of labor. As polities enter into more hierarchic relationships, they can choose to pursue these greater joint economies even though they incur more specific assets as well. In short, greater hierarchy allows polities to invest in greater joint economies, further increasing the benefits of cooperation. In this way, the joint economies of cooperation are partly endogenous to the choice of security relationship.

Figure 3.1b illustrates the case of positively related specific assets and joint economies. In this figure, $\Phi'$ represents the special case of constant expected costs of opportunism, where the increase in asset specificity—and, thus, the actual costs of opportunism, should it occur—is exactly offset by the decline in the probability of opportunism from greater hierarchy. If the increase in the joint economies is sufficiently large, the expected benefits will remain the same ($\beta' - \Phi' = \beta - \Phi$) or be larger ($\beta'' - \Phi' > \beta - \Phi$). In those cases where the increase in the joint economies is not sufficiently large relative to the increase in the expected costs of opportunism, and where the expected benefits of cooperation would actually be reduced by greater investments in joint economies, polities will choose not to make more relationally specific investments. Constant joint economies ($\beta$) and declining expected costs of opportunism ($\Phi$), illustrated in Figure 3.1a, form the baseline case against which other investment possibilities are measured.

Not only may polities choose hierarchy to reduce the expected costs of opportunism but they may also create hierarchies to expand their joint economies when rising asset specificity would otherwise thwart cooperation. Thus, reductions in the expected costs of opportunism may be "traded" for greater joint economies, depending upon the precise relationship between such economies and asset specificity.

The expected costs of opportunism are crucial in shaping the choice between unilateralism and cooperation, on the one hand, and among alternative security relationships, on the other. The expected costs of opportunism also condition the willingness of polities to invest in greater joint economies, and thus interact to define the expected benefits of cooperation. As the expected costs of opportunism fall or the expected benefits of cooperation rise with relational hierarchy, polities should normally prefer more hierarchic security relationships and we should observe, over time, a trend toward empires. One could argue, although I do not myself hold strongly to this view, that the consolidation of the modern world into multipolity states organized as internal hierarchies is evidence for this trend.[64] At the same time, there is certainly no movement toward universal hierarchy. That this is not the case is the result of governance costs.

### Governance Costs

Polities incur governance costs in creating and maintaining all security relationships. Governance costs are a type of transactions costs. According to one widely cited definition, "The fundamental idea of transactions costs is that they consist of the cost of arranging a contract ex ante and monitoring and enforcing it ex post, as opposed to production costs, which are the costs

---

[64] On the superiority of the sovereign territorial state over rival city-states and confederations, see Spruyt 1994.

of executing a contract."[65] Transactions costs are often taken to include such diverse activities as searching for buyers and sellers, acquiring information about the price and quality of goods, and bargaining to find the true position of the parties when prices are endogenous.[66] In focusing here on governance costs, I am primarily concerned with the costs of making agreements, monitoring partners, and enforcing agreements—the core purposes behind security relationships.

Governance costs take three distinct forms: lost autonomy and distorted incentives in the subordinate partner, safeguards on the dominant polity, and coercion.[67] Despite the prominence attached to coercion in international relations—defined broadly to include all threats or actions designed to reduce the welfare of the partner unless certain behaviors are performed (compellence) or not performed (deterrence)—its role and importance is more easily understood once the logic of voluntary contracting is explicated. Governance costs increase with relational hierarchy, and deter polities from pursuing more hierarchic relationships.

### THE SUBORDINATE PARTNER

The primary costs to the subordinate polity of cooperation and hierarchy are, first, a loss of autonomy or security and, second, distorted incentives and reduced welfare. These costs are low in anarchic relationships, and increase with greater hierarchy. To enter voluntarily into a hierarchic relationship, in turn, the subordinate polity requires compensation from the dominant polity at least equal to the welfare it could achieve in a unilateral strategy. This compensation is a governance cost to the dominant polity.

The great irony of cooperation is that dominant polities pose progressively greater threats to subordinate polities as security relationships move from anarchy to hierarchy. As defined in Chapter 2, security is, in part, the ability to accumulate and allocate wealth as a polity desires and this, in turn, requires both the freedom to possess wealth and the freedom to choose one's own form of rule. As the rights of residual control shift from the subordinate polity to the dominant polity, the freedom of the former to decide autonomously how to accumulate and use its wealth is increasingly constrained. The dominant polity exercises control over more areas of policy and limits the subordinate polity's ability to decide its own fate. To produce security against a predatory third party, the subordinate polity in a hierarchic security relationship exposes itself to threats from the dominant polity.

Polities are likely to behave differently when in positions of dominance, with some being more exploitative and therefore more threatening than

---

[65] Matthews 1986, 906. For other definitions, see Dahlman 1979.

[66] Eggertsson 1990, 15.

[67] There may also be maladaption costs when circumstances change and render existing agreements between polities less appropriate. See Williamson 1985, 21; and North 1990.

others. In gauging the degree of threat, the subordinate polity will estimate how the dominant polity is likely to use its greater residual rights of control. In 1945, for example, many German soldiers fled before the advancing Red Army into the arms of American troops, preferring to trust their fate to the Western democracies rather than the Soviet dictatorship. Although the theory of relational contracting posed here cannot account for why such variations in the behavior of dominant polities arise, that they do vary is not inconsistent with the theory (I return to this point in Chapter 7). Regardless of this variation, however, the loss of residual control or security to any other party is a substantial cost to the subordinate polity, and that polity will demand some form of compensation if it is to enter voluntarily a hierarchical relationship.

The shift of decision-making authority to the dominant polity also distorts incentives for the efficient use of resources in the subordinate member of the dyad, creating an indirect governance cost. With complete decision-making authority, as in anarchy, parties to an agreement are motivated to produce security in the most efficient manner possible, as the resources thereby "saved" from less productive alternatives can be used for other valued purposes.[68] As the subordinate party's authority shrinks, its incentives are altered; the resources released by efficient production are subject to increasing control by the dominant polity and, thus, less valuable to the subordinate. As the subordinate party's authority recedes, incentives in other areas of economic and political life are distorted, as well. By definition, as residual rights decline, the dominant polity is exercising control over a greater range of behavior and, by implication, directing resources to uses the subordinate party would not choose on its own. As decision-making authority shifts from one party to the other, distortions in the subordinate member multiply.[69]

These distortions—both in the production of security and other areas—can, in part, be corrected by additional oversight provisions that mandate certain specified actions by the subordinate party. When this solution is adopted, however, the dominant polity must employ additional resources to monitor and safeguard the new provisions. As the distortions increase with relational hierarchy, the resources employed by and, therefore, the costs to the dominant polity must increase as well.[70] With costly information, distor-

---

[68] This argument parallels the assumption in microeconomic theory that individuals are best motivated when they are claimants on the profits of a firm. In the same way, polities are best motivated by the freedom to use their resources in any way they choose.

[69] This argument has a direct analog in the case of private firms; see Grossman and Hart 1986. Under hierarchy, subordinate polities have greater incentives to engage in strategic misrepresentation or shirk in unmonitored areas; see Miller and Cook 1994, 47. The distortions are roughly equivalent to the directly unproductive activities found in many rent-seeking enterprises; Bhagwati 1982 and 1983.

[70] In turn, when heavily monitored and controlled, the subordinate party may choose to shirk

tions cannot be removed entirely. Monitoring and safeguarding additional areas of behavior are subject to diminishing marginal returns. It is also efficient to shift the locus of residual control from one party to the other precisely when it is difficult to specify future contingencies. As a result, it is very costly to safeguard against all possible distortions.

The loss of autonomy and security and the inherent and uncorrectable distortions created within its society are substantial costs to the subordinate polity in any security relationship. These costs also increase rapidly with relational hierarchy. To gain the subordinate party's willing consent to a cooperative and hierarchic relationship, these costs must be compensated by some transfer or sidepayment from the dominant polity at least equal to the difference between the welfare of the subordinate member under unilateralism and its new level of welfare under cooperation. Presumably, the subordinate polity shares in the joint gains from cooperation, but it is precisely the fear that the dominant party will expropriate these gains and others that poses the threat in the first place. Moreover, since the joint gains are shared, and only the subordinate polity loses autonomy and confronts distortions, the subordinate polity will often require substantial compensation to gain its willing adherence to the relationship. As the subordinate partner's residual control declines, the compensation package offered by the dominant party must grow. That the costs of voluntarily negotiated hierarchies may be nearly prohibitive for dominant states may explain why coercion, discussed below, has historically played such an important role in the process of empire building.

These distortions in the subordinate polity will also accumulate over time, ultimately undermining the basis for a hierarchic relationship. Indeed, in part because of these accumulating distortions, hierarchy becomes an "obsolescing bargain" eventually doomed to failure.[71] Each distortion requires actors within the subordinate party to adjust their own behavior in individually rational but nonetheless socially inefficient ways, thereby producing further distortions in the economy. Over time, in a way similar to Mancur Olson's ossification thesis, the accumulated distortions become manifest in declining growth rates and economic stagnation (if not absolute decline).[72] At any moment in time, the dominant polity will offer a compensation package sufficient to keep the subordinate party from rebelling or otherwise breaking the relationship. As the distortions increase with time, the compensation package must also increase, raising the net cost of the relationship to the

---

by violating the spirit but not the rule of the agreement, "working to rule" or following the dominant polity's imposed edicts to the letter; but since agreements are necessarily incomplete over a wide range of circumstances, the subordinate polity's efforts must also be less productive. See Miller and Cook 1994, 41–42; also Miller 1992.

[71] The phrase is from Vernon 1971. It is equally appropriate here.

[72] Olson 1982.

dominant member. In this way, empires and other hierarchic relationships eventually become obsolete; from the dominant polity's point of view, a structure of costs and benefits that was attractive early in the relationship becomes ever less appealing as the relationship matures and the distortions and compensating sidepayments grow—as eventually occurred even in the Russian empire.[73] All else held constant, any hierarchic relationship will eventually become costly on net to the dominant polity. The more hierarchic the relationship, the sooner the break-even point will be reached.[74]

### SAFEGUARDS ON THE DOMINANT POLITY

Relational hierarchy shifts the locus of opportunism from the subordinate partner to the dominant state. As the partner's rights of residual control decline, the rights of the dominant polity over it expand, thereby increasing the potential that the latter will act opportunistically toward the former.[75] Especially important here is the enhanced ability of the dominant polity to exploit the subordinate party; by using its expanded decision-making authority, the polity can alter the terms of the initial contract to its advantage. In the absence of coercion, the subordinate partner will not submit to this vulnerable position unless the behavior of the dominant polity is adequately constrained in the agreement. In other words, the dominant polity must commit itself not to act opportunistically toward its subordinate, and it must construct safeguards to make this commitment credible.[76]

Central to any agreement are safeguards employed by both parties to protect their interests, ensure compliance, and thereby render the agreement enforceable. As Williamson suggests, such safeguards typically include first, actions designed to modify opportunity costs (sanctions for failing to perform the required actions, the exchange of hostages, sidepayments, and so on); second, "specialized governance structure(s) to which to refer and resolve disputes;" and third, "regularities that support and signal continuity intentions."[77] Safeguards can apply both to the items in the agreement and to the residual rights of control. They impose costs on polities directly by committing them to particular undertakings designed to modify opportunity

---

[73] See Bunce 1985; and Lake 1997.

[74] The discount rates of polities will obviously matter here. Given the obsolescing bargain in hierarchy, polities with a high discount factor (that is, they do not value the future heavily) will tend toward more hierarchic relationships, whereas polities with a low discount factor (that is, they do value the future heavily) will tend toward more anarchic relationships.

[75] Dow 1987.

[76] On the problem of credible commitments in international relations, see Powell 1990; Bueno de Mesquita and Lalman 1992; Cowhey 1993; and Fearon 1995. Fearon 1993 focuses on precisely the problem here—that after consolidation the weaker party will become even weaker—and finds that under a wide range of circumstances the weaker side will choose to fight rather than accept an agreement that is not credible.

[77] Williamson 1985, 34.

costs and signal continuity intentions, such as deploying troops in exposed "tripwire" positions to assuage allied fears of abandonment. Safeguards also produce costs through the creation and maintenance of specialized governance structures, ranging from, say, NATO today to Britain's imperial offices at home and abroad in the nineteenth century. All three types of safeguards come together in international coalitions, a complex institution that binds— to some extent—potentially dominant powers to consenual goals and strategies (in Chapter 6, I suggest that this particular safeguard has been critical to America's post-Cold War security relationships). The more extensive and severe the safeguards, the more costly they are; the greater the safeguards, in other words, the greater the resources that are employed to alter opportunity costs, signal continuity intentions, and create and maintain specialized institutions.

Any partner will insist upon adequate safeguards against future opportunism prior to entering voluntarily into a relationship. Given the shift in the locus of decision making, subordinate partners will be increasingly attentive to this need as the degree of relational hierarchy increases. As a result, dominant polities must undertake costly actions to bind themselves to the terms of the contract and, especially, to commit themselves to exercise their expanded decision-making authority in a nonopportunistic manner. Again, the latter requirement is particularly difficult to meet, as it is most efficient to shift rights of residual control from one polity to another under conditions of uncertainty; if future contingencies cannot be specified in the contract, neither can the circumstances under which the safeguards will be employed. By their very nature, safeguards on the enhanced ability of the dominant polity to exploit its subordinate partner will tend not to be credible—suggesting why coercion is so prevalent in relational hierarchies. Nonetheless, the relationship between increasing hierarchy and increasing safeguards on the dominant party is continuous; the greater the relational hierarchy, the greater the safeguards the dominant polity must accept on its own behavior in order to gain the voluntary compliance of its subordinate partner.

## COERCION

Although it fits awkwardly within the neoclassical economic approach that informs relational contracting theories, coercion is a fact of life in international relations (and elsewhere).[78] The governance costs incurred in correct-

---

[78] It is in this area that the analogy between firms contracting in markets and states contracting in anarchic international systems ultimately breaks down. Firms do use coercive tactics, as exemplified in the sometimes colorful language of the "takeover wars" of the 1980s: at various times, firms were besieged in hostile takeovers, they employed poison pill and white knight defenses, and numerous other strategies evocative of traditional battlefields. Such tactics were designed to alter the incentives of the players, make various proposals or positions more or less attractive, and thereby shape the outcome of the struggle. They all carried some cost to the

ing and compensating distortions in the subordinate party and safeguarding against the potential for exploitation by the dominant party are both rooted in problems of costly information. Coercion is a substitute for voluntary negotiations between polities. It can be used by the dominant polity to promote cooperation without compensation for the subordinate polity. When coercion prevails, autonomy is simply forfeited and distortions tolerated—and even potentially corrected by eliciting desired behaviors in difficult-to-specify contingencies. Coercion can also substitute for effective safeguards on the dominant polity, allowing for cooperation without constraints. Rather than binding itself to costly actions that alter opportunity costs, demonstrate commitment, or create specialized governance structures, the dominant polity can force its partner to accept an agreement that lacks the safeguards that would be necessary in an otherwise voluntary relationship. In short, coercion is an alternative to the concessions and compromises that would normally be required in any voluntarily negotiated relationship between two parties. That coercion is quite common in international relations does not vitiate this analytic insight.

Coercion can also enable polities to overcome differences in their preferred relationships by forcing the weaker party to acquiesce to the wishes of the stronger. Just as a mugger forces his victim to choose between his money and his life, so can a powerful polity force another to choose between a subordinate position in a hierarchic relationship and enormous harm. The asymmetrical ability to use coercion often leaves the weaker party with only the illusion of choice—and sometimes not even that. Nonetheless, the alternative relationships and their determinants described in the theory remain salient, defining both the advantages to the weaker party of not conceding to the other and the amount of force the stronger must employ. Given the costs of compensating subordinate polities for their lost autonomy and distorted in-

---

participants. Nonetheless, the coercion used by firms was governed by domestic legal rules that limit the use of force and violence in market transactions. In international politics, limitations on the use of force and violence are considerably looser.

When coercion is prevalent, and especially when it is overt, it challenges the language of "rights" and "authority" heretofore used to describe security relationships. Clearly, the subordinate is giving up rights and authority it previously possessed, but it is admittedly somewhat inconsistent with common language to describe the increased influence of the dominant polity as an increase in its rights or authority when hierarchy is achieved at gunpoint. Most of the time, however, coercion remains latent. When the parties understand that one side can use coercion more cheaply and effectively than the other, there is no need to make it manifest; the potential or "shadow" of force structures their relationship, even though force itself is never actually used. But it is precisely this mutual understanding that makes security relationships *social* relationships and justifies, in a more technical usage of the words, the terms *rights* and *authority*. Moreover, in domestic politics, we routinely speak of coercive dictatorships as possessing authority within their polities and of oppressed peoples as possessing limited political rights. My usage here does not differ from this practice.

centives, and the difficulty of safeguarding subordinates against the potential for future exploitation by the dominant polity, coercion may be the only means of effectively establishing informal and formal empires. Throughout history, the terms of the peace have been written by the victors, not the losers—the powerful, not the weak. The same holds for hierarchical relationships.

Like voluntarily negotiated relationships, coercion requires the use of scarce resources and, therefore, is costly to polities that use or threaten to use it. This is clearly true for direct military action, but it holds equally for other sanctions such as trade embargoes (which, if effective, reduce the sanctioning country's terms of trade). Polities will choose between negotiations and coercion according to their relative costs. Those that possess a "comparative advantage" in coercion—whether from sheer size, military prowess, or resource endowments—will tend to rely upon this instrument. Although any general statement is open to challenge, coercion does appear to have been, in some cases, the more cost effective and, perhaps, the only feasible instrument to build hierarchical security relationships. The process of consolidating political authority into larger territorial units, the "state-building" process that produced the modern states in today's developed world, was frequently violent.[79] Likewise, the threat of coercion by technologically superior European polities was key to the process of empire building in the periphery of the global system.

As with the other governance costs, the costs of creating and maintaining a relationship through coercion typically increase with hierarchy. The more hierarchic the imposed relationship, the smaller the subordinate actor's rights of residual control and the more it can be expected to resist both at the outset and throughout the course of the relationship. The greater the resistance, the greater the coercion necessary to support a given relationship. Thus, the governance costs of acquiring control over others and maintaining a relationship through coercion increase as relations move from anarchy to hierarchy.

For all three reasons, then, governance costs are likely to increase with greater hierarchy. Giving up their valued autonomy and fearful of distorted incentives, subordinate polities will demand greater compensation from their dominant partners as hierarchy increases. Dominant polities, in turn, will need to incur more costly constraints on their own potential for opportunism as their decision-making authority expands. To the extent that coercion is a substitute for voluntary negotiations between parties, replacing compensation from and constraints on the dominant polity, it too will increase and become more costly with hierarchy. These costs can be summed up in a governance cost schedule, denoted as $\gamma$ in Figure 3.2 and drawn to reflect increasing marginal costs of hierarchy.

[79] Tilly 1985 and 1990.

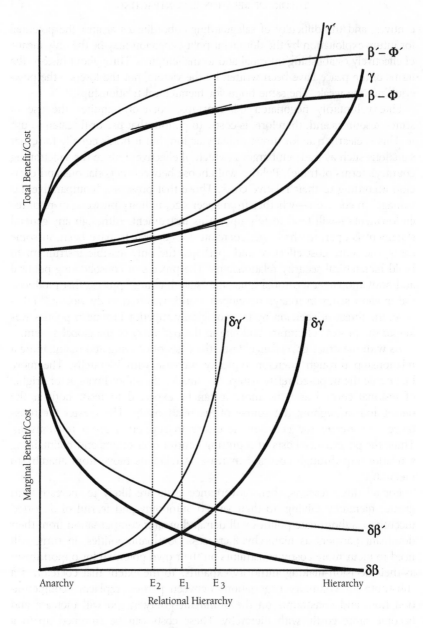

Figure 3.2. Optimal Security Relationships

## Optimal Security Relationships

To produce security, polities choose between unilateralism and cooperation and, within the latter, along a continuum of security relationships that ranges from anarchy to hierarchy. The optimal choice for any polity is a function of its joint production economies, expected costs of opportunism, and governance costs. Joint economies form the basis for all cooperation, and may differ across security relationships if polities choose to invest more heavily in such economies as the probability of opportunism declines. The expected costs of opportunism and governance costs are both nil in unilateralism, since by definition there are no partners to act opportunistically or to govern. Holding the degree of asset specificity constant, the expected costs of opportunism decline with relational hierarchy. If polities invest in more specific assets as hierarchy increases, the expected costs may decline more slowly or remain constant. The expected benefits of cooperation, that is, the benefits from joint production minus the expected costs of opportunism, increase with relational hierarchy. Governance costs rise with hierarchy. Joint economies, expected costs of opportunism, and governance costs are all necessary, but none alone is sufficient, to explain the choice of security relationship.

The individual variables, and their interaction, are illustrated in Figure 3.2. The optimal relationship equalizes the marginal benefit from an additional increment of hierarchy, whether from a reduction in the probability of opportunism or greater joint economies, with the marginal governance cost of that unit. In Figure 3.2, this occurs at $E_1$ where the difference between $\beta - \Phi$ and $\gamma$ is maximized (the point where two tangent line segments are parallel) or the marginal expected benefit ($\delta\beta$) and marginal cost ($\delta\gamma$) curves intersect.[80] If the governance costs of hierarchy increase ($\gamma'$ and $\delta\gamma'$), the preferred relationship will shift toward anarchy ($E_2$). If expected benefits increase with hierarchy ($\beta' - \Phi'$ and $\delta\beta'$), perhaps because joint economies increase relative to the level of relationally specific assets, the preferred relationship will shift toward hierarchy ($E_3$). Shifts in overall joint economies, expected costs of opportunism, and governance costs—that is, exogenous changes in these variables that apply equally to all security relationships, illustrated by shifts in the curves so that they intersect the vertical axis in different places—will have similar effects.

Setting the benefits from unilateralism at the origin, as long as the expected benefits of cooperation are at least equal to or greater than governance costs somewhere along the continuum of security relationships, there will be some optimal security relationship that is preferred to unilateralism. This would be represented in Figure 3.2 by a point of tangency between the expected benefits curve and the governance cost curve or, more likely, by the

---

[80] For reasons of clarity, the tangents for the other equilibria are not drawn here.

intersection of these two curves, creating an open "petal" (as drawn) that depicts the net benefits of entering into a security relationship. Thus, unilateralism will be chosen when governance costs are comparatively high, with all points on the governance cost curve lying above the expected benefits curve, or when benefits are comparatively low, with all points on the expected benefits curve lying below the governance cost curve. The latter can occur either when the joint economies in cooperation are small or when the expected costs of opportunism are high.

The arguments above can also be summarized in a series of comparative static hypotheses, all including the traditional ceteris paribus clause. These hypotheses are not intended to be exhaustive but to illustrate the core logic of the theory, especially as it applies to the empirical assessments in Chapters 4 through 6.

> $H_1$: *The greater the joint production economies, the more likely polities are to cooperate.*

All else held constant, the greater the joint economies, the larger the gains from cooperation, and the greater the incentive for polities to pool their resources and efforts. As the expected benefits curve $(\beta - \Phi)$ intersects the vertical axis higher, the more likely it is to exceed governance costs for some security relationship.

> $H_2$: *The greater the expected costs of opportunism, the less likely polities are to cooperate.*

Overall, the more costly opportunism by its partner is to a polity, or the more specific assets that would be at risk in the relationship, the less willing it is to cooperate. The greater the expected costs of opportunism, the lower the expected benefits curve $(\beta - \Phi)$ will intersect the vertical axis; this decreases the chance that expected benefits will exceed governance costs for at least one possible security relationship. As the risks of pooling resources and efforts with others increase, polities are less likely to choose cooperation.

> $H_3$: *The more rapidly the expected costs of opportunism decline with hierarchy, the more likely polities are to choose hierarchical security relationships.*

It is, of course, precisely the desire to reduce the probability of opportunism that leads polities to form hierarchic security relationships. By doing do, they constrain the ability of their partners to act opportunistically, reduce the expected costs of opportunism, and increase the expected benefits of cooperation. The more efficacious hierarchy is in reducing the probability of opportunism, the more likely polities are to form hierarchical relationships. This would be reflected by a more steeply (negatively) sloped $\Phi$ curve in Figure

3.1 or a more steeply (positively) sloped $\beta - \Phi$ curve in Figure 3.2 ($\beta' - \Phi'$ > $\beta - \Phi$; $E_3$ is more hierarchic than $E_1$).

H$_4$:  *The more specific the assets at risk in cooperation, the more likely politics are to form hierarchical security relationships.*

By the same logic as used in hypothesis three, highly specific assets create strong incentives for polities to create hierarchical security relationships to reduce the expected costs of opportunism. When assets are highly specific, polities will either create hierarchical security relationships or act unilaterally, depending on the net benefits of cooperation relative to the governance costs of hierarchy.

H$_5$:  *The greater the probability of opportunism by partners, the less likely polities are to invest in relationally specific assets.*

The prospect of costly opportunism by partners inhibits polities from investing in highly specific assets. When hierarchical security relationships are prohibitively costly, or when they are not sufficiently effective at reducing opportunism, polities will be reluctant to make specific investments. To the extent that larger joint production economies depend upon more specific assets, as is likely to be the case for a broad range of technologies, positive externalities, and especially divisions of labor, a high probability of opportunism not only reduces directly the net benefits of cooperation but, indirectly, the feasible joint production economies. In this way, joint production economies are, as noted above, partly endogenous to the choice of security relationships.

H$_6$:  *The larger the governance costs, the less likely polities are to cooperate.*

High governance costs decrease the possibilities for cooperation. As the costs to the dominant polity for compensating and coercing the subordinate polity and constraining itself increase, cooperation becomes less attractive. In this way, the governance cost curve ($\gamma$) intersects the vertical axis at a higher level and increases the likelihood that unilateralism will be preferred to any security relationship.

H$_7$:  *The less rapidly governance costs increase with hierarchy, the more likely polities are to choose hierarchical security relationships.*

The less costly hierarchic security relationships are relative to anarchic security relationships, the more able polities are to absorb such costs and the less unattractive an additional unit of hierarchy becomes. The governance cost curve ($\gamma$) becomes flatter, as does the marginal cost curve, and the optimal strategy moves toward greater hierarchy ($\gamma' > \gamma$ and $\delta\gamma' > \delta\gamma$; $E_2$ is less hierarchic than $E_1$).

Although these hypotheses are phrased in comparative static terms, it is

TABLE 3.1
Summary of Predictions by Security Relationship

| Policy or Relationship | Most Likely When |
|---|---|
| Unilateralism | • Joint Production Economies small<br>• Expected Costs of Opportunism high<br>• Governance Costs high |
| Alliance | • Joint Production Economies large<br>• Expected Costs of Opportunism low and do not fall significantly with hierarchy<br>• Governance Costs low but rise rapidly with hierarchy |
| Empire | • Joint Production Economies large<br>• Joint Production Economies expand rapidly with hierarchy relative to asset specificity<br>• Expected Costs of Opportunism high (but not too high) and decline significantly with hierarchy<br>• Governance Costs low and rise slowly with hierarchy |

important to recognize that it is the combined effects of all three variables—joint production economies, expected costs of opportunism, and governance costs—that determine the choice of policy or security relationship. Each variable is necessary for any complete explanation. Table 3.1 identifies the joint conditions under which unilateralism, alliances, and empires are "most likely" to be chosen.

The interaction of these three variables is seen most clearly, perhaps, in the conundrum identified above in the common core of international relations. Placing the extant literatures on alliances and empires side by side suggests a seeming paradox: the same variable, opportunism, simultaneously deters polities from entering into an alliance and propels them into an empire. The conundrum dissolves once we recognize that the effects of opportunism are contingent upon the joint production economies and governance costs. For any given expected cost of opportunism, the theory here suggests that when joint economies are small and governance costs high, polities will generally prefer unilateralism over an alliance. In this instance, the expected costs of opportunism will vitiate the gains from cooperation, appearing to drive states into unilateralism. Conversely, with the same expected costs of opportunism, when joint economies are large and governance costs small, polities will prefer some measure of hierarchy over an alliance or unilateralism. Under these circumstances, the potential for opportunism seemingly leads polities into an empire. Likewise, holding joint economies and governance costs constant, increasing the expected costs of opportunism will drive polities either toward unilateralism, as the net benefits of cooperation turn negative, or toward hierarchy, as the only possible way of dealing with the greater risks. The choice between alternative policies and relationships is a function of all three variables and each must be included in the analysis. Focusing on only one factor at a time, as is common in many theories of international relations, seriously distorts our analyses.

## METHOD AND EVALUATION

This book is an exercise in theory-driven history. The theory has been outlined above. Chapters 4 through 6 present a history of American foreign policy as seen through the lens of the theory. The principal criterion for evaluating such a history is the ability of the theory to shed new light on the historical reality, to reveal new dimensions and causes, and to allow us to see events from a different perspective. In short, the theory must provide some empirical "value-added" or, more colloquially, it must tell us something interesting about the data or history that we would have otherwise missed.

The case studies in Chapters 4 through 6 are not, strictly speaking, tests of the theory developed in this chapter.[81] The research does meet many of the traditional standards of social scientific inquiry. The theory was developed in its essentials prior to undertaking the empirical research. Although personal interest played an important role in case selection, the periods examined here were nonetheless chosen to ensure variation in the dependent variable, namely, the type of security relationship, if any, formed between the United States and its partners. The cases were selected prior to collecting information on the independent variables. Finally, although the analysis is entirely verbal, it is in fact a "large-n" study. The theory is dyadic in construction and based on the relationship between any polity and each of its partners. In the case of current American security relationships, for example, there are at least as many potential observations as there are states, coded either for "no relationship," defined as unilateralism, or along the continuum of security

---

[81] I also do not attempt to assess systematically the present theory against its plausible rivals. In each chapter, I briefly outline existing explanations, but in most cases they fail because they do not address the choice between alternative security relationships. Moreover, the present theory is often synthetic, subsuming insights from other perspectives within a common framework—suggesting that so-called alternatives should often not be treated as independent explanations. By selecting cases from a single country over time, however, many dispositional factors are effectively held constant. That is, variables like American ideology, values, social purpose, identity—if they have any empirical content at all—should remain absolutely fixed across different dyads at a moment in time and relatively fixed across time. Such fixed features of the American political landscape cannot then explain synchronic and diachronic differences. Nonetheless, many factors differ across the three periods examined here—much varies between the United States in the world in 1919 and 1991. These differences are noted, where appropriate, in the cases below.

relationships in Chapter 2. Moreover, there is considerable variation in relationships across dyads. In the Persian Gulf coalition, for instance, the United States created protectorates with Saudi Arabia and the other regional states, and alliances with Britain, France, and the remaining members of the coalition. I often use regional shorthands in the case studies because of the widely shared characteristics of the relationships in these areas. To repeat the full list of dyads when referring to, say, America's essentially homogenous relationships with the various countries of Europe would be infelicitous, to say the least. Nonetheless, even though I refer to regions, readers should remember that such shorthands summarize characteristics of a larger number of dyads. Thus, although there are only three cases in the book, the number of actual observations is substantially larger.[82]

While attempting to follow, where possible, the strictures of social science, the cases nonetheless fall short of rigorous tests of the theory for three reasons. First, the variables are not easy to operationalize. Problems of operationalizing the dependent variable—security relationships—were discussed in Chapter 2. Similar problems arise with the independent variables. Joint production economies, the expected costs of opportunism, and governance costs are difficult to measure precisely; in turn, we generally lack systematic data. This same problem has bedeviled tests of relational contracting theories in economics, as well.[83] In Chapter 7, I outline two more formal assessments of the theory intended to point toward more precise tests in the future. But for the present, we are mostly limited to case studies that probe the comparative static predictions of the theory across dyads and time periods.

The second reason that the cases fall short of being rigorous tests of the theory is that the independent variables, as noted above, are actually defined as probability distributions: states do not know their joint production economies, expected costs of opportunism, or governance costs with certainty. Rather, they base their decisions on some set of prior beliefs which they update as new information is received. The probabilistic nature of the variables makes measurement difficult. It also makes case selection extremely consequential. For example, focusing on prominent historical events—especially noteworthy policy "failures" where actual strategies grossly underperformed expectations—risks limiting analysis to cases with extreme values on the variables (discussed in Chapter 7). Fortunately, the dyadic nature of the present theory greatly multiplies the number of possible cases, but this does not fully solve problems of descriptive and causal inference.

Third, and perhaps most important, we can observe the relationship chosen by a polity, but we cannot observe the relationships *not* chosen and the

---

[82] On the difference between cases and observations, see King, Keohane, Verba 1994, 217–28.
[83] Shelanski and Klein 1995.

costs and benefits associated with these counterfactuals.[84] When a polity chooses unilateralism, for instance, we cannot inspect the costs and benefits of any actual security relationship; or if a polity pursues an empire, we cannot measure the costs and benefits of either unilateralism or any of the less hierarchical alternatives. In other words, we can observe, presumably, the intersection of the marginal benefit and marginal cost curves in Figure 3.2, but we cannot observe the other points along each curve. Yet, these "unobservables" are central to the theory and, as argued above, structure the choice of relations by polities.

All three of these problems are actually common in the social sciences, but are typically glossed over. They are certainly not unique to the current theory. The difficulties of measuring national capabilities are admitted even by those for whom they are crucial.[85] Buck passing, chain ganging, and imperial overextension are all based on probabilistic decisions made by imperfectly informed political leaders (see Chapter 7). At both the micro and macro levels, alternative institutions can never be observed directly, often giving rise to charges of "functionalism."[86] The point here is not to condemn other studies because of their methodological difficulties—or excuse this one—but to point out that the problems identified above are general and defy simple solution.

Given these methodological problems, one appropriate research strategy is to examine the comparative static predictions of the theory in periods of major policy change. Through such cases, we can observe the direction of change in the independent variables and probe the range of possible variation in relations, even if we cannot assign precise values or fully explicate the counterfactuals. This is the research strategy used here. In each case, I assemble the available evidence to identify the direction of change in the independent variables and predict the range of likely outcomes. This often requires using several different kinds of evidence and considerable judgment, especially when estimating the "unobservable" ranges of the independent variables. It also requires comparisons across time periods and, within each era, across dyads. In all cases, I try to be explicit about how and why I draw the estimates I do. This evidence is then assessed against the security relationships chosen by the United States. Every effort is made to avoid reason-

[84] This is a form of the fundamental problem of causal inference. See King, Keohane, and Verba 1994, 79. On counterfactual reasoning in international relations, see Fearon 1991, and Tetlock and Belkin 1996.

[85] Waltz 1979, 131.

[86] Katzenstein 1985 argues that, through a process of contingent historical choice, the small states of Europe have evolved nearly unique corporatist institutions to cope with the rigors of dependence on international markets. Katzenstein's argument ultimately succeeds because of the remarkable similarity he identifies between similarly situated states and his counterfactual estimates of the costs and benefits of other choices. For another "functionalist" arguments, see Keohane 1984.

ing "backward" from known outcomes; that is, to avoid using observed changes in policy to establish the changes in the independent variables. As I argue below, the available evidence is largely consistent with the theory, and the theory helps illuminate new dimensions of the cases, providing some confidence that the theory is capturing important real-world phenomena.

### Political Debate and the Testing of Systemic-Level Theory

In addition to an examination of the comparative static predictions of the theory, I also assess the theory by probing the public debates surrounding changes in foreign policy. This is, I admit, a somewhat unorthodox method of assessment. I do not examine public debates to trace the process by which policy gets made or to derive additional implications of the theory, since it does not make any predictions on this score.[87] Rather, in a democracy (at least), public debate can be used as a means of assessing the motives of policy makers and, in turn, of the polity as a whole. Public debate provides an additional source of data and an empirical check on our theoretical expectations.

If the variables in the theory are hard for us to measure after the fact, they are equally if not more difficult for policy makers to assess beforehand. With incomplete information, moreover, no one policy maker will necessarily possess the same information as another, leading them to make different assessments of the optimal relationship for the polity. When faced with a choice, then, policy makers must resolve their conflicting estimates. In a democratic political system, part of this process involves political debate and persuasion, which I interpret here as a means of sharing information and moving toward a common estimate of the levels and distributions of key variables. As John Stuart Mill believed, only from such debates can "true," unprejudiced, and undogmatic opinions emerge.[88]

Understood in this way, policy debates can be used to help evaluate theory by revealing whether policy makers were worrying about the kinds of concerns and tradeoffs highlighted by the theory. Were they, for instance, trying to estimate the probability of opportunism under alternative security relationships? Were they concerned about what kinds of compensation would be required by subordinate polities or how extensive the constraints on their activities might be? Did they understand that the potential for opportunism by others could be mitigated, but only at the cost of imposing greater constraints on their own country? Did they recognize that relatively anarchic security relationships limited their incentives to invest in additional joint production economies? If policy makers were, in fact, concerned with

[87] See King, Keohane, and Verba 1994, 226–27.
[88] Mill 1978, especially 50.

such issues, it would not confirm the theory, but it would help establish the plausibility of the theory and reassure us that it was capturing something meaningful about the real world. The absence of such evidence would be even more revealing. I am skeptical of any theory of social interaction that lacks individual-level support; if policy makers or contemporary analysts do not recognize and understand the kinds of causal forces and tradeoffs indicated by the theory, the theory is most likely wrong.

With this method in mind, I intentionally select periods of flux in international affairs and, especially, in American foreign policy. The years following World War I, World War II, and the Cold War are characterized by uncommon openness in policy and policy debates. These are times of great struggle between individuals holding differing views on the appropriate direction of American foreign policy. In the heat of these great debates, assumptions normally left implicit in policy are laid bare and self-consciously examined and questioned. For these reasons, the three periods are exceptionally good at revealing the considerations, calculations, and judgments of the decision makers charged with formulating policy. One must be cautious in generalizing from such periods, however, because they are not randomly chosen. Indeed, they are chosen precisely because they are exceptional, in the full sense of this overused word. Although caution is required, I cannot think of any reason why the theory should systematically work better in such exceptional periods than others, and thus am relatively confident that examining eras of flux will not bias the results obtained.

Although the theory, by assumption, is mute on why different groups within society or different sets of policy makers within the government reach the assessments they do, that individuals vary in the information they possess and in their estimates of the optimal relationship for their country is entirely consistent with the approach. Assuming that information is costly and, therefore, incomplete does not imply that all individuals possess (or lack) precisely the same information. Yet, why Congressional representatives from the American Mid-west, presumably reflecting the views of their constituents, are consistently more skeptical of cooperation with Europe and consistently reach higher estimates of the probability of European opportunism remains something of a mystery, and lies outside the current theory.[89] Such systematic differences cannot be explained by the rational, unitary actor model that underlies the approach used here. That such differences do exist, however, leads to illuminating debates and allows us to access another type of data to apply to the theory.

There is, however, one consistent division between branches of the American government that warrants consideration here. In all of the cases below, the executive has been more supportive of cooperation with others than has

[89] For a regionalist approach to American foreign policy, see Trubowitz 1998.

Congress. This cleavage may be a function of two factors. First, within the division of labor embedded in the American government, the executive is charged with the conduct (but not necessarily the formulation) of foreign policy. Specializing in this area, it follows that the executive would have more and "better" information about potential partners, and would therefore feel more confident in its ability to estimate their probabilities of opportunism and to design agreements to control this potential.

Second, because it specializes in the conduct of foreign affairs, cooperation in any form may favor the executive relative to Congress in the subsequent formulation of policy. The executive may be able to manipulate to its own advantage opportunism by others or the safeguards designed to control opportunism by others. Recognizing this, Congress fears opportunistic behavior not only by the foreign partner but also by its own executive. As we shall see in Chapter 4, for instance, Congress was reluctant to approve the League of Nations for fear that the executive, not the legislature, would represent the United States within the institution, and this might subtly but significantly shift the balance of power between the branches of government. Security cooperation threatened, in this instance, to upset the domestic political balance. This division between Congress and the executive is not decisive in the cases below. Moreover, it is a structural feature of the American political system, and therefore is generally constant over time. In times of "divided" government, the distrust between Congress and the president may be higher than normal. Even so, cooperation was voted down in one such instance, the League of Nations, approved in another, the Persian Gulf War, and conducted in a spirit of bipartisanship for much of a third, the Cold War. Nonetheless, the division between the legislative and executive branches heightens the domestic political debate and forms an enduring pattern. This division between the branches of government is not anticipated by the theory. Fortunately, it is also not inconsistent with the theory and should not bias the results below.

Although readers are free to hold this research to their chosen standards, my criterion for evaluation, as noted, is primarily theoretical value-added. In focusing on this criterion, I have purposely chosen cases that are already well understood. As any student of American foreign policy knows, there are voluminous literatures on the League of Nations debate and interwar isolationism, the early postwar years and the origins of the Cold War, and, increasingly, the post-Cold War period. In the United States, and probably elsewhere as well, even scholars who have not focused on American foreign policy are presumably aware of the broad contours of these cases. Yet, if I can demonstrate that the predictions of the theory are broadly consistent with the empirical record, plausible given our available historical knowledge, and helpful in understanding new dimensions of international politics, I will judge the enterprise at least partially successful.

## CONCLUSION

The strength of the theory developed here, in my view, is not that it outlines a wholly original perspective on international relations. Indeed, as discussed above, problems of aggregating capabilities and opportunism are central to existing theories of international relations. Rather, the theory provides a set of analytic tools for bridging different islands of theory and predicting when polities will prefer unilateralism or cooperation and, within the latter, anarchic or hierarchic security relationships. In short, it provides a unifying perspective on international relations.

At the same time, the theory does emphasize political problems different from those examined by others. The gains from cooperation are not fixed or given, but vary across time and space as a function of joint economies and the expected costs of opportunism. Although virtually ignored in what I called the common core above, governance costs are central to the problem of international cooperation. Such costs are overlooked even in regime theory, which tends to emphasize how regimes lower transactions costs rather than how such costs vary across alternative forms of governance. Most important, the theory calls our attention to how polities seek to organize themselves to reap the largest gains from cooperation at the lowest possible cost. The question of how states attempt to control one another is placed at center stage. In this view, international cooperation cannot proceed unless some effective governance structure can be constructed at an acceptable cost. In an opportunistic world, controlling the behavior of others is critical.

## Chapter 4

## THE LONE HAND

FOR OVER A CENTURY, the United States eschewed entangling security relationships. From 1790, when it disavowed its alliance with France, the nation maintained a strictly unilateral foreign policy in thought as well as deed. This nearly sacred principle of American foreign policy was challenged, however, by World War I and its aftermath. The debate over the most appropriate postwar policy for the United States focused primarily on whether to join the new League of Nations. The struggle over the League, in turn, is profoundly revealing of America's foreign policy motivations and calculations. The United States considered two alternative security relationships in the context of the League in 1919–1920—a mildly hierarchic vision of the League advocated by progressive internationalists, and a strictly anarchic vision championed by conservative internationalists. Both were ultimately rejected. America's traditional unilateralism triumphed by default. Nonetheless, this decision was reaffirmed numerous times in the 1920s and 1930s, suggesting that the rejection of the League was not simply an historical accident or the play of personalities and partisan politics.

American foreign policy between the wars is often described as "isolationist," implying that the United States withdrew from international affairs and sought a kind of international political autarky. This description is, at best, appropriate only for the mid-1930s, when the United States did turn inward and tried to ignore the more threatening world growing up around it. But as historians have demonstrated, the isolationist label distorts the reality of interwar foreign policy.[1] Walter McDougall states the case strongly: "American isolationism is a myth. The word—which did not come into common use until the 1890s, when propagandists for empire flung it at their Mugwump critics—should be struck from America's vocabulary."[2] The United States was deeply involved in international affairs, especially in the 1920s, but to a significant degree even in the 1930s. Rather than isolationist, American foreign policy between the wars is more accurately described as unilateral. "Its main aim" was not withdrawal, Manfred Jonas writes, but "the avoidance of political and military commitments to, or alliances with, foreign powers."[3] Its closest synonym, Albert K. Weinberg concludes, is "non-entanglement."[4]

---

[1] See especially Jonas 1990, and Adler 1966.
[2] McDougall 1997, 137.
[3] Jonas 1990, viii.
[4] Quoted in Guinsburg 1982, 4.

The debate over the League of Nations was not between isolationists and internationalists but between advocates of unilateralism and cooperation, at one level, and between partisans of moderately different security relationships, at another. As Gilbert M. Hitchcock (NE), leader of the Senate Democrats, declared during the League fight, "internationalism has come and we must choose what form the internationalism is to take."[5] After a long and vigorous debate, they decided not on isolationism but on unilateralism.

This chapter, as do all of the case studies in this book, begins by setting out the expectations of the theory developed in Chapter 3. This is followed by a brief historical survey intended to provide necessary background for the analysis that follows. I then highlight alternative explanations and discuss how they relate to the interpretation offered here. In the main part of the chapter, I organize the analytic discussion around the three key independent variables: joint economies, the expected costs of opportunism, and governance costs. The final section carries the analysis from the debate over the League of Nations up to the outbreak of World War II.

## Theoretical Expectations

World War I is often understood as a political watershed, the violent break between the "Pax Britannica" and the "American century." In the security environment of the United States, however, there was less change than commonly supposed, and what change did occur was more evolutionary than revolutionary. The seeds of change were sown during the war, but they required several decades to germinate, grow, and eventually flower into the conditions necessary for security cooperation. The theory outlined in Chapter 3 suggests that the prospects for cooperation were quite limited in the interwar years and that unilateralism was still the most likely policy for the United States.

Even after the war, the joint production economies—and, thus, the potential gains from pooling resources and effort with the Europeans—were at best modest. There were few significant changes from the prewar period, when unilateralism reigned. Despite substantial technological innovation on the European battlefield, there was little change in the costs of projecting force over long distance; this would require further developments in both air and naval power. Similarly, there were positive externalities produced by stability in Europe, but the United States could still free ride effectively in unilateralism. On this dimension, therefore, there was little reason to expect the United States to alter its security policy in 1919 or endorse cooperation with others during the interwar period. As the joint economies were quite limited, cooperation in any form was unlikely (Hypothesis 1).

The probability that Europe would act opportunistically against the United

[5] Quoted in Knock 1992, 229.

States was quite large. Despite vigorous debates over how best to reduce this potential, there was relatively little disagreement on this basic point—Europe could not be trusted. The war did little to improve America's view of the "old world" as a cesspool of competing antagonisms and perfidious diplomats. On the other hand, there were few specific assets at risk in cooperation with Europe, at least in the plans under active discussion. But although the actual costs of opportunism might not have been substantial, the probability that Europe would abandon, entrap, or exploit the United States was sufficient to make the expected costs of opportunism positive and politically significant. This inhibited cooperation (Hypothesis 2).

As expected, the high probability of opportunism also deterred investments in greater joint economies (Hypothesis 5). The difficulties of projecting force could have been mitigated, in part, by pre-positioning equipment in Europe and stationing American troops overseas, much as was done after World War II. Yet such a forward presence required American bases in Europe, and thus considerably deeper "entanglements." A division of labor was also possible, as in NATO after 1945, but this would have entailed even more relationally specific assets; anticipating that Europe would act opportunistically, the United States declined to make investments in relationally specific assets. The absence of such investments, in turn, severely limited the joint production economies possible during the interwar years. Together, the high probability of opportunism and the small joint economies ensured that, at best, the net benefits from cooperation would be small indeed.

Finally, governance costs were high, at least relative to the net benefits from cooperation, and rose rapidly with hierarchy. These high and rising governance costs impeded cooperation and limited the United States to relatively anarchic security relationships (Hypotheses 6 and 7). Although the United States established itself as a great power during the war, imposing a security relationship on the Europeans was simply not a viable option. Although Wilson's vision of the League would have placed some constraints on Europe's freedom of action in foreign policy, the latter remained strong enough to repel any American attempt to limit significantly their sovereign powers. The constraints on Europe had to be voluntarily negotiated, and would have come only at the cost of nearly equal constraints on the United States.

To summarize, with a high risk of opportunism, the United States would have been likely to invest in the joint production economies necessary to make cooperation worthwhile only within a hierarchic security relationship. The high and escalating governance costs, on the other hand, limited the United States to relatively anarchic security relationships, none of which was likely to reduce substantially the risks of opportunism. These are close to the "most likely conditions" for unilateralism (see Table 3.1). That the League was ultimately rejected conforms with the expectations of the theory.

The debate over the League, in turn, illuminates these expectations. As anticipated, the issues at the center of the political debate focused precisely on the tradeoffs highlighted by the theory, and especially on how effective the League would be in controlling opportunism by partners and how costly it would be to govern the security relationships embodied within it. That the League was proposed at all, and subjected to vigorous debate, suggests that the considerations stressed by the theory were not obvious. The debate itself grew out of the uncertainties of the postwar world and the unknown capabilities of international organizations. In this environment of sparse information and high uncertainty, it is not surprising that different analysts had competing visions of an unknown future, and America's role within it, and drew conflicting estimates of the expected costs of opportunism and governance costs.

Moreover, as we shall see, there was not a single vision of the League under consideration, but two. President Woodrow Wilson, the League's principal architect, and other progressive internationalists envisioned a binding collective security organization.[6] Their plan included elements of hierarchy that would have limited, at the margin, the decision-making authorities of other countries, especially over foreign policy. Even though its powers were highly circumscribed and narrow, the progressives saw the League as a limited and partial American-led protectorate that would significantly reduce the potential for opportunism by the nation's partners. In formal terms, progressives estimated that the expected costs of opportunism were quite high, but declined sharply with hierarchy, at least in its initial stages. At the same time, the governance costs of the League were expected to be manageable; although it might constrain the United States, the United States would control the League and the country would never be compelled to act against its will. Although they never claimed that the military benefits from pooling resources and efforts with others would be large, the progressives nonetheless anticipated that effective cooperation could be obtained at a cost acceptable to the United States.

Conservative internationalists, in turn, backed the League as a discretionary and purely anarchic organization intended only to facilitate America's participation in the European balance of power. The progressive vision of the League, conservatives believed, would not significantly reduce European opportunism. Not only would the League be ineffective at controlling the behavior of others but the binding commitment proposed by the progressives would open the United States to greater risks of entrapment. Substantial

---

[6] The terms "progressive" and "conservative" internationalism are from Knock 1992. They accurately capture the different philosophical origins of the two groups, and are used here. Unfortunately, the labels also leave the incorrect impression that the "irreconcilables" were not "internationalists"—an inference that is true only for some of the senators usually listed in this group.

hierarchy might reduce the risk of opportunism, but the minimalist plans being evaluated would not. In their view, the expected costs of opportunism were quite high and "flat," at least in the still relatively anarchic range of relationships embodied in the plans under discussion. Moreover, the conservatives estimated that the governance costs of cooperation would be high and increase rapidly with hierarchy. Not only would the League greatly constrain the United States but it was also an organic institution—indeed, it was supported as such by the progressives—that might over time gain new powers and further control the United States. Better, the conservatives argued, that the United States maintain the maximum flexibility of action under a purely anarchic security relationship.

The disagreement between progressives and conservatives, as we shall see, was rooted not only in the uncertainties of the postwar era but also in the structure of collective security. Both visions of international cooperation were eventually revealed to contain only weak safeguards that were nonetheless too costly relative to the net gains. Moreover, the differences between these plans could not be reconciled or compromised. Solving the problems revealed by one set of critics only exacerbated the problems highlighted by the other: binding commitments to the League opened the United States to a greater risk of entrapment, but anarchy did nothing to alleviate the risk of opportunism more generally. The architects of cooperation were unable to bridge the gap between progressives and conservatives. Unilateralism eventually triumphed.

The principled supporters of unilateralism—the so-called irreconcilables—were actually few in number. Their political victory is often regarded as a paradox, perhaps even a tragedy. Nonetheless, they won not by the force of their arguments but because they were the defenders of the status quo. The failure by either the progressives or conservatives to win wide support for security cooperation necessarily implied continued unilateralism.

American foreign policy in the interwar period demonstrates clearly that it is the interaction between the variables identified in Chapter 3 that determines the choice of security relationships. The probability of opportunism was too high to permit investment in any division of labor or technology that would incur assets specific to the European relationships. The net benefits of cooperation, in turn, were too low to offset the governance costs of the progressive and conservative internationalist programs. Ultimately, the United States chose unilateralism because both visions of interwar cooperation failed to offer a better plan for producing the country's security. This result contrasts with that following World War II. As we shall see in Chapter 5, the safeguards embodied in the North Atlantic Treaty Organization and other post-World War II relationships were not obviously cheaper or more effective than those of the League. What differed, in this case, were the substantially greater joint economies and the lower probability of opportunism, which produced net benefits of cooperation large enough to justify the governance costs of cooperation.

## A RE-DECLARATION OF INDEPENDENCE

From its ill-fated treaty with France onward, the United States eschewed international restraints on its freedom of action. With a special legitimacy rooted in the legacy of the founding fathers, the principle of unilateralism had many defenders before 1914. Indeed, it was virtually unchallenged prior to the "Great War."

America's rise as a world power in the late nineteenth century was carefully designed not to jeopardize its international independence. Its overseas expansion in the late 1890s was undertaken unilaterally and without consultation with or commitments to the established European powers. And although the United States attended the international peace conferences at The Hague in 1899 and 1907 and accepted the convention creating the Permanent Court of International Arbitration, for instance, its adherence was nonetheless qualified by the "unequivocal" reservation that no part of the agreement "shall be so construed as to require the United States to depart from the traditional policy of not intruding upon, interfering with, or entangling itself in the political questions or policy or internal administration of any foreign state."[7]

Even when war broke out in Europe in August 1914, the United States, demonstrating the success of its historic policy of foreign policy independence, was initially unaffected by the conflagration.[8] As the war unfolded, however, the United States became involved, ironically, because it sought to adhere to strict neutrality: coming into conflict, first, with its eventual allies—and especially Britain—over neutral shipping rights and, later, with Germany over the rules of submarine warfare.[9] After deciding to join the fray in April 1917, the United States fought only as an "associated" power. When the president subsequently discovered that government agencies were seeking to build support for the war by using slogans that referred to "our Allies," Wilson commanded that the phrase be changed to "our Associates . . . because we have no allies."[10] Despite numerous requests, and the recognition that American troops could be deployed more quickly and effectively if integrated into existing European divisions, and although the position of the allies was weakening in the fall of 1917, the United States also refused to amalgamate its forces with those of Britain and France.[11] Senator William E.

---

[7] Dulles 1963, 58–60; quote at 60.
[8] Iriye 1993, 19.
[9] Buehrig 1955; Duroselle 1963, 42; Iriye 1993, 23.
[10] Quoted in LaFeber 1994, 303.
[11] Kennedy 1980, 93–94 and 172; LaFeber 1994, 304.

Borah (R-ID), later a leading irreconcilable, captured concisely the American position at the outbreak of the war. "I join no crusade," he declared; "I seek or accept no alliance; I obligate this government to no other power. I make war alone for my countrymen and their rights, for my country and its honor."[12] Throughout the conflict, the United States remained what it had been for over a century: an independent party, acting only according to the dictates of unilateralism.[13]

Yet the war also produced the first important cracks in the domestic consensus supporting unilateralism.[14] Defined in narrow, neutralist terms, the Great War initially failed to attract enthusiastic support in the United States. For most people, the defense of neutral rights remained a questionable basis for fighting. The public nonetheless supported intervention out of deference to the presidency, patriotism, and the faith that the antiwar president had tried every other decent alternative.[15]

The "realists" around former president Theodore Roosevelt had long advocated a more aggressive American stance in favor of Great Britain and against Germany, and quickly rallied around Wilson.[16] As the former Rough Rider wrote a British friend three days after Wilson's war address to Congress, "thank God we are in, and are able to look men in the eyes without flinching!"[17] It was not just the glory of war that cheered Roosevelt, however, it was also the apparent willingness of the United States to take up its rightful and, in his view, necessary responsibilities in the European balance of power.

Prominent liberals in the United States, who events would reveal as progressives first and pacifists second, were initially less enthusiastic.[18] Key to their eventual support for the war was the transformational potential of the conflict. This theme was first raised in Wilson's "Peace without Victory" speech (January 1917) and again in his war message (April 1917)—where in one of several arguments made to justify American intervention the president rallied supporters to "make the world safe for democracy." Wilson's progressive war aims were elaborated most clearly in his famous "Fourteen Points," issued in January 1918. In addition to specific territorial accommodations, the Fourteen Points included calls for open covenants of peace, freedom of the seas, the removal of "all economic barriers" between countries, the reduction of armaments, the "adjustment of all colonial claims"

---

[12] Quoted in Dulles 1963, 103.

[13] Knock 1992, 138, correctly notes that by not making its participation conditional upon agreed principles or European actions prior to entering the hostilities, the United States forfeited an important source of leverage over the postwar peace.

[14] On Wilson's evolving views during the war, see Ambrosius 1991.

[15] Osgood 1953, 258–59.

[16] Buehrig 1955, 150–67; Dallek 1983, 76–77.

[17] Quoted in Osgood 1953, 270.

[18] Kennedy 1980, 42; Ambrosius 1987; Knock 1992.

with the colonial people themselves having "equal weight" in determining their fate, and a "general association of nations . . . for the purposes of affording mutual guarantees of political independence and territorial integrity to great and small states alike."[19] These goals promised progressives an end to the old European balance of power politics that had, in their view, produced the current slaughter. As Robert Osgood concludes, it was Wilson's moral leadership under the banner of the Fourteen Points that finally enabled progressives "to reconcile themselves completely to the unpleasant fact of American participation in a world war. . . . Only the opportunity for international reform made war bearable."[20]

Once it was redefined in progressive terms, Wilson fought the war with support from both his left and right. In the process of building public support, however, he turned the defense of neutral rights into a righteous crusade not only against Germany but against Europe.[21] In the end, Americans did not fight a war, they fought against imperialism, feudalism, autocracy, secrecy, and the very idea of war itself. In doing so, they legitimated at home a role for the United States in European affairs and opened up the possibility of cooperation after victory.

Opinion on postwar American policy clustered around three positions, similar to those that prevailed prior to 1917: progressive internationalism, conservative internationalism, and unilateralism.[22] Patriotism and hypernationalism served to paper over differences between advocates of these alternative views during the war. All submerged their competing conceptions of the peace in the interests of victory. Their differences, however, were never far below the surface and quickly reemerged with the armistice in November 1918. Their rival conceptions of the peace and postwar international order crystallized around Wilson's fourteenth point, the League of Nations, and it is in the debate over the League that America's security policy and its determinants are most clearly revealed.

The idea for a league of nations dates from the earliest days of the war. Although he later opposed Wilson's league bitterly, Roosevelt, in September 1914, was the first prominent political leader to propose such an organization.[23] Colonel Edward House, Wilson's trusted friend and advisor until the closing stages of the Versailles conference, discussed the concept of some "general guarantee" of the peace with the British, at their initiative, several times in late 1914 and early 1915, and he subsequently informed the British of Wilson's approval of the league idea in January 1916.[24] In the meantime,

---

[19] Quoted in LaFeber 1994, 309–10.
[20] Osgood 1953, 274–75.
[21] Kennedy 1980, 42; Ambrosius 1987, 33.
[22] Britain experienced similar splits; Kennedy 1983, 19–20.
[23] Cooper 1983, 279.
[24] Ambrosius 1987, 16–20.

former president William Howard Taft and other advocates of a legalistic solution to the problem of war formed the League to Enforce Peace, an organization intended to bolster public support for international dispute settlement.[25] Wilson declared his support for a league at the first national assembly of the League to Enforce Peace in May 1916, proposing a "universal association of nations" to defend freedom of the seas and to prevent war; such an organization, he concluded, would provide "a virtual guarantee of territorial integrity and political independence." Wilson's speech received wide assent. Walter Lippmann wrote that "in historic significance it is easily the most important diplomatic event that our generation has known."[26] The league idea was a prominent theme in Wilson's reelection campaign in 1916, when the issue was already turned to partisan advantage, and it was reiterated in his Peace without Victory speech.[27] Once America entered the war, however, Wilson's public advocacy diminished. Although it secured final position in his Fourteen Points, and received passing reference elsewhere, Wilson made only one major speech on the topic during the war, the Fourth Liberty Loan address in September 1918. Given the League's later prominence, Wilson was uncharacteristically silent. He thereby lost an important opportunity to build domestic support for the cause.[28]

Wilson's negotiation of the Treaty of Versailles, of which the covenant of the League of Nations was part, is well known. Soon after the armistice, Wilson sailed to Europe at the head of the American Commission to Negotiate Peace. Also included on the commission were Colonel House; Secretary of State Robert Lansing, who was overshadowed by the president; General Tasker H. Bliss, a former army chief of staff; and Henry White, a career diplomat and the only Republican on the team. There were no senators and no elected leaders of the Republican party on the commission.

After a triumphant tour of Europe, the first order of business in Paris—at Wilson's insistence—was the League.[29] The covenant was written with substantial input from Lord Robert Cecil and Jan Christiaan Smuts, both members of Britain's Imperial War Cabinet; this input suggests flexibility in Wilson's views at this stage and an important degree of overlap in his and, especially, Smuts's thinking.[30] A draft of the covenant was completed by February 1919, when Wilson was forced by pressing domestic business and legislative necessities to return to the United States for a brief visit.

The draft covenant met a cool reception from the new Congress, in which Republicans now held majorities in both houses. Especially chilly was a

[25] Divine 1967, 7.
[26] Quoted in Ambrosius 1987, 23–24.
[27] Duroselle 1963, 53; Knock 1992, 95.
[28] Knock 1992, ix.
[29] Dallek 1983, 87.
[30] Knock 1992, 204 and 208.

White House dinner for thirty-four legislative critics held on February 26. Two days later, taking a carefully calibrated position designed to cultivate moderates, Senator Henry Cabot Lodge (R-MA), a close friend and follower of Roosevelt and the new chairman of the Senate Foreign Relations Committee, criticized the draft covenant on the floor of the Senate. The president, he stated, was prone to "enticing generalities" and "shrill shrieks" when "facts, details, and sharp, clear-cut definitions" were necessary. While acknowledging that a league might be advantageous, he asked for "consideration, time, and thought."[31] At this stage, critics identified four unsatisfactory provisions in the draft covenant. It should, they argued, be modified to preserve the Monroe Doctrine, protect exclusive national control over "domestic" issues (especially immigration and the tariff), allow for the peaceful withdrawal of any member, and avoid ambiguous obligations for the use of armed force.[32] All of these objections were designed to ensure that no decision-making authority was transferred from the United States to the new organization and that the League would remain a strictly anarchic institution. Building upon these criticisms, Lodge then attacked in the so-called Round Robin, introduced on March 3, which rejected the draft covenant and called for an immediate peace treaty with Germany. The resolution was signed by thirty-seven (later thirty-nine) senators, more than the one-third of the upper chamber required to prevent ratification. The Round Robin was a tremendous blow to Wilson's position and credibility with his European counterparts. After championing the League in Paris, Wilson now faced a minority at home sufficient to veto the treaty and on record against the covenant "in the form now proposed."[33] Wilson responded angrily, declaring on the eve of his return to Europe that once completed it would be impossible to "dissect" the covenant from the peace treaty "without destroying the whole vital structure."[34]

Back in Paris, Wilson charged once again into the diplomatic fray. Nearly all of the difficult issues, especially those that conflicted with the principles of the Fourteen Points, had either been deferred or remained unresolved in what was, from the American point of view, the "first round" of the negotiations. Yet, it was precisely these issues to which the Europeans attached the greatest importance. Significant compromises would undoubtedly have been necessary under any circumstances, but Wilson's hand had been considerably weakened by the domestic dissension.[35] Knowing both the president's com-

---

[31] Quoted ibid., 240–41.

[32] Ambrosius 1987, 95.

[33] Quoted in Knock 1992, 241.

[34] Quoted ibid., 244.

[35] Not only had the Round Robin undercut the League, but House, who led the American delegation during the president's absence, had already made important concessions to the Europeans. Perhaps the president's closest advisor believed he represented adequately Wilson's views,

mitment and his lack of support at home, the Europeans now held the League hostage to their other demands.[36] Forced to reopen the draft covenant to obtain the changes demanded by the Senate, Wilson had to give way to Allied demands in order to "save" the League—and it was these compromises that would lose Wilson and the treaty so much support when they became known.[37]

While denying the port city of Fiume to Italy, Wilson nonetheless acquiesced in most of the Italian claims originally contained in the secret Treaty of London. After defeating a Japanese amendment on racial equality in the League Commission, which would have been strongly opposed in the United States as undue interference in domestic affairs, Wilson was forced to agree to transfer German rights in China's Shantung peninsula to Japan. Likewise, Britain withheld agreement on an amendment protecting the Monroe Doctrine to obtain an Anglo-American naval understanding.[38] Finally, Wilson and French Prime Minister Georges Clemenceau disagreed on many issues. Indeed, despite a certain grudging respect, Wilson regarded the Frenchman as his primary nemesis in Paris. Although often depicted as bellicose even after the war, France was actually defensive and nervous; the president was forced to make numerous compromises to calm French fears.[39] Most important, in order to temper Clemenceau's demands for the permanent demilitarization of areas east of the Rhine and intrusive League investigations of potential treaty violations, Wilson was obliged to accept with France a bilateral security treaty against unprovoked German aggression, negotiated in tandem with a similar Anglo-French treaty.

Wilson submitted the Treaty of Versailles to the Senate two days after his return to the United States in July 1919. As Wilson entered the chamber carrying the bulky document, Lodge asked "Mr. President, can I carry the treaty for you?" "Not on your life," Wilson responded with a smile. Everyone

---

sought to place his own stamp on the negotiations, or was simply caught up in the need to make diplomatic progress—or, perhaps, the president underestimated his own need to compromise—but Wilson supposedly declared to his wife upon their return that "House has given away everything I won before we left Paris. He has compromised on every side, and I have to start all over again, and this time it will be harder"; quoted in Schulte Nordholt 1991, 123. The story comes originally from Edith Bolling Galt Wilson's rather self-serving and defensive autobiography. Mrs. Wilson's antipathy for House is well known, rendering the statement somewhat suspect.

[36] Ambrosius 1987, 123.

[37] Kennedy 1980, 358; Dallek 1983, 89. Duroselle 1963, 98, identified three classes of issues for Wilson: "(1) those in which he finally gave in to his European colleagues, for example, reparations; (2) those in which he refused to give in on the substance but accepted some compromise, such as the questions of the Saar and the Rhineland; (3) those in which he remained intransigent to the end, such as the questions of Fiume and Dalmatia."

[38] Ambrosius 1987, 123; Knock 1992, 246–50.

[39] Schuker 1976, 5; Leffler 1979.

roared, but the levity quickly passed.[40] The treaty met immediate resistance from the president's right and left.

Conservative internationalists and irreconcilables rejected the president's vision of a "new order." In their judgment, the covenant, despite Wilson's hard-won revisions in Paris, did not satisfy their earlier objections. The new provision for withdrawal upon twenty-four months' notice was inadequate, as was the exclusion of domestic questions from the League, because it reserved to the Executive Council the right to determine the standing of an issue. The Monroe Doctrine amendment, in Lodge's words, was "worthless."[41] Throughout, the concern was that transferring decision-making authority to the League might constrain future American actions.

The most important failing, from the critics' view, was Article 10 of the covenant, and it was this issue that would most clearly divide opinion and, ultimately, sink the treaty. As the principal purpose of the League was to oppose aggression, all members bound themselves "to respect and preserve as against external aggression the territorial integrity and existing political independence of all States members of the League." At Wilson's direct suggestion, the article went on to state that "In case of any such aggression the Executive Council shall advise upon the means by which this obligation shall be fulfilled."[42] Although Article 16 provided for the use of economic sanctions, the use of force remained a possibility.[43] Without a doubt, Article 10 represented a significant break with America's traditional unilateralism. Not only would the United States be committed to defend other countries, but the Executive Council of the League would advise upon the means. Wilson defended Article 10 as a moral obligation, which implied a degree of discretion, rather than a legal obligation, which did not.[44] Yet for conservative internationalists and even more for irreconcilables, the strategy of international cooperation embodied in Article 10 was far too great a commitment, and threatened to constrain the United States too much.

Progressive internationalists, on the other hand, were in principle willing to undertake the commitment entailed in Article 10. But for many, the unsavory compromises reached in the "second round" of negotiations in Paris threatened to drag the United States into the defense of an unjust and unprincipled status quo. Under the banner "THIS IS NOT PEACE," the progressive editors of the New Republic turned their backs on the League they had previously supported. "Americans would be fools if they permitted themselves to be embroiled in a system of European alliances," they declared. "America promised to underwrite a stable peace. Mr. Wilson has failed. The

---

[40] Quoted in Knock 1992, 251.
[41] Ambrosius 1987, 137.
[42] Quoted in Schulte Nordholt 1991, 296; see Ambrosius 1987, 73.
[43] LaFeber 1994, 321.
[44] Ambrosius 1987, 165; Schulte Nordholt 1991, 386.

peace cannot last. America should withdraw from all commitments which would impair her freedom of action."[45] The fear here, it is important to note, was not the entangling nature of the commitments in the League per se, but rather the failure to resolve political issues in Europe in a way that would preserve peace into the future. The progressives feared entrapment, but for reasons very different from those of the conservatives.

Assaulted from both sides, the treaty was in serious jeopardy. Sensing that public support for the treaty was eroding, Lodge stalled for time, reading aloud the entire 246-page document to an almost empty committee chamber, and parading a seemingly endless stream of mostly irrelevant and hostile witnesses through the hearings.[46] On September 10, 1919, the Foreign Relations Committee reported the treaty to the Senate with forty-five technical amendments and four reservations.[47] In the words of the majority committee report, these changes were designed to transform the "entangling alliance" into a genuine "League of Peace"—felicitous phrases that underscored the deep division between progressive and conservative internationalists on the best way to ensure America's interests in the postwar era.[48] By early November, Lodge had pared the committee amendments and reservations down, curiously, to fourteen reservations.

There is considerable disagreement on whether these reservations were merely symbolic or substantive, as maintained by the participants themselves.[49] Although many of Wilson's supporters claimed that the United States would have to reopen negotiations if the reservations were approved, emphasizing their substantive nature, this view was not necessarily shared by Britain and France.[50] Clearly, many reservations were only sharpened versions of issues discussed virtually from the outset: the right of withdrawal, the Monroe Doctrine, immigration, and the freedom to reject mandates. Again, Article 10 was the most important, with Lodge's second reservation declaring that "the United States assumes no obligation to preserve the territorial integrity or political independence of any other country, unless in any particular case the Congress, which under the Constitution, has the sole power to declare war or authorize the employment of the military or naval forces of the United States, shall by act or joint resolution so provide."[51]

With the executive-legislative battle joined, and confident that the public shared his vision or could be brought round to his views, Wilson set out on a national speaking tour. Having already suffered a possible stroke in April

---

[45] Quoted in Dulles 1963, 117 fn.16; see also Knock 1992, 254.
[46] Kennedy 1980, 360–61; Schulte Nordholt 1991, 381–82.
[47] Duroselle 1963, 122.
[48] Barnet 1990, 180.
[49] See Schulte Nordholt 1991, 399.
[50] Stromberg 1963, 35–36; Leffler 1979, 17; Schulte Nordholt 1991, 404.
[51] Quoted in Schulte Nordholt 1991, 400.

while in Paris, the rigors of the trip finally broke the president's health. Scholars differ in their estimates of the effect that Wilson's numerous speeches were having on public opinion.[52] In any event, the strain was too much, and he was forced to cut short his trip and return to Washington. Days later the president suffered the massive stroke that left him an invalid for the remainder of his life.

On November 19, the Senate voted down the Treaty of Versailles and, with it, the Covenant of the League of Nations. Considering the treaty first with the Lodge reservations, the Senate voted against it, 39 aye–55 nay—the irreconcilables voting with the Democrats to defeat it. Twenty-four senators would have had to change their votes to approve the treaty with reservations. On a motion to approve the treaty without the reservations, the irreconcilables voted with the Republicans, 38 to 53, 25 votes short of the necessary two-thirds majority.[53] Thus, although roughly 80 percent of the Senate approved of the treaty in some form, neither version could muster even a simple majority. The Senate and public were, if not surprised, clearly confused by this outcome. Over the winter pressure built for reconsideration. Lodge appeared to be moderating his position, but was pulled back by the irreconcilables in his party.[54] Wilson remained obdurate. On March 19, 1920, the Senate voted again, but only on the treaty with reservations. This time, ratification failed 49–35—still far short of the required two-thirds.[55]

Wilson then declared the upcoming presidential election "a great and solemn referendum" on the League.[56] But although the Democratic nominees, James M. Cox and Franklin D. Roosevelt, supported the covenant vigorously, Republicans Warren G. Harding and Calvin Coolidge equivocated. Even as the election was determined largely by local and economic issues, Harding— winning the biggest electoral landslide to that date in American history— interpreted the results as a verdict against the League.[57] In April 1921, he announced that he was abandoning the treaty and later signed separate peace treaties with Germany and Austria.[58] In doing so, he brought to an end both America's first European war and its first attempt at international security cooperation. Although the United States would participate in European affairs throughout the 1920s and, to a lesser extent, 1930s, it would maintain a steady unilateral course until its next call to arms.

[52] Cf. Kennedy 1980, 361; and Schulte Nordholt 1991, 394–95.

[53] The vote totals for the treaty with and without reservations were 94 and 91, respectively. Three senators chose not to vote on the latter. The votes necessary for a two-thirds majority are calculated on the basis of the 94 total votes, as these three senators would undoubtedly have been pressed into taking a stand on a close decision.

[54] Ambrosius 1987, 228–30.

[55] Knock 1992, 263–64; LaFeber 1994, 329.

[56] Quoted in Knock 1992, 264.

[57] Ambrosius 1987, 270–89.

[58] Leffler 1979, 32.

### The Fight over the League

This paradox of failed ratification despite extensive and widespread support for the principle of a league, magnified by the events of the late 1930s and 1940s, has stimulated an extensive debate on the causes of American rejection. Although there is considerable variation within each approach, and many authors draw upon more than one, five general explanations can be identified for the failure of the United States to join the League: constitutional, personal, partisan, ideological, and realist.[59] None is intended to explain variations in the security relationships identified in Chapter 2, making comparative assessments of their explanatory power difficult.

The constitutional explanation focuses on the institutions of Senate ratification, including the division of authority between the executive and legislature, the two-thirds supermajority requirement, and the simple majority requirement for amendments.[60] Although institutions privilege and empower some political actors over others and create a peculiar politics of ratification, this explanation fails for the simple fact that some treaties are ratified—including some in the interwar period that were clearly "internationalist" in orientation, such as the Four-, Five-, and Nine-Power pacts negotiated at the Washington Conference for the Limitation of Armaments (see the final section of this chapter). Under the same rules, the North Atlantic Treaty was easily ratified in 1949 (see Chapter 5). Clearly, the constitutional rules governing ratification mattered in the failure of the League, but they were not decisive.

Personal explanations emphasize Wilson's intransigent personality, the effects of the president's deteriorating physical health, including the possible stroke of April and the massive stroke of November 1919, and enmity between the president and, first, Theodore Roosevelt and, later, Lodge.[61] Considerations of personal health and hatred (the term is not too strong) were clearly important in the League fight. Yet, as Knock concludes, "Wilson's illness may have been the decisive factor behind the treaty's defeat. But it does not necessarily follow (all other factors remaining the same) that the absence of the stroke would have produced a different (or happier) out-

---

[59] Developed at a slightly more general level, *regional* and *ethnic* explanations of America's so-called isolationism have been widely criticized in the literature. See especially Jonas 1990; and Guinsburg 1982. These explanations will not be addressed here. *Economic* explanations are also offered for America's interwar isolationism; see, among others, Wilson 1971; Williams 1972; Leffler 1979; and Frieden 1988. Although helpful on many trade and financial issues, these analyses shed less light on questions of security cooperation, as defined here, and tend to underestimate the domestic support for internationalism.

[60] See Haynes 1938, 694–703, 713–18.

[61] On Wilson's health, see Laukhuff 1956; George and George 1964 [1956]; and Weinstein 1981. On personal enmity, see Widenor 1980; Parsons 1989; and Schulte Nordholt 1991, 319.

come."[62] The same holds, I would add, for other personal factors. The deep divide between progressive internationalists, conservative internationalists, and irreconcilables was evident from the earliest debates on the League and remained throughout the course of deliberations. Even after he was repudiated by a majority of the voters in the 1918 congressional election, which he had hoped to use as a personal "vote of confidence" on the eve of the Paris peace talks, and later as he lay in bed debilitated by a stroke, the politically and physically weakened president was able to hold a core of twenty-three senators to his vision of a progressive League. If personal factors mattered, they appear to have been shared by a significant fraction of the Senate.[63]

The partisan explanation points to the struggle between the two major parties for dominance.[64] In various guises, scholars have argued that the Republicans were, in fact, the natural majority party of the era, and the Wilsonian interlude is the real anomaly; that Lodge and other Republicans were loathe to let Wilson win the peace as well as the war; and that Wilson—by arrogance or mistake—inappropriately politicized the peace talks in the 1918 election and compounded this error by failing to include any senators or Republican leaders on the peace commission.[65] Although promising, this explanation ultimately founders on the same point as the previous one. How was a weakened president able to maintain such tight control over his party, especially when he appears not to have exercised any of the powers of his office other than the "bully pulpit"?

This explanation is further complicated by the heavy substantive content of the debate. Many have sought to downplay the policy differences between the parties.[66] But, as we shall see below, the parties were not just fighting, they were fighting over issues that they, at least, deemed important to the future of American foreign policy. The division of the government into a Republican legislature and a Democratic executive obviously did influence the politics and prospects of ratification. Had the Democrats controlled the Senate and the presidency, ratification would have been far more likely. Given the importance of the League and Wilson's foreign policy in the 1918 mid-term elections that produced a Republican Senate, however, "divided

---

[62] Knock 1992, 267.

[63] By the time of its Senate defeat, Wilson, perhaps troubled by his "phase two" compromises or perceived European perfidy, may have become disillusioned with his own League construct. See Costigliola, 1984, 54; and Ambrosius 1987, 172. Dallek 1983, 91, extends this possibility to suggest that Wilson actually willed the defeat of the League by his intransigence rather than risk having the flaws in his vision revealed through practice. Although it is difficult to evaluate the empirical accuracy of this hypothesis, it nonetheless falls prey to the criticism made of other personal explanations.

[64] See Holt 1933, 292–307.

[65] On Republican dominance, see Kennedy 1980, 241–44; on the battle to win the peace, see Knock 1992, 240; on the lack of cooperation with the Senate, see LaFeber 1994, 314.

[66] Osgood 1953, 294; Schulte Nordholt 1991, 399.

government" itself reveals a profound mistrust and skepticism by the public over the progressives' vision of the future. Divided government is as much a consequence as a cause of the League's failure.

Several historians have recently elaborated an ideological explanation highlighting the international consequences of the deep intellectual chasm between progressivism and conservatism that defined American politics at this time.[67] In this, I think, largely correct view, both Wilson and Lodge are seen as constrained by their respective progressive and conservative constituencies. If Wilson strayed too far from the "transformational" purpose of the war or League, he risked alienating the progressives central to the new Democratic coalition cobbled together in 1916. Likewise, Lodge was held back by the conservatives, as was most apparent in his seemingly sincere willingness to compromise important issues following the League's first senatorial defeat. These coalitions, in turn, were rooted in specific ideologies—in the case of the progressives, one drawn almost entirely from the domestic political economy.

Although it captures important dimensions of the debate, this view cannot account for the irreconcilables, some of whom, like Lawrence Y. Sherman (R-IL), Bert M. Fernald (R-ME), and Albert B. Fall (R-NM), were traditional conservatives and others, such as Robert M. La Follette (R-WI) and George W. Norris (R-NE), who were clearly progressives.[68] These principled defenders of unilateralism bridged the political divide then dominating the Senate, and were united only by their deep distrust of Europe. In foreign affairs, at least, there appears to be a second dimension of political cleavage. More important, the ideological explanation generally ignores the specifics of the international environment confronting the United States. In their assessments of the League debate, revisionist historians fail to ask whether the progressive or conservative vision actually conformed to the needs of American foreign policy in the interwar period.[69]

A final, realist explanation, well known to scholars of international politics, argues that America's idealism was intellectually flawed, and led directly

---

[67] Ambrosius 1987; Knock 1992.

[68] Guinsburg 1982, 25.

[69] This exclusive focus on domestic considerations is not limited to the ideological explanation. Guinsburg's 1982, 289, summary is typical in its failure to address the international determinants of security strategy. "Regional sentiments, with ethnic emotions a significant but by no means dominant component, served as an essential foundation for the survival of isolationism in the interwar years. Partisan ambitions, defects of presidential leadership, and the national climate of opinion frequently abetted the cause. Yet if the senatorial isolationists could not have succeeded without these assets, neither could isolationism have survived without the talent and zeal of its senatorial champions and the vulnerability of the Senate to the influence of a determined minority." In short, everything matters except the international environment and America's interests in that arena.

to the disaster of the 1930s.[70] Although appealing to American values and aspirations, the realists argue, the progressive vision embodied in the League was insufficiently attentive to the needs of international power politics. What was required, and would have worked better had it been chosen, was the balance-of-power politics advocated by the conservative internationalists.[71] Implicit in this critique is the proposition that the League failed because a sufficient number of Senators recognized the needs of the balance-of-power system and refused to be swayed by the idealists.

For reasons explained below, I disagree. Where realists tend to point to contradictions in the logic of collective security, I focus here more on the lack of congruence between the progressive program for the League and the particular environment in which the United States found itself in 1919. The progressive internationalist vision was not unfounded; it possessed a logical core and might have been appropriate at another time and under only slightly different circumstances. The conservative internationalist program, in turn, was equally sound—and equally inappropriate. The question is not whether realism or the institutional solutions labeled "idealist" in this partic-ular debate are appropriate under all circumstances, but rather what condi-tions favor the choice of which type of security relationship. Both versions of the League were rejected because of the small joint production economies then in existence, which limited the gains from cooperation; the significant probability of opportunism by Europe, which threatened to overwhelm whatever gains might accrue to the country; and the governance costs of cooperation, which both limited the feasible options to relatively anarchic security relationships and threatened to constrain the United States greatly in the conduct of its foreign policy.

The debate over the League was vigorous because the issues were substan-tial and all sides could claim important confirming evidence for their posi-tions—even if it was mostly counterfactual. The League was rejected not only because of personal factors, partisanship, or ideology. Rather, the League in both its progressive and conservative visions failed because the limited benefits for the United States, rooted in the joint economies of the time and significant fears of European opportunism, could not offset the difficulties and costs of adequately safeguarding American interests. Despite significant support for the idea of security cooperation, Americans wanted the League, in the end, only if it could overcome problems it was ill suited to solve. The League ultimately foundered on the small gains from cooperation, high risks of opportunism, and high governance costs it inevitably entailed. After con-

---

[70] Carr 1939; Osgood 1953; Morgenthau 1978.

[71] For a current example of this same discussion, see Kupchan and Kupchan 1991; and Betts 1992.

templating the alternatives, unilateralism reemerged as the optimal policy for the United States. Although its principled advocates—the irreconcilables—were small in number, unilateralism remained the default option or second choice for both the conservative and progressive internationalists. When neither could make a convincing case for their vision, the country reverted to its historic independence.

## JOINT PRODUCTION ECONOMIES

The joint economies in producing security in the interwar period were relatively small, and thus the possible benefits from cooperation were severely restricted. Although the absolute magnitude of these joint economies is hard to discern, as discussed in Chapter 3, we can more readily observe and compare changes in the direction and magnitude of this variable. At the end of World War I, I argue here, the joint production economies were not significantly larger than before 1914. The war set in train tremendous changes, but these were accompanied by high uncertainty about their likely effects. They also took two decades to mature. Not until the mid- to late 1930s were the innovations begun in World War I fully realized. Conversely, after World War II the joint economies were substantially greater than in 1919. That war was the final catalyst that brought the emerging changes together, and thereafter altered the economics of security in profound ways.

Prior to World War I, the United States relied primarily upon its geographic isolation and its navy to protect itself from foreign threats. In 1883, the United States Navy consisted of 90 ships, 48 of which were capable of firing a gun, and 38 of which were made of wood—all at a time when the British Navy numbered 367 modern warships. At the end of that decade, America's navy was rated twelfth in the world, behind that of Turkey, China, and Austria-Hungary.[72] Even then, however, the tide had begun to turn. By 1890, construction plans were underway for a new fleet of 15 cruisers and 6 battleships, which were expected to put the United States on par with Germany.[73] The navy's fortunes improved further when Theodore Roosevelt ascended to the presidency in 1901, and promptly proceeded to press Congress for two new battleships a year. By the time he left office eight years later, Roosevelt could boast that he had doubled the size of the navy.[74] To show off his achievements, the president sent the "Great White fleet," now consisting of 22 modern battleships, on a round-the-world tour in 1907–1908.[75]

This deep-water navy gave the United States the strategic reach necessary

---

[72] LaFeber 1993, 114–15, and LaFeber 1994, 187.
[73] May 1973, 7.
[74] Dulles 1963, 67–68.
[75] LaFeber 1993, 207.

to defend its self-proclaimed security zone. By the turn of the century, the United States was committed under various doctrines to defend unilaterally the entire Western Hemisphere and portions of the Pacific, including its imperial possessions in the Philippines and Guam. This defense area, Walter Lippmann estimated in 1943, comprised roughly 40 percent of the land surface of the earth.[76] These commitments, along with the construction of a modern navy, demonstrate a not insignificant ability by the United States to project force over distance even before World War I.

The Great War saw tremendous technological changes and immense increases in firepower deployed on the battlefield. The first truly "industrial" war, World War I brought forth several new tools of death—poison gas, land mines, and other weapons—and greatly improved others, especially ordnance and submarines.[77] Once the opposing armies were fully joined on the continent, these technologies conspired to raise the costs of projecting force and advantaged the defense. Armies dug into their trenches and millions of soldiers died for small territorial gains. By the end of the war, the ability to project force gradually began to improve, especially with the development of new ways of breaching enemy lines, the creation of mechanized and motorized armies, and improvements in military aviation.[78] It is on this basis that some analysts speak of a "military revolution," but World War I is more accurately described as the beginnings of an important military evolution.[79]

These new war-induced technologies were of limited import, at least in the short run. First, the lessons of the war were by no means clear. Even the introduction of the tank in 1916, which in the late 1930s "overthrew the entire balance of power in Europe," remained at the end of the war "a weapon of potential and promise rather than performance on the battlefield."[80] Much the same can be said about air power. Even though "all of the missions that make up the employment of air power had appeared by 1918," the "full potential . . . remained unclear."[81] In a perverse way, World War I ended too soon for the full development and realization of the new technologies.

More importantly, the individual innovations were less significant than their eventual integration into "combined systems" or "combined-arms" forms of warfare, a more difficult and unpredictable undertaking. The many different technologies and different organizational structures produced by the war needed to be melded into a coherent whole. This was a new hurdle for

---

[76] Lippmann cited in White 1996, 18.

[77] Submarines were eventually countered by the use of convoys. With the success of the latter, few in the interwar years expected submarines to pose an effective threat to shipping and force projection.

[78] Quester 1977, 140; van Creveld 1989, 177.

[79] Doughty and Gruber 1996, 638.

[80] Murray and Millett 1996, 2; and Murray 1996a, 7.

[81] Doughty and Gruber 1996, 644.

the various militaries, and was an open-ended process without a clearly envisioned outcome. As Barry Watts and Williamson Murray write, "Beyond the time required for the fragile airplane and unreliable tanks of World War I to evolve into more mature weapons by the late 1930s, military services had to develop new organizational structures such as the panzer division or Fighter Command's organizational arrangements for the command and control of Britain's air defenses." Such changes, they conclude, were often "the result of ad hoc improvisation" and were "extraordinarily difficult to execute and fraught with profound uncertainties."[82] Not until the late 1930s did the new innovations finally bear fruit in these complex systems for war. Indeed, the new technologies, once realized, may have fed the desires of the axis powers for imperial expansion and contributed in important ways to the outbreak of World War II.

Second, the scale economies of many new technologies, although larger, were nonetheless still limited. Even after the increased firepower and mobility of the tank was joined with innovations in doctrine, which did not occur until Germany developed the Blitzkrieg strategy in the 1930s, the mechanized army's greater need for ammunition, spare parts, and fuel, coupled with limited logistics, continued to restrict its offensive reach.[83] Germany's push into the Soviet Union in 1941 failed largely for these reasons. Other innovations may even have decreased strategic reach; the Royal Air Force's development of radar and advanced fighters allowed it to assemble the integrated air defense system that defeated Germany in the "Battle of Britain."[84] Even France, the most likely target of any German revanchism and the most heavily armed European state, sought to produce security for itself not by projecting force but by demilitarizing German border areas, searching for allies, and—most important for the point here—hiding behind its fixed Maginot Line.

Third, and central for the United States, most innovations during this period were limited to the actual battlefield, and did little to alter the ability of countries—and especially offshore countries—to project force over long distances. Tanks were instruments of continental warfare, and though they might influence how the United States fought once there, the rise of mechanized warfare did not change its ability to deploy force across the Atlantic. Similarly, aircraft possessed only limited ranges; aviator Charles A. Lindbergh, we must remember, did not cross the Atlantic until 1927. Three innovations

[82] Watts and Murray 1996, 372.

[83] Doughty and Gruber 1996, 639, find the origins of the Blitzkrieg in doctrinal manuals published in 1924 that distill the lessons of World War I. On limited logistics, see van Creveld 1989, 177–78. As Murray 1996a, 46–47, writes, only 20 percent of the German forces were motorized; the rest "remained a foot and horse-drawn army." Also Doughty and Gruber 1996, 693 ff.

[84] Doughty and Gruber 1996, 668 ff.

did have important implications that, once refined, did create new strategic reach. But like the battlefield technologies discussed above, they too required decades before they were fully realized and effectively employed.

By 1917, the Germans and, later, the British were waging direct air attacks on one another's territory, demonstrating the potential for long-range aircraft and strategic aerial bombardment. This was, according to one analyst, the only innovation of the interwar period that "represented a truly new approach to war-waging."[85] Nonetheless, as with other new technologies, "the extent of such attacks and their results left room for considerable debate as to [their] potential effects on future warfare."[86] The pace of technological change remained gradual over the 1920s, and accelerated in the 1930s, as metal replaced wood-and-canvas construction, wings were redesigned, and power plants improved. By 1939, Germany was flying the first jet aircraft.[87] Yet, despite the enthusiasm of initial proponents of air power, the ability to deliver large amounts of force over distance remained limited. Even in World War II, long-range bombers were both of dubious effectiveness and subject to high loss rates, at least until the Luffwafte had been destroyed.[88]

During World War I, Britain also made important advances in naval air power. Entering the war with only improvised seaplanes, by 1918 Britain had twelve aircraft carriers, at a time when no other country possessed even one, and was "conducting carrier operations with aircraft that were operationally effective in shooting down enemy aircraft, conducting reconnaissance patrols, and dropping bombs and torpedoes."[89] Britain allowed its naval air capabilities to languish after the war, and passed the initiative, such as it was, to the United States and Japan. Again, the pace of innovation was slow in the 1920s, but by the mid-1930s both the United States and Japan had "developed sophisticated concepts for carrier operations that would soon change the face of naval war." As demonstrated by the successful attack by Japan on Pearl Harbor, aircraft carriers eventually allowed those states that possessed them to extend their reach greatly. Also important to the ultimate success of the carrier, however, was the decision by the Americans to build a vast armada of supply ships, thereby allowing their fleet to stay continuously at sea.[90]

World War I also saw innovations in amphibious landing capabilities, which permitted battles to be brought to the enemy.[91] The record here is even more mixed than elsewhere. Despite earlier successes, Britain, France, and

---

[85] Millett 1996b, 331. See also Murray 1996b, 97.
[86] Murray 1996b, 97.
[87] Ibid., 98.
[88] Doughty and Gruber 1996, 734 ff.
[89] Till 1996, 194.
[90] Doughty and Gruber 1996, 646, 708–13, 820–21.
[91] Millett 1996a, 50–95.

Australia-New Zealand suffered tremendous loses in an amphibious landing at Gallipoli in 1915, an ill-fated attempt to seize the Straits of the Dardanelles from Turkey. The British alone suffered more than 200,000 casualties in this effort.[92] Again, the rate of innovation in amphibious warfare remained low through the 1920s, especially for the allied states. In 1921, Japan possessed "the world's foremost amphibious force," and in 1939, "Japan alone possessed the doctrine, tactical concepts, and forces for such operations."[93] But by 1941, the United States had surpassed its rival. Amphibious warfare is one of the most complex forms of combat, requiring coordinated air and naval support to protect the troops going ashore, bombardment to disrupt defending forces, and rapid reinforcements complete with artillery and tanks. The integration of forces and capabilities that slowed the pace of innovation after World War I and produced such high uncertainty about the effectiveness of alternative technologies was most acute in this area. Even into World War II, the problems of complexity and uncertainty were nearly overwhelming, and the potential for amphibious warfare remained just that—potential.

Thus, the revolution in warfare begun in World War I was a long-drawn-out process. In 1919, this revolution remained in embryonic form, full of potential but requiring considerable growth and maturation before its benefits could be clearly seen. The technological scale economies of producing security did not expand greatly during World War I, if they grew at all. Two decades later, the situation facing states was quite different, but in 1919 there was no particular reason to expect the changes to be as profound as they eventually were. Decision makers, and especially those in the United States who were most distant from the sites of future conflicts, were quite justified in assuming that the gains from security cooperation would be quite modest.[94]

Civilian transportation costs provide an indirect way of measuring the costs of projecting force over distance. This is discussed more thoroughly in Chapter 7, but the important point here is that there is no particular reason to believe that the costs of shipping goods differed in any systematic way from those of shipping troops and equipment. Although freight rates declined steadily over the late nineteenth and twentieth centuries, there is no decisive break between prewar and postwar costs. The costs of shipping grain from Chicago to New York by rail and then to Liverpool by ship averaged $.0364 per hundred pounds in 1900–1913 (in constant 1996 dollars);

---

[92] Doughty and Gruber 1996, 563–65.

[93] Millett 1996a, 50.

[94] Christensen and Snyder 1990 argue that in the interwar years civil authorities incorrectly believed in defense dominance, when the balance had actually shifted to the offense. In my reading, the evidence is much more ambiguous, and no misperception is necessary to account for the interpretations of technology that dominated in this period. On offense and defense dominance and military doctrine more generally, see Posen 1984; J. Snyder 1984; Van Evera 1984 and 1986.

they averaged $.0316 between 1922–1935, a 13 percent decline.[95] By contrast, freight costs averaged $0.0632 between 1880 and 1889, and fell by 50 percent prior to World War I. Neither in terms of the available technologies nor as reflected in freight rates is there any persuasive evidence that it was significantly less costly to project force over distance after the war than before.

The difficulties of projecting force over distance were recognized by many in the United States. For most analysts, America's oceanic buffers both insulated the country and hindered its ability to act in Europe and Asia. As late as 1939, then former President Herbert Hoover, a leader in the "fortress America" school, maintained that the Western Hemisphere was protected by a virtually insurmountable barrier, a "moat of three thousand miles of ocean on the east, and six thousand miles on the west."[96] Accordingly, the need for constant vigilance was minimal. Secure behind their oceanic buffers, Americans throughout the interwar period rejoiced that the war was over, the Germans were defeated, and Europe was far away. Even with the wartime innovations, Americans believed that fighting away from home remained a costly and difficult enterprise.

Conversely, in the interwar period the United States enjoyed substantial positive externalities from European security efforts. Before, during, and after World War I, the United States possessed an interest in preventing the emergence of a dominant European power. This was also in the interests of the Europeans themselves, and it would remain in their interests regardless of what the United States did. In the absence of an American commitment, the Europeans had to provide for their own defense. Without incurring cost or effort, the United States would then be protected against the rise of a new European hegemon. Through unilateralism, the United States could free ride effectively on Europe. That the Europeans suffered from the same incentives, and would ultimately choose to "pass the buck" to one another, does not alter the calculus of the United States. Had it chosen to make a substantial contribution to European security after World War I, America's partners would have had strong incentives simply to pass the burden in its direction rather than to one another. That free riding ultimately produces suboptimal outcomes—in this case contributing to the absence of an effective European deterrent and, therefore, to the beginning of World War II—does not mitigate the collective action dilemma that prompts "buck passing" in the first place.

This free ride for the United States was made possible, in part, by its large but not overwhelming size. According to the logic of collective action, large

---

[95] Freight rates were reasonably stable within each of these periods. During the war the rates climbed dramatically, reflecting the greater risk of shipping during the conflict. They did not stabilize until 1922. For sources, see Chapter 7.

[96] Quoted in DeConde 1957, 25.

TABLE 4.1
United States GDP Relative to Other Great Powers

| Year | United States : United Kingdom, France, and Germany | United States : United Kingdom, France, Germany, and Japan |
|------|:---:|:---:|
| 1913 | 1.12 | .97 |
| 1919 | 1.52 | 1.21 |
| 1920 | 1.49 | 1.20 |
| 1949 | 1.97 | 1.65 |
| 1950 | 2.00 | 1.67 |

*Source:* Calculated from Maddison 1982, Table A2, p. 161; Table A7, pp. 174–75; and Table A8, pp. 176–77.

states will tend to bear a disproportionate share of the burden of providing positive externalities—and such goods can be provided effectively if one state is sufficiently large that its private interests lead it to contribute even though others still ride free.[97] The United States is often described as "hegemonic" in the interwar years, but there are no precise measures of hegemony and scholars disagree on the relevant dimensions and breakpoints.[98] Nonetheless, comparing the Gross Domestic Product of the United States, a standard measure of aggregate international power and size, with that of others in this period suggests that although it was undoubtedly larger than others in 1919 than in 1913, it was less large relative to others in 1919 than in 1949, when free riding was clearly less possible (see Table 4.1). Without a clear consensus on what it means to be hegemonic, and without measures of the private benefits and costs to countries of providing the positive externality of European security, such aggregate figures cannot be decisive; at the very least, the greater interests of the Europeans in their own stability should lead us to discount the intensity of America's desires for the positive externality and, in turn, the effects of size. These figures do suggest, however, that the United States would be more strongly motivated to provide the positive externality of European stability after World War II than after World War I. Moreover, as we shall see in Chapter 5, whereas Europe could be reasonably expected to defend itself after 1919, no such expectation could be held after 1945. One central lesson of World War I was that, left to their own devices, the Europeans could only fight to a standstill, and the prospects of any one state achieving continental dominance were slim. After World War II, with

[97] Olson and Zeckhauser 1966; Snidal 1985; Lake 1988, 33–88.
[98] See various descriptions and datings of hegemony in Kindleberger 1973; Krasner 1976; Russett 1985; Gilpin 1987; and Strange 1987. This literature is reviewed in D. Lake 1993.

the continent facing a far larger Soviet army, the United States was essential
to maintaining a stable and effective balance. In short, although generalized
free riding may have contributed to Europe's instability after World War I,
the United States was nonetheless in a better position to free ride in 1919
than in 1945. This reinforced incentives for unilateralism during the interwar
years.

As suggested by the theory, joint production economies are partly endogenous. Some of the costs of projecting force could have been offset, at least
in principle, by forward deployments of troops and pre-positioning of matériel—actions effectively carried out by the United States after World War II.
Yet, such a forward-based approach would have required a network of bases
and resupply facilities in both the United States and Europe, entailing at least
some relationally specific assets. In practice, such advanced stationing would
have required a vastly greater role for the United States in European affairs
than was envisioned at the time by even the most extreme advocates of
cooperation. Fear of European opportunism restrained the United States
from even considering options that would have incurred more specific assets.
It is important to note that no one on either the progressive or conservative
side of the debate advocated forward deployments to capture the larger joint
economies potentially available in a forward-based strategy. This contrasts
sharply with the post-1945 policy debate.

A potential division of labor also existed after the war. As a continental
and largely regional struggle, the roles and tasks available to the United
States and the several European powers in the interwar period were less
diverse than they would be under the global competition of the Cold War,
but some division of effort and responsibility would still have improved the
welfare of all parties. Nonetheless, the division of labor was limited for political reasons. As with the question of forward deployment, a division of labor
would have entailed some asset specificity in United States-European relations. And for this reason, the cooperation proposed after World War I did
not envision a division of labor in the international production of security.
Neither the progressive plan embodied in the League Covenant nor the conservative vision laid out in the Lodge reservations included a division of
tasks, responsibilities, or forces. Indeed, when France early in the peace conference proposed an international army under the League and, later, an international general staff, both of which might have contained the institutional
seeds of a division of labor, Wilson flatly rejected the proposals.[99]

The failure to consider forward deployments or a division of labor may
have resulted not only from the high probability of European opportunism

---

[99] Duroselle 1963, 94 and 97; Leffler 1979, 5. Kissinger 1994, 236 and 275, notes that
Wilson did on occasion imply an openness to such a force, but also notes that the absence of a
clearly identified potential aggressor "rendered advanced military planning impossible."

but also from the overly general nature of the League and the ambiguous nature of the threats confronting it. Alternatively, it may have reflected the overconfidence of League advocates; many, Wilson included, expected the League to be such an effective deterrent to aggression that little effort was expended discussing how and in what ways it would exercise force if ever called upon to do so.[100] In any event, the consequence of this failure was that the United States did not seek to take advantage of potentially greater joint economies with Europe. It could, of course, always throw its weight into the scales and contribute to the defense of Europe, much as it had done in the Great War. This would augment but not magnify the effectiveness of the cumulative American and European military might, however, and could be done as easily under strict unilateralism as cooperation.

As the chief architect of the League, Wilson appears to have been cognizant of the joint economies available to the United States through cooperation, and aware that the actual economies produced by the League were likely to be small. In discussing the role of the United States as a possible mediator of the European conflict, House cited the Pan-American Pact, then under discussion but eventually blocked by Chile,[101] and told the British that Wilson had "arranged a closer union of the Americas so if it was thought best not to enter a world wide sphere, we could safely lead an isolated life of our own. If this were decided upon . . . we would increase our army and navy and remain within our hemisphere."[102] Similarly, in one of his preliminary discussions of a possible league, Wilson stated to a delegation from the American Union Against Militarism that "if the world ever comes to combine its force for the purpose of maintaining peace, the individual contributions of each nation will be much less, necessarily, naturally less, than they would be in other circumstances."[103] In Montana during his national speaking tour on the League, Wilson solemnly declared "It is either this treaty or a lone hand, and the lone hand must have a weapon in it," and elsewhere he declared it is either "armed isolation or peaceful partnership," and that if the United States chose splendid geographic isolation, then "we must be physically ready for anything that comes."[104] Finally, while supporting in 1918 and 1919 an unprecedented naval building program designed to make the United States the world's largest sea power, Wilson fought anti-League forces with the threat that far greater naval appropriations would be necessary unless the country joined the new international organization.[105] At the same time, it is important

---

[100] Leffler 1979, 12. The contradiction here is obvious. If the League was not institutionally and politically prepared to use force, threats to do so would not be credible.

[101] Knock 1992, 39–44.

[102] Quoted in Ambrosius 1987, 19–20.

[103] Quoted in Knock 1992, 66.

[104] Quoted in Ambrosius 1987, 178; Calhoun 1986, 253.

[105] On the naval building program, see Parsons 1978, 168–71, and Iriye 1993, 39. On the navy program and the League, see Dulles 1963, 138.

to note that these statements were not elaborated and justified and did not constitute a major theme in the League debate.[106] Despite his awareness of the issue, and the possibility of greater joint economies, Wilson and his domestic allies did not use this argument to sway undecided legislators or voters. In a debate in which virtually every possible argument was offered for examination, this suggests either that the benefits created by cooperation were not salient to the intended audience—although it is not clear why this should be the case—or that the actual benefits were not expected to be significant and the case for the League could not rest on this foundation.

In the end, unilateralism was not an unattractive policy for the United States in the interwar period. The limited joint economies placed significant limits on both the expected costs of opportunism and the governance costs the United States was willing to bear, ultimately undermining both the progressive and conservative conceptions of the League of Nations and tilting the United States toward continued unilateralism.

## SAFEGUARDING AMERICAN SECURITY

How best to protect the United States from European opportunism and how to build an effective security relationship at an acceptable cost were the key issues in the postwar debate about American foreign policy and the proposed League of Nations. There was considerable uncertainty about both the expected costs of European opportunism and the likely governance costs of alternative security relationships. This uncertainty was further complicated by the differing proposals advanced by the progressive and conservative internationalists, which were themselves based on differing assessments of the likely costs and benefits of cooperation. After a brief survey of the overall expected costs of opportunism and governance costs, I turn to the competing views and specific plans proposed by the principal factions.

The probability that Europe would act opportunistically toward the United States was significant during the interwar period. Fears of entrapment were the driving force behind the League of Nations debate at home. Given the unstable peace, the harshness of the treaty toward Germany, unsatisfied demands of the Allies for territory and security, weak successor states to the Habsburg empire in eastern Europe, the retreat of Russia into communist-led isolation, and general economic instability, Americans correctly feared being drawn into another European misadventure. As reflected in the turnabout by the editors of the *New Republic*, it was not only historic distrust of Europe but also the instability of the postwar environment that produced in the United States significant and quite reasonable fears of entrapment into costly and dangerous European conflicts.

---

[106] Calhoun 1986, 254, notes that this was a "favorite theme" of Wilson during his national speaking tour; nonetheless, it later disappeared from the Senate debate.

Fears of abandonment and exploitation were less severe. The Europeans were not likely to abandon the United States, as America's concerns in the region were much the same as theirs; in fact, Europeans had a real fear that the United States would retreat into unilateralism and abandon them—as in fact happened. At the same time, the United States did fear exploitation by its European allies. Just as the United States could free ride on Europe because of their shared goals and aspirations, the countries of Europe could free ride on any commitment made by the United States—underscoring the general potential for buck passing in the interwar period.[107] Even if the relevant countries collectively agreed to defend stability on the continent, they could still exploit the United States by free riding.

Although the various factions in the League debate differed in their particular assessments, nearly all agreed that, absent some effective security relationship, the probability of European opportunism was very high. Cooperation threatened to entrap the United States into unwanted wars and exploit its resources. At the same time, the League was expected to create few relationally specific assets. As already discussed, this was largely endogenous, as the fear of European opportunism inhibited the United States from considering any cooperative undertakings that would, in fact, be costly if its partners acted opportunistically. This prevented the United States from investing in the joint production economies that might have made cooperation viable. The probability of opportunism was sufficiently high that the expected costs were positive and a significant factor in the choice of security relationships. The repressing of investments in greater joint production economies may have been more consequential in the long run.

In turn, as we shall see shortly, the progressive and conservative internationalists differed in how effective they believed the League would be in constraining the potential for European opportunism. As Ambrosius highlights, "The question of control, not isolationism versus internationalism, was the central issue in the treaty fight."[108] On the one hand, the progressives anticipated that the League would be very effective in controlling the Europeans and lowering the risk of opportunism. Wilson's vision of the League contained a measure of hierarchy, and progressives believed this would transform the nature of international politics and significantly reduce the likelihood that the United States would be drawn into unwanted conflicts. On the other hand, the conservatives argued that this limited hierarchy would be insufficient and would, in fact, prove counterproductive: by committing the United States to collective security, it would inevitably be drawn into Europe's antagonisms. At best, in their view, the expected costs of opportunism would decline only slightly—if at all—over the range of still generally anar-

---

[107] Posen 1984, 102 and 111; Christensen and Snyder 1990.
[108] Ambrosius 1987, 162.

chic security relationships under discussion. Better, the conservatives argued, to maintain America's freedom of action within a purely anarchic League. In the end, many analysts recognized the truth in both positions. The failure to transform international politics exposed the United States to unacceptable risks, whereas participating in a traditional balance-of-power mechanism, as proposed by the conservatives, would do little to alleviate the danger of entrapment.

Without a significantly more hierarchical relationship than proposed by either group, it was simply impossible to safeguard American interests effectively.[109] This was not because American planners were unimaginative and uncreative—that they missed some innovative institution that would have allowed them to monitor and control the Europeans effectively. In presenting the American people, and the world, with a radical vision of the transformation of international politics, the president certainly did not lack imagination, and his program challenged others to think creatively about alternative possibilities. Constrained to relatively anarchic security relationships by rapidly rising governance costs, however, there was no effective solution to the dilemma facing American policy makers at this time. With only small potential gains from pooling resources with others and inhibitions on investments in further joint production economies, almost any risk of opportunism was sufficient to undermine the benefits of cooperation.

Governance costs were also significant, at least relative to the net benefits of cooperation. First, although the problem of measuring such costs are bedeviled by the methodological problems discussed in Chapter 3, they appear to have risen rapidly with hierarchy. Reflecting these anticipated costs, an imperialist strategy was never seriously discussed. The United States did not occupy or control any territory in Europe as a result of the war, and the fixed costs of conquering other countries to build an American empire on the continent were so high that any mention of the idea, even today, seems ludicrous. Even in the periphery of the international system, the United States actively refused an empire. Wilson wanted the United States to administer a mandate under the League of Nations, and in fact accepted a mandate in Armenia, and submitted the necessary legislation to Congress. Opinion across the spectrum, however, was highly antagonistic. Not only was the risk of further entrapment very large but proponents and opponents of the League alike were acutely aware of the direct costs of governing one of the world's political and economic troublespots; Secretary of State Robert Lansing estimated that it would take 50,000 troops to control the area.[110] With governance costs that rose rapidly with greater hierarchy, the United States, as a practical matter, was limited to relatively anarchic security relationships.

Second, even in anarchic relationships the governance costs of security

[109] Stromberg 1963, 32.
[110] LaFeber 1994, 320.

cooperation were substantial. All factions in the League debate recognized that security cooperation with Europe necessarily entailed some restrictions on America's freedom of action in foreign policy. To control the potential for opportunism by others, the United States had to bind its own hands as well, to a greater or lesser extent. This was a cost the progressive internationalists thought worth paying, but all groups recognized that the costs were real.

Had the joint economies been larger, the probability of opportunism lower, or governance costs less consequential, perhaps United States would have found it possible to live with one or the other vision of the League. As it was, after much contestation, unilateralism was reaffirmed.

## The Progressive Plan

Through the League of Nations, progressive internationalists—and especially President Wilson—sought to continue the crusade begun in the war to transform international relations and transcend Europe's traditional balance of power politics. Two features of the League, often remarked upon but too seldom appreciated, were central to this purpose. They were also the focus of the conflict between progressives and, on this score, both conservative internationalists and the irreconcilables.

In its first principal feature, the League was intended to transform the nature of international relations.[111] To do this, it was necessary to establish a strong commitment on the part of all states, including the United States, to participate in the League's collective security actions. As stated in Article 10, member states were bound to preserve the integrity and independence of others. Partisans of all positions agreed that this the was "heart" of the Covenant. This binding commitment was, of course, necessary for the League to provide a credible deterrent to aggression, a point that was made at the time and has remained central to subsequent discussions of collective security agreements.[112] If national commitments to the League were tenuous, then the old European balance of power politics would continue unabated, and the instability inherent in this mechanism might entrap the United States into another European war.[113] Likewise, if important states remained outside the League, the potential for free riding and other forms of opportunism would continue. Thus, the League could function only as a multilateral institution in which all were bound by the same set of rules: tailoring contracts to the needs of individual states would open up sufficient room for ambiguity as to gut the intent of the organization. Only by making the League binding and universal could the "old" ways be transcended, but if the bindings were sufficiently tight, in the views of the progressives, war would become obso-

---

[111] Iriye 1993, 28.
[112] Leffler 1979, 12; Ambrosius 1987, 237.
[113] Leffler 1979, 12.

lete. Progressive internationalists firmly believed this was the best way to deter conflict and thereby mitigate the risk of future American entrapment into continental affairs.

In turn, this binding and universal image of the League was complemented by a measure of hierarchy within the organization. As outlined in Article 10 and elsewhere in the covenant, the Council of the League, acting as an executive body, could call upon member states to act and advise them of their obligations.[114] This shift in authority from the individual members to the Council was intended to overcome, in part, the problems of collective action that would otherwise thwart universal efforts. To the extent that Council directives were binding, however, this constituted an important shift in rights of residual control from members to the League itself, creating a limited protectorate in which the authority of states to reach independent foreign policy decisions would be partially constrained. The extent of this transfer of residual rights, of course, was a hotly contested issue. Article 11 notes that "Any war or threat of war, whether immediately affecting any of the Members of the League or not, is hereby declared a matter of concern to the whole League," suggesting that its purview was limited to issues of war and peace. At the same time, this article continues that it is the right of any member to bring to the attention of the League or Council "any circumstance whatever affecting international relations which threatens to disturb international peace or the good understanding between nations upon which peace depends." Article 4, paragraph 4, also states that the Council may deal with any matter "affecting the peace of the world." Most galling to critics of the League, however, is that the Council itself was free to define the limits of its own mandate, thereby transferring real political authority to the organization.

In his conflict with the Senate, Wilson was somewhat evasive on how tightly the United States was bound by the advice of the Council.[115] The president denied to opponents that the United States had any *legal* obligation

---

[114] Under some specified conditions, such as those outlined in Article 15, paragraph 10, the assembly of the League of Nations could also issue directives to members, but the council was by far the more important body for this purpose. The council was composed of representatives of the Principal Allied and Associated Powers, together with four members elected by the assembly on a nonpermanent basis.

[115] Somewhat disingenuously, but apparently sincerely, Wilson often referred to the League as a "disentangling alliance"; see Ambrosius 1987, 28 and 46. "I shall never, myself, consent to an entangling alliance," Wilson declared in May 1916. "But I would gladly assent to a disentangling alliance—an alliance which would disentangle the people of the world from those combinations in which they seek their own separate and private interests and unite the people of the world to preserve the peace of the world upon a basis of common right and justice"; quoted in Cooper 1983, 301–2. In this and other similar statements, Wilson appears to be stating the truism that when there is a harmony of interest, no state acts with others against its will. The question, of course, is whether the mere existence of a league would produce such a harmony; Wilson's insistence on carefully constructed safeguards suggests that he believed otherwise, or at least thought it prudent to hedge his bets.

to follow League directives, which in his view would have been automatically binding. Rather, he maintained that the country was bound only by a *moral* obligation that was discretionary but nonetheless superior to a legal obligation.[116] This novel political doctrine and wordplay, which Roland Stromberg terms "unreal," captures an important point.[117] Although Wilson recognized the need for Congressional approval for certain types of actions recommended by the League, he also maintained that Article 10 did create an obligation for action. Thus, he carefully constructed a presumption that the United States would follow League directives; should the United States chose to ignore such a directive, the country's reputation would be severely damaged. As we shall see, his critics sought to create the opposite presumption and, thereby, lower the reputational costs should the United States choose an independent path. What Wilson intended was to harness the reputation of the United States to the League so as to bind Congress and future administrations as much as possible within the constraints of the national constitution.[118] Although the United States retained its formal rights of residual control, Wilson nonetheless sought to limit those rights de facto by creating an obligation to act within the bounds of the international consensus as it might exist on any given issue and at any time. Wilson, of course, did not necessarily desire to constrain the freedom of action of the United States. Rather, the League was designed to control the behavior of others, and the constraints on the United States were the necessary price of achieving that influence over its partners.

The second principal feature of the League was the safeguards to protect American interests and influence within the organization.[119] As envisioned by Wilson, despite the degree of hierarchy central to his vision of political transformation, American interests would be protected within the League in three ways. First, the United States could use its favored position of asymmetrical interdependence to coerce the Europeans, as necessary, into abiding by American wishes. Wilson calibrated America's involvement in the war to maximize his postwar influence; according to Edward B. Parsons, Wilson contributed "the minimum necessary to the prevention of a German victory," and in doing so husbanded the country's military, financial, and manpower resources to ensure leverage in the peace conference and afterwards.[120] And after the war, as Ambrosius writes, Wilson believed that "other nations de-

---

[116] Schulte Nordholt 1991, 386.

[117] Stromberg 1963, 37.

[118] Ibid., 36–38. On reputation as a means of rendering international agreements self-enforcing, see Lipson 1991.

[119] Leffler 1979, 5.

[120] Parsons 1978, viii. Recent studies of Wilson's diplomacy emphasize not his idealism but his realism; for example, Calhoun 1986 and 1993.

pended upon the United States, but not the reverse."[121] This was especially true in the economic realm, where the president clearly intended to use the nation's new economic power as a weapon. As he told House in mid-1917, "When the war is over, we can force [England and France] to our way of thinking, because by that time they will be financially in our hands."[122] Echoing this same idea, Wilson later declared publicly that, although the United States might be "partners" with other powers, "let me predict we will be the senior partner. The financial leadership will be ours. The industrial primacy will be ours. The commercial advantage will be ours. The other countries of the world are looking to us for leadership and direction."[123] Reflecting the small net benefits of the League to the United States, Wilson also believed that the Europeans needed the proposed organization more than the United States did, and that this would provide him with significant political influence. Again according to Ambrosius, Wilson believed that although "the League could facilitate the projection of American influence throughout the world," the United States "could protect its own vital interests without the new League."[124] This asymmetrical interdependence was also recognized by the Europeans. As Lord Cecil, a member of the British delegation at Versailles, told Leon Bourgeois, the United States "had nothing to gain from the League of Nations . . . she could let European affairs go and take care of her own; the offer that was made by America for support was practically a present to France."[125] In short, the United States could use its lower opportunity costs of abandoning the League (that is, returning to unilateralism) as a source of leverage in Europe.

Second, within the League Commission in Paris, Wilson fought to require all binding decisions of the Council to be unanimous, thereby giving the United States (and other members) a veto.[126] Thus, the entity that would recommend sanctions to be applied by members would be controlled by the United States. The country did not need to fear League directives to do something it would otherwise prefer not to do, for the League could not recommend action without the explicit, prior consent of the United States. In the "ablest" Democratic defense of the covenant in the Senate, Hitchcock,

---

[121] Ambrosius 1987, 79.

[122] Quoted in LaFeber 1994, 315.

[123] Quoted in White 1996, 22.

[124] Ambrosius 1987, 79.

[125] Quoted in Kissinger 1994, 236.

[126] Leffler 1979, 5. Knock 1992, 247, attributes the veto to Cecil, but Ambrosius 1987, 74, suggests that this provision was sustained only through Wilson's active support. On the construction of the veto, a comparison of Article 15, paragraphs 6 and 7 is instructive, dealing with dispute settlement procedures. In the former, a unanimous council report prohibits other league members from going to war with any country that complies with the recommendations of the council report, but in the latter a split council decision allows each country "the right to take such action as they shall consider necessary for the maintenance of right and justice."

then chair of the Foreign Relations Committee, emphasized precisely this point. As Senator Albert B. Cummins (R-IA), a critic of the League, correctly discerned, "The President of the United States believes that this compact should be made because he is sincerely of the opinion that the United States can and will control the league of nations."[127]

Third, Wilson built an organic, flexible League, premised on morally binding commitments, that would grow in responsibility, authority, and possibly hierarchy.[128] Recognizing that the territorial settlements and peace terms of the Treaty of Versailles would have to be reconsidered as errors were revealed and conditions changed, Wilson did not believe that all contingencies could be specified in advance.[129] More important, in his view, was that the League be an institution for collective decision making that could adapt to its environment. In this effort, some measure of hierarchy was necessary, as the theory would lead us to expect. Where critics decried this flexibility and hierarchy, Wilson understood it as integral to the postwar peace. Since future contingencies could not be foreseen, the League was designed to grow as necessary to maintain international stability, and thus to continue to limit the risks of entrapment into unwanted European conflicts.

Within this organic League, Wilson was willing to cede some degree of national sovereignty to obtain control over the behavior of others. This was, in fact, the principal governance cost of the limited protectorate he consciously constructed, and was recognized as such.[130] At the White House dinner, Wilson assured his critics that Congress's constitutional powers were not infringed, but he also argued that the United States, like all nations, would have to give up some sovereignty "for the good of the world."[131] He concluded by noting that the League "would never be carried out successfully if the objection of sovereignty was insisted upon by the Senate."[132] Thus, although Wilson recognized that there would be governance costs for the United States from participating in the League, this was a cost he was willing to pay to reduce the risks of European opportunism.

It was through this organic institution that Wilson expected to transform international politics and control opportunism by the countries of Europe. Constraints on America's freedom of action were a necessary price for control over others. Yet, because of the first two safeguards—asymmetric interdependence and the veto—Wilson was confident that the price would not be too high. The League would control the policies of all, and the United States

---

[127] Quoted in Ambrosius 1987, 93.

[128] Dulles 1963, 111; Schulte Nordholt 1991, 285 and 293–94; Knock 1992, 207.

[129] Schulte Nordholt 1991, 298.

[130] Wilson had already encountered the need to absorb such costs to make collective security work in the interventions in Russia in 1918; Calhoun 1993, 109.

[131] Quoted in Schulte Nordholt 1991, 322.

[132] Quoted in Knock 1992, 233.

would control the League. In this way, America's interests in an uncertain world would be protected.

### The Critics Respond

The conservative internationalists and irreconcilables, together, rejected virtually every plank in Wilson's platform for peace. Believing that there was a high intrinsic risk of European opportunism, critics of the League feared that the United States was creating a costly new Frankenstein—and one with global powers. Although many other issues were also raised, and although conservative internationalists and irreconcilables parted company on the appropriate alternative to Wilson's vision, this fear was the core of the group's individual and joint objections. According to Lodge, his fourteen reservations were designed, most generally, to "release us from obligations which might not be kept," and to "preserve rights which ought not to be infringed."[133]

First, opponents emphasized that the costs of the progressive safeguards, and especially the loss of sovereignty admitted by Wilson, were greater than the president either acknowledged or understood. The veto in the League Council was extensively discussed in the Senate and found wanting. It is on this issue that the split between legislators and the executive, noted in Chapter 3, found its principal form. The critics did not dispute, in the first instance, whether the veto would protect the United States from other states. Rather, they argued that the veto did not respect the division of authority within the American government, long recognized as the centerpiece of the remarkable system of democratic rule created by the founding fathers. Nor did it protect Congress or the public from a capricious president who might use the authority of the League to buttress his own misguided schemes and hinder actions supported by majorities in Congress. As Knock describes it, opponents "could easily envision situations in which a Wilsonian on the League's council might cast a vote that would set a precedent of interfering with the prerogative of the United States to take independent coercive action." *The Nation* summarized the issue more bluntly: Senator Fall of New Mexico opposed the League, the editors wrote, "because at bottom he desires to see the United States free to make war on Mexico, whenever his constituents demand it."[134] Thus, although the veto protected America's national interests as the president might define them, it did not protect Congress's constitutional prerogatives or its definition of the national interests should it disagree with the president. Indeed, the League promised to strengthen the power of the presidency at home while weakening the legislature. The loss of sovereignty would not be borne equally across the branches of government.

---

[133] Quoted ibid., 266.
[134] Ibid., 266–67.

Thus, it is no coincidence that this objection was raised most vigorously by members of Congress, but it cut more broadly at the distinctive division of authority that lies at the heart of the American constitution. Nonetheless, this objection is qualified by the robust support that Wilson's vision of the League continued to receive from Democrats in the Senate. Although they must have recognized that they might eventually lose control over the presidency, many Democrats continued to support this possible transfer of authority to the executive. Even after Wilson was struck down by a stroke and could no longer lead his party effectively, twenty-three senators continued to support the covenant as originally negotiated.

This uneven distribution of the governance costs of the League, central to nearly all histories of the ratification fight, clearly colored the debate and divided the executive from the legislature. But nearly one-quarter of the Senate voted against their "institutional" interests. In turn, the issue of congressional versus executive control over representation in international organizations were reprised in the debate over the United Nations in 1945, but to only minor effect. What mattered more, in the long run, was that critics believed the costs in terms of lost sovereignty were substantially greater than the gains from cooperation in the guise of the League.

Second, and more important, the critics charged that an organic League was dangerous and carried with it unpredictable costs. If the organization was flexible enough to counter unforeseen problems, it might also be capable of evolving into an even more hierarchical entity able to impose even greater constraints on the United States in the future. Indeed, Wilson himself noted the possibility that the League might eventually move away from unanimity to some form of majority rule. The fear of accepting open-ended commitments to a League whose initial purposes were left intentionally vague and whose authority might grow over time was widespread among conservative internationalists and irreconcilables.[135] The United States, they maintained, must strictly decide its own contributions. As Lodge stated, "Surely it is not too much to insist that when we are offered nothing but the opportunity to give and aid others [as Wilson's moralism often seemed to imply] we should have the right to say what sacrifices we shall make and what the magnitude of our gifts should be." Borah made a similar point. "I may be willing to help my neighbor, though he be improvident or unfortunate," the irreconcilable Senator announced to the chamber, "but I do not necessarily want him for a business partner. I may be willing to give liberally of my means, my counsel and advice, even of my strength or blood, to protect his family from attack or injustice, but I do not want him placed in a position where he may decide for me when and how I shall act or to what extent I shall make sacrifice."[136] It

---

[135] Ibid., 257.
[136] Quoted in Osgood 1953, 286.

was the open-ended nature of the commitment to the League that worried critics, and it was the high level of uncertainty about the future that prevented the progressives from offering a persuasive response.

This fear of an organic League, and its possibly escalating governance costs, contrasts sharply with attitudes on the French Security treaty, which cut across the progressive-conservative divide.[137] Although some progressives accepted the treaty as a logical extension of the League, others opposed it as inconsistent, unnecessary, or—worse—a fall from America's principled position into the dangerous balance of power system. Wilson himself was initially reluctant and never mustered any enthusiasm for the agreement. "As you know," he stated to White, "all that I promised is to try to get it."[138]

In his message to the Senate accompanying the treaty, Wilson explained that the alliance would obligate the United States to provide "immediate military assistance to France" against unprovoked German aggression. Although the Council of the League would not need to offer advice under Article 10, the French treaty was nonetheless "to be an arrangement, not independent of the League of Nations, but under it."[139] Despite the obviously entangling nature of the alliance—Wilson acknowledged its "legal" and automatic rather than "moral" and discretionary nature[140]—it received significant support from conservative internationalists, but not, it should be noted, from the irreconcilables who feared that Britain and France would "control the alliance at all times and on all questions."[141]

Several prominent conservatives actually supported the treaty in principle but wanted to break its link with the League. As Lodge wrote to Senator Albert J. Beveridge (R-IN),

> If there had been no proposition such as is included in Article 10, but a simple proposition that it would be our intention to aid France, which is our barrier and outpost, when attacked without provocation by Germany, I should have strongly favored it for I feel very keenly the sacrifices of France and the immense value her gallant defense was to the whole world. But they have made the French treaty subject to the authority of the League, which is not to be tolerated. If we ever are called upon to go to the assistance of France as we were two years ago, we will go without asking anybody's leave. It is humiliating to be put in such an attitude and not the least of the mischief done by the League is that Article 10 will probably make it impossible to do anything for France . . . as many of our Senators desire. That would be a distinct and separate thing which we could well

[137] Ambrosius 1987, 159; Dulles 1963, 113.

[138] Quoted in Ambrosius 1987, 112. On Wilson's views of the treaty, see Calhoun 1986, 263–64. Leffler 1979, 15, notes that subsequent French actions on the Rhineland angered Wilson and dissuaded him from seeking ratification of the treaty.

[139] Quoted in Ambrosius 1987, 159–60.

[140] Schulte Nordholt 1991, 386.

[141] Ambrosius 1987, 212.

afford to do. When it is already wrapped up in that unending promise to go to the assistance of anybody it becomes intolerable.[142]

Elihu Root, a Republican elder statesman, legal scholar, and senator from New York, urged Lodge to support the agreement in similar terms. "I hope to the Lord, you are going to consent to the French treaty, striking out of course the provision for submission to the League Council," he wrote. "It seems to me that it is desirable to accompany the opposition which you are making to the *vague and indefinite commitments of the League Covenant* with an exhibition of willingness to do the *definite certain specific things which are a proper part of true American policy*, and which are necessary to secure the results of the War upon which America has expended so much life and treasure."[143]

The treaty died an ignominious death, "permanently pigeonholed in the dark recesses of the files of the Committee on Foreign Relations." This "curious incident" in the history of the Treaty of Versailles, as Dulles terms it, is primarily important here as an example of what the conservative internationalists were willing to support.[144] The French treaty demonstrates that binding, automatic commitments to respond militarily to unprovoked aggression were tolerable, as long as that commitment was clear, unambiguous, and limited. In the view of conservative internationalists, the progressive's organic League satisfied none of these conditions and promised only increasing constraints on American sovereignty.

Third, the conservatives challenged the efficacy of the progressives' binding commitment to collective security. Where Wilson and other supporters believed a strong commitment by the United States to the organization was necessary to induce Europe into the transforming and controlling web of the League, opponents argued that the tighter the commitment, the greater the likelihood of entrapment. In their view, the League itself magnified general fears of European opportunism; importantly, the covenant froze the inherently unstable status quo in Europe and committed the United States to defend it.[145] Moreover, critics correctly charged that a binding commitment would actually increase the incentives for the Europeans to act opportunistically. The critics understood that a guarantee of League and, in turn, American involvement, while perhaps suppressing some conflicts, might increase the risk of others and allow the Europeans to free ride more effectively on the United States. On this issue, the irreconcilables and conservative internationalists were in perfect agreement.

Through the League commitment, critics argued, the United States would lose its independence and discretion. In Article 10, Senator Borah asserted,

---

[142] Quoted ibid., 160.
[143] Quoted ibid., 212, emphasis added.
[144] Dulles 1963, 113.
[145] Iriye 1993, 63 and 69.

we "are pledging ourselves, our honor, our sacred lives, to the preservation of the territorial possessions the world over and not leaving it to the judgment and sense of the American people but to the diplomats of Europe."[146] Lodge agreed. "It is easy to talk about a league of nations and the beauty and necessity of peace, but the hard practical demand is, Are you ready to put your soldiers and your sailors at the disposition of other nations? . . . This is the heart of the whole question."[147]

This lack of discretion, opponents continued, would serve to stimulate and expand international conflicts. Calling attention to a recent statement by Andrew Bonar Law, the Conservative leader of the British Parliament, Borah emphasized that there were twenty-three different wars in progress in Europe even after the so-called armistice. Under the League, escalation was inevitable. "The whole world will be called to act under article 10 at just the same moment any particular nation is called upon to act under article 10, and instead of localizing a war, instead of circumscribing its activities, any controversy will immediately spring into a world conflict."[148] Building on the same theme, Senator Hiram W. Johnson (R-CA) argued that the British empire, through the League, would "demand American blood to subdue Ireland."[149] Again Lodge echoed the irreconcilables' views. In a major address, he noted that any revolution or insurrection threatened to entangle the United States under the League. What the United States needed was not commitment but prudent involvement. "Nobody expects to isolate the United States or to make it a hermit Nation, which is a sheer absurdity. But there is a wide difference," he concluded, "between taking a suitable part and bearing a due responsibility in world affairs and plunging the United States into every controversy and conflict on the face of the globe."[150]

In short, the conservatives maintained that a binding commitment to the League would be counterproductive, that it would not reduce the risk of European opportunism and might, perhaps only as a rhetorical point, increase that risk. In analytic terms, and as expected by the theory, critics charged that a binding commitment created a problem of "moral hazard," in which guarantees, once given, cause the recipient to act in a more risky fashion than before. Rather than transforming international relations and controlling Europe, the conservatives concluded, the League actually threatened to excite conflicts and further entrap the United States. In the view of the critics, the United States would not control the League, the League would control the United States. It would stimulate conflict, and drag the United

---

[146] Quoted in Ambrosius 1987, 90.
[147] Quoted in Schulte Nordholt 1991, 321.
[148] Quoted in Ambrosius 1987, 161.
[149] Quoted in Barnet 1990, 166.
[150] Quoted in Ambrosius 1987, 162.

States in through its moral obligations.[151] In their eyes, imperfect safeguards, combined with their high and potentially escalating governance costs, undercut the president's case for the League. This was especially true, they believed, given the existence of viable alternatives.

### The Conservatives' Limited Vision

Conservative internationalists believed it possible to live within the League, duly amended, but they advocated a strictly anarchic form of cooperation with Europe. Where Wilson sought to control others through a binding and partially hierarchical League, conservative internationalists countered that the best way to control others and protect the country's interests was to make the actions of the United States discretionary and conditional. Only by making America's actions contingent upon European behavior, they argued, could the United States effectively control events outside its borders. By offering both the "carrot" of involvement and the "stick" of abstention the United States could adequately sway the course of European diplomacy. In direct opposition to the progressive vision of the League, discretion was the conservative internationalists' primary—indeed, exclusive—safeguard for international cooperation. The conservatives correctly noted that the governance costs of their strategy were considerably lower. Where Wilson was willing to cede some sovereignty to obtain control over other countries, the conservatives claimed that their discretionary League would leave America's freedom of maneuver in international politics unimpaired.

The debate between progressive and conservative internationalists crystallized around Article 10. Wilson wanted to construct a superior, moral commitment with a presumption of action that nonetheless allowed the United States some discretion. Lodge and the conservative internationalists—through the instrument of clarifying Congress's constitutional powers—wanted to preclude any such presumption. As the second of Lodge's fourteen reservations stated, the United States would not be obligated to give support to other countries unless Congress "shall by act or joint resolution so provide."[152] This reservation replaced Wilson's positive presumption of action with a negative presumption. "In effect," Stromberg concludes, "Wilson and the Democrats wanted to accept an obligation that we might thereafter refuse, while Lodge and the Republicans wanted to refuse an obligation we might thereafter accept."[153]

Underneath the wordplay lay two opposed versions of how to safeguard American interests in an opportunistic world. By insisting on discretion, the conservative internationalists weakened the principles and international po-

---

[151] Ibid., 93.
[152] Schulte Nordholt 1991, 400, quoted in full above.
[153] Stromberg 1963, 37.

litical mechanism through which the progressives hoped to control and transform European foreign policy. Nonetheless, in their view, discretion was superior, or at least less costly in terms of the constraints on America's freedom of action. Although the "carrot-and-stick" approach might or might not be as effective in controlling Europe as the progressive's League—and this is difficult to determine from the debate—conservatives clearly believed it was less costly, offering some restraints on European behavior in exchange for much weaker constraints on American sovereignty.[154]

Progressives countered that discretionary involvement did little to deter disputes or resolve the underlying sources of conflict in Europe. "The real question," Senator Peter G. Gerry (D-RI) proposed, "is whether we believe that it is not better for the United States to have a say in European matters and thus try to prevent another horrible war or to keep our hands off and wait until the world is aflame and then endeavor to assert our might to protect our rights."[155] Wilson defended Article 10 as central to the transformational purpose of the League. In its absence, he stated during his national speaking tour, "we have guaranteed that any imperialist enterprise may revive, we have guaranteed that there is no barrier to the ambition of nations (including the United States) that have the power to dominate, we have abdicated the whole position of right and substituted the principle of might." The Lodge reservation to Article 10 was nothing short of "a rejection of the covenant," he declared at another stop, for it would "change the entire meaning of the Treaty and exempt the United States from all responsibility for the preservation of peace."[156] In Wilson's view, discretion was dangerous, for it undercut the potential of the League and was therefore likely to lead to more opportunism in the long run. Article 10 was more than "a renunciation of wrong ambition on the part of powerful nations," Wilson declared as the Senate was about to vote on the treaty, it was "the bulwark, the only bulwark, of the rising democracy of the world against the forces of imperialism and reaction."[157] Compromise was impossible not just because the president became more intransigent after his stroke, but because the Lodge reservations, and the conservative view of the League that they embodied, failed to transcend the old European balance-of-power politics.

### The Irreconcilable Victory

The irreconcilables, the principled defenders of continued unilateralism in American foreign policy, opposed even the conservatives' vision of the League as a strictly anarchic security relationship. Their task was made eas-

---

[154] Knock 1992, 58.
[155] Quoted in Ambrosius 1987, 161–62.
[156] Quoted in Knock 1992, 261–62.
[157] Quoted ibid., 268.

ier, in a sense, by the failure of the Senate conservatives to articulate a positive justification for their vision. The conservatives developed their ideas almost entirely in opposition to the progressive proposal, and failed to address how and in what ways a discretionary international organization would facilitate America's responsibilities in the European balance of power.[158] The irreconcilables did not open new ground or raise new issues, but simply took the critique developed jointly with the conservatives to its logical conclusion.[159] Any league would constrain America's freedom of action. If discretion were necessary to safeguard the country's interests, they asked, why agree to any restraints? If Wilson's safeguards were inadequate and too costly, why join at all? Unilateralism, the irreconcilables claimed, would be the cheapest and most effective safeguard of all, and frequently quoted Washington's Farewell Address to make their point. All the irreconcilables wanted, Senator Johnson argued, was the right to "respond to humanity's cry or civilization's appeal . . . as we ourselves see fit, in our own time and our own mode." Unilateralists did not seek to abandon America's duties, he continued, but they did insist upon the "unentangled freedom of a great nation to determine for itself and in its own way where duty lies."[160]

The progressive and conservative internationalists effectively revealed the weaknesses in each other's vision. The conservative internationalists persuaded many that the costs of the League safeguards were too high, especially as the institution threatened to evolve over time, and that binding commitments would stimulate entrapment and facilitate exploitation. Emphasizing the inevitability of renewed war in Europe if the League failed, the progressive internationalists maintained that only by controlling and transforming European behavior through the League would the cycle of conflict be broken.[161] These positions could not be reconciled. Effective safeguards proved impossible to construct at an acceptable cost.

If the joint economies had been larger or potential for opportunism smaller, and therefore the net benefits from cooperation greater, perhaps the United States would have been willing to accept the risk inherent in one or the other postwar vision or to invest in more hierarchic forms of governance. Circumstances thus conspired against America's participation in the League. The irreconcilables won not because they persuaded others of the value of unilateralism but because of the difficulties they and others identified in international security cooperation. Unilateralism triumphed by default. Cooperation required positive action; a decision to "do nothing" was a decision in favor of continued unilateralism in American foreign policy.

---

[158] Although the "legalists" around the League to Enforce Peace did develop a coherent position, it was lost in the Senate furor.

[159] Guinsburg 1982, 19–50.

[160] Quoted ibid., 21–22.

[161] Leffler 1979, 12.

Personalities, partisanship, and other factors no doubt played a role in the fate of the League. But they loomed large at the time and remain so in the historiography not because the issues themselves were trivial or unimportant but because the tradeoffs captured in the debate were and remain today central to the choice of security relationships. That there was a heated debate over the League is not surprising. Questions of policy are typically decided "at the margin," and there was considerable uncertainty at the time. Not only were decision makers unsure of the likely security challenges in the interwar years, but they were equally if not more uncertain about how the League itself would actually work. Typically, "obvious" choices, those in which the costs and benefits of alternatives are clear and unambiguously weighted in favor of one option, are not politicized. This is evident, in the case here, by the absence of any discussion of imperial relationships with the countries of Europe; the League was problematic, however, and it thus became an issue of considerable contention. The debate over the League, in turn, served important purposes of communication, clarification, and collective reasoning. By providing information and insight and assessing alternatives, the debate revealed the flaws in both proposed forms of cooperation.

With two opposed visions of the postwar order, and with neither vision able to withstand scrutiny on its own, the United States chose to maintain the status quo. Advocates of unilateralism did not win because of their legislative savvy.[162] Rather, the status quo was superior because the alternatives, under the international circumstances of the time, were both flawed. Whether the alternative visions would, in the end, have been more effective in stabilizing the European order is an open question. What we do know, however, is that, in Jonas's words, unilateralism was the "considered response . . . of a large, responsible, and respectable segment of the American public."[163]

### AFTER THE LEAGUE

Throughout the 1920s and 1930s, the United States adhered to a strategy of unilateralism, and reaffirmed the decisions of 1919–1920. The rejection of the League was not an anomaly, or simply the result of idiosyncratic factors. Long after Wilson's departure from office and the end of partisan gridlock in 1921—the Republicans dominated the legislative and executive branches in the 1920s, the Democrats in the 1930s—the nation continued to hew to its traditional policy of eschewing foreign entanglements. Unilateralism remained the touchstone of American policy. This is demonstrated most clearly, perhaps, by the country's rejection of the World Court, reliance on private

---

[162] Guinsburg 1982.
[163] Jonas 1990, xiv.

economic diplomacy in Europe, and its central role in the Washington Conference for the Limitation of Armaments.

Although rejecting the League, many in the United States still sought to
play an active role in promoting world peace. For some, joining the Permanent Court of International Justice seemed an appropriate vehicle. Launching
an active campaign for membership in 1923, the Harding administration
was, in the president's words, seeking "the right course . . . whereby our
favored nation may make its largest feasible contribution to the stabilization
of civilization."[164] Supported by both the Democratic and Republican parties,
the proposal passed the Senate, but only with substantial reservations.

The Harding administration itself proposed four reservations, clarifying
that the United States would still be free of all relations with and obligations
to the League, demanding that the United States receive a role equal to that
of League members in electing judges, affirming that only Congress could
determine the share of Court expenditures the United States would bear,
and—clearly guarding against organic international institutions—stating that
all changes in the Court's statute would require American approval.[165] Although supporters of the Court beat back irreconcilable-sponsored reservations of a crippling nature, additional reservations were added in the Senate,
including a fifth that declared the Court could not "without the consent of
the United States entertain any request for an advisory opinion touching any
dispute or question in which the United States has or claims an interest."[166]

Foreign signatories to the Court charter found these reservations difficult
to accept, particularly the fifth, which seemed to give the United States privileges and immunities that they themselves lacked. When negotiations were
proposed, President Calvin Coolidge—who had assumed office upon Harding's death—declined the invitation.

In 1927, Root negotiated with Court members a new protocol governing
American accession. Subsequently supported by the administration of Franklin Delano Roosevelt, but not actively pushed, the question of Court membership again came before the Senate in 1935. This time, however, the proposal failed to receive the necessary two-thirds majority.[167] According to at
least one Senator, this vote reflected "the public mind as it has stood for
many years."[168] The Senate held fast to American unilateralism.

Seeking to fashion a more activist but strictly unilateral policy to stabilize
economic and political conditions in Europe, the Republican administrations
of the 1920s relied principally upon private, economic diplomacy.[169] The

---

[164] Quoted in Guinsburg 1982, 82.
[165] Ibid., 83.
[166] Quoted ibid., 104–5.
[167] See ibid., 155–76
[168] Quoted in Dulles 1963, 171.
[169] This private diplomacy has been widely dissected by revisionist and postrevisionist histo-

United States officially eschewed participation in any international economic conferences or undertakings, lest such actions be construed as obligating the United States in any way or entangling it in the affairs of Europe. Nonetheless, under the careful guidance of Secretary of Commerce Herbert Hoover and Secretary of State Charles Evans Hughes, private citizens and American business were free and, in fact, encouraged to participate. The so-called Dawes Plan exemplifies this pattern.

As many had predicted, the high and open-ended reparations imposed on Germany by the Treaty of Versailles proved to be a source of continuing political friction and economic instability. In 1923, when Germany proved unable to meet its obligations, France seized the strategic Ruhr Valley, Germany retaliated in a massive strike, and European exchange markets panicked. Secretary of State Hughes agreed to a conference to resolve the crisis, but stipulated that American participation would be strictly private. Although the American delegates were officially chosen by the Reparations Commission, the State Department actually made the selection and cabled the names of the delegation to the commission for official announcement. Composed of Charles G. Dawes, then a Chicago banker and later vice president under Coolidge; Owen D. Young, a New York industrialist and Wilsonian; and Henry M. Robinson, a prominent west-coast financier and vice president of the Chamber of Commerce of the United States, the delegation met extensively with State Department officials prior to its departure and was accompanied in Paris by staff from the Commerce and State departments. The Coolidge administration officially endorsed the "Experts Report" issued at the conclusion of the conference.[170] In the plan, France was allowed to continue its occupation of the Ruhr and German reparations were significantly reduced (but were also slated to increase once again with the return of prosperity). To facilitate reconstruction, Germany received a $200 million loan, divided equally between American and foreign banks. Through the Dawes Plan and other such private arrangements, the United States government did help stabilize Europe's faltering economy. Yet it remained in the background, deeply involved in European affairs but avoiding any hint of entanglement.

The unilateral but activist nature of American foreign policy is also revealed in the Washington Conference. Although the United States and Britain had reached an initial accord on naval programs at Paris, the tremendous cost of the continuing naval buildup continued to worry American policy makers. In December 1920, Senator Borah introduced a resolution calling for

---

rians. Among others, see Parrini 1969; Wilson 1971; Hogan 1977; Leffler 1979; and Costigliola 1984. On the problems of Europe and the effects of America's economic diplomacy, see also Schuker 1976; Silverman 1982; and McNeil 1986. For a review of the literature on private economic diplomacy between the wars, see Burk 1981.

[170] Leffler 1979, 82–120.

a conference with Britain and Japan to reduce armaments; it quickly passed.[171] With widespread support in an economy-minded Congress, Harding was forced to act.[172] At this same time, Britain was concerned with the renewal of the Anglo-Japanese alliance and was considering a meeting to address both naval and Far Eastern questions. Searching for ways of reducing military spending, and strongly opposing any renewal of the Anglo-Japanese treaty, the Harding administration seized the initiative and called a conference for fall 1921.[173] The meeting would include all participants with interests in the Pacific except the Soviet Union (which was not invited), and possess a broad agenda, considering political questions as well as disarmament.

The Washington Conference was convened on November 12, and Hughes startled participants by offering a far-reaching proposal for limiting capital ships (that is, battleships) in his opening remarks. Under the secretary of state's leadership, the Washington Conference produced three related treaties. In the Four Power Treaty, which replaced the Anglo-Japanese treaty, the United States, Britain, France, and Japan agreed to respect each others' insular possessions in the Pacific and to consult together should their rights in this regard be threatened. Article 2 stated that if a member's rights were challenged, the four powers would "communicate with one another fully and frankly in order to arrive at an understanding as to the most efficient measures to be taken, jointly or separately, to meet the exigencies of the particular situation."[174] In the Five Power Treaty, which also included Italy, the governments agreed not to fortify their bases in the Pacific and to reduce the total tonnage of their capital ships to specific numerical limits. This was one of the most significant arms-control agreements in history.[175] In the Nine Power Treaty, the five plus China, Belgium, the Netherlands, and Portugal agreed to respect the sovereignty and independence of China and the principle of the Open Door.[176] Although virtually all participants except the United States made unhappy compromises, the conference was an enormous success.

While demonstrating America's willingness and ability to act internationally when it suited its interests, the Washington treaties also highlight the commitment to unilateralism. In submitting the treaties to the Senate, Harding announced that nothing in the agreements "commits the United States, or any other Power, to any kind of an alliance, entanglement or involvement. It does not require us or any Power to surrender a worthwhile tradition. . . . The Senate's concern for freedom from entanglements, for preserved tradi-

---

[171] Guinsburg 1982, 55.
[172] Dulles 1963, 149.
[173] Iriye 1993, 76.
[174] Quoted in Guinsburg 1982, 57.
[175] Goldman 1994.
[176] Dulles 1963, 150–51.

tions, for maintained independence, was never once forgotten by the American delegates."[177] Even so, the Four Power Treaty was worrisome to irreconcilables and some conservative internationalists. The Senate clarified the American commitment by passing a resolution stating that the United States undertook "no commitment to armed force, no alliance, no obligation to join in any defense."[178] So reserved, the treaties, despite significant debate, were ratified by wide margins.

The United States did become more "isolationist" in the 1930s. As historian Robert Dallek writes, the manifestations of this attitude are well known:

> the neutrality laws of 1935–37 barring meaningful American support to victims of attack as well as aggressors; rejection of League overtures for joint sanctions punishing Italy's invasion of Ethiopia; indifference and neutrality toward the existing Republican government and the Fascist rebels in Spain's Civil War; passive acceptance of Japanese aggression in China, including an attack on the American gunboat *Panay*; acquiescence in German reoccupation of the Rhineland and annexations of Austria and Czechoslovakia's Sudetenland; narrowly defeated demands for a national referendum on any congressional declaration of war; and the failure of neutrality revision in the summer of 1939, or the rejection of pleas to allow Anglo-French arms purchases from the United States should Hitler drive them into a war.[179]

As is clear from this cogent summary, these policies represented not a change of policy, which remained unilateral, or even a lack of concern with European affairs, as all the underlying events continued to receive wide attention in the United States.

Although emphasizing withdrawal or a lack of activity, the isolationism of the mid-1930s can be interpreted within the definition of security offered in Chapter 2 as a willingness to run a greater risk of challenge to vital security interests and a direct consequence of the Great Depression. As the economy collapsed and the national wealth contracted, the demand for all goods fell—including security. This is reflected in the trends in military personnel and major national security outlays. Growing slowly over the late 1920s, military personnel peaked in 1930 and then declined. Military expenditures, measured in constant 1958 dollars, reached their high in 1932, but fell by 27 percent over the next two years.[180] Simply put, during the depression, Americans were unwilling to reduce their consumption of other commodities fur-

---

[177] Quoted in Dulles 1963, 152.

[178] Quoted in Guinsburg 1982, 67.

[179] Dallek 1983, 118–19.

[180] Nominal defense expenditures peaked in 1930. Facing a more hostile world, these trends were reversed in the late 1930s. Defense expenditures and military personnel returned to levels not seen since before the demobilization was completed in 1922. U.S. Department of Commerce 1975, Series F5 (p. 224); Y467 (p. 1,115); Y 904 (p. 1,141).

ther in order to maintain the same level of security as before, so they demanded less. In this sense, isolationism represents not a change in means of producing security, which remained unilateral in any event, but rather a decline in the absolute demand for security.[181]

Both unilateralism and the depression-induced decline in the demand for security were shattered by the rapid fall of France in June 1940 and Japan's attack on Pearl Harbor in December 1941.[182] The German victory in France altered the European balance of power and demonstrated the battlefield potential of the new military technologies. The Japanese attack on the fleet at Pearl Harbor revealed the dawn of a new age in which foreign powers could now project significant force across America's oceanic moats. As we shall see in the next chapter, the seeds of America's post-1945 shift to cooperation lay not only in the communist threat, which is underdetermining, but in the changes manifested in these early axis victories.

## Conclusion

The failure of the United States to join the League of Nations remains one of the great puzzles of the American century. The League embodied many of the ideals for which Americans fought and died in the Great War. Wilson, the scholar-president, staked his political career—even his life—on the League, and his defeat is one of the great human tragedies of American politics. Despite widespread popular support for the idea of the League, the treaty consistently failed to muster the necessary majority in the Senate. Given the political tragedies of the late 1930s, we cannot help but wonder if the League was a missed opportunity to build lasting peace. For these reasons and more, the League continues to attract scholarly and popular attention.

In seeking to piece together this puzzle, many analysts have minimized the substantive differences between the progressive and conservative internationalists and have emphasized the domestic sources of the ratification fight. Those who highlight international considerations point primarily to a misplaced idealism in progressive thought and the American public at large. Without denying that such factors contributed to the failure of the League, the theory here emphasizes other considerations and calls attention to questions prominent in the debate but often submerged in the histories.

As emphasized throughout this book, no one factor in the theory accounts for the failure of security cooperation in the interwar years. Modest joint production economies, moderate expected costs of opportunism, and high

---

[181] The risk to American security increases, of course, only if other polities do not decrease their military expenditures by a proportionate amount. If all reduce defense effort equally, no greater risk is created. Given the robust nature of German and Japanese military spending and preparations during the depression, however, the risk to the United States did increase.

[182] Jonas 1990, 276; see also Gaddis 1997, 35–36.

and rapidly rising governance costs combined to limit the feasible relationships to the anarchic end of the continuum posed in Chapter 2 and, more generally, to make cooperation difficult and unilateralism likely. The expectations of the theory are borne out in this case.

Moreover, the debate over the League of Nations focused precisely on the concerns and tradeoffs highlighted by the theory. Although decision makers were aware of the limited joint production economies, this factor did not figure in the deliberations. However, the issues of European opportunism, institutional effectiveness, and the costs of alternative security relationships were central to the legislative and national debates over the League. Not only are the expectations of the theory generally supported by interwar policy, but the theory appears to be capturing salient concerns of contemporary policy makers and analysts, providing confirming evidence of another, more indirect sort.

If any one causal factor was more important than the others in this period, it was the high probability of European opportunism. Across the spectrum of American opinion, analysts agreed that, absent some form of hierarchical control, the risk that Europe would entrap or exploit the United States was very high. Cooperation was risky. On its own, this reduced the net benefits of cooperation. More importantly, however, the high probability of opportunism also inhibited the United States from investing in the joint economies that might have made cooperation attractive. Yet even here it is the combined effects of the variables that are important. Had the joint economies been larger—perhaps if the new technologies stimulated by the war had been available sooner—the United States might have been willing to tolerate the expected costs of opportunism and governance costs of an anarchic relationship, much as it did after 1945. Or, if governance costs were lower or did not rise as rapidly, some more hierarchical relationship able to reduce significantly the probability of opportunism might have been possible. It was the confluence of these forces that ultimately doomed cooperation.

## Chapter 5

# COLD WAR COOPERATION

FOLLOWING the second World War, the United States adopted a new foreign policy of international cooperation, embodied in the North Atlantic Treaty Organization (NATO) and a series of bilateral security relationships in the Pacific. Despite a continuing distrust of Europe and the strong clamor in many conservative circles for a return to "fortress America," albeit one protected by an atomic shield, the United States broke decisively with its traditional strategy of unilateralism. Although it evolved over time, security cooperation remained the centerpiece of American foreign policy throughout the Cold War.

For the most part, the United States chose relatively anarchic security relationships with its partners in Europe and the Pacific. With Europe, the United States entered into alliances with like-minded states, principally Britain, and asserted a sphere of influence over others. In both Germany and Japan, the United States, as an occupying power, erected more hierarchical relationships, but from the outset these were intended to be temporary mechanisms for, first, taming the defeated powers and, second, transforming them into partial American protectorates. In the Philippines, the United States carried through on a prior commitment to independence for the islands, although they too remained in a de facto protectorate. Only in Micronesia did the United States seek a full hierarchy, creating the Trust Territory of the Pacific Islands in 1949—an empire in all but name.

This chapter explores this historic shift in American foreign policy from unilateralism to cooperation and examines the choice of security relationships across partners. It focuses primarily upon the period from 1947 to 1951, when the key decisions shaping American postwar policy were made and implemented. Although virtually all histories of this period have focused on the threat of Soviet expansionism, often seeking to assign responsibility for the Cold War to one, the other, or both of the superpowers, the Soviet threat itself cannot account for the postwar security relationships constructed by the United States.

Relatively anarchic relations were eventually chosen everywhere but in the Trust Territory, I argue, because of large joint production economies, moderate expected costs of opportunism that did not decline significantly with hierarchy, and low governance costs that increased rapidly with hierarchy. Although Micronesia also promised large joint economies for the United

States, the other considerations were reversed—thus creating this apparent anomaly in American policy.

## THEORETICAL EXPECTATIONS

Emerging from its second global conflagration in a generation, the United States in 1945 faced a world transformed, and it seized the opportunity to build a world in its image. This was, as Secretary of State Dean Acheson later phrased it, a moment of "creation."[1] In this new world, conditions were propitious for a new policy of international cooperation and for relatively anarchic security relationships. The United States recognized the possibilities and manipulated conditions to make cooperation even more attractive.

In terms of the theory laid out in Chapter 3, there were two fundamental changes that led the United States to select a policy in 1949 different from that in 1919. First, there was a significant increase in the joint economies of producing security. The technological changes begun in World War I had reached fruition by World War II, and may even have contributed to the outbreak of that war. During World War II, even more new technologies became effective, including the atomic bomb and (rudimentary) missiles— further extending the strategic reach of the countries that possessed these new weapons. Similarly, deterring the Soviet Union provided broad positive externalities for potential targets. Unlike the situation after 1919, when the United States could free ride on others, few now believed Europe could carry the burden of protecting itself from Soviet expansionism, at least in the near term, and the weight necessarily fell on the United States. Given this dispro-portionate responsibility, the United States could engage in effective "burden sharing" and get others to contribute more than they otherwise might only through explicit policies of cooperation. Both the new technologies and the expanded positive externalities greatly strengthened the incentives for the United States to engage in some form of security cooperation (Hypothesis 1).

Second, the probability that its partners would act opportunistically fell substantially. The United States now dwarfed its potential partners. Drawn together by the common threat from the Soviet Union, the United States shared new interests with its collaborators. Its ability to set the international agenda and hold its partners to that agenda was almost unprecedented. Where in the interwar years the United States strongly believed that Europe could not be trusted, the United States now assumed that its partners, though they might act opportunistically, were nonetheless generally reliable.

As a consequence of this low probability of opportunism, the United States could now invest in greater joint production economies, despite the more specific assets such investments entailed (Hypothesis 5). A forward-

[1] Acheson 1969.

based strategy, possible but not considered during the interwar years, could now be taken up, thus making the most effective use of the new technologies. A division of labor could also be introduced. Together, these new investments further increased the gains from cooperation.

With a low probability of opportunism and now considerable specific assets at risk, it is difficult to compare the expected costs of opportunism in the interwar and Cold War periods. The observed investments in specific assets suggest that the probability of opportunism fell more sharply from the interwar years than asset specificity rose with greater joint economies. With the probability of opportunism and asset specificity moving in opposite directions in this period, however, it remains hard to discern—independently of the outcomes we wish to explain—whether the expected costs, on average, were higher or lower than in the interwar years. Hypothesis 2 is, thus, difficult to evaluate in this case.

On the other hand, it seems reasonably clear, and there was a widespread consensus among policy makers to support this inference, that the probability of opportunism did not decline significantly with greater hierarchy (Hypothesis 3). Indeed, as we shall see in the American occupations of Germany and Japan, there were significant and widely shared fears that hierarchy would itself create incentives for future opportunism. As hierarchy was believed to be generally ineffective in reducing the probability of opportunism, the United States had little incentive to expend the resources necessary to build and maintain such security relationships. Nonetheless, where assets were highly specific, as in the forward bases in the Pacific, the United States chose more hierarchic security relationships (Hypothesis 4).

Finally, governance costs were low after 1945 but, as before, rose rapidly with hierarchy (Hypotheses 6 and 7). As we shall see, the United States typically relied upon inducing others to cooperate. The costs of these inducements were significant, but not large. The United States also employed a series of safeguards in its relatively anarchic relationships, and these most likely provided net benefits to all. Finally, the constraints on its own behavior were minor. At the same time, the governance costs of hierarchy were quite high. Even in the occupations of Germany and Japan, where the cost of establishing hierarchies over others had already been absorbed or "sunk," the costs of control were prohibitive, at least compared to the alternatives. Again, this suggests that if cooperation were chosen, it would tend to be more anarchic than hierarchic.

Large joint production economies, moderate expected costs of opportunism that did not decline significantly with hierarchy, and low governance costs that escalated rapidly with hierarchy suggest that cooperation was likely after World War II and, moreover, that it would be comparatively anarchic. With the exception of the moderate expected costs of opportunism—difficult to estimate in this case, in any event—these conditions match those most likely to produce alliances and other anarchic relationships (see Table 3.1).

There was, of course, considerable variance in the individual variables across dyads during this period, creating differences in optimal security relationships. Whereas the League of Nations was designed as a single security relationship to be employed uniformly across a large number of partners, there was much greater variety in the new relationships adopted by the United States. This allows us to assess the theory in a large number of observations within a single case study. These variations are discussed below.

The debate over American foreign policy, in turn, was less vociferous than in the interwar years. There was some disagreement, of course, with the unilateralists dissenting from the policy of emerging cooperation at least through the Korean War in 1951. There are three reasons why opinion was less divided. First, there was significantly less uncertainty both about military technology and international politics after World War II—and this uncertainty was quickly resolved by 1947, when the Cold War emerged, or by 1949, when the Soviet Union followed the United States in testing an atomic bomb. Although it was never seen with clarity, the future was less hard to predict than in 1919. Second, the choice between anarchic cooperation and its principal rival, unilateralism, was more obvious. The factors pushing toward cooperation were stronger, and analysts soon realized that unilateralism was far less appropriate for the United States than anarchic forms of security cooperation. Since vigorous debate tends to arise only on the margins of policy, when the costs and benefits of alternative policies are hard to discern or are more nearly equal, the clarity of the postwar incentives suppressed deep policy disagreements. Third, the greater variety of security relationships found in the Cold War may also have subdued debate, as relationships could be tailored to circumstances rather than imposed in a "one-size-fits-all" manner as in the League. As a result, where debate itself provided important indirect evidence for the theory in the case of the League—and such evidence is also used in this chapter, where appropriate—the assessment here relies more on comparisons between the interwar and postwar cases and between dyads during the Cold War.

## PATTERNS OF COOPERATION

Between 1945 and 1947, American foreign policy was adrift. The Truman administration rapidly demobilized the military and the economy, abruptly canceled the lend-lease program, and continued the atomic bomb program even after Japan's capitulation. Concurrently, and in a more cooperative vein, the United States and Great Britain opened secret talks to coordinate their strategic planning for future wars and, in October 1946, Secretary of the Navy James Forrestal announced the creation of the first permanent American Naval Command for the Mediterranean.[2] No clear direction in policy existed.

The drift in policy was mirrored in the political debate. A small band of "bedrock isolationists" advocated retreating once again from the vicissitudes of European politics and concentrating on pressing domestic problems. Having opposed American involvement in World War II on the grounds that it was not "within the range of possibility that the United States of America [could] be invaded by any single nation or combination of nations in Europe, or Asia, or both," as one Congressman declared, the bedrockers continued to believe that the country could safely stand aloof from international conflicts.[3] Although many were vehemently anti-Communist, they strongly opposed American security guarantees to other countries and all entangling alliances.[4] As H. M. Griffith, vice president of the National Economic Council, put it, any surrendering of America's "freedom of action may well lead to our death as a Nation."[5]

A somewhat larger group of unilateralists, with roots in the conservative internationalist tradition espoused by Senator Henry Cabot Lodge and others in the interwar period, sought to respond to emerging threats in the international arena through an aggressive unilateralism that relied primarily on America's nuclear monopoly. Recognizing both the importance of the Soviet threat and America's new global security interests, the unilateralists opposed formal alliances with other countries, favoring instead an extended "Monroe Doctrine" that would now stretch beyond the Western hemisphere to Europe and the Pacific. Senator Robert Taft (R-OH), the intellectual and political leader of this group, argued strongly that the United States should stand aloof from potential allies, fortify itself, and build a nuclear arsenal capable of "pulverizing Russia" if the communist power sought to expand abroad at the expense of American interests.[6] Although firmly committed to an active policy in the world arena, the old conservative internationalists now backed off from foreign entanglements, retreating into a position of strict unilateralism.

The emerging majority of so-called internationalists, including stalwarts from the progressive tradition and those in the throes of conversion, called for cooperation with Europe and recognized the value of security relationships despite their entangling nature. Throughout the internationalist ranks flowed a new political realism. Once the "spirit of Yalta" evaporated in the harsh light of victory, reflected in the tensions and hard bargaining at the Potsdam peace conference, few internationalists believed that the United States or even the United Nations could transform international politics or

[2] Cook 1989, 44–45.
[3] Quoted in Dallek 1983, 127.
[4] Ireland 1981, 119.
[5] Quoted in Kaplan 1984, 21.
[6] Ireland 1981, 209.

end war. Rather, cooperation was now advocated by the internationalists on quite pragmatic grounds. Alliances and other anarchic security relationships were seen simply as the most effective way to secure the United States. Yes, the internationalists recognized, partners might act opportunistically, but the probability was low and, in any event, the United States could construct effective safeguards to limit the risk at acceptable cost.

This debate continued until at least the spring of 1951. Yet, starting in early 1947, the drift in American policy slowly ceased and a clear trend toward security cooperation with both Europe and the Pacific emerged. As the postwar era matured, a firm internationalist majority developed behind the new entanglements—a majority that was to endure until the end of the Cold War some forty-five years later.

### The Atlantic Alliance

America's new strategy of cooperation with Europe emerged incrementally. Four significant steps can be identified: the Truman Doctrine and Marshall Plan in spring 1947; the Vandenberg Resolution of June 1948; the negotiation, signing, and ratification of the North Atlantic Treaty in 1949; and the so-called Great Debate over American troops in Europe in 1950–1951.

In the spring of 1947, the United States acknowledged that its postwar security was interdependent with that of Europe and took its first moves toward rebuilding its former wartime allies as strong and co-equal partners in the emerging Cold War with the Soviet Union. The devastating winter of 1946–1947, when severe cold and acute shortages threatened much of Europe with starvation, set two related trains in motion.[7] First, the winter crisis forced Britain to reassess the gap between its capabilities and overseas commitments. Seeking to scale back the country's foreign policy, Foreign Secretary Ernest Bevin decided to yield to indigenous and foreign demands and grant India an early and prompt independence. He also decided to terminate British aid to Greece and Turkey. Whereas the United States welcomed the first move, the second caught it by surprise. It was, as then Undersecretary of State Acheson acknowledges, a "shocker."[8]

Acting quickly to bolster congressional support for a major policy initiative, the Truman administration, and especially Acheson, briefed legislative leaders about the rapidly evolving events in Greece and Turkey and painted the deteriorating situation in stark, anticommunist colors.[9] This same theme was carried forward by President Truman in his address to Congress on March 12, 1947, where he enunciated the doctrine that bears his name.

---

[7] See Cohen 1993, 34.

[8] Acheson 1969, 217.

[9] This meeting is one of the most widely described and cited episodes in the literature on the early Cold War. See ibid., 219, for a firsthand account.

Stating that the world was presently torn between the forces of freedom and tyranny, Truman pronounced "that it must be the policy of the United States to support free peoples who are resisting attempted subjugation by armed minorities or by outside pressures. . . . Should we fail to aid Greece and Turkey in this fateful hour," he continued, "the effect will be far-reaching to the West as well as to the East." Despite his willingness to pick up Britain's mantle in the Near East, Truman hastened to add that "our help should be primarily through economic and financial aid" and not a direct American presence.[10]

Second, on his way home from the Moscow foreign ministers' meeting of the "Big Four" wartime allies (March 10–April 24, 1947), Secretary of State George C. Marshall toured Europe and was deeply moved by its plight. Fearful that economic and political instability would create a vacuum into which Soviet influence would flow—a fear highlighted by the presence of communist parties in the coalition governments of both France and Italy—Marshall asked George Kennan and his newly created Policy Planning Staff to develop a strategy for getting Europe back on its feet. Kennan's report subsequently formed the basis for the so-called Marshall Plan, outlined in the secretary's commencement address at Harvard University on June 5.[11] Premised upon the belief that greater European integration was necessary for successful economic recovery, and seeking to avoid any deeper American involvement in the implementation of aid, the plan suggested only that the Europeans submit a joint and integrated request for assistance.[12] Although the door was left open for full Soviet and East European participation, and Soviet Foreign Minister Vyacheslav Molotov did join in initial deliberations with Britain and France, the Soviets and their clients quickly withdrew. The fourteen countries that did elect to participate in the plan formed the Organization of European Economic Cooperation and submitted a unified request in September. One month later President Truman submitted an interim aid bill to Congress; a long-range program was presented in December and enacted into law in April 1948. In tandem with the Truman Doctrine, the Marshall Plan was the first overt manifestation of the new, more cooperative American policy—albeit one that did not yet directly entangle the United States in European affairs.

The Vandenberg Resolution, passed by the Senate on June 11, 1948, terminated the debate, at least in the Truman administration and among congressional leaders, on the question of unilateralism versus cooperation.[13] By a vote of 64–4, the Senate in effect gave its prior consent to any regional

---

[10] Quoted in Cook 1989, 74.

[11] On the Marshall Plan, see the fiftieth anniversary symposium in *Foreign Affairs* 76, 3 (May/June 1997).

[12] Cook 1989, 84.

[13] Kaplan 1984, 75.

security arrangements the president might negotiate, and granted new impetus to the behind-the-scenes talks already underway between the United States, Britain, and Canada on an Atlantic area pact.

By the spring of 1948, the Cold War was becoming more intense. On February 25, a communist-led coup toppled the democratically elected government of Czechoslovakia.[14] Two days later, the Soviet Union demanded that Finland sign a "friendship" treaty. This sparked fears in Norway, reported to both Britain and the United States on March 8, that it was likely to face a similar demand in the near future. And on March 5, General Lucius D. Clay, commander-in-chief of the American troops in Europe and military governor of the United States occupation zone in Germany, cabled Washington that war with the Soviet Union might "come with dramatic suddenness."[15]

Under the press of these events, the United States gradually warmed to the idea of a formal security arrangement with its former wartime allies. The idea for such an arrangement was first raised, in vague form, by Bevin in talks with Marshall following the London foreign ministers' conference in December 1947. On January 13, Bevin went further, instructing Britain's ambassadors to France, Canada, and the United States to inform their respective governments that he would soon be proposing to the House of Commons that the Soviet Union be contained by "some form of union in Western Europe, whether of a formal or informal character, backed by the Americans and the Dominions."[16] Although one analyst claims that "this was the diplomatic communication that launched the making of the Atlantic Alliance," Marshall's reply one week later was scarcely enthusiastic.[17] Misreading the signals from Washington, Bevin went even further—in fact, too far—instructing Lord Inverchapel on January 26 to see Undersecretary of State Robert A. Lovett to propose, in essence, a military alliance with Britain; this idea was quickly dismissed by the American. Although the United States was, at best, lukewarm to the idea of a regional security arrangement, the events of the next month would rapidly alter the American position. In the context of the Norwegian inquiry as to whether assistance would be forthcoming if it chose to resist Soviet pressure for a friendship treaty, Bevin again—and even more explicitly—raised the question of a security agreement with the United States, a suggestion Marshall now heartily endorsed. On March 22, secret talks began at the Pentagon between the United States, Britain, and Canada, resulting in a recommendation to undertake more formal talks leading up to a possible treaty.[18]

At this point, the Truman administration, and Undersecretary Lovett in

[14] On the Czech coup and American policy, see Leffler 1992, 205.
[15] Reprinted in Smith 1974, 568.
[16] Quoted in Cook 1989, 114.
[17] Ibid.
[18] Ibid., 114–31. See Wiebes and Zeeman 1983.

particular, began to cultivate congressional support for a regional security arrangement through Senator Arthur H. Vandenberg (R-MI), the powerful chair of the Foreign Relations Committee and, previously, a moderate unilateralist. Although Truman, a Democrat, was running for election less than seven months hence, the president passed the initiative to the senator, thereby helping to forge a bipartisan consensus on the alliance issue. Written by the State Department with considerable input from Vandenberg, the resolution was kept deliberately vague and noncommittal, a point emphasized by both Lovett and Vandenberg in hearings before the Senate Foreign Relations Committee. Indeed, the resolution only encouraged the United States to pursue "such regional and other collective arrangements as are based on continuous and effective self-help and mutual aid, and as affect its national security."[19] It is unlikely that many senators were aware of the larger context in which the resolution was already placed. Although the Soviets undoubtedly knew of the gestating treaty through their spy in the British Foreign Service, Donald Maclean, who was participating in the so-called Pentagon talks, the negotiations had not, at this point, been revealed to the American public. Nonetheless, by passing the resolution, the Senate gave an unequivocal green light to the treaty talks.

On January 23, 1948, one day before the start of the Berlin blockade, the United States informed Britain that it was now ready to begin formal negotiations on an Atlantic security pact—taking the third step toward a strategy of cooperation with Europe. Along with Lovett, the ambassadors from Britain, France, Canada, Belgium, Holland, and Luxembourg gathered in Washington on July 6 for a general discussion of the issues. After five days they turned the deliberations over to a working group composed of senior diplomatic staff, which submitted its report to the seven governments on September 9. The ambassadors met again on December 10 and charged the working group with writing a first draft of the treaty. This draft was circulated and discussed with the Foreign Relations Committee in early 1949. After substantial changes, Acheson, now secretary of state, announced the treaty on March 18. It was signed on April 4, 1949. After twelve days of debate, the Senate ratified the treaty by a vote of 82 to 13 on July 21.

With Truman's surprise election in 1948, all the pieces were in place for a rapid conclusion of the North Atlantic Treaty. As Don Cook observes, "it had become an accepted public fact that the United States was well on its way to joining some kind of entangling defense alliance with Europe, and this . . . generate[d] remarkably little editorial opposition or heated rumblings of isolationist denunciation."[20] Just as important, Truman had the votes in the Senate for ratification—if acceptable treaty language could be found. The exten-

---

[19] Reprinted in Kaplan 1984, 226.
[20] Cook 1989, 200–1.

sive negotiations between the State Department, foreign governments, and the Senate focused on two issues: the mandated response to foreign aggression against treaty members (Article 5) and the requirement for mutual aid (Article 3).

As detailed below, the Americans wanted to maintain the largest possible freedom of action to limit the constraints and, therefore, the governance costs that could be imposed upon the United States. Some, such as George Kennan, initially opposed any treaty, believing that the American troops stationed in Germany provided a sufficient guarantee of American involvement in any future hostilities.[21] Others, such as Taft, favored a simple extension of the Monroe Doctrine to Western Europe.[22] The Europeans, on the other hand, feared that despite current trends the United States would eventually withdraw from the continent. As a result, they—and especially the French—wanted the strongest possible guarantee of American support, particularly in the early stages of conflict. The final treaty language was a compromise, albeit one reflecting more closely the American position. Article 5 simply states that "the Parties agree that an armed attack against one or more of them in Europe or North America shall be considered an attack against them all" and calls upon each member to "assist the Party or Parties so attacked by taking forthwith . . . such action as it deems necessary, including the use of armed force, to restore and maintain the security of the North Atlantic area."[23] Although it was based upon the broad individual discretion demanded by the United States, the Europeans succeeded in including the provisions that action would be taken promptly and that it would include possible armed force.

Having essentially accepted the American version of Article 5, the Europeans next focused on Article 3, and were substantially more successful. For the Europeans, the concept of a weak American commitment without adequate economic and material aid was meaningless. Many American officials agreed, but they were opposed again by Kennan, the isolationists, and the unilateralists—as well as the military. Kennan feared that the emphasis on military assistance risked turning the Atlantic relationship into a military alliance that would, in turn, alienate the Soviet Union.[24] The unilateralists shared Kennan's concern and worried over the deeper involvement in European affairs that increased aid implied. The military, on the other hand, feared that the Europeans would use Article 3 to shift even more of the burden of rearmament onto the United States and drain America's limited

[21] Ibid., 165.

[22] Kaplan 1984, 125.

[23] Reprinted in ibid., 228.

[24] Ireland 1981, 120. At the same time, Kennan recognized the need for military staff talks to develop a coordinated response to a possible Soviet invasion of Western Europe; Cook 1989, 165.

stocks of military equipment. Despite this opposition, the administration was able to focus the debate on Article 5 and stress the self-help and mutual aid provisions of the treaty, thereby gaining senatorial support for the strong language preferred by the Europeans in Article 3.[25]

The outbreak of the Korean War on June 25, 1950, prompted the United States to take the fourth and final step toward security cooperation with Europe: the assignment of American troops to NATO and the appointment of General Dwight D. Eisenhower as Supreme Allied Commander, Europe (SACEUR). Prior to the war, there was little desire to integrate American forces directly into a unified military command structure.[26] Indeed, during the hearings on ratification, Secretary of State Acheson explicitly denied that any such move was being considered. This detachment was also reflected in the earliest organizational form of the alliance. Of the five regional planning groups created at the first North Atlantic Council meeting in November 1949, the United States joined only two as a full member, the North Atlantic Ocean and Canada-United States groups, choosing to participate only "as appropriate" in the others.[27] With the outbreak of hostilities in Korea, this reluctance to become more deeply involved in the permanent, ongoing defense of Western Europe evaporated. On September 9, 1950, President Truman announced that additional American troops would be assigned to Europe. At a meeting of the North Atlantic Council several days later, the organization's highest political body adopted the principle of forward defense in Europe, proposing to stand against a Soviet invasion as far to the east as practicable, and created a corresponding central command to coordinate planning, deployments, and possibly combat—actions that are often referred to as putting the "O" in NATO.[28] At the request of the Council, in turn, Truman nominated Eisenhower for the newly created post of SACEUR on December 19. In return for this deeper American commitment to the alliance, the Europeans agreed to greater military contributions and the eventual integration of Germany into the continental defense effort, a development that would occur only in 1955 after substantial delay and equivocation, especially by France. Perhaps most significant, an important if nonetheless limited element of hierarchy was introduced into the alliance through the central command, and the Europeans accepted American dominance of this mechanism both in principle and in fact.

Truman's actions in late 1950 occasioned the Great Debate in American foreign policy. Although focused on the president's constitutional authority to

[25] Ireland 1981, 121.

[26] On March 7, 1950, however, Acheson and John J. McCloy, the United States high commissioner in Germany, did discuss the idea of setting up a secretariat for NATO; Barnet 1983, 133. Acheson was also contemplating sending five additional divisions to Europe; Leffler 1992, 346.

[27] Kaplan 1984, 140; Ireland 1981, 162.

[28] Weber 1991, 33; Fox and Fox 1967, 15.

deploy troops overseas without congressional approval, the underlying concern was the deepening American involvement. Again, the unilateralists around Senator Taft called for a more aloof role, insisting that the American contribution to Europe should consist primarily of air and naval forces. This view was undercut, however, by Eisenhower, who—just back from a whirlwind tour of the continent—argued that an effective land defense could be established but that it would require additional American troops. Such forces, he maintained, were also a moral commitment that would give the Europeans the courage of their convictions.[29] On April 4, 1951, the Senate finally approved the stationing of four additional divisions in Europe under NATO command and endorsed Eisenhower's appointment as SACEUR by a vote of 69–21.

Despite its appellation, the Great Debate was anticlimatic. Although the Korean War and its aftermath considerably broadened the scope and magnitude of the American involvement in Europe, it did not alter the fundamental nature of the strategy that had evolved between 1947 and 1949. Even four additional American divisions would have been insufficient to repel successfully a Soviet attack on Europe; their primary contribution, recognized by all at the time, was as a tripwire or "hostage." Yet, the American occupation troops in Germany were already effectively serving in that capacity de facto from 1945 and de jure from May 1950, when the three high commissioners for Germany stated that an armed attack on the western occupation forces in Germany would be considered as an armed attack on all parties to the North Atlantic Treaty, and that Article 5 would immediately be brought into play.[30] Moreover, these occupation forces were seen as relatively permanent fixtures on the European landscape. As early as 1946, Secretary of State James Byrnes stated that "Security forces will probably have to remain in Germany for a long period. . . . We are not withdrawing. . . . As long as there is an occupation army in Germany, American armed forces will be part of that occupation army."[31] And in the same announcement quoted above, the commissioners further stated that "the three Allied Powers have no intention in the present European situation of withdrawing their occupation forces from Germany."[32] The differences are further blurred when it is recognized that the assignment of ground troops to NATO did not contain any greater or more permanent commitment; nothing in NATO precluded the United States from reducing or eliminating its assigned forces in Europe. Indeed, during the Great Debate both Eisenhower and Marshall, now secretary of defense, suggested that when the Europeans had regained their strength and the secu-

---

[29] Wells 1985, 189.
[30] Ireland 1981, 176.
[31] Reprinted in U.S. Congress, Senate 1961, 60. See Leffler 1992, 120.
[32] Quoted in Ireland 1981, 176.

rity situation had improved, the United States might be able to withdraw its troops from Europe.[33]

The Korean War was not decisive in the move to cooperation with Europe, although it coincided with and facilitated NATO's turn from a simple mutual defense pact into a "command-in-being."[34] The real entanglements had already been entered into prior to the outbreak of hostilities: American troops were already hostages to a Soviet attack and the treaty bound the United States to respond. Nonetheless, the Great Debate was important for its symbolic implications. After watching an open congressional and public debate that resolved on greater involvement on the continent, the Europeans could be more confident of the existing American commitment. The debate thus served to signal America's future intentions.

Through these four steps, the United States gradually built relatively anarchic security relationships with the countries of Europe. This was a decisive turn away from Washington's dictum of eschewing foreign entanglements and represents one of the most important foreign policy initiatives of the twentieth century.

Some observers, however, describe America's security relationships with Europe in more hierarchic terms. This is particularly true for analysts—on both sides of the Atlantic—opposed to the disproportionate role of and burden on the United States in the alliance. David Calleo, for instance, depicts NATO as "a hegemonic American protectorate." There is an element of truth in this perspective. As Calleo notes, an American has always served as SACEUR and "Europe's defense depends upon the willingness of the United States to initiate a nuclear war rather than see Europe overrun."[35]

The relationships between the United States and its European partners were more than pure and simple alliances. Throughout all of the Cold War, the United States imposed a proscription on its partners. Although they might choose not to ally actively with the United States, like Sweden, partners were prohibited from allying with the Soviet Union, suggesting that Europe, at least, was embedded in an American sphere of influence.[36] In many dyads, of course, something close to an alliance prevailed: Britain, for instance, had no desire to ally with the Soviet Union, and therefore was not constrained in any way by the American proscription. In some cases, however, the United States went further and restrained partners from potentially moving to ally with the Soviet Union or, possibly, to a neutral position in the superpower competition. This is clearest in the cases of France and, especially, Italy, where the United States acted both broadly under the Marshall

---

[33] Ibid., 210.

[34] For a similar view on the importance of the Korean War, see Kaplan 1984, 8–9. For a contrary view, see Stein 1993.

[35] Calleo 1989, 19.

[36] Gaddis 1997, 44, 149.

Plan and more specifically through diplomatic, covert, and short-term economic channels to expel the elected communist parties from the governing coalitions and ensure their defeat in future elections. Although the United States now appears to have been more a bystander or, perhaps, just another interest group during the French political crisis, it was clearly more aggressive and active in Italy; the United States even began planning for direct intervention should northern Italy fall into communist-led instability.[37]

The United States also used its influence and resources not only to proscribe the relationships of others but to control their foreign policy initiatives, suggesting that Europe might be seen as a partial protectorate. The classic example is the Suez crisis of 1956, when the United States humiliated its ostensible allies and forced Britain and France to withdraw from their intervention in Egypt. Stepping outside the boundaries of what the United States considered acceptable brought swift retribution.[38]

In some cases, the United States assumed even wider powers over the foreign policies of its partners. Even after its return to sovereignty, Germany did not possess independent military forces and depended upon the United States for protection from foreign threats. Unlike any other member, German forces were fully integrated into NATO and did not possess an autonomous national command structure. Nonetheless, Germany retained or, over time, earned some measure of foreign policy autonomy, with its policy of Ostpolitik preceding America's own detente with the East by several crucial years. In the end, Germany remained for much of the Cold War a limited but never entirely complete American protectorate.

Yet, whereas the Soviet Union periodically intervened to maintain control over its partners in Eastern Europe, the United States did not exercise similar instruments of imperial rule. In 1956, Iceland elected a coalition of parties on a platform of ousting the American bases. Only the Hungarian revolt and the financial implications of the base closures led Icelanders to pull back from withdrawal. Surprisingly, the United States was quite prepared to bow before the wishes of a population of 150,000. Similarly, in 1966, France withdrew its forces from NATO without calling forth the American equivalent of the Soviet's Brezhnev Doctrine.[39]

Although constrained in important ways, the states of Europe, with the possible exception of Germany, did not lose their ability to conduct their own foreign policies—as France's "singularity" over the history of the alliance vividly illustrates. In many areas, including economic relations with the Soviet Union, the United States was unable to control the foreign policies of its partners, and consistently subordinated its own desires in the interests of

---

[37] Leffler 1992, 157, 196, 206, and 213. On the French case, the now standard work is Wall 1991, esp. 2–4 and 63–95; on Italy, see Miller 1986, 213–49.

[38] The most detailed account is Kunz 1991.

[39] Kaplan 1984, 182–83; Gaddis 1997, 219.

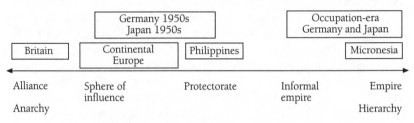

Figure 5.1. American Security Relationships during the Early Cold War

harmony.[40] Even the Suez crisis of 1956 carried a double-edged lesson. In the short term, the United States was able to force its will upon Britain and France. In the long term, however, the crisis sparked new efforts in London and especially Paris to lessen their dependence upon the United States, ultimately leading to greater autonomy.

It is, as discussed in Chapter 2, difficult to identify precisely the nature of informal relationships. As Geir Lundestad recognizes, if the United States did dominate Europe after the war, it was an "empire by invitation" in which the Europeans were active accomplices in their own subordination.[41] Differentiating the freedom to exercise rights of residual control from the failure to challenge the effective transfer of such rights from one party to another is admittedly a difficult and somewhat subjective enterprise. America's European partners appear to have retained at least some and often substantial decision-making authority in foreign policy. Although often unappreciated elements of hierarchy existed, America's security relationships with its partners in Europe clustered toward the anarchic end of the continuum, constituting a sphere of influence for most and a partial protectorate only in the case of Germany. These relationships are summarized in Figure 5.1.

### The Pacific Perimeter

The United States was already a major presence in the Pacific before the outbreak of World War II—holding the Philippines as a colony and Guam as an unincorporated territory, having acquired both island outposts as a result of its war with Spain in 1898. After 1945 even many isolationists, who opposed deeper ties to Europe, recognized America's important interests in Asia.[42]

As early as 1943, army and navy planners resolved to establish a forward

[40] See Mastanduno 1988 and 1992.
[41] Lundestad 1986 and 1992.
[42] See Schaller 1985, 72–74.

defense in Asia fortified by an offshore security perimeter composed of Japan, the Philippines, and Micronesia.[43] This defense vision was widely shared within the Roosevelt and, later, Truman administrations; the only debate was over how best to structure the necessary security relationships. The result was a loose protectorate with Japan, embodied in the United States-Japan security pact signed in September 1951; a protectorate in the Philippines, reflected in the long-term base agreements imposed as a condition for independence and postwar aid; and the creation of a "strategic trusteeship" or formal empire over Micronesia.

The initial American planning documents envisioned a punitive peace for Japan, focusing on the demilitarization of society, the democratization of politics, and the deconcentration of industry. Substantial reparations were also anticipated for those countries which had suffered under Japanese occupation during the war. These relatively harsh measures were embodied in the Initial Post-Surrender Policy (document 150/4/A), drafted by the State, War, Navy Coordinating Committee (SWNCC) and issued to General Douglas MacArthur, the Supreme Commander for the Allied Powers (SCAP), in September 1945.[44]

By late 1947, however, the punitive peace outlined for Japan was giving way to an alternative vision. Described as "the turning point in American policy toward Japan" and issued in October 1948, National Security Council Directive NSC 13/2 codified this view and directed SCAP to promote Japan's economic recovery, so that the country could rejoin the family of nations as a supportive and contributing member of the American security community.[45] It also raised for the first time the issue of Japanese rearmament.[46]

This "reverse course" in American policy toward Japan, however, did not solve the lingering problem of the political status of Japan, especially the issue of when and how the country would recover its sovereignty. Although not questioning the assumption that Japan would eventually regain its independence, the Department of Defense and Armed Services favored a prolonged occupation so that the United States could continue to enjoy unimpeded military use of Japan's territory. The State Department, on the other hand, while concurring in the need for post-occupation military bases in Japan, favored an early peace treaty so as not to alienate the Japanese population. Over the long term, the diplomats preferred an indebted partner to a disaffected appendage. MacArthur also favored terminating the occupation as soon as possible, most likely to demonstrate the efficacy of his policies and administration.

A way out of this impasse, a nonpunitive peace treaty joined with a secu-

---

[43] Ibid., 54.
[44] Harries and Harries 1987, 200; Dunn 1963, 39–40.
[45] Dunn 1963, 77.
[46] Harries and Harries 1987, 194.

rity pact guaranteeing postoccupation bases to the United States was first suggested by the British in September 1949.[47] This same idea was formally broached by Japanese negotiators in May 1950 in an attempt to break America's bureaucratic logjam and hasten their country's return to sovereignty.[48]

With this proposal on the table, John Foster Dulles, brought into the State Department to help build a bipartisan consensus on foreign policy, was given full responsibility for negotiating a peace treaty with Japan. Building upon a draft treaty completed within the State Department the previous October, Dulles began his task in May 1950—one month before the outbreak of the Korean War—and completed it in May 1951. The peace treaty with Japan was signed by all the participants in the Pacific war except Poland, Czechoslovakia, and the Soviet Union on September 8, 1951, in San Francisco. Simultaneously, the United States signed a security pact with Japan that guaranteed American forces extensive base rights for an indefinite period of time, ostensibly to deter armed attack upon Japan.[49]

As in Europe, the Korean War may have stimulated the participants in the American-led cooperative enterprise on to greater efforts. The manifest Soviet threat may also have blocked domestic opposition within the United States to the new security commitments extended to Japan. But, as in Europe, the essential framework and commitments for cooperation in the Pacific had already been settled prior to the outbreak of hostilities.

America's security relationship with Japan was more anarchic than hierarchic, but more than a simple alliance between sovereign equals. The security pact codified Japan's status as a partial American protectorate. Japan was prohibited by Article 9 of its so-called peace constitution from possessing offensive military forces, and therefore was not expected to defend the United States, as NATO members were. The security agreement was clearly a one-sided obligation. In exchange for its commitment to defend Japan, the United States was permitted to station troops in Japan, maintain bases, and use its forces not only to defend the island nation but to support its interests throughout the Far East.[50] In a separate agreement, held apart from the formal security pact to avoid legislative debate in Japan, American forces were also allowed to put down riots and disturbances at the request of the Japanese government, a provision "so loosely drawn that for the rest of the 1950s the Japanese complained that the United States could use force whenever it desired within Japan."[51] In yet another agreement extracted as the price of ending the formal occupation—the infamous Yoshida letter, drafted by

[47] Dunn 1963, 82.
[48] Dower 1979, 374.
[49] See Schaller 1985, 294.
[50] Leffler 1992, 464–65.
[51] LaFeber 1997, 291.

Dulles himself—Japan pledged not to "conclude a bilateral treaty with the Communist regime of China."[52] As the historian John Dower concludes, the restoration of Japanese sovereignty did not mean that Japan had recovered "the capability of pursuing an independent foreign policy."[53] Although it did not cede all of its foreign policy authority to the United States, and retained at least some limited autonomy, Japan escaped from the direct control of the United States only to enter into a limited protectorate. As Dulles remarked to British officials, the 1951 security agreements "amounted to a voluntary continuation of the Occupation."[54]

The Philippines were obtained by the United States as one of the spoils of the Spanish-American War in 1898. Somewhat ambivalent about its imperial role, the United States soon looked forward to the day when it could judge the Philippines ready for self-rule. The Organic Act of 1916, commonly called the Jones Law and intended as a basic charter for Philippine freedom and independence, stated in its preamble that it was the intention of the United States to award independence to the Philippines as soon as a stable government should be set up.[55] Not surprisingly, Filipinos believed that they had already fulfilled this criterion, and pressed throughout the interwar period for independence.

Independence was finally granted in 1934 in the Tydings-McDuffie Act, which established a ten-year transition to full sovereignty. Supported by an economic coalition of protectionists, who opposed the duty-free entry of Philippine goods into the United States, and labor, who in conjunction with west coast nativists opposed Filipino immigration, the Tydings-McDuffie Act also drew wide support from isolationists, who desired to draw back into the American "homeland" and, especially, to escape from a potential flashpoint in the increasingly ominous struggle with Japan in the Pacific.[56] Passed at the one moment of true isolationism in American history, the Tydings-McDuffie Act did not specify future base rights for the United States, but left this for discussion at the end of the ten-year transition period.[57] Under the press of isolationism, the United States wanted not freedom for the Philippines but freedom from the Philippines. As President Franklin Roosevelt stated in a confidential meeting with the congressional leadership over the Tydings-McDuffie bill, "Let's get rid of the Philippines—that's the most important thing. Let's be frank about it."[58]

The Japanese quickly conquered the Philippines during World War II. The

---

[52] Quoted ibid., 293.
[53] Dower 1979, 371.
[54] Quoted in LaFeber 1997, 297.
[55] Smith 1958, 76.
[56] Brands 1992, 152; Friend 1965, 85.
[57] Brands 1992, 156.
[58] Quoted ibid., 163.

United States retook the islands only with considerable effort. Nonetheless, the United States held to the original schedule for independence, although not without new reservations based upon "the sea change that had occurred in world affairs since the passage of the Tydings Act."[59] Even before the end of the war, Congress now urged that "the President . . . [be] authorized . . . to withhold and acquire and to retain such bases and the right incident thereto as he may deem necessary for the mutual protection of the Philippine islands and the United States."[60] Almost ignored in 1934, bases now became a precondition for independence.

Independence was granted on July 4, 1946. Even afterward, however, the United States continued to exert a profound influence over the islands. The Philippines remained economically dependent upon the United States, both for trade and reconstruction aid. As a result, "there was never any doubt that the Americans would get their bases. The only questions were how many and where."[61] In exchange for aid, the Philippines agreed in 1945 that the United States could establish and develop bases at fourteen sites requested by the navy and twelve requested by the army.[62] In addition, the Philippines agreed not to allow third countries to establish bases in the islands without Washington's permission, a clear indicator of a sphere of influence.[63] The Bases Agreement formally reached in March 1947 authorized the United States to hold twenty-three bases in the Philippines under a ninety-nine-year rent-free lease, and affirmed America's continued responsibility for the strategic defense of the islands.[64] In addition, the agreement gave complete operational control of the bases to the United States, contained no provisions for early termination, granted extraterritorial rights to American personnel, and even gave the United States jurisdiction over Filipino civilians for offenses committed on the bases. As one Filipino negotiator noted in reflection, "It was not so much a treaty between two sovereign nations as it was the extension of American sovereignty in the Philippines through the establishment of U.S. enclaves of extraterritoriality on her soil."[65] The bases, and the extensive rights thereto, suggest that the United States went beyond the negative proscriptions of a sphere of influence, reflected in the veto over third-party bases, toward a tighter form of control over defense and foreign policy in the

---

[59] Ibid., 221. Concerned about Filipino support for the American war effort, Congress even authorized the president in June 1944 to advance the date of Philippine independence if it were deemed advisable; Smith 1958, 113.

[60] Quoted in Gregor and Aganon 1987, 6.

[61] Brands 1992, 221.

[62] Leffler 1992, 170–71, suggests that the army was less enthusiastic about bases in the Philippines.

[63] Brands 1992, 222.

[64] McCoy 1981, 58; Stromseth 1989, 164–65.

[65] Quoted in Stromseth 1989, 165.

Philippines, signaled by its responsibility for the continuing defense of the islands. When the formal empire ended, a protectorate arose to take its place.

Covering approximately 3,000,000 square miles of ocean, an area larger than the United States, the islands of Micronesia total only 700 square miles of surface area, a land mass less than half the size of the state of Rhode Island. In close proximity to most major Pacific trade routes and, after 1945, within striking distance of Southeast Asia, China, and Japan, the Trust Territory of the Pacific, along with Guam, is strategically placed in the South Pacific.

Objects of considerable struggle in the war, there was widespread consensus during and after the hostilities that Micronesia should remain an American possession, at least for the foreseeable future. As with Japan and the Philippines, American military planners and statesmen were from the outset determined not to lose access to the actual and potential bases on the islands. With widespread public support within the United States for permanent occupation of the islands, the only issue was how, under what circumstances, and for how long American control would be extended over the territory.[66]

As elsewhere, the military wanted a more permanent and wider range of control than the State Department thought prudent. While this debate raged at the cabinet level, the State, Navy, Army, and Interior departments began to formulate a compromise soon after the Yalta summit. The result, called a strategic trust, envisioned a unique political entity under the general supervision of the United Nations, and therefore internationally legitimate like other trusteeship agreements, but completely under the practical control of the occupying power. As enacted by the United Nations, a strategic trust differs from other trusteeship agreements by first, allowing the administering power to fortify the territory and to close parts of it at will for security purposes; second, making the Security Council, rather than the General Assembly, the site of United Nations control, permitting the United States to exercise its veto if necessary; and third, specifying that the state "concerned" would have final authority regarding any alteration in the status of the territory.[67] The second and third provisions of this agreement constituted a "double guarantee" of American control over the future of Micronesia.

In November 1946, President Truman announced his intention to place the islands under trusteeship. On April 2, 1949, the Strategic Trusteeship agreement for Micronesia was approved by the Security Council. Despite the deepening Cold War, the support of the Soviet Union was secured by a deal brokered earlier by Secretary of State Byrnes, trading Russia's support for American control of Micronesia for America's support for Russian control of

---

[66] Gale 1979, 49–52.
[67] Ibid., 54.

the Kuriles and South Sakhalin islands.[68] The strategic trust agreement was ratified by Congress on July 18 and signed into law the same day. This was the only strategic trust ever created by the United Nations, and the only territory to come under direct American control during this era of new-found cooperation. With complete rights of residual control vested in the dominant partner, Micronesia became a formal empire of the United States.

During the first postwar years, the United States considered and eventually rejected a return to unilateralism. Likewise, an American empire in Europe or Japan was never seriously considered, and the Philippines were actually granted independence, albeit under continuing constraints. Only in Micronesia did the United States establish an imperial relationship after the war. Despite the opposition of both the isolationists and unilateralists, a consensus gradually emerged—even before the outbreak of the Korean War in June 1950—that cooperation with Europe and the Pacific within relatively anarchic security relationships was the most efficient way to protect America's security interests. Within this general blueprint, however, there was also considerable variation in the types of security relationships employed by the United States. We now turn to explaining America's historic shift to cooperation, as well as the country's varying security relationships.

## ALTERNATIVE EXPLANATIONS

America's postwar security relationships are most commonly explained as a function of either the threat posed by the Soviet Union or the bipolar structure of the international system. The arguments of both historians and political scientists, however, are underdetermining. Although the Soviet threat and bipolarity clearly mattered, neither can account for the choice of one security relationship rather than another. The theory developed here provides a more complete understanding of the choice of security relationships and, possibly, a challenge to structuralist accounts.

In the views of most Americans, the Soviet Union constituted the primary threat to Western security after 1945. Indeed, Soviet behavior during and immediately after the war lent credence to American fears.[69] The creation of the Comecon economic bloc and Cominform in 1947, the Soviet-backed coup in Czechoslovakia in February 1948, the Berlin Blockade imposed in June 1948, the Soviet-backed invasion of South Korea in June 1950 and, throughout, Soviet obstructionism over Germany all served to reinforce America's views on the innate aggressiveness of the Russian regime. Likewise, Moscow's conventional military superiority, its test of an atomic weapon in September 1949, and its alliance with the newly triumphant communists in

---

[68] LaFeber 1997, 263.
[69] Leffler 1992, 3–10 and 100–4.

China suggested that Soviet leaders might actually have the wherewithal to succeed in some of the territorial ambitions attributed to them by Western observers.

American decision makers also feared that the Europeans, devastated and demoralized by the war, could not or would not put up much of a fight against internal or external communist aggression—and would thereby provide the Soviet Union an opportunity to expand its influence at relatively little cost. The Greek civil war, which prompted the Truman Doctrine, appeared to confirm this view, as did the presence of communists in the French and Italian governments.

Taken together, these trends do suggest that the Soviet Union was a threat, as defined in Chapter 2, to the security of North America, Western Europe, and noncommunist Asia. Fears of Soviet expansionism were not entirely unfounded. It is on this basis that "traditionalists" or "realists" place the primary burden for the Cold War on the Soviet Union.[70] As John Lewis Gaddis concludes in a recent reaffirmation of traditionalism, "once Stalin wound up at the top in Moscow and once it was clear his state would survive the war, then it looks equally clear that there was going to be a Cold War whatever the west did. Who then was responsible? The answer . . . is authoritarianism in general, and Stalin in particular."[71]

On the other hand, there is equally clear evidence that the American government inflated the Soviet threat and engaged in purposefully provocative behavior.[72] American intelligence officials were (or should have been) confident that the Soviet Union could not, immediately after the war, mount a successful attack on Europe, given their "20 million dead, 70,000 villages destroyed, and the absence of usable railroad track across Poland."[73] Likewise, the Marshall Plan and, specifically, the rebuilding of Germany were at least partial stimuli for Soviet policies in Eastern Europe, especially the consolidation of power in Czechoslovakia; nonetheless, these actions were subsequently presented to the public by American statesmen as unprovoked and aggressive actions.[74] Accordingly, "revisionists" place primary responsibility for the Cold War squarely on the United States.

Postrevisionist historians and neorealist political scientists locate the origins of the Cold War in the bipolar structure of the international system. Whereas postrevisionists accept that there may have been important misperceptions and overreactions on both sides of the Cold War, and that ideas,

[70] See MacDonald 1995/96.

[71] Gaddis 1997, 294.

[72] LaFeber 1985 and 1994; Lowi 1967. For a recent theoretical and comparative study, see Christensen 1996. For a more tempered view, see Leffler 1992, 144–46.

[73] Barnet 1983, 130; see also Evangelista, 1982/83. For a contrary view, see Karber and Combs, n.d.

[74] Barnet 1983, 127.

personalities, and domestic politics matter as well, they essentially agree with the neorealists that the political competition between the United States and Soviet Union was rooted in bipolarity—a distribution of capabilities defined by only two superpowers.[75] In this "no-fault" view of history, the Cold War was the inevitable result of the struggle for security between two similarly situated titans. Until the collapse of the Soviet Union and the beginning of the "new Cold War history," this postrevisionist/neorealist synthesis had become something of a new orthodoxy.[76]

For most analysts, the desire to ally with the countries of Europe and the Pacific follows unproblematically from the emerging superpower hostilities. As Timothy Ireland notes, "the emergence of the American commitment to western Europe has been viewed as a cause-and-effect relationship in response to Soviet actions in the Near East, the Balkans, eastern Europe, and Germany. Even 'revisionist' historians view the creation of the Atlantic Alliance almost exclusively in terms of the cold war."[77] The literature on the Pacific perimeter focuses on similar themes.[78] The existing historiography has focused primarily on the origins of the Cold War and the question of which side was more threatening to the other and, therefore, more culpable. Unfortunately, it does not take America's security relationships with its partners as problematic and in need of explanation.

Despite its obvious importance, the Soviet threat is insufficient as an explanation of American security relations.[79] Whatever its origins, the Soviet threat required a response. As the presence of an active debate between the unilateralists and internationalists suggests, however, the United States possessed viable alternatives. It could have remained unencumbered by relationships with Europe and the Pacific, built up its conventional forces, and threatened to destroy any aggressor through its nuclear monopoly and, later, nuclear superiority. This was, in fact, the position of Taft and his followers. Or, taking the Soviet lead, the United States could have enlarged its empire beyond the Trust Territory, building even more hierarchical relations with Japan, Europe, and their former colonies. Although alliances, spheres of influence and even protectorates were eventually chosen, either a fortress America or a more extensive empire could have provided similar levels of security for the United States, albeit at differing costs.

Neorealists do attempt to offer an explanation for the security relationships pursued by states. In my view, however, they misinterpret the nature of

---

[75] See Leffler 1992; Waltz 1979.

[76] For an interesting evolution of these arguments, see Gaddis 1982, 1987, and 1997.

[77] Ireland 1981, 4.

[78] See Schaller 1985.

[79] Although he focuses on the decision of the United States to accommodate or challenge the Soviet Union, Messer 1977 makes a similar point. Historians are only now beginning to address this issue; see Gaddis 1997.

America's security relationships after World War II and offer only an incomplete explanation. Neorealism posits that bipolarity will be characterized primarily by internal balancing, closely related to what is described here as unilateralism. This hypothesis is developed most fully by Kenneth Waltz, but in his characteristically subtle way. Waltz deduces that "where two powers contend, imbalances can be righted only by their internal efforts" and "in a two-power system the politics of balance continue, but the way to compensate for an incipient external disequilibrium is primarily by intensifying one's internal efforts."[80] Yet bipolarity need not preclude alliances. He recognizes that "alliance leaders may try to elicit maximum contributions from their associates. The contributions are useful even in a bipolar world, but they are not indispensable."[81] In Waltz's view, then, some alliances may be found under bipolarity, but they will not be the *primary* means of producing security.

The United States clearly did not rely exclusively on its internal abilities, suggesting that a strong form of the neorealist thesis is incorrect. Moreover, although Waltz and other neorealists do not rule out alliances under bipolarity, the considerable attention devoted by the United States to constructing security relationships and strengthening its ties with others is at least somewhat inconsistent with the central thrust of the theory. This is, of course, a matter of emphasis and interpretation, resting largely on the definition of "primary." In my reading of history, relationships between the United States and its partners in Europe and the Pacific were one of the centerpieces of American foreign policy during the Cold War. The United States also relied upon the cooperation and assistance of its partners to a considerable degree. The United States typically contributed just under 70 percent of total NATO defense expenditures, a large share to be sure; but at the same time, this figure indicates that the partners contributed just over 30 percent of total expenditures, a not insignificant amount.[82] I argue below that the partners also contributed important forward bases that are not reflected in such figures. The considerable attention and effort devoted by the United States to constructing and maintaining its postwar security relationships, moreover, suggest that American leaders, at any rate, saw these partnerships as something less than dispensable. If this is the case, then the observed relationships cut against the spirit of neorealist theory.

More problematic, however, is the difference in security relationships forged by the United States across various dyads and the difference between the United States and Soviet Union. As noted above, America's relationships ranged from alliances to at least one formal empire, but were generally anarchic. The Soviet Union, on the other hand, chose to construct far more

[80] Waltz 1979, 163 and 118.
[81] Ibid., 169.
[82] Adams and Munz 1988.

hierarchic security relationships.[83] Whereas the United States choose alliances and spheres of influence in its relationships with the Europeans, the Soviet Union generally choose informal empires with its partners in Eastern Europe and formal empires with polities adjacent to itself. In its present form, neo-realism would suggest that, first, a country ought to construct similar relationships with its various partners and, second, two states occupying roughly equivalent positions within the international structure will adopt similar and perhaps even identical security relationships. Neither of these expectations is supported.

Neorealists possess, at best, an incomplete theory of security relationships. Bipolarity was, of course, important to the choice of anarchic security relationships, especially as it tended to reduce the exit options of partners and, thereby, the probability of opportunism. But bipolarity was not the sole or even the most important determinant of America's decisive break with uni-lateralism. To understand this historic shift in policy, it is important to consider a broader range of alternative security relationships and a more complex calculus of interests, one that integrates joint production economies, expected costs of opportunism, and governance costs.

### JOINT PRODUCTION ECONOMIES

Cooperation depends on the joint economies in producing security. The larger the joint economies, the greater the returns from pooling resources and efforts with others, and the more attractive cooperation is to a polity. The joint economies available to the United States expanded greatly around the time of World War II. This created a strong incentive for the United States to adopt some form of cooperation after the war.

#### Technology

As discussed in Chapter 4, World War I spurred important changes in the technology of war. These changes evolved slowly over the interwar years, as they often required integrating innovations into complex systems to reach their full potential. Thus, the development of mechanized ground forces, military aviation, and naval air power, all begun during the Great War, and refinements in amphibious warfare required several decades to mature. By the late 1930s, these technologies gave states an unprecedented ability to project force over distance. Germany could not have carried out its offensives of 1939 without the mechanization and motorization of its army. Japan could not have carried out its successful attack on Pearl Harbor absent its advances in naval air power. During the course of World War II, these technologies

---

[83] On the contrast between the American and Soviet empires, see Gaddis 1997, especially 283–89. For an application of the theory here to the Soviet case, see Lake 1996 and 1997.

were continuously refined, increasing the strategic reach of states even farther.

World War II also stimulated new technological innovations. Most importantly, rockets and heavy bombers now allowed combatants to bypass troops on the ground, strike behind enemy lines to disrupt operations in the rear, and ultimately to attack "strategic" targets—especially a state's leadership, industrial capacity, and popular morale. Although strategic bombing originated in World War I, the scale and destructiveness of such efforts increased exponentially in the years before and during World War II, making this conflict unlike any known previously.[84]

Atomic (later nuclear) weapons magnified this strategic capability. At one level, atomic weapons did not constitute a new form of warfare, only a more efficient and destructive version of weapons already in use. As but one example, almost as many people died in the firebombing of Tokyo on March 8, 1945 (estimated at 83,000), as by the atomic bombs dropped on Hiroshima on August 6 (estimated at 90,000) and Nagasaki on August 9 (estimated at 35,000).[85] At a second level, however, atomic weapons, and certainly their thermonuclear cousins first tested in 1951, were unique. Their destructive power and horrific potential could now deter war itself in a way that previous weapons could not. This was surely something new in the history of international relations.

These "modern" technologies of war greatly extended the security perimeters of states. To capture the effects of changing technology, we can again refer to civilian transport costs as a rough guide. Given the shift in technologies from sea and land to air, ocean and rail freight rates are no longer appropriate. The ease of projecting force is now better reflected in air transport costs, which fell dramatically over this period. Between 1930 and 1940, average air transportation revenue per passenger mile fell from approximately $0.68 to $.046, a 32 percent decline; by 1950, revenue per passenger mile fell to $0.30, a further 35 percent drop.[86] When we consider that the destructive power of the weapons carried by long-distance bombers was rising exponentially over this same period, it would appear that the costs of projecting force over distance declined rapidly indeed.

The new technologies and enlarged security perimeter for the United States dramatically increased incentives for international cooperation.[87] Defensively, there was a new premium on forward bases to contain foreign

[84] Quester 1966.

[85] Doughty and Gruber 1996, 837–38.

[86] Herring and Litan 1995, 14. Costs in constant 1990 dollars.

[87] On technology and the forward-basing strategy, see Harkavy 1993. Even after the United States had fully converted to long-range bombers, intercontinental missiles, and nuclear ships with minimal refueling needs, Harkavy argues, the United States still needed forward bases for command, control, communications, and intelligence.

powers and intercept foreign attacks. For most Americans, Pearl Harbor shattered the belief that the United States was protected behind its oceanic moats. Forward bases were necessary to prevent a repeat. General "Hap" Arnold, for instance, advocated meeting "attacks as far from our own borders as possible to insure against any part of the United States mainland being visited by the sudden devastation beyond any Pearl Harbor experience."[88] From bases in Japan, for instance, it would be possible to dominate the Yellow Sea and the Sea of Japan, thereby controlling Asian ports from Shanghai to Vladivostok.[89] "The object of these defensive bases," historian Melvyn P. Leffler concludes, "was to enable the United States to possess complete control of the Atlantic and Pacific oceans and keep hostile powers far from American territory."[90]

Offensively, forward bases were also necessary to bring force to the enemy. Although the new technologies greatly extended the security perimeter, they did not immediately erase all issues of distance. Until further refinements in aircraft and the development of intercontinental ballistic missiles, effective ranges of the new weapons systems remained limited. Until mid-1950, for instance, the United States relied heavily upon the B–29 bomber, which could not fly safely from North America to targets in the Soviet Union. According to James T. Patterson, "Military experts privately estimated that in a war it could take two weeks to drop an atomic bomb on the USSR, by which time the large Russian armies could have swept to Paris."[91] To utilize the new technologies most effectively in an offensive capacity, then, also required that the United States acquire forward bases in the Pacific and Europe. In an overall review of base requirements conducted in September 1945, the Joint War Plans Committee concluded that, in fact, the new technologies demanded that forward bases be established in "areas well removed from the United States, so as to project our operations, with new weapons or otherwise, nearer the enemy."[92]

For some in the United States, the new technologies promised to preserve the country's traditional freedom of action. Taft, for instance, believed that the United States could employ the new technologies to avoid entangling overseas commitments. For the internationalist majority, however, the gains from cooperation were obvious. In responding to the criticism that the United States was abandoning its historic policy of unilateralism, Secretary of State Acheson declared that technology had shrunk the Atlantic Ocean to the size of the Caribbean.[93] As a report to Congress phrased it, Japan now acted

---

[88] Quoted in Duke 1993, 26.
[89] Harries and Harries 1987, 190; Schaller 1985, 54.
[90] Leffler 1984, 350.
[91] Patterson 1996, 122.
[92] Quoted in Leffler 1984, 351.
[93] Kaplan 1988, 35.

as the "west coast" of the United States, or as Secretary of the Navy James Forrestal remarked, exhibiting a distinct confusion over America's place in the world, "China is now our Eastern frontier."[94] As the United States was drawn to a forward-based strategy with outposts both in the Pacific and on the European continent, this strategy required the pooling of American resources with those of other states, combining American weapons and manpower, at least, with foreign territory.[95]

The larger security perimeter adopted by the United States was not only a reflection of political commitments made to others but a cause of those commitments. America's willingness to engage in a forward-based strategy, of course, is partly endogenous. Had the risk of opportunism by its partners been sufficiently high, as in the interwar years, such a strategy might well have been impossible. However, the technological advances that reduced the costs of projecting force also played an independent role. For any given expectation of opportunism, the technological innovations enlarged the security perimeter and made cooperation more attractive. The ability and willingness of the United States to make political commitments to others were conditioned by the larger joint economies produced by the new technologies.

One important implication of the forward-based strategy, and the increased joint economies that followed from it, was a tendency to universalize cooperation. There was widespread agreement among Defense and State Department planners that a larger rather than smaller security perimeter would now best serve America's interests. As the Joint Chiefs of Staff (JCS) summarized the case in 1947, the most distant and peripheral islands are actually the most important, because the goal of a forward strategy is to begin operations "from points farther from our own vital areas and nearest those of the enemy."[96] This did not imply, however, that America's reach was unlimited, as demonstrated by Acheson's important speech in January 1950, in which he declared the Asian mainland and the island of Taiwan outside of the country's defense perimeter—a position that many later criticized as a costly catalyst for the Korean War.[97]

Any effective perimeter also required a complete network of bases. As discovered in 1941, Guam, the largest island in Micronesia and the one most capable of supporting a forward base, was virtually useless without control over the smaller surrounding islands. Thus, as the JCS reasoned, any gaps "tend greatly to weaken if not vitiate the effectiveness of the system as a whole."[98] At the same time, within the largest feasible perimeter, American

---

[94] Quoted in LaFeber 1997, 282 and 257.
[95] See Leffler 1992, 41, 56–59, 112–14, and 226.
[96] Schaller 1985, 57.
[97] Cohen 1993, 55 and 63–65.
[98] Quoted in Schaller 1985, 57.

military predominance had to remain inviolate.[99] As Undersecretary of State Lovett stated in the initial debates over membership in a European alliance, "Greenland and Iceland [are] more important than some countries in western Europe to the security of the United States and Canada." Amplifying, Charles Bohlen, Counselor of the Department of State, argued that "without the Azores [which belonged to Portugal], Iceland and Greenland, help could not be got to Europe in significant quantities at all."[100] If the gains from the new technologies were to be realized, cooperation within the extended perimeter had to be universal.[101]

### Positive Externalities

As in the interwar years, there were significant positive externalities generated from deterring expansionist powers. Two features differed between the periods, however. First, the Soviet threat after 1945 appeared to be more salient and "real" than threats in the early interwar years. Whereas German revanchism after 1919 was a concern, especially to France, most believed the defeated power was unlikely to resuscitate its drive for continental hegemony. The optimists were proved wrong by the events of the 1930s, and the lessons drawn were quickly projected—correctly or incorrectly—onto the Soviet Union. Thus, where the League of Nations was designed as a general deterrent against challenges to the status quo from wherever they might arise, the United States and others quickly singled out the Soviet Union as the most likely challenger. By drawing clearer lines of political division, the positive externalities produced by deterring the Soviet Union were more apparent both to the United States and its partners.

Second, in the interwar period, the United States was able to free ride on Europe effectively, whereas after 1945 it was necessarily in the position of leading the effort to counter the Soviet Union. After World War I, the Europeans had intense preferences for maintaining balance on the continent. After World War II, on the other hand, the United States worried that the Europeans, and to a lesser extent the Japanese, lacked the will and resources to defend themselves against an expansionist Soviet Union. Americans also worried that the internal weakness of many regimes would create a political vacuum into which communist influence would flow, perhaps allowing the

[99] Leffler 1984, 349.

[100] Quoted in Kaplan 1984, 83.

[101] This universalizing tendency in American policy, much criticized by contemporary and later scholars, also followed directly from the need to diversify investments in base sites and reduce potential quasi rents (see below). It tended, however, to make even the most trivial outpost a "vital" American interest—for without these alternate base sites, perhaps inconsequential on their own terms, the price for *existing* bases could be raised significantly; it was also an important impetus behind the over-extended American foreign policy discredited in the Vietnam War. On "overextension," see Snyder 1991 and Chapter 7 below.

Soviet Union to achieve political gains in the West even without using force. The United States also inferred from World War I that the European equipoise, which had resulted in a costly military stalemate, could be decisively shaped by American intervention. After 1945, the fragile states of Europe and Asia were so weak that, even together, they would be quickly overwhelmed by any Soviet offensive. The United States could not stand aside and hope to tip the balance in whatever direction was necessary; rather, its full weight was essential to achieve balance. In 1920, the United States was clearly first among equals, and perhaps even hegemonic (see Table 4.1). By 1949, however, it was almost twice as large as its likely partners taken together. As the largest Western power with the most to gain (in absolute terms), a greater share of the burden would necessarily fall on the United States. After World War II, if the positive externality of deterring Soviet expansion was to be produced, it would have to be done by the United States.

The American policy of "containment," in turn, did create significant benefits for the countries of Europe and Asia. They enjoyed greater security, a reduction in the probability that the Soviets would expand at their expense, without bearing the cost. Although the United States might have provided this public good even in the absence of material support from other states, a position recommended even by the unilateralists, it could reduce its own defense burden by increasing the contributions of others over what they would otherwise choose to provide. Through cooperation, in other words, the United States could hope to increase the production of others or the proportion of their efforts that benefited itself. Although it is impossible to know with certainty what the contributions of others to the joint defense would have been in the absence of explicit cooperation, it was clearly a major ambition of the United States to use its leverage over its partners to ensure that the collective burden was shared, if not equally at least more equally than would otherwise have been the case. Thus the question is not whether the partners got a free ride—which of course they did, in part—but whether cooperation shifted onto them a greater share of the burden than would have obtained if the United States had limited itself to unilateralism.

In the early postwar years, the United States, with some justification, felt that it was carrying the collective defense burden virtually alone. As a Policy Planning Staff report counseled in November 1947, the United States has "borne almost single handed the burden of the international effort to stop the Kremlin's political advance. But this has stretched our resources dangerously far in several respects. . . . In these circumstances it is clearly unwise for us to continue to attempt to carry alone, or largely single handed, the opposition to Soviet expansion."[102]

At American insistence, Article 3 of the North Atlantic treaty specified that

[102] Quoted in Ireland 1981, 54–55.

countries should engage in "continuous and effective self-help and mutual aid."[103] For the Europeans, this article promised them access to the American aid and military resources they so desperately needed. Yet, while its partners focused only on the last word of the phrase, the United States emphasized the concepts of *effective self-help* and *mutual* aid. According to Timothy Ireland, the purpose of this clause, in part, was to signal the Europeans "that once adequate defense levels had been achieved cutbacks in potential American efforts could be expected."[104]

Indeed, the clause was used with some effect to pry greater contributions out of Europe. Even before the final draft of the treaty had been approved, the departments of State and Defense had agreed among themselves "that a clear connection [should] be established between the granting of military aid and negotiations for base rights."[105] And in early March 1949, the American ambassadors to London and Paris were instructed by Acheson to communicate the administration's views on military aid to their respective foreign ministers. Emphasizing that the principle of reciprocity would be central in any aid program, Acheson informed his ambassadors that the Truman administration was "not thinking in terms of 'lend-lease' but of 'mutual aid,'" and that this implied a "coordinated program" in which each ally would contribute "what it most effectively can in manpower, resources, productive capacity or facilities to strengthen the defense capacity of the entire group."[106] Accordingly, under Section 402 of the Mutual Defense Assistance Act of 1949, the United States negotiated bilateral agreements with its partners, signed in January 1950, which specified among other terms "arrangements for securing base and other specific military operating rights" and "a commitment assuring the United States of reciprocal aid, with each party supplying the other with materials it needed for defense production."[107] Although many provisions of the bilateral treaties smacked of nineteenth-century imperialism, base rights, extraterritorial privileges, and—particularly irksome—American oversight of aid utilization through the Military Assistance Advisory Groups, the United States felt they were necessary both to ensure that aid was used effectively and to extract the maximum contributions by the Europeans to the common defense effort.[108]

The ongoing pressure on partners to increase their defense contributions and honor fully their commitments to NATO was institutionalized in the so-called Annual Review, an exercise intended to survey alliance targets and assess the efforts of each member in fulfilling these goals. Although no sanc-

---

[103] Reprinted in Kaplan 1984, 227.

[104] Ireland 1981, 85.

[105] Lovett quoted ibid., 127.

[106] Quoted ibid., 129.

[107] Kaplan 1980, 60.

[108] Ibid., 60–65.

tions for failure could be imposed, members were put in the uncomfortable position of having to justify publicly any shortfalls they might have incurred. This allowed the combined weight of the membership to be brought to bear on significant laggards, even though it also diminished American leverage when *all* members failed to live up to the goals that had been established.[109]

The United States also sought to increase the contributions of others and reduce its own defense burden by rearming the Federal Republic of Germany and Japan. From the earliest days of the Atlantic alliance, the United States maintained that an effective defense of Europe would have to include German rearmament and the deployment of German forces along the central front. Without a German contribution, the kind of forward territorial defense advocated by the Europeans was impossible. France, on the other hand, was adamantly opposed to German rearmament and preferred that the United States supply the additional resources and troops to make a defense at the Rhine possible. As the American contribution to Europe increased and deepened in September 1950, the issue of German rearmament was forced onto the agenda. Indeed, at the foreign ministers' meeting on September 12, only days after Truman announced that additional troops would be stationed in Europe, the American representatives explicitly linked deployment and German rearmament—putting them on a collision course with the French. After some delay, France responded with the Pleven Plan, which proposed that German troops participate in a European Army at the smallest unit level possible and that this army be deployed only after the creation of a European Council of Defense Ministers, a European Minister of Defense, and a European Parliament capable of voting a defense budget. The American and French positions were eventually reconciled in the Spofford compromise, a bargain in which the United States decoupled its troop commitments and the question of immediate German rearmament while France accepted the principle that the additional American troops in Europe were part of a larger effort that included German rearmament in the near future.[110] After a longer delay than the United States originally thought acceptable, German troops entered NATO in 1955.[111]

In Japan, America's ability to control the problem of free riding by rearming the defeated nation was complicated but not thwarted by Article 9 of the Japanese constitution.[112] Apparently drafted and inserted into the constitution

---

[109] Fox and Fox 1967, 143 and 253.

[110] Ireland 1981, 202–7.

[111] For a contemporary review of this debate, see Craig 1955.

[112] America's ability to control Japanese free riding was also hampered by the fears of Japanese revanchism held by other Asian states. Australia and New Zealand were particularly vocal in their concern over possible Japanese imperialism. Far removed from the likely sites of Russian expansionism, and confident that the United States would protect them against external communist threats in any event, these countries feared "that a revived and rearmed Japan would

by MacArthur, Article 9 renounced "war as a sovereign right of the nation and the threat or use of force as a means of settling international disputes" and promised that "land, sea, and air forces, as well as other war potential will never be maintained."[113] It was used to great effect by Prime Minister Shigeru Yoshida to break the political strength of the militarists to his right and resist American calls for rearmament—calls that started soon after the occupation began.[114]

Although the occupation authorities were formally charged to demilitarize the former enemy, at least one high-ranking occupation official—General Charles Willoughby, head of the Far East Command's G-2/Intelligence Section—nonetheless moved immediately upon his arrival in Tokyo to maintain intact the nucleus of the Japanese military.[115] And as in other areas, the limited policies of demilitarization set forth in SWNCC 150/4/A were overturned in NSC 13/2, which stated that "it may well become extremely important to our national security for Japan to be capable of providing some degree of military assistance to the United States, at least to the extent of Japan's self-defense," and called for the creation of a 150,000-man national police force in Japan.[116]

The pressure for Japanese rearmament intensified as the negotiations for a peace treaty shifted into high gear under Dulles. In mid-1950, Dulles made clear to Yoshida that the United States wanted Japan to construct an army, explicitly mentioning a figure of 350,000 men.[117] And during the San Francisco Peace Conference, Dulles endeavored unsuccessfully to persuade Yoshida to draft plans for a force of 300,000 soldiers.[118] Reflecting this continued pressure, the security pact, signed concurrently with the peace treaty, explicitly referred to the "expectation . . . that Japan will itself increasingly assume responsibility for its own defense against direct and indirect aggression."[119]

Although MacArthur initially stonewalled Washington's calls for Japanese rearmament, he too finally relented, withdrawing his opposition to the rearming of Japan just days before the outbreak of the Korean War. On July 8, 1950, he finally ordered Prime Minister Yoshida to create a National Police Reserve of 75,000 men to be equipped and trained by the United States, but

---

again be looking to expand in the South Pacific"; Dunn 1963, 128. To assuage this fear and gain their support for the peace treaty with Japan, the United States negotiated the Tripartite Security Pact (ANZUS) with Australia and New Zealand.

[113] Reprinted in Harries and Harries 1987, xxiv and 216. On Japanese security norms and institutions, see Katzenstein 1996b; and Berger 1996.

[114] Dower 1979.

[115] Harries and Harries 1987, 220–27.

[116] Quoted ibid., 231.

[117] Ibid., 235.

[118] Dower 1979, 386.

[119] U.S. Department of State 1952, 3,331.

TABLE 5.1
Allied and Non-Allied Defense Burdens, 1963

|  | All NATO | NATO Europe | Other Europe[a] |
|---|---|---|---|
| Military Expenditures as a percent of GNP | 7.22 | 5.03 | 3.20 |
| Military Expenditures per capita (constant U.S. dollars) | 208.27 | 102.60 | 45.64 |
| Armed Forces per 1,000 people | 12.24 | 11.29 | 12.23 |

*Source:* U.S. Arms Control and Disarmament Agency 1975, Table 1: 15 and 17.

[a]Although "other Europe" is not formally defined in the source, country data later in the same volume (Table 2) indicate that the category is composed of Albania, Austria, Finland, Ireland, Spain, Sweden, Switzerland, and Yugoslavia.

designated to preserve internal security.[120] In 1952, the National Police Reserve was expanded to 110,000 men, armed with tanks and heavy artillery, combined with an embryonic navy, and renamed the National Security Force.[121]

No one expected Japan or Europe to carry a defense burden equal to that of the United States. At home and abroad, it was recognized that unequal size carries unequal responsibilities, and that a disproportionate burden would necessarily fall on the United States. Nonetheless, the efforts of the United States to ensure that its partners contributed to the joint defense appear to have enjoyed at least some measure of success. Most concretely, the defense burdens of the European members of NATO were substantially greater than those of the non-NATO European states, who also enjoyed some or all of the positive externalities provided by the United States (see Table 5.1). In 1963, the earliest year for which consistent data are available, the European members of NATO spent 57 percent more of their GNP and 124 percent more per capita on defense than European states that were not members of NATO or the Warsaw Pact. Only in the share of the population in the mili-

[120] Harries and Harries 1987, 198 and 234.

[121] Ibid., 198. Under continuing American pressure, Japan signed a Mutual Security Assistance agreement with the United States in March 1954, in which it promised to take "all reasonable measures which may be needed to develop its defense capacities." Quoted ibid., 238. By agreement, the 1954 accord was soon followed by two basic defense laws, which remain the foundation for Japan's armed forces today. Dower 1979, 417. The Defense Agency Law created a de facto Ministry of Defense in the Japan Defense Agency. The Self-Defense Forces Law legitimized the maintenance of permanent armed forces under the constitution, further enlarged the army to 130,000, and for the first time explicitly authorized the emergent military to defend Japan against external aggression. Harries and Harries 1987, 238. In return for these policy initiatives, the United States agreed to supply Japan with $150 million in weapons and military equipment and roughly $100 million in other aid during the coming year. Dower 1979, 467.

tary do the non-NATO states exceed the members, but this higher ratio is driven almost entirely by the case of Yugoslavia (with 18.42 armed forces per 1,000 people) and, in any event, the relative positions were reversed by 1968. Thus, in several dimensions, the European members of NATO carried a substantially greater defense burden than nonmembers. The United States did bear a disproportionate burden, as indicated by the higher averages for all NATO members, but it also appears to have used alliance instruments successfully to shift at least some of the cost onto its partners.[122]

## The Division of Labor

The differing geographic positions and factor endowments of the United States and its prospective partners also created the basis for a division of labor in the production of security. A division of labor, of course, is always available to security partners. The question is whether they take up this opportunity to specialize in particular types of defense effort. In the interwar period, as I argued in Chapter 4, the United States and its potential European partners, facing moderately high risks of opportunism, never contemplated a division of labor in security affairs, and thus deprived themselves of these potential gains from cooperation. After World War II, and with a substantially smaller risk of opportunism, the United States and its partners chose differently and adopted a modest division of labor in producing security. Clearly, the United States and its partners did not specialize fully, as the efforts of Britain and France to develop costly but independent nuclear arsenals dramatically attests.[123] But the question is whether America's security relationships allowed a greater division of labor than would have been possible in their absence. Although the counterfactual is unknowable, the reluctance of countries to specialize even in the context of enduring relationships suggests that the modicum of specialization that did occur was substantially greater than would have otherwise been the case.[124] As William T. R. Fox and

[122] The United States may also have pressed non-NATO European states for greater contributions than they would otherwise have made, but the disproportionate burdens still suggest that pressure within NATO was comparatively more effective. Included here as one of the non-NATO European states, Spain had bilateral security ties to the United States at this time, but was below the mean for its category on every indicator.

[123] On continuing problems of technological innovation and the limited division of labor, see Hobbs 1989.

[124] Estimating the division of labor within NATO, of course, depends upon the choice of the relevant counterfactual—what the deployment of forces across the various services would have been absent the security relationships between partners. If unilateralism was the alternative in many of these relationships, as it appeared to be at the time, two separate defense goals or strategies would have been available to the United States, each of which has different implications for the deployment of forces. One vision of unilateralism was a strict continental defense, as advocated by the small band of bedrock isolationists. In this view, defense efforts would be

Annette Baker Fox conclude, achieving the kind of balanced and collective defense envisioned in NATO "implies some specialization according to capacity, i.e., more specialization than would be likely if each state tried to protect itself and more than would be likely if the implicit or explicit sharing of common objectives was not accompanied by the sharing of plans to realize those objectives."[125]

One basis for the division of labor was the exchange of foreign bases for American troops and the security umbrella they provide. Foreign bases, as discussed above, were central to the strategy of forward defense. But by accepting American bases, the participating countries "specialized . . . by supplying territory and accepting a specific vulnerability to retaliation."[126] The exchange of American aid for foreign bases was an early part of America's postwar strategy, continuing a policy begun in 1940 in the "destroyers for bases" deal with Britain, and further developed in the lend-lease program.[127] Securing bases after the war was central to the negotiations over "mutual aid" under Article 3 of the NATO treaty.

The second and, perhaps, more important basis for the division of labor was specialization by role and capacity. Such specialization was important only with Europe. Micronesia and the Philippines—impoverished, resource-poor, and unable to defend themselves—were expected to depend completely upon the United States for protection. Although they were an essential part of the Pacific perimeter, they could not contribute resources beyond their bases to the American defense effort. Although Japan was expected to be less of a burden, as the aspiration of American planners was to develop Japan's economy and military to the point at which the country could defend itself and thereby relieve the United States of the necessity, the country was not ex-

---

entirely devoted to deterring and, if that failed, coping with a direct foreign attack on American soil. In this case, a strong navy would have been the centerpiece of defense planning, and the unilateral force structure would have been biased in this direction. If this is the baseline, there would appear to have been no division of labor within NATO as it actually existed. This conclusion, however, is based on a very different defense goal than that actually pursued by the United States at this time; it is not the security relationship that is varying in this counterfactual, but the goals of policy. A second vision of unilateralism sought to deter Soviet expansionism and, if necessary, to defend Europe by American arms alone. This was generally the position of the so-called isolationists led by Taft. In this scenario, the United States would have required many more forces and, most likely, many more ground forces than it actually deployed under NATO; the United States might have looked more like Britain, with the army constituting the largest service. This implies that the actual division of labor within NATO was quite substantial. Of the two counterfactuals, only the second holds the goals of American policy constant, and thus allows us to infer the magnitude of the division of labor. Through this lens, it appears that the real division of labor, though far from complete, was nonetheless significant.

[125] Fox and Fox 1967, 128.
[126] Ibid., 129.
[127] Duke 1993, 25 and 36.

pected to contribute to any larger division of labor. In Europe, on the other hand, the expectation was quite different.

From the earliest days of NATO, the United States envisioned a division of labor within the alliance. In 1949, Secretary of State Acheson testified before Congress that the defense efforts of NATO members were to be based on a "logical and practical division of labor" in which "each member of the Alliance will specialize in the kinds of forces and the production of weapons for which it is best suited and which will fit into a pattern of integrated defense."[128] The specific features of the division were then laid out by General Omar Bradley. The United States would assume primary responsibility for the nuclear deterrent and naval forces, whereas Europe would take responsibility for land forces and tactical air power. On the principle that "the man in the best position and with the capability should do the job for which he is best suited," the division would be, according to Bradley,

> First, the United States will be charged with the strategic bombing. We have repeatedly recognized in this country that the first priority of the joint defense is our ability to deliver the atomic bomb.
>
> Second, the US Navy and the Western Union naval powers [i.e., Britain] will conduct essential naval operations, including keeping sea lanes clear. The Western Union and other nations will maintain their own harbor and coastal defense.
>
> Third, we recognize that the hard core of the ground power in being will come from Europe, aided by other nations as they can mobilize.
>
> Fourth, England and France and the closer countries will have the bulk of the short-range bombardment and air defense. We, of course, will maintain the tactical air force for our own ground and naval forces, and United States defense.[129]

The division was obviously not complete; for instance, each country would retain responsibility for its own logistical support.[130] The United States nonetheless envisioned a substantial specialization and sharing of responsibility. This vision, in turn, became the basis for military planning within NATO.[131] The division of labor was somewhat attenuated with the outbreak of the Korean War and the sending of additional American ground troops to Europe, but the principle of specialization remained central to the alliance.[132]

The practice of specialization is reflected in the composition of forces

---

[128] Quoted in Lunn 1983, 10.

[129] Quoted ibid., 10–11.

[130] Fox and Fox 1967, 144.

[131] Kaplan 1988, 39.

[132] Williams 1985, 57. The alliance also made strides, early in its history, in standardizing the production and deployment of weapons; Carlton 1981, 201. Through its postwar assistance to Europe, which often took the form of surplus military equipment, the United States created de facto standardization within the alliance. See Duke 1993, 37; Fox and Fox 1967, 150. Paradoxically, as the European economies rebounded, and defense industries loomed more important in those economies, standardization became more difficult to maintain. Carlton 1981, 203.

TABLE 5.2
Military Personnel by Service, 1955–1961 (in percent)

|              | Army | Air Force | Navy/Marines |
|--------------|------|-----------|--------------|
| United States | 35.6 | 33.0 | 31.3 |
| Britain | 51.5 | 31.2 | 17.2 |
| France[a] | 76.9 | 11.5 | 11.5 |

Sources: United States, Lewis 1989, 23; Britain, Greenwood 1977, 190; France, Martin 1981, 370.

Note: Rows may not add to 100 due to rounding.

[a]The variance within each cell is quite low except for France, where a decisive shift occurs in 1958: Air Force, 1955–1957 = 8.1 percent, 1958–1961 = 14.1 percent; Navy 1955–1957 = 16.1 percent, 1958–1961 = 8.1 percent.

deployed by the NATO states. Figures on the early years of NATO are scarce, and those that can be obtained are generally not directly comparable. One gross measure of the degree of specialization is the distribution of personnel across the various services, depicted for the United States, Britain, and France for the years 1955–1961 in Table 5.2. As is immediately clear, even after the Korean War buildup, the United States employed far fewer of its military personnel in the army than either Britain, which shared naval responsibilities with America, or France, which concentrated almost exclusively on continental defense. Looking across these three states suggests that there was, indeed, a significant division of labor within NATO.

Cooperation promised large benefits to the United States after World War II. The joint economies of producing security were significantly larger after 1945 than before, and thus cooperation was far more attractive during the Cold War than in the interwar years, and far more likely to be chosen by American policy makers. But as the theory in Chapter 3 suggests, joint economies are a necessary but not a sufficient condition for cooperation. Security relationships also depend upon the expected costs of opportunism and governance costs.

OPPORTUNISM

As noted above, the expected costs of opportunism during the Cold War were somewhat ambiguous. The probability of opportunism was quite low. Although it did not fear abandonment by its partners, the United States did face some potential for entrapment and exploitation, both in Europe and the Pacific, but this was not expected to pose a significant problem. On the other hand, precisely because the probability of opportunism was low, the United States was able to invest in the most efficient technologies, even though these required specialized forward bases, and to create a modest division of labor with Europe, even though specialization produced specific assets as a by-product. On net, the benefits of additional investments in technology and the division of labor probably outweighed the increased costs of opportunism—but this reading is based, in part, on a knowledge of the outcome. Even compared to the interwar period, the overall expected costs of opportunism are difficult to estimate.

More clearly, the expected costs of opportunism did not decline significantly with hierarchy, creating little incentive for the United States to pursue more imperial relationships. Modest safeguards could be applied even in anarchic security relationships to manage effectively the risks of opportunism. The occupations of Germany and Japan, in turn, demonstrate that hierarchy was expected to breed resentment that, in the long run, would make it more rather than less difficult to control the potential for opportunism. Exceptions to the relatively anarchic security relationships built by the United States after World War II are of limited analytic utility precisely because they are, in fact, exceptional. The Trust Territory of the Pacific, however, may be the proverbial proof of the rule: in Micronesia, for reasons that are not found in any other significant partner of the United States at this time, hierarchy promised to reduce significantly the potential for opportunism.

## The Risks of Anarchy

The United States did not fear abandonment by its partners, even under the relatively anarchic relationships it chose to adopt. As widely noted, bipolarity restricts the number of viable partners for states.[133] Unable to affect the balance of power materially through their own actions and combinations, states are left to align with one or the other superpower. Britain, at least, was very much aware of this structural constraint. As Bevin wrote his fellow ministers in his bleak summation of the world situation at the end of 1945, "there are two mighty countries in the world which, by the very nature of things, are following the present policy which is certain to see them line up against each other. We in Great Britain who have had the brunt of two great wars will be left to take sides with either one or the other."[134] For states living in the shadow of the Soviet Union, the United States was by far the more attractive pole of the postwar magnet. Given its political and economic dominance, geographic distance and, as we shall see, rapidly escalating governance costs, the United States possessed few imperialist ambitions in the postwar system, whereas the Soviet Union was pursuing precisely this course in Eastern

---

[133] Waltz 1979; G. Snyder 1984 and 1990; Gowa 1994.
[134] Quoted in Cook 1989, 22–23.

Europe. Anarchic relationships with the United States seemed far more promising than unilateralism, which would entail higher defense burdens on populations already exhausted by war, or more hierarchic relationships with the Russians.

The opportunity costs to the partners of terminating cooperation with the United States were also relatively high. As discussed above, the benefits of cooperation for the United States were large—as they were for its partners. The gains from a division of labor were potentially great. And although the partners would receive some benefit from even a unilateral commitment by the United States to contain the Soviet Union, America made clear that its willingness to defend them and its level of aid were dependent upon their participation in a joint, cooperative endeavor. Had America's partners chosen to forgo cooperation, they would have forfeited substantial benefits. Although the Europeans might have been able to counter the Soviet threat on their own, an option of regional cooperation that was entirely lacking in the Pacific, this would have required substantially greater defense burdens and the earlier and more extensive rearmament of Germany. Just such a vision informed the early European discussions of the Brussels Pact, although the rearmament of Germany was still difficult for France and others to contemplate. As the least devastated of the once-great European powers, Britain soon realized that much of the regional burden would fall on its shoulders—a burden that by early 1946 it knew it was ill-prepared to carry. Britain soon became the most vigorous advocate of greater American involvement on the continent.

Thus the United States expected to have relatively loyal partners in both Europe and the Pacific. Pooling resources with the United States promised to be a far more efficient means of producing security than any unilateral or even regional initiatives. By participating in the division of labor, states could conserve scarce resources. By increasing the American contribution to their defense, they could spare themselves an onerous burden. As a result, the United States had little reason to fear abandonment in any form by its partners.

The United States, on the other hand, possessed only moderate opportunity costs for abandoning cooperation. As suggested by the political strength of its advocates at home, unilateralism was a feasible if more costly option. If the costs of opportunism became too high or the costs of constructing and maintaining security relationships grew too large, America's external ties could be jettisoned. Although constrained by bipolarity, the United States also possessed a wide array of middle- and small-sized partners, giving it an additional measure of flexibility. Because of these lower opportunity costs, the Europeans, especially, feared that the United States might abandon them and retreat once again into unilateralism. This fear gave the United States even more leverage over its partners. Since it could go it alone more easily, the United States could link its commitment to its partners to substantial concessions, as it did in the periodic wrangles over burden sharing.

Although the United States did not fear abandonment, it did face a real risk of entrapment or exploitation by its partners. Since it received net benefits, once the United States committed to cooperation it would suffer some cost if its partners defected, and this induced dependence could be manipulated by its partners for their own ends. The joint economies from the forward bases and division of labor also created relationally specific assets and, thus, quasi rents for the United States, which again exposed it to the risk of opportunism by its partners.

The opportunity costs of cooperation created the potential for its partners to entrap or exploit the United States. As Senator Taft warned, the Atlantic alliance threatened to place the United States "at the mercy of the foreign policies of 11 other nations."[135] With the American contribution to their defense, for instance, the Europeans and Japanese did not bear the full cost of any potential conflict. As a result, they had an incentive to engage in riskier or more aggressive actions, knowing that the costs would be borne in part by the United States (up to the point where the gains from cooperation had been entirely appropriated). The Federal Republic of Germany, for instance, could take a tougher stand against the Soviets on the issue of Berlin than would otherwise be possible. Such actions, although rational for the states themselves, threatened to call forth conflicts with the Soviet Union that American efforts were, in part, designed to avoid.

Its partners could also seek to free ride on the United States by urging it to increase its overall defense contribution and assume a larger share of the collective burden. They could also exploit the United States by agreeing to an equitable share of the defense burden and then failing to deliver, either explicitly—by ignoring target force levels, for instance, a problem throughout the history of NATO—or implicitly—by not investing in less easily observed but nonetheless costly activities like training and morale. Indeed, the partners could attempt to shift the collective burden onto the United States until the latter was indifferent between maintaining cooperation and retreating into unilateralism.

As noted in Chapter 3, any division of labor creates some quasi rents, at least equal to the transactions costs of rebuilding a diversified defense capability. The presence (if not the magnitude) of such quasi rents can be inferred from the military plans for the defense of Europe adopted by United States. As embodied in OFFTACKLE, the principal military plan for the late 1940s and early 1950s, the United States envisioned a pullback of NATO forces to the periphery of the continent, a complete American mobilization as in

[135] Quoted in Kaplan 1968, 18.

World Wars I and II, and then a full offensive designed to push the Soviets from the West. The American counteroffensive was not expected to take place until two years after the start of hostilities.[136] Even within a continuing division of labor, the American mobilization for war was expected to be a difficult and costly process. In the absence of specialization, the initial and ongoing costs of a fully diversified American defense capability would have been even larger.

The forward defense strategy also created substantial quasi rents for the United States, especially in the Pacific. As noted above, this strategy required a chain of naval and air bases along the entire western fringe of the Pacific: any break in the chain threatened to undermine the entire strategy. If a large number of suitable base sites had existed, the United States could have chosen among its potential partners; in this hypothetically "thick" market, the quasi rents incurred by the United States would have been relatively low. In reality, however, there were an extremely limited number of first-class sites, particularly in the South Pacific. In this "thin" market, the forward strategy adopted by the United States produced large quasi rents. Whereas base rights in Japan were secured by treaties imposed as a condition of independence, the Philippines remained highly dependent upon the United States, and Guam continued to be an American dependency, the islands of Micronesia were critical free agents. Without control over the surrounding area, as demonstrated in World War II, Guam was of little use; without Guam, the forward defense strategy would be ineffective. As a result, the Micronesian islands as a collective, or even any single intransigent holdout, could potentially appropriate all of the gains earned by the United States from its entire Pacific perimeter. Thus, although the United States enjoyed substantial gains from cooperation, these gains could also be exploited by its partners.

Critics of America's alliance commitments were particularly concerned with the potential for future entrapment and exploitation. In the Great Debate, for instance, Taft worried not about the exigencies of the moment—the Korean War—that necessitated sending additional troops to Europe but, rather, about the tendency of commitments to develop a life of their own and grow with time. Just as the conservative internationalists had opposed an "organic" League of Nations, Taft feared that security commitments made for reasons of expediency could take on independent momentum and prove more enduring or substantial than was prudent. In his view, it was important to safeguard the principles of, first, assistance but not entanglement in European affairs and, second, Congressional supremacy over foreign policy.[137]

Unilateralism remained a potent force in postwar American politics because it articulated forcefully the risk and consequences of opportunism. The

[136] Griener 1985, 151–52.
[137] Williams 1985, 55.

unilateralists maintained that the risk of entrapment and exploitation by partners was too great, even after the war, and that the United States ought to retain its traditional aloofness. These critics of cooperation ensured a full debate in the United States of the twin fears that entangling alliances would put the country at risk through partners it could not control, and that they would force it to bear a disproportionate share of the common defense burden. The internationalists, in turn, estimated that cooperation was preferable to unilateralism despite the risks of entanglement, acknowledged implicitly in the anarchic governance structures created to control the risk of opportunism.

## Safeguarding Anarchy

As noted in Chapter 3, safeguards can be adopted to create specialized governance structures, signal intentions of continuity, and alter the incentives of the parties to any agreement, even anarchic security relationships. Much of the political debate within the United States and the diplomatic struggle between the United States and Europe, on the one hand, and the United States and its Pacific partners, on the other, focused precisely on how to construct effective safeguards within what were still relatively anarchic security relationships.

To safeguard against the risks of entrapment, the United States relied primarily upon its right to withdraw from agreements; the defensive nature of its commitments, as it was required to respond only if an ally was directly attacked; and its right to define unilaterally its appropriate response to unknown contingencies. This can be seen most clearly in Article 5 of the NATO treaty, which specifies the mutual commitments of the partners. The Europeans, of course, wanted formal binding guarantees that an attack on any member would bring a prompt American response—in other words, an immediate and inextricable entanglement. The United States, on the other hand, wanted to avoid any automatic commitment, desiring instead to retain its freedom of action to respond at the time and in the manner of its own choosing.[138] Backed by superior power, and Europe's dependence on American economic and military aid, the position of the United States prevailed.

Although protected by the discretionary nature of its commitments, the United States also developed more extensive institutional safeguards against possible entrapment. As the United States deepened its involvement on the European continent during the fall of 1950, it constructed within NATO a more formal, American-led decision-making structure.[139] In its original form,

---

[138] Ireland 1981, 81; Kaplan 1984, 84.
[139] Ismay 1956; Pedlow 1993.

the alliance was headed by the North Atlantic Council, composed of the foreign ministers of the various members. Subordinate to the Council were the Defense Committee, composed of the defense ministers, and the Defense Financial and Economic Committee, composed of the finance ministers. Under the Defense Committee, in turn, there was a Military Committee, composed of the chiefs of staff. At the lowest rung of the organizational ladder stood the Regional Planning Groups, divided into separate committees for the North Atlantic Ocean, Canada-United States, Western Europe, Northern Europe, and Southern Europe and Western Mediterranean. Within this structure, the Regional Planning Groups were expected to be the center of activity, with the majority of the planning and integrating of forces occurring at this level.[140]

As the Atlantic alliance got on its feet, and especially as the Korean War accelerated the defense plans of the member states, the cumbersome nature of the original design was revealed. In September 1950, member states decided to integrate their forces under a centralized command, and General Dwight D. Eisenhower was appointed to the position of SACEUR, responsible to the Military Committee. SACEUR gradually emerged as "the most influential center for military policy," replacing the Regional Policy Groups.[141] NATO decision making was further consolidated in 1951 when the Defense and Defense Financial and Economic Committees were consolidated into the North Atlantic Council. A further consolidation occurred in 1954, when a secretary general, always a European, and a permanent secretariat were created, along with a Supreme Allied Commander Atlantic, Canada-United States Regional Planning Group, and a Channel Committee.

Decisions within the North Atlantic Council require unanimity, thus giving each member a veto.[142] Despite this anarchic rule, the United States occupies critical nodes, especially the position of SACEUR, giving it a decisive voice in the formulation of policy and deployment of forces and introducing a small element of hierarchy into the alliance. Whereas the secretary general and permanent secretariat are responsible to the Council alone and not intended to represent their countries within NATO, the SACEUR serves simultaneously as the commander of all NATO forces in Europe, responsible ultimately to the Council, and commander of all American forces in Europe, responsible to the president.[143] This divided responsibility and loyalty, in turn, implicitly gives the United States a check on how its integrated forces are employed as well as how the other national contingents within NATO are used, reduc-

---

[140] In May 1950, the Council created the Council Deputies, who thereafter met in continuous session. The Council Deputies selected Ambassador Charles M. Spofford, an American, as their permanent chair.

[141] Fox and Fox 1967, 27.

[142] Ibid., 26.

[143] Ismay 1956, 55.

ing the likelihood that the United States could be entrapped by the organization or by errant members pursuing their own agendas. Through this small degree of hierarchy, NATO forces are prevented from acting in ways that might contravene the interests of the United States. Although the Europeans could still on their own act more provocatively than the United States might desire, the president would at least have some advance warning and an ability to restrain his more adventuresome partners.[144]

The United States also sought to change European and Japanese incentives in order to safeguard against abandonment by its partners. It pursued three broad strategies to increase the attractiveness of cooperation to the Europeans and, to a lesser extent, the Japanese, and thereby increase the costs of abandoning the United States.[145]

First, security cooperation was embedded into a larger series of economic agreements. Even before the war ended, the United States, Britain, and other countries began planning for and negotiating a series of regimes governing relations in international trade, money, and finance.[146] The Bretton Woods international monetary regime, creating the International Monetary Fund and International Bank for Reconstruction and Development, was signed in 1944 and the General Agreements on Tariffs and Trade in 1947. These regimes, negotiated prior to the NATO treaty, eventually facilitated an unprecedented level of international economic exchange. They also enhanced the value of cooperation more generally. Not only did they create cross-issue linkages and the basis for strategies of reciprocal punishment (such as "tit for tat"), but they also raised the costs of breaking the external security relationship with the United States. If Europe and Japan were to defect from their security commitments to the United States, they would place their economic gains at risk as well.

Second, the United States also increased the opportunity costs of the Europeans by backing independence for their remaining colonies. After the war, the United States feared that the Europeans, and particularly Britain and France, would turn inward, both economically and politically, upon their empires, threatening American plans for an economically open and politically aligned Atlantic community. Through its anti-imperialist rhetoric and, in some cases, material support for noncommunist independence movements,

---

[144] The institutional constraints imposed by NATO on European adventurism contrast sharply with the behavior of America's partners elsewhere in the world. With American aid in Europe, for instance, both the French and Dutch were freed to fight colonial wars in Southeast Asia— conflicts which, some American officials believed at the time, diverted necessary resources from Europe and threatened to embroil the United States in areas outside of its self-defined security perimeter. In this particular case, the unilateralists were all too prescient.

[145] On the integrated nature of the grand strategy pursued by the Truman administration, see Leffler 1992.

[146] See Gardner 1980.

the United States sought to raise the costs of empire to the Europeans, thereby making a policy of Atlantic cooperation comparatively more attractive.[147]

Finally, in addition to the specific safeguards embodied in Article 3, emphasizing mutual aid and the rearming of Germany and Japan, the United States more generally sought to limit future free riding by rebuilding Europe and Japan as co-equal partners in the fight against communism. In Japan, this took the form of reversing the punitive economic policies adopted early in the occupation. In Europe, it took the form of direct aid.

Planning for the occupation of Japan began several years before the war ended and culminated in the Potsdam Protocol. In SWNCC 150/4/A, the SCAP was instructed to dismantle Japan's armed forces, establish a representative government, and promote individual liberties, free speech, and a free press. Seeking to go beyond mere demilitarization and the elimination of direct war potential, the SWNCC directive and other early instructions also sought to eradicate the Japanese social structures that had fueled the country's expansionist tendencies. In this task, the central building blocks were to be the construction of a democratic political system with secure individual freedoms and economic reform, with the latter focusing on reparations and deconcentration.[148]

By the summer of 1947, as noted above, the Truman administration had already begun to reconsider the wisdom of its economic policies in Japan. As America's new strategy of cooperation began to take shape, military and civilian planners concluded that the United States had little alternative but to promote recovery in Japan as its first priority. In April 1948, total reparations were scaled back from targets of 990 million yen to only 102 million.[149] NSC 13/2, issued in October, further reduced this total. The program was declared "successfully terminated" in May 1949. Deconcentration also fell into increasing disfavor. MacArthur initially opposed the breakup of the Zaibatsu or industrial combines that, in American opinion, bore substantial responsibility for Japan's militarism. A reluctant convert to deconcentration, his efforts in this area, ironically, now came under vicious attack as "socialistic." In May 1948, the Deconcentration Review Board overturned or amended almost all of the original 325 reorganization decrees issued under the new Japanese legislation. As Edward C. Welsch, head of SCAP's Anti-Trust and Cartels division summarized, "What was initially considered . . . a major objective of the Occupation [had] become . . . a major embarrassment."[150] Coupled with this reversal was the beginning of substantial economic assistance modeled on the Marshall Plan. Whereas previous American aid was

---

[147] On the security dimensions of decolonization, see Lake 1987; and Hager and Lake, forthcoming.

[148] Schaller 1985, 24–25.

[149] Ibid., 35.

[150] Quoted ibid., 130.

limited to humanitarian assistance, Congress approved direct economic aid and raw materials credits in June 1948, thereby completing Japan's transition from enemy to ally.[151]

The effort to rebuild Europe, initiated earlier, was far more extensive.[152] Embodied in the Marshall Plan, American aid was designed to get Europe back on its feet, undercut the political appeal of communism, and rehabilitate the "old world" as an effective actor on the international scene.[153] America's partners would then be better able to provide for their own defense and the United States could shift a larger share of the common burden onto their shoulders.[154]

In the early postwar period, before the Cold War had become fully engaged, the American aid program emphasized restoring Europe as an independent—but Western-oriented—center of power capable of meeting its own defense needs. As Kennan wrote in October 1947, "it should be a cardinal point in our policy to see to it that other elements of independent power are developed on the Eurasian land mass as rapidly as possible in order to take off our shoulders some of the burden of 'bi-polarity.'"[155] This same point was repeated, not surprisingly, in an influential report of the Policy Planning Staff issued the next month.[156]

The emphasis on economic recovery remained even after the Cold War was underway and the alliance was formed, although now it was explicitly understood that European resources would be marshaled in tandem with those of the United States. "Recovery is the first objective," Secretary of State Acheson stated before the Senate Foreign Relations Committee in April 1949, "and therefore the new military production, the military efforts we are talking about here, are all limited and controlled by the prior necessity for recovery in Europe."[157]

Throughout both periods, it was widely accepted that European economic recovery was a necessary alternative to greater American rearmament and

---

[151] Ibid., 132.

[152] Although treated here as part of the larger project of European recovery, American policy toward Germany paralleled that in Japan.

[153] The effort at European reconstruction was also reflected in American support for and, indeed, advocacy of political and economic integration, which would enable Europe to develop the economic vitality latent in a continent-wide market. Integration would also help solve the "German problem" by embedding the defeated country's economic and military might in supranational institutions of control.

[154] Weber 1991 attributes the attempt by the United States to rehabilitate Europe as a major international pole to an innate belief, held by American leaders, in the superiority of multipolar international systems. In my view, the rehabilitation of Europe was attractive only because this third pole was expected to be firmly allied with the United States, and thus the system was not expected or desired to be multipolar in the traditional sense.

[155] Quoted in Gaddis 1987, 58.

[156] Ireland 1981, 55.

[157] Quoted in Gaddis 1982, 62–63.

involvement in European defense. This is seen most clearly, perhaps, in the testimony of Secretary of State Marshall, Secretary of the Army Kenneth Royall, and Secretary of Defense James Forrestal on the Marshall Plan before the Senate in January 1948. Repeating a theme raised by all three, and clearly against his own bureaucratic self-interest, Royall explicitly argued that European recovery would go "a long way toward reducing the necessity for a larger national armament in the future and probably reducing our present armament."[158] Only one senator, Bourke Hickenlooper (R-IA), even bothered to challenge the view that a restoration of Europe would ease the American defense burden.[159]

Cooperation between the United States and others did not emerge of its own accord. Rather, it was actively constructed and nurtured by building effective but nonetheless broadly anarchic safeguards against the risk of opportunism. Protected by a general convergence of interests, the United States employed a network of commitments designed to secure the advantages of cooperation at an acceptable cost. Resting on the self-interest of the participating states, these safeguards helped shape and maintain a pattern of cooperation that persisted from 1947 to the end of the Cold War.

## The Limits of Empire

In the American occupation zone of Germany, in Japan, and in Micronesia, the United States faced conditions conducive to postwar imperialism. All three partners were essential to a forward defense strategy, due to geography in the cases of Japan and Micronesia and pressure from other European states in the case of Germany. Japan and Germany were despised and defeated enemies—usually infertile ground for building trust between partners. Yet only in Micronesia did the United States annex territory. In Germany and Japan it sought to speed their return to sovereignty and full partnerships in the "family of nations"—a favorite phase of American diplomats of the period.

The occupations of Germany and Japan suggest that empire was typically ineffective in restraining the potential for opportunism by America's partners. In the views of nearly all officials, a prolonged period of American rule threatened to turn Germany and Japan against the United States, strengthen support for the local communist parties, and increase the likelihood that each would seek to align itself with the Soviet Union.[160] By failing to hasten the rehabilitation of Germany and Japan, the United States would increase

---

[158] Quoted in Ireland 1981, 59.

[159] Ibid., 60.

[160] This "enlightened" and long-term perspective contrasts sharply with that of the Soviet Union in Eastern Europe, which repressed its partners and made, over the long term, unwilling partners out of possible friends. See Gaddis 1997, esp. 284–87.

the chances that, once they did reacquire their sovereignty, they would with-draw from America's sphere of influence. This implies that the probability of opportunism did not decline significantly with greater hierarchy.

In the unusual circumstances of Micronesia, on the other hand, the ex-pected costs of opportunism in anarchy were high and fell dramatically with hierarchy, helping to explain this anomaly in American policy. In Micronesia, independence threatened opportunism of another kind. In the absence of any indigenous state to ally with, an agreement made with anyone claiming to represent the region would quickly become worthless in the vacuum of Micronesian political life. Imperial rule was the best and perhaps only way to secure an American presence in the islands.[161] The case of Micronesia sug-gests that American restraint after World War II was not simply the result of a philosophical aversion to imperialism, as often implied by analysts, but rather followed from a careful calculus of costs and benefits.

### GERMANY

In the "Declaration Regarding the Defeat of Germany," prepared after the unconditional surrender of Germany, the victors claimed complete sover-eignty over the defeated territory.[162] Yet, despite Germany's subordinate status under the occupation, permanent domination or the melding of the defeated areas into a formal American empire was never considered. Indeed, one of the most remarkable features of the American occupation was the consistent assumption that, duly de-Nazified and democratized, Germany would return to the family of nations as a full and equal partner. In the Declaration, the blunt sentence assuming full sovereignty in Germany by the allies is followed immediately by another, noting that this "does not effect the annexation of Germany."[163] Likewise, in the protocol issued on August 1, 1945, at the Pot-sdam Conference of the Big Three, the allies agreed that one of the four purposes of the occupation was "[t]o prepare for the eventual reconstruction of German political life on a democratic basis and for eventual peaceful co-operation in international life by Germany."[164] Elaborating, the joint declara-tion stated that

> [I]t is not the intention of the Allies to destroy or enslave the German people. It
> is the intention of the Allies that the German people be given the opportunity to
> prepare for the eventual reconstruction of their life on a democratic and peaceful
> basis. If their own efforts are steadily directed to this, it will be feasible for them
> in due course to take their place among the free and peaceful peoples of the
> world.[165]

---

[161] This argument obviously parallels the Gallagher and Robinson 1953 thesis on the "imperi-alism of free trade."

[162] Reproduced in Stares 1990, 40–45.

[163] Ibid., 40.

[164] Reprinted in U.S. Congress, Senate 1961, 31.

[165] Quoted in Botting 1985, 153.

Finally, in an important address at Stuttgart in September 1946—a speech that marked the end of the Carthaginian peace envisioned by the "Morgenthau Plan"—Secretary of State James Byrnes echoed this same position. "Freedom from militarism," he declared, "will give the German people the opportunity, if they will but seize it . . . to show themselves worthy of the respect and friendship of peace-loving nations, and in time, to take an honorable place among the members of the United Nations."[166] Although some officials debated whether the reorientation of German social, political, and economic life would take three, five, forty, or—in the view of at least one military officer on the ground in postwar Babenhausen—three hundred years, no one questioned either Germany's eventual return to sovereignty or that the occupation should be and was in fact designed to facilitate this end.[167]

Central to this calculus was a widely shared belief that a permanent occupation of Germany promised to be counterproductive, either threatening a permanent revisionism or driving a disaffected populace into support for the communists in East Germany and the Soviet Union. The best way to secure a peaceful Western-oriented Germany, many American officials believed, was to begin devolving political power onto indigenous leaders as soon as possible. This view was neatly captured in a policy summary authored by General Lucius D. Clay, then deputy military governor of Germany and later elevated to governor, in July 1946.

> No country can regain its self-respect nor progress in maturity in democratic processes in the presence of large occupying forces. . . . Basically, the most important objective to the peace of the world is to create a democratic state in Germany which can be received in confidence as a member of the United Nations. This objective can be accomplished best with a minimum of outside control and with token forces, provided that the occupying powers stand firmly together so that Germany will recognize that any deviation from Allied objectives will bring swift retribution. Allied control over Germany should be exercised at the earliest possible date through leadership and not through command.[168]

This view was seconded by Byrnes in his Stuttgart speech. "It is the view of the American Government," he declared, "that the German people throughout Germany, under proper safeguards, should now be given the primary

---

[166] Reprinted in U.S. Congress, Senate 1961, 56.

[167] Forty years was the period most commonly used by high American officials to estimate the necessary length of the occupation. See Byrnes speech at Stuttgart, ibid., 55–62, and Clay's memorandum in Smith 1974, 242. The outside estimate of three hundred years is from an anecdote in Davis 1967, 18, and is based on the period of time that Rome occupied England.

[168] Reprinted in Smith 1974, 243. This policy summary was suppressed by the State Department because Clay had deviated from several points in JCS 1067 and the Potsdam agreements. Clay nonetheless argued that this was, in fact, the policy he had been operating under as deputy military governor. Although Clay subsequently threw it "in the waste basket," this policy memorandum appears to have formed the basis for Byrnes's Stuttgart speech the following September. See ibid., 254–55.

responsibility for the running of their own affairs. . . . The American Government has supported and will continue to support the necessary measures to de-Nazify and demilitarize Germany, but it does not believe that large armies of foreign soldiers or alien bureaucrats, however well motivated and disciplined, are in the long run the most reliable guardians of another country's democracy."[169]

Failure to devolve political responsibility, on the other hand, would have dire consequences for the political future of Germany and the balance of power between East and West. According to Clay, an admitted "cold warrior," the United States should move quickly to establish an indigenous government for western Germany. "The resentment of the Germans against colonial administration," he wrote in November 1947, "is increasing daily and those democratic Germans who hate communism and would prefer to establish the type and kind of government which we desire will soon lose their positions of leadership with their own people." While noting that there was no precedent for what the United States was trying to do in Germany, Clay concluded that "I cannot emphasize too strongly that a failure on our part to take the lead in establishing such a government will not only seriously damage our position of prestige in Germany, which now stands at an all-time high, but in doing so will encourage Communist penetration which we may not be able to stave off. The Germans can do a better job of fighting communism in Germany than we can as an occupying power, and they do want this opportunity."[170] Whereas an early return to self-rule would have the positive effect of solidifying democratic forces in Germany, prolonged occupation would have the negative consequence of increasing Soviet influence in the territory, with deleterious consequences for American interests.[171]

Thus, the concern that western Germany might become disaffected and, at best, neutral rather than a supporter of the West in its emerging struggle with the Soviet Union vitiated any possibility of a prolonged occupation. As

---

[169] Reprinted in U.S. Congress, Senate 1961, 60.

[170] Reprinted in Smith 1974, 476–77.

[171] This same logic held on both sides of the emerging "Iron Curtain," creating a competition between the Western powers and the Soviet Union to transfer political power from the allies to local German authorities—regardless of whether or not society had been sufficiently prepared to support democratic institutions. This competitive process appears to have been initiated, perhaps unwittingly, by the Soviet Union, which was more interested in reparations than in punishing Germany's transgressions. As Brigadier General Frank Hawley, the American commandant in Berlin, noted in his diary, "The Russians . . . from the start freely recognized the Germans as liberated, whereas we have considered them a conquered people." Quoted in Barnet 1983, 29. Compelled to respond to the more liberal Soviet policy, the United States accelerated the process of devolving self-rule onto the Federal Republic. As Alfred Grosser 1955, 39, concludes, "the reacquisition of sovereignty by Germany had been intended to follow the growth of democratic sentiment and achievement. In reality, however, it began immediately the east-west schism developed."

Acheson reflected, "Our best hope was to make [our] former enemies willing and strong supporters of a free-world structure. Germany should be welcomed into Western Europe, not kept outside in limbo . . . relegated to maneuvering between the Soviet Union and the allies."[172] Sounding a similar theme, Henry Byroade, overseeing German affairs at the State Department, warned that "If we fail to inspire the Germans . . . with a genuine conviction that they are on the road to full restoration of their legitimate prerogatives as a nation, they will almost certainly turn to the East. In that event we would lose Germany by default and Russia would make a long stride toward the battle for Europe."[173] Cooperation with a sovereign Germany, even one in which the roots of democracy remained tender, appeared to be a more viable long term strategy than imperial domination. The longer the United States held onto Germany the more likely it was to resent and resist American leadership.

While steadily loosening the reins and moving away from formal control, the United States, in conjunction with its wartime allies, nonetheless retained a hierarchical security relationship with Germany for almost two decades. Given Germany's past wars against its neighbors, its potential for revanchism in hopes of reunifying the country and regaining territories lost to Poland, and the country's position in the forward defense of Europe and its contribution of ground troops critical to the shared allied effort, the allies felt it necessary to hold onto important rights of residual control.[174]

Full sovereignty was retained by the allies for four years until the promulgation of the Occupation Statute in September 1949, which authorized and recognized the Federal Republic of Germany. While conveying full legislative, executive, and judicial powers to the Federal and Lander governments, the allies nonetheless reserved broad powers for themselves, including the right to veto all internal legislation and withdraw all powers conferred by the statute in case of emergency.[175] Although this statute stopped short of creating an empire, the allies nonetheless held significant residual rights of control over a broad range of domestic issues. The Occupation Statute was subsequently revised in March 1951, when the Federal Republic obtained partial sovereignty over its external relations, further reducing the rights of residual control and transforming Germany into an incomplete protectorate.[176]

[172] Acheson 1969, 338. See also Leffler 1992, 280.
[173] Quoted in Leffler 1992, 319.
[174] See Stares 1990, 1–19.
[175] Grosser 1955, 44; Clay 1950, 428–29.
[176] Grosser 1971, 294. The allied occupation was officially terminated in the Bonn Convention, signed in Paris in October 1954. At this same time, the Federal Republic became a member of the reorganized Western European Union (WEU), formerly the Brussels Pact, and NATO (effective May 1955). In joining the WEU, the Federal Republic agreed to incorporate all of its military forces into NATO (a requirement not imposed on any other member), forswear the right

It is important to note that Germany did not greatly resist this lingering hierarchy. It readily accepted, even actively embraced, the restraints on its freedom of action. Germany recognized that these reduced rights of residual control were the price it had to pay for economic and political integration into the "West," integration that the nascent regime desired to protect itself from threats both at home and abroad. This acceptance makes it difficult to define the relationship between Germany and the United States, as hierarchy is often evident only when the subordinate party strains against its fetters (see Chapter 2). It is unlikely, for instance, that the United States would have tolerated a unified but neutral Germany in the center of Europe had Konrad Adenauer and other early postwar German leaders supported Stalin's efforts in this direction. It is even more difficult to imagine that the United States would have accepted any security relationship between West Germany and the Soviet Union—clearly revealing that, even at its most autonomous, the Federal Republic remained firmly embedded within an American sphere of influence. In any event, the United States did not need to restrain Germany greatly, as all parties recognized and accepted the constraints as they existed.

JAPAN

The American occupation of Japan, although differing in its particulars, paralleled that of Germany in its essentials. As in Germany, the United States assumed that Japan would eventually return to the family of nations as a full and equal partner. A February 1944 planning document asserted that Japan's status would evolve through three stages: one of complete subordination, a second of close surveillance but relaxed direct control, and a third of full independence in which the vanquished country would "properly discharge her responsibilities in a peaceful family of nations."[177] Similarly, the Potsdam Proclamation declared that after Japan had been duly demilitarized and democratized, the occupying forces were to be removed.[178] The only question was not if but when Japan would regain its sovereignty.

Many American policy planners feared that in Japan a prolonged occupation would prove counterproductive, strengthen the hand of the communists

---

to manufacture atomic, biological, or chemical weapons on its territory, and abstain from the use of force to achieve reunification or the modification of its frontiers. Balfour 1982, 184; Grosser 1971, 307. Thus, Germany was allowed to rearm, but only under significant restraints, thereby abridging its ability to conduct an independent foreign policy. On the other hand, Stares 1990, 15–17, argues that German forces are not wholly controlled by NATO and, indeed, their relationship to NATO is not dissimilar from that of other countries. In July 1963, the Status of Forces Agreement officially transformed American forces stationed in Germany from an occupation army into invited guests of the Federal Republic. Davis 1967, 278. Finally, in May 1968, the three allies informed the Federal Republic that their rights of intervention in an emergency had lapsed—leaving it an almost but not quite sovereign state. Grosser 1971, 79.

[177] Dunn 1963, 32–33.
[178] Ibid, 39–40.

internally, and increase the likelihood that a resentful Japan, once freed from American occupation, would align itself with China or the Soviet Union. This view dominated in the State Department. By early 1949, Acheson and his advisors became convinced that the occupation was nearly past its prime, given the apparent success of the reverse course, and that it would soon pay diminishing rewards while eliciting greater Japanese resentment.[179] Holding that a treaty was necessary to ease the "growing uneasiness and restiveness among the Japs," especially in light of the communist advance in China, Acheson warned that unless Japan recovered its sovereignty soon it might prefer an accommodation with the "Commie system in Asia." The longer the occupation dragged on, the more "easy prey to Commie ideologies" Japan would become.[180] In Acheson's view, the occupation "was a wasting asset" that, if continued, would eventually strengthen anti-American sentiments and drive Japan into the communist bloc.[181]

The military, however, strongly disagreed with this assessment.[182] Maintaining that Japan was essential to the newly adopted forward defense strategy, the JCS, Defense Secretary Louis Johnson, and Under Secretary of the Army Tracy Voorhees all opposed an early American withdrawal and doubted that a prolonged occupation would sacrifice Japan's future friendship.[183] Far from fearing Japanese alienation from the United States, the JCS maintained that— given the "debacle" in China and the "developing chaos on the Asian mainland, together with its communistic trend"—America must not let Japan slip from its grasp.[184] Suspicious of Japan's loyalty and fearful of potential opportunism, Pentagon officials warned that Tokyo might take advantage of its sovereignty to become neutral or align itself with the Soviet Union.[185] Better, the military argued, that a peace treaty be postponed as long as possible.

By early 1950, however, the differences between the State and Defense Departments had begun to narrow and the British suggestion of separate peace and security treaties was already on the table. The final logjam was broken by Dulles's appointment in May 1950 to negotiate a Japanese peace treaty. Clearly identified with conservative Republican circles, Dulles nonetheless delighted State Department officials by dismissing most of the military's case against an early peace treaty with Japan. Believing it vital to retain

[179] Schaller 1985, 165.

[180] Quoted ibid., 166; see Dunn 1963, 82.

[181] Acheson 1969, 428–29.

[182] MacArthur, most likely for reasons of personal expediency, dissented from the prevailing view of the military, a position that did much to alienate his superiors in the Pentagon. Buckley 1982, 72; and Schaller 1985, 215.

[183] Schaller 1985, 165; Dunn 1963, 86–87.

[184] Quoted in Schaller 1985, 167.

[185] Ibid., 248. Officials in the army's Civil Affairs Division, responsible for occupation policy, generally shared the State Department's views on the counterproductive nature of the occupation. Leffler 1992, 255.

Japan's goodwill and friendship for the future, Dulles echoed Acheson's fears that further delays might permanently undermine Tokyo's willingness and ability to align with the United States. Should Japan become anti-American, he asserted, no number of foreign troops or bases would make a difference.[186]

With Dulles's support and through his efforts, the peace treaty was rapidly negotiated, and full sovereignty was returned to Japan. Unlike the situation in Germany, where important residual powers were retained, the United States possessed formal rights only over the military bases that it negotiated as a condition of peace and sovereignty. As in Germany, the absence of effective resistance makes it hard to establish the precise nature of the security relationship between the United States and Japan. The United States was unlikely to accept a neutral Japan or, worse, one allied with the Soviet Union, suggesting that Japan at least fell squarely within an American sphere of influence. Moreover, its dependence on the United States for security suggests that a truly autonomous foreign policy was not possible. Important restraints on what it could (and could not) do in foreign policy remained, even after the return to sovereignty. As Dulles wrote to Acheson, "it is inconceivable that . . . Japan should pursue foreign policies which cut across those of the United States."[187] Despite strong neutralist and pacifist blocs within the country, Japanese leaders wisely chose not to press the limits of American tolerance, and accepted the restraints of the protectorate imposed upon them.

In summary, the United States had much to lose and little to gain from a postwar strategy of imperialism in Germany and Japan. In both, the costs of rule were sunk. In a strong consensus, however, imperialism was believed to be counterproductive. The risk of opportunism would not be significantly lower in empire than in spheres of influence or loose protectorates—or not sufficiently lower to justify the substantial costs of imperial rule (discussed below). To the extent that this calculus held in Germany and Japan, it was even more true in the rest of Europe and the Pacific, where the costs of obtaining imperial control had not yet been absorbed. Although the counterfactuals of actual anarchic security relationships are normally impossible to observe, the occupations of Germany and Japan clearly demonstrate that, in American eyes at least, hierarchy was not an effective tool over the long term for reducing the probability of opportunism.

### TRUST TERRITORY OF THE PACIFIC

Micronesia has had a long history of imperial rule. Granted to Spain in 1493 by Pope Alexander VI in the papal bull that divided the non-European world between the Iberian powers, it was only in 1521 that the islands were actu-

---

[186] Schaller 1985, 254.
[187] Quoted in LaFeber 1997, 293.

ally "discovered" by Magellan. Not subdued and brought under direct Spanish domination until after 1668, Spanish rule lasted a little over two centuries, coming to an end in the late nineteenth century: in 1885, Germany established a protectorate over the Marshall Islands, the United States seized Guam in the Spanish-American War of 1898, and Germany took advantage of Spain's subsequent weakness to purchase the Caroline Islands for $4.5 million. Under a secret agreement with Great Britain, Japan occupied all of Micronesia except Guam during the opening days of World War I; Japan later governed the islands under a class "C" League of Nations mandate. The United States, in turn, fought a series of hard and costly battles to conquer the islands during World War II.

As early as 1942, the army and navy began preparations for the occupation of Micronesia, but it was not until February 1947 that a draft trusteeship agreement for the islands was submitted to the United Nations.[188] The strategic trusteeship eventually extended over Micronesia gave the United States a status Secretary of State Byrnes described as "tantamount to sovereignty."[189]

There was a wide consensus within the United States government at this time on both the strategic value of the islands and the need to keep them under American control. As in the case of Japan, military planners argued for the permanent incorporation of the islands so as to retain indefinitely unfettered control of all potential base sites in the region.[190] In early 1946, the JCS informed the secretary of state that, in their view, it was "essential to national defense . . . to gain strategic control of the Japanese Mandated Islands by assuming full sovereignty over them"; Secretary of War Henry Stimson concurred, arguing that the islands "must belong to the United States with absolute power to rule and fortify them."[191] Yet, as we have already seen in the occupation of Japan, strategic necessity need not produce imperialism. Even given the strategic advantages of Micronesia, we must still answer the question why, in this exceptional instance, the United States chose imperialism over cooperation.

---

[188] Gale 1979, 47.

[189] Quoted ibid., 47.

[190] Ibid., 53–59; Heine 1974, 4.

[191] Quoted in Gale 1979, 56. More cognizant of the diplomatic repercussions of the military's demands, the State Department opposed outright annexation for two reasons. See Louis 1977, 68–87 and 512–31. State Department officials feared that formal incorporation of Micronesia would stimulate similar actions by the Soviet Union elsewhere in the Pacific. As Secretary of State Cordell Hull noted, if the United States were to annex Micronesia, "Russia would thereupon use this acquisition as an example and precedent for similar acquisitions by herself." Quoted in Gale 1979, 52. This position was later undercut when the Soviet Union announced in February 1946 that it planned to retain control of Japan's northern islands. Ibid., 59. As discussed above, the broader American strategy of decolonization, backed by President Franklin D. Roosevelt, Truman, the State Department, and, in other contexts, the military, also constrained American options in the South Pacific.

Where American officials feared that in Germany and Japan prolonged foreign rule would increase the eventual risk of opportunism, these same officials were convinced that in Micronesia the absence of imperial rule would culminate in a different form of abandonment—the immediate political collapse of the region. Although the United States might otherwise have preferred anarchy over hierarchy, there was no state in Micronesia to ally with, a problem not found elsewhere within the American defense perimeter. Even in the Philippines, reflecting earlier success, a strong indigenous leadership had emerged by the 1930s and was ready to rule in America's stead. It was not that the costs of opportunism, if it were to occur, were any greater in Micronesia than in Germany, Japan, or the Philippines. Especially in the latter two partners, the necessary ports were equally "strategic"—that is, specific and central to the relationship with the United States. What differed in Micronesia was the absence of a state with whom to enter into a relatively anarchic security relationship.

There were three areas of concern for American policy makers, all stemming from the legacy of colonial rule.[192] First, the islands could not produce the economic surplus necessary to support a regionwide political infrastructure. Unlike the first and second imperial rulers of Micronesia, Japan had actually begun to develop the islands and integrate them into its economy. With Japan destroyed as a regional and economic power, the islands were left without an infrastructure, as the Japanese had controlled all interisland transport and trade, and without an export market, as all produce had been shipped north to Tokyo. In addition, many of the islands were severely damaged as a result of the fighting between American and Japanese troops. With a subsistence economy and the devastation of the war, the prospects for development appeared dim.

Second, there was no tradition or mechanism for self-rule in the islands. Although it is not clear what precolonial political forms existed, the islands had failed to develop an indigenous political elite or local political institutions during their four centuries of imperial governance. In 1945, Micronesia was, in a very real sense, a political tabula rosa. Before the islands could hope to enter into international agreements some form of local political rule had to be created and institutionalized.[193]

Third, there was no national or "Micronesian" identity through which to forge a unified political entity. Under previous rulers, the individual islands had been discouraged or sometimes prohibited from interacting with one another. The many different regional languages also impeded unity, as did the absence of a indigenous, territory-wide newspaper. Even symbols of

---

[192] See Gale 1979, 47.

[193] In addition, whereas American officials feared that in Germany and Japan a continued occupation would strengthen the local communists, there were no indigenous political movements of any stripe in Micronesia, with the possible exception of Modekgnei, a Palauan religious cult that began as an anti-Japanese movement. Ibid., 111.

unity were lacking. As late as the 1960s, Micronesia had no flag, no anthem, nor any of the other trappings of a nation state. Without the centralizing presence of a foreign ruler, the islands, spread across an area the size of the United States, might have fractured into a series of smaller political units and undermined America's interests in the area, for the strategic value of the islands lay in their potential as staging areas from which hostile powers could mount operations against Guam.[194]

Thus, at the time the trusteeship was adopted, there was no state in Micronesia. This constituted a severe threat of opportunism to the United States—not a threat of conscious defection, as elsewhere, but one of unintentional default through political collapse. Even if an indigenous leader had emerged, it was unlikely that anyone could secure power for long in Micronesia's political vacuum. Combined with the quasi rents generated by America's forward defense strategy, this threat of political instability indicated that the expected costs of opportunism would be substantial in an anarchic security relationship, but substantially lower in more hierarchic and direct forms of rule. Empire was, thus, perhaps the only security relationship that could uphold America's interests in the region.

In conclusion, the probability of opportunism after 1945, while not insignificant, was clearly lower than in the interwar period. This permitted the United States to invest in greater joint economies and enjoy greater benefits from cooperation. For most partners, the expected costs of opportunism did not decline significantly with hierarchy. Outside of Micronesia, imperialism threatened to be counterproductive. These features suggest that the United States would be inclined toward both cooperation and relatively anarchic security relationships after World War II. Nonetheless, the specific form that cooperation would take depended, as well, on governance costs.

## GOVERNANCE COSTS

The governance costs of anarchic security relationships were relatively low in the postwar era. The United States was able to safeguard against opportunistic behavior by its partners effectively and at minimal cost to itself. The governance costs of more hierarchical security relationships, on the other hand, threatened to be quite high—except in the Trust Territory of the Pacific.

### The Costs of Anarchy

A key question in the postwar policy debate was whether it was possible to safeguard relatively anarchic security relationships at a cost that did not exhaust the gains from cooperation. Given the high costs of hierarchy (see

[194] Nevin 1977, 71.

below), nearly all analysts recognized that with most countries in Europe and the Pacific, the United States was limited to relatively anarchic security relationships.

The unilateralists, and even more so the isolationists, were pessimistic: the gains from cooperation were small, the risks of opportunism large, and most important, the costs of safeguarding American interests high. The internationalist majority, on the other hand, drew a more optimistic and, as later events confirmed, largely correct conclusion. In important ways, the internationalists recognized that anarchic relationships could be embedded in and safeguarded through a broader network of international economic and political ties that were desirable on their own terms. In this way, security cooperation could be reinforced at little cost and, in turn, security relationships could be used to bolster other forms of cooperation as well. This minimized the direct costs of safeguarding these security relationships. The United States also absorbed the potentially significant costs of signaling its intentions to its partners and, in turn, restraining its own behavior. Given the dominant position of the United States after the war, however, these costs were not large, either.

As noted above, the United States sought to draw its partners into American-led security relationships by enmeshing them into a series of larger economic relationships and dismantling their imperial systems. Given its economic hegemony, and its belief that it would benefit from an open and stable international economy, these are actions the United States might well have taken anyway, even if security cooperation had not been an additional aspiration.[195] The United States also sought to reduce incentives for free riding by rebuilding Europe and Japan as strong, coequal partners. In light of its need for foreign markets, and the lessons drawn from the economic instabilities of the interwar period, this too was a policy the United States might have followed even had it chosen to pursue security unilaterally. America's international economic leadership, well described by others, was not simply a byproduct of its security policies.[196] That economic leadership was otherwise in the interests of the United States clearly implies that its cost as a safeguard on security cooperation was minimal. Indeed, given the mutual benefits received by the United States and its partners, economic openness might not have imposed any real costs at all. The issue of whether economic desires drove security relationships or vice versa, which has tortured many histories of the Cold War, need not be resolved here. Rather, what is important is that America's economic and security relationships reinforced each other in a mutually beneficial way that served to minimize the governance costs of cooperation.

---

[195] This is based on the theory of economic hegemony. See Gilpin 1975 for a classic statement dealing with much of this period. For a review of this literature, see Lake 1993.

[196] Calleo and Rowland 1973; Krasner 1976; Gilpin 1987.

More costly to the United States was the need to signal its intentions to its partners and constrain its own freedom of action. The United States primarily demonstrated its commitment not to abandon its partners through the negotiation and ratification of the North Atlantic Treaty and the Great Debate. From the perspective of traditional international relations theory, formal treaties are curious documents.[197] Since no third party exists to enforce treaty commitments, states will live up to their promises only if it is in their interest to do so, but if it is in their interest to carry out promised actions, then the document itself is irrelevant. Yet the North Atlantic Treaty was critical to solidifying United States-European relations after World War II. Although not codified into a formal document, Truman's actions in the fall of 1950, which precipitated the Great Debate, had much the same character. These actions did not change the effective role of the United States in Europe, no greater commitment was undertaken, and the right to change the future status of the American troops assigned to NATO was not abridged. Rather, Truman merely augmented and changed the symbolic status of the American troops. Why then did the Great Debate matter?

In both the formal treaty ratification and the Great Debate the actions of the Truman administration were potentially costly, both to the reputation of the country as a whole and to Truman personally, who would have been politically weakened and humiliated had the measures failed in Congress. By demonstrating a willingness to absorb these political costs, the Truman administration and, later, Congress signaled the value they placed on the new security ties to Europe and the Pacific. By putting the country's reputation "on the line," and risking an important legislative defeat, Truman and to a lesser extent Congress indicated they were willing to pay some significant cost to come to the aid of their partners. Having witnessed the willingness of the Truman administration and, by Congressional ratification, the country as a whole to pay these costs, the partners in turn could be more confident that the United States would come to their aid if ever called upon to do so. The informal relationship that existed prior to 1949, which did not explicitly tie the reputation of the United States to the defense of its partners, or even an executive agreement that would have allowed Truman to escape the domestic costs of a legislative rebuke would not have signaled the same commitment. Recognizing this, the partners, and especially Britain, continually pushed the United States to enter into a formal treaty, arguing that only such a document, duly ratified by the Senate, would quell lingering European fears of American abandonment.[198] That the United States and the Truman administration did not, in the end, actually absorb these political costs, which would have been imposed only if the country or Congress rejected the obligation to defend Europe, is somewhat immaterial. Rather, the important point is that

[197] Morrow forthcoming.
[198] Ireland 1981, 83–85.

the administration placed itself and the country at risk of bearing such costs. In ratifying the treaty and supporting the commitment of troops to NATO, Congress and the public at large proved that America's promise to aid Europe was credible, and not simply "cheap talk."

Its partners also imposed costly constraints on the foreign policy of the United States. The restraining effects of America's partners were clearly evident, according to William T. R. Fox and Annette Baker Fox, in the case of Berlin, where after the wall went up critics complained "that the United States was being held back from a bolder course by allies who were less eager to take 'tough' and perhaps provocative measures."[199] In other cases, the constraints on American policy are more difficult to estimate. Fox and Fox nonetheless conclude that "the calculations of American officials were modified" by the reactions of NATO members, with some effects on defense policy. They quickly add, however, that "to what extent and specifically by whom, even the policy makers might have difficulty in saying."[200] Reflecting on the Cold War, Gaddis has recently argued that the constraints on the United States, especially in NATO, were deep and profound. In his more expansive view, America's partners shaped which countries would enjoy its protection—Italy, but not Spain; the form that protection would take, especially the placing of American troops in exposed, tripwire positions and the delayed rearming of Germany; and, partly, the heavy reliance on nuclear forces. Even more telling, in his retrospective,

> The Americans even allowed NATO's concerns to shape their policies outside [Europe]. Objections from allies, as much as anything else, kept the United States from escalating the Korean War after Chinese intervention. Fears of a backlash within NATO discouraged Washington from pressing the French to end their debilitating colonial wars in Indochina and Algeria. Eisenhower gave Adenauer a veto over negotiations with Moscow on German reunification, even as he gave in to pressures from other NATO allies to meet the new Soviet leader at the 1955 Geneva summit. And surely Eisenhower's and Kennedy's responses to the alleged strategic missile "gap" of the late 1950s and early 1960s would make little sense without taking into account their hypersensitivity to NATO's interests.[201]

As the more qualified position of Fox and Fox suggests, estimating the constraints imposed on the United States is difficult, as it depends upon a counterfactual analysis of what the country would have done in the absence of partners. The United States might have checked itself from, say, using atomic weapons in Korea even if its partners had not exerted substantial pressure to avoid this breach of the nuclear "firewall." On balance, the United States was constrained at the margin by its partners. As with the broader economic and

---

[199] Fox and Fox 1967, 122.
[200] Ibid., 105.
[201] Gaddis 1997, 201–2.

political strategies adopted to modify the incentives of its partners, however, many of these supposed constraints were in the country's own self-interest. As a result, they carried few significant governance costs.

As a final piece of the puzzle, it is important to note that most of these constraints emanated from America's European partners. Not only were these partners stronger than those in the Pacific, and better able to assert their wishes against American resistance, but the coalitional structure of NATO, welcomed by the United States, may well have served to magnify their leverage. By itself, multilateralism is not necessarily a more efficient organizational form. As Steve Weber suggests with particular reference to NATO, "multilateral institutions may substantially increase the transactions costs of making decisions, particularly when the alliance must negotiate contributions to its budget or the collective provision of scarce resources like manpower." Coalitions also dilute the power of the dominant state. "If security is indivisible and an attack on one is an attack on all," Weber reasons, "the hegemon loses the ability to differentiate among its allies. . . . This minimizes the hegemon's coercive power and its ability to extract payment for protection. It makes the sanctioning of free-riders difficult, because the threat to abandon any particular state as punishment loses credibility."[202] Thus, at first blush, multilateralism in NATO can be understood to cut against America's interests.[203] Together, the member states can more readily restrain the United States when it seeks to act against their interests. In this sense, the coalitional form of NATO may have served to strengthen the constraints on the United States. Where the United States prompted the Europeans to act multilaterally in the economic arena, making Marshall Plan aid contingent on a joint request, the Europeans were the primary advocates of multilateralism in the security arena. Even Britain was intent upon diluting its "special relationship" with the United States by broadening the Atlantic alliance into a nearly European-wide entity. This same mechanism is central to America's security relationships in the post–Cold War era (see Chapter 6).

In summary, there were governance costs for the United States even in its relatively anarchic relationships. The country paid to alter the incentives of its partners and accepted constraints on its own freedom of action. These costs, however, were not very significant, largely because the United States might well have pursued quite similar policies anyway. Empire promised to be quite different.

---

[202] Weber 1991, 7–8; see Fox and Fox 1967, 26.

[203] But note that the United States insisted that all military assistance be negotiated bilaterally between itself and the recipient country. This ensured that the leverage of the United States remained robust on the issue of free riding—which in many ways was more politically sensitive in the United States than the security guarantee itself.

## The Costs of Empire

At the end of World War II, the United States found itself in control of the territory of Germany, Japan, and Micronesia. It had absorbed the costs of conquering these areas for reasons entirely unrelated to postwar security relationships. The costs of creating hierarchies in these states were already "sunk," and therefore could be safely left aside. The United States needed to calculate only the continuing costs of rule. In this section, I focus on the direct costs of rule in the occupied territories. There are also substantial indirect costs that stem from distorted incentives in the subordinate partner—some but not all of which are likely to be compensated by the dominant state. For reasons discussed in Chapter 3, these distortions are likely to multiply over time, and the periods under review here are quite short. Thus, the costs discussed here are the minimum, not the maximum, costs of hierarchy. Even so, the costs of empire were substantial, at least in Germany and Japan. Generalizing to other cases in which the costs of establishing control over others were not already absorbed, this suggests that hierarchical security relationships were almost prohibitively expensive during the Cold War.

Although it is difficult to find exact figures, the United States appears to have operated its occupation forces in Germany at a deficit, failing even to recover its expenses.[204] The Germans were expected to pay all costs associated with the occupation, and they bore a substantial burden during a period in which many Germans were living at or below the subsistence level: between 1946 and 1950, between 26 and 42 percent of all tax revenue collected in Germany was reserved to pay for the occupation and in 1951–52, occupation costs amounted to 6.3 percent of Germany's gross national product.[205] Yet, the United States, noting that it paid the salaries of its troops and provided them with all necessary personal and military equipment, consistently maintained that it was spending far more than it received from Germany in reimbursements, and may have been spending four times more than the Germans for the occupation forces.[206]

Given the economic devastation of the war, Germany could hardly have paid more. Indeed, the opposite was the case, as substantial financial assistance became necessary soon after the end of hostilities simply to keep the population alive. Between 1945 and the end of the occupation in 1955, the United States alone contributed over $4 billion to the Federal Republic in

---

[204] Occupation costs were not budgeted separately from other military costs in the United States and the value of matériel provided by the Germans and Japanese—often through requisitions—is difficult to ascertain. For both of these reasons, even "ballpark" figures should be treated skeptically.

[205] Grosser 1955, 90; Davidson 1961, 265.

[206] Davidson 1961, 261, 265, and 297.

Marshall Plan and other economic aid.[207] Far from being a source of gain for the United States, the war-devastated German economy could not even support the costs of daily rule. The Anglo-American occupation zones, merged in "Bizonia" in 1946, were costing taxpayers in the United States and Britain over $600 million per year—a level of subsidy from victors to vanquished unparalleled in world history. Germany was clearly a case where, in a strict pecuniary sense, empire did not pay.[208]

Similarly, although again exact figures are not available, the cost of the American occupation of Japan is estimated to have cost more than one million dollars a day. Not including army expenses, direct American aid rose from $108 million in 1945/46, to $294 million in 1946/47, and to $357 million in 1947/48.[209] In 1949, overall occupation expenses amounted to approximately $900 million.[210] As in Germany, the occupation of Japan was very costly.

Governing the Trust Territory of the Pacific, however, was not exorbitantly expensive. In 1948, the first full year of American rule, Congress appropriated only $1 million for all expenses in the territory. Throughout the 1950s, Congress authorized a yearly ceiling of $7.5 million, but appropriations never met this cap, reaching a high of $6.15 million only in 1958.[211] Moreover, of these expenditures approximately $1.5 million was raised in local revenues each year from transportation and other user fees.[212] Although the actual costs of rule were greater than the revenues generated in the territory, expenditures were not large, and pale by comparison to those in Germany and Japan.

The lower cost of empire in Micronesia was not simply a function of the devastation of the war. In the island-to-island fighting of World War II, Micronesia suffered equal if not greater damage than Germany or Japan. Likewise, the lower costs were not the product of the level of development or geography. Sharing many characteristics, the Philippines received far greater aid after the war than Micronesia, even though it was now an independent

---

[207] Ibid., 259; Zink 1957, 263.

[208] Botting 1985, 216 and 110. This should be contrasted with the case of France, which appears to have at least broken even in running its occupation zone. In 1948, *Die Welt* published figures showing the occupation costs in the American zone were approximately 122 Reichsmarks a year per German in 1946–1947, while those in the French zone were 194 Reichsmarks (this still contrasts favorably with the Soviet zone, in which occupation costs were 438 Reichsmarks per capita). The *Stuttgarter Zeitung*, in turn, calculated that the whole French Army in 1949 had cost France about 4.5 billion deutsche marks, or 10,000 marks per soldier (this included the war in Indochina). This was almost exactly the cost of the occupation per soldier to the Germans in the French zone. Davidson 1961, 261–63.

[209] Dunn 1963, 62 and 67.

[210] Schaller 1985, 82.

[211] Figures do not include expenditures on Guam.

[212] Nevin 1977, 81; Gale 1979, 104.

state embedded within an American protectorate. In the first eight years after independence (1946–1953), total American aid to the Philippines is usually placed at about $2 billion dollars, or roughly $250 million per year—more than fifty times greater than similar expenditures in Micronesia.[213] Thinly populated with few aspirations of economic development, Micronesia was easy to rule and required only a minimal infrastructure. Only after 1962, when new demands for independence began to be heard, did the United States expand its programs of political and economic development, and only then did the price tag of empire begin to rise.[214]

That the Trust Territory would not be self-supporting was recognized early on. A 1948 navy document observed, for instance, that the "islands cannot be expected to be self-supporting. . . . [they] are a liability and an inevitable charge on the public purse."[215] But with the joint economies produced by possession of the islands—which, with Guam, were most likely comparable to those derived from bases in Japan or the Philippines—it is not unreasonable to conclude that the Trust Territory provided net benefits.

In all three cases examined here, imperial relationships were costly, but far less so in the Trust Territory than in Japan and Germany. In the absence of an indigenous state and in the presence of large quasi rents, an anarchic security relationship with Micronesia would have entailed very high expected costs of opportunism. Low governance costs allowed the United States to choose an empire in this exceptional case. In Germany and Japan, and by extension in the rest of Europe and Asia, American decision makers calculated that a prolonged occupation was almost certain to stimulate defection and alienate potential supporters of the United States. With the high cost of rule, an empire could not be long endured. Anarchic relationships appeared far more promising.

## CONCLUSION

American security cooperation after World War II was rooted in the large joint economies of producing security, especially those created by the new technologies and the positive externalities of deterring possible Soviet expansionism, and the low probability of opportunism, which allowed the United States to create even larger joint economies by investing in forward bases and a division of labor despite the relationally specific assets these investments entailed. Compared to the interwar years, the benefits of cooperation were substantially greater. This permitted the United States to break with its traditional unilateralism and enter into new security relationships in both Europe and the Pacific. No policy, of course, is the result of a single variable. As

[213] Smith 1958, 118.
[214] Gaffaney 1995.
[215] Quoted in Nevin 1977, 82.

outlined in the theory, and shown in this case, joint production economies and the expected costs of opportunism are interactive. Moreover, had the expected costs of opportunism or the governance costs been larger, cooperation would have been far less promising, irrespective of the joint economies available to the United States. At the very least, policy would have been far more contested, perhaps sparking a repeat of the deep political divisions of the interwar period. At most, high expected costs of opportunism or governance costs could have caused cooperation to be rejected once again. Cooperation was likely but not inevitable after 1945.

The choice of security relationships, in turn, was driven by the expected costs of opportunism and governance costs. The expected costs of opportunism are, as noted above, difficult to measure. As revealed by the occupations of Germany and Japan, however, American decision makers clearly estimated that these costs would not decline significantly with greater hierarchy. Imperialism of any sort, in their view, would prove counterproductive. This produced only limited incentives for more hierarchical security relationships.

Around this general expectation, however, there was considerable variance. Where interests were closely aligned, as between the United States and Britain, there were few expectations of significant opportunism. Britain was "trusted" because its goals and aspirations matched those of the United States, and because it was dependent upon the United States militarily, politically, and economically. Under such circumstances, all else held constant, we would expect an alliance to be the preferred security relationship, and of all of America's partners, Britain comes closest to this ideal. Where support for an Atlantic partnership was less evident, and especially in France or Italy where domestic instability was high and some future relationship with the Soviet Union was not entirely out of the question, a sphere of influence was constructed to ensure continued American control.

Elsewhere, there were substantial specific assets at risk, raising the expected costs of opportunism. Especially in the Pacific, but also in central Europe, forward bases created large quasi rents that could be easily appropriated by America's partners. In these dyads, we would anticipate more hierarchic relationships to control the risks of opportunism. As expected, we find a formal empire in Micronesia, a temporary empire evolving quickly into a less than full protectorate in Germany and Japan, and a protectorate in the Philippines.

Governance costs were low, on average, but they rose rapidly with greater hierarchy. For most dyads, the governance costs of anarchic relationships were quite small. America's interests could be safeguarded easily within its broader strategies of economic recovery and openness. On the other hand, empire was prohibitively expensive, as the occupations of Germany and Japan again demonstrate. Rapidly escalating governance costs inhibited the United States from seeking greater control over its partners. Why subordinate Britain or France when the need was small and the costs of building anything other than a largely anarchic security relationship enormous? The answer is sufficiently obvious that, in most cases, hierarchy was never consciously considered—although the deep involvement of the United States in Italy's internal affairs in 1947 suggests that this might be a marginal instance. The costs of keeping Germany and Japan in subordinated positions compelled the United States to return them to sovereignty quickly and govern them lightly. Even the Philippines proved to require substantial subsidies. Only in the Trust Territory of the Pacific were the governance costs of empire sufficiently low to justify an American empire.

One of the most remarkable features of American foreign policy during the Cold War was its essential continuity.[216] The policies adopted during the crucial years detailed above endured with few significant changes until the final collapse of the Soviet Union's informal empire in Eastern Europe in 1989. The Atlantic bargain forged during the founding of NATO and the Great Debate remained intact, while the American-Japanese security relationship stayed strong.

Only in Micronesia did American policy change appreciably prior to the end of the Cold War. As domestic political institutions were cultivated under American rule, indigenous demands for greater autonomy and, in some cases, independence grew as well.[217] Recognizing again the risk of disaffection inherent in imperial rule, the United States moved without significant hesitation, beginning in the late 1960s, to reestablish its regional ties along less hierarchical lines. Micronesia is today organized into five political units. Guam remains an unincorporated territory of the United States and the Republic of Palau, while currently acquiring the institutions of self-rule, is still under the strategic trusteeship. The Federated States of Micronesia and the Republic of the Marshall Islands became sovereign, self-governing states in "free association" with the United States in 1986; under this status, the United States is responsible for their defense and other specified services and for providing economic assistance. At this same time, the Northern Mariana Islands became a commonwealth in political union with the United States. For these latter states, America's imperial rule has evolved into protectorates.

In terms of the analysis developed in this chapter, this overall continuity in American security relationships is not unexpected. Joint economies, although reduced, remained large and significant throughout the Cold War. The expected costs of opportunism stayed moderate and "flat." Governance costs were low, and almost always rose sharply with hierarchy.

Yet NATO was continually described as unraveling, in a state of perpetual

---

[216] Krasner 1989; McCalla 1996; Wallander and Keohane 1995. On changes in NATO over time, see Treverton 1985; and Duffield 1995.

[217] Gaffaney 1995.

crisis, or on the brink of disaster.[218] Tensions over security issues with Japan were also high. Many of the disagreements that plagued America's relations with its partners were rooted in the positive externalities and, correspondingly, issues of burden sharing discussed above. Whenever positive externalities are created, states can reduce their individual costs by shifting the burden onto others. The sense of attendant crisis in NATO was often simply atmospherics created by members as they jockeyed for advantageous positions from which to bargain over their shares of the costs and benefits of producing security. Although disagreements threatened to undermine friendly relations between partners, disputes over burden sharing were not necessarily signs of imminent collapse. Rather, they suggested that substantial joint gains were being produced by the cooperative enterprise, and that they remained significant enough that states were willing to devote resources and risk diplomatic conflict in order to appropriate a greater share.[219]

Three exogenous changes, however, exacerbated the problem of burden sharing among the United States and its partners. First, the gradual decline of American hegemony, a process underway since the early 1950s, forced a nearly constant reconsideration of the "appropriate" burdens carried by individual states. Whereas the United States sought to reduce its relative contribution in line with its declining capacity, its partners, as might be expected, resisted any expansion of their burden, despite their now greater ability to carry a heavier load. Although its share of NATO defense expenditures remained approximately 25 percent greater than average until the end of the Cold War, the United States did come to bear a less disproportionate defense burden than in the early postwar years.[220] This reduction was, obviously, a source of conflict. Moreover, the decline in the American defense burden was reversed in the late 1970s and early 1980s, as the United States, but not its partners, met the collective pledge of May 1977 to expand defense spending by 3 percent a year. Although the Reagan administration steadfastly avoided politicizing this issue for fear of undermining domestic support for its rearmament program, this trend further magnified tensions within the alliance.

Second, even before the historic collapse of the Soviet Union, the changing nature and level of the Soviet threat reduced the magnitude of the positive externalities produced by the policy of containment. By the late 1960s, the West correctly perceived that Soviet expansionism was wanning and now posed a reduced threat to the countries of Europe and the Pacific. Policies of Ostpolitik and détente appropriately followed. Despite the failure of détente, Soviet activities in Africa during the mid-1970s, the Soviet invasion of Afghanistan in 1978, and President Ronald Reagan's "evil empire" rhetoric, this

[218] Among others, see Calleo 1987.
[219] On burden-sharing struggles in NATO, see Treverton 1978.
[220] Oneal and Elrod 1989, 446.

sanguine view of the Soviet Union endured. Beset by mounting domestic problems, the Soviet Union was increasingly perceived to be a status quo power; although it might seek to take advantage of opportunities within the periphery, it was unlikely to expand directly east or west. Although this "mellowing" of the Soviet Union had been a key objective of American foreign policy since the war, it nonetheless magnified tensions over burden sharing. To the extent that the Soviet Union no longer desired expansion, it no longer needed to be deterred. The positive externalities produced by containment were proportionately reduced—but not, of course, eliminated, as few argued that the Soviet Union harbored absolutely no designs on Western Europe. Prudence also dictated that some deterrent force remain in place. Nonetheless, the net benefits of cooperation were reduced by the shrinking positive externalities.

Third, as the Soviet Union attained nuclear parity with the United States in the late 1960s, military strategy shifted from massive retaliation to flexible response, which allowed for graduated escalation and reemphasized conventional war-fighting capabilities.[221] At the extreme, deterrence based upon massive retaliation is purely public in nature: any transgression against any partner would elicit an American first strike on the Soviet Union. Deterrence based upon flexible response is less public, as the actual decision to defend any specific territory is determined only in the management of the overall level of risk. Necessary to maintain credibility in the face of Soviet nuclear parity, a flexible deterrent reduced the magnitude of the positive externalities previously captured by the alliance, further politicizing issues of burden sharing.

With the changes in both the level and nature of the Soviet threat, the benefits of continued cooperation, while still substantial, shrank over the 1970s and 1980s, and the basis for the relationships maintained by the United States since 1947 was weakened. Although the United States might not have formed the same security relationships in, say, 1970 that it chose in the immediate postwar years, cooperation and its relatively anarchic security relationships endured. Nonetheless, when the Berlin wall was torn down and the Cold War ended in 1989, the relationships constructed and maintained by the United States were already fragile. The end of the Cold War further reduced the positive externalities provided by deterring the Soviet Union. Relations became more fractious, and the probability of opportunism rose. Analysts quite reasonably concluded that the remaining years of America's postwar security relationships were numbered.[222]

Contemporary internationalists, however, are loathe to let the considerable postwar investment in international cooperation depreciate (for a more com-

---

[221] On flexible response and positive externalities, see ibid., 440; and Murdock and Sandler 1984. On the politics of flexible response, see Duffield 1995; Kugler 1991; and Stromseth 1988.
[222] Waltz 1993, 76.

plete discussion of the current debate, see Chapter 8). Internationalists see NATO, in particular, as an effective instrument that will allow the United States to continue to reap the benefits of the substantial joint production economies built and reinforced during the Cold War. To sustain these relationships in the absence of the Soviet threat, internationalists propose two futures for NATO.

First, NATO can go "out-of-area," that is, deploy force under the auspices of the alliance outside its member states. The substantial joint production economies created through the organization would be used as the foundation for a more general strategy of collective security, but one firmly under the control of the United States and its current partners.[223] The theory above suggests that this is a wise and sensible strategy, but the United States must think carefully about how to safeguard itself against partners with now more diverse security interests.

Second, NATO can be "enlarged" by inviting former Warsaw Pact states to become members of the organization.[224] As we saw above, NATO always had the dual purpose of containing the Soviet Union and integrating Germany into Europe. The hope is that the organization can continue these roles by containing Russia and folding the nascent capitalist democracies of the East into the West. This strategy has two flaws that are highlighted by the theory. At least in the short run, the new Eastern European members will lack the economic capacity to upgrade their militaries to Western technological standards, will not participate in the division of labor, and will not contribute significantly to the public good of collective defense; indeed, their primary reason for joining is to free ride, in one form or another, more effectively on the Western members. Expanding membership will reduce the joint economies produced by the alliance as a whole, even if existing members can segregate the newcomers in ways that do not dissipate completely the gains from cooperation. In addition, inviting in fragile states with substantial internal problems, different geopolitical interests, and little desire to participate in the sorts of out-of-area operations noted above threatens to increase the risks of opportunism for all—old and new alike. Existing members may get drawn into disputes in the East they might otherwise avoid and new members may feel compelled to participate in operations far from home. Both problems threaten to reduce significantly the expected benefits of cooperation and may fatally weaken the organization. In this case, rather than strengthening existing security relationships and wedding the United States more firmly to a policy of international security cooperation, NATO expansion may ultimately prompt the United States to retreat, once again, into unilateralism.

---

[223] Not only would taking NATO out-of-area enable a division of labor to be sustained, but it might also reduce Europe's free riding on the United States in other areas of the globe. See Gombert and Kugler 1995.

[224] For the a history of the decision to enlarge NATO, see Goldgeier 1998.

## Chapter 6

## GULLIVER'S TRIUMPH

IN NOVEMBER 1989, the Berlin Wall fell, symbolically ending the Cold War that had divided East and West since World War II. The collapse of the Soviet Union following an attempted coup in August 1991 further eroded the bipolar division of the postwar era. These events were greeted in the United States with a sense of relief, even wonderment.

In 1968, as the public consensus that had sustained America's foreign policy during the Cold War was breaking apart on the shoals of Vietnam, Stanley Hoffman wrote of a "crisis of complexity" in world affairs.[1] Like Gulliver in the classic story by Jonathan Swift, Hoffman suggested, the United States was a giant bound by an international system that it understood only poorly.

Today, although the world is no less complex, the United States possesses an unprecedented freedom of action in international affairs. Released from the constraints of Cold War competition, it is the dominant superpower, free to act where and when its interests and desires lead. Ironically, the greatest challenge to the United States today is to tie its own hands—to bind itself against the potential for opportunism inherent in its "unipolar moment," lest it scare smaller states, the Lilliputians, into rising up against it.[2]

The primary restraint on American power, sometimes eagerly embraced by the United States, has been an unprecedented willingness to shape but then work within the prevailing international consensus on the ends and means of foreign policy. Most concretely, the United States has willingly and actively constructed ad hoc coalitions whenever it has chosen to use force in the post-Cold War era. It has also appealed to and received authority from the United Nations to lead these coalitions. This strategy is not only the product of burden sharing, the desire to internalize the widely shared benefits of policing the world. Nor is it simply a normative response, the product of a peculiarly American way of projecting power onto the world stage. For the United States, building coalitions and securing international support is also a self-conscious attempt to safeguard others—and itself—from the potential for opportunism that inheres in its present position of global dominance.

Enjoying unparalleled capabilities and the ability to act unilaterally in world affairs if it so chooses, why is the United States cooperating with others rather than acting alone? Why is it building generally anarchic relationships rather than hierarchies under its control? In September 1993, in a

[1] Hoffman 1968.
[2] The phrase is from Krauthammer 1990/91.

speech widely recognized as outlining the foreign policy foundations of the first Clinton administration, Anthony Lake, then assistant to the president for National Security affairs, stated that "only one overriding factor can determine whether the U.S. should act multilaterally or unilaterally, and that is America's interests. We should act multilaterally where doing so advances our interests, and we should act unilaterally when that will serve our purpose." He concluded by observing that "the simple question in each instance is this: What works best?"[3] This is certainly the right question, but unfortunately Lake did not offer an answer.

In this chapter, I pose a preliminary response by examining two defining instances of recent American foreign policy: the Persian Gulf War in 1990–1991 and the intervention into Somalia in 1992–1993. Despite the clear differences in the these conflicts and in the magnitude of the American response, they are strikingly similar. In both, the United States evinced a new willingness to work with the international community in setting its foreign policy goals, and formed ad hoc coalitions of states to carry out the missions. It adopted a clear policy of international cooperation and, with the exception of the Persian Gulf states during the war, generally anarchic security relationships.

The two cases suggest that the same variables can, when taking different values, nonetheless combine to create similar outcomes. In the Persian Gulf War, large joint production economies interacted with high (in the Gulf) and moderate-to-low (with others) expected costs of opportunism that declined slowly with hierarchy, and high governance costs that rose rapidly with hierarchy to produce protectorates over the Gulf states and alliances with others. In this case, the coalition resulted from both the substantial joint economies in cooperation and the need to safeguard dependent and subordinate Gulf states against American opportunism. In Somalia, with negligible joint production economies (which might normally be expected to result in unilateralism), low expected costs of opportunism (which declined slowly with hierarchy), and low governance costs (which rose rapidly with hierarchy), the United States chose anarchic alliances. Cooperation proceeded in this unfavorable environment only because the expected costs of opportunism, even in anarchy, and governance costs were virtually nil. In Somalia, the coalition did not constrain the United States, but served only to signal Washington's limited and humanitarian ambitions in the region.

## THEORETICAL EXPECTATIONS

The Cold War competition between the United States and the Soviet Union was like a "black hole," a collapsed star of sufficient weight that it traps

---

[3] A. Lake 1993, 663.

everything—including light—within its gravitational field. For most of the postwar era, the pull of the superpower competition was strongly felt. Regional conflicts that might have escaped the attention of great powers and remained autonomous under other circumstances were seized and inevitably drawn into the Cold War's grasp. Each superpower feared that the other might gain some advantage by intervening in a regional conflict. To block such gains, each superpower had to be ready to intervene, even preemptively. Reputational concerns reinforced this incentive: many feared that forsaking a potential partner in need would undermine commitments to other partners. Regional disputants, in turn, could gain substantial and perhaps decisive assistance by appealing to one or the other superpower. Knowing this, each regional party was compelled to make such an appeal lest its opponent gain at its expense. In this dangerous courtship, regional parties were compelled to request aid and the superpowers were bound to grant it. Regional conflicts quickly escalated into tests of superpower will and capacity, and a single, overarching cleavage was imposed upon international politics.[4]

The collapse of the Soviet Union and the end of the Cold War broke this black hole apart, freeing each superpower from the need to anticipate the actions of the other and liberating regional conflicts. This had two primary effects on the United States of concern to the analysis here. First, the single, overarching threat from the Soviet Union dissolved into multiple threats from numerous regional powers. The world did not suddenly become a less threatening place, although stepping back from the brink of nuclear annihilation is a significant change. Rather, regional conflicts regained their autonomy and, perhaps, even expanded as local parties moved to take advantage of the international political flux and the stockpiles of weapons accumulated earlier. Iraq's invasion of Kuwait, its challenge to the principle of sovereignty, and its possible control of 40 percent of the world's proven oil reserves was the first major challenge of this kind.

Second, no longer concerned that it would be checked at every possible turn, the United States was freed to intervene in conflicts around the globe according to its inner lights and desires. Today, with a substantially lower danger of superpower escalation, the United States is more able to intervene in international and regional conflicts with the aim of ending the hostilities or, at least, the personal suffering. "Humanitarian" interventions are now possible, as are political interventions designed to promote democracy or halt internal wars. Released from the constant need to balance power internationally, the United States can now act on the basis of its domestic political needs and whims—even when its aspirations are opposed by regional actors.

---

[4] On regional conflicts during and after the Cold War, see the essays in Lake and Morgan 1997. On the Cold War as an "overlay" on regional conflicts, see Buzan 1991, 186–229.

America's "rescue" of Somalia, motivated primarily by a domestic concern over politically induced mass suffering in a foreign land, exemplifies this new form of intervention.[5]

Just as the Soviet threat after World War II did not determine the nature of the American response, however, the more diffuse threats of the post-Cold War world do not mandate a particular policy or set of security relationships. Unilateralism is possible and supported by diverse groups, including isolationists, who wish the United States to withdraw from world affairs, and activists, who want it to stay involved. Cooperation is also possible, and supporters differ in their preferred relationships. Some desire to preserve Cold War forms, like NATO, whereas others envision an expanded security community through NATO enlargement or a reinvigorated United Nations. As in 1919–1920 and 1945–1947, there is no clear consensus on the proper course of American foreign policy, reflecting a high degree of uncertainty in the world and the existence of several competing policy alternatives. We are witnessing, of course, a "quiet" debate, lacking the decisive turn of the Senate's failed ratification of the League of Nations or the incremental but clearly articulated steps toward international cooperation after World War II. Yet we are nonetheless witnessing an important debate. As in the other postwar periods examined in this book, the means of policy are proving equally if not more contentious than the ends. The correct course for America's post-Cold War foreign policy is difficult to discern, but it is subject to the same considerations revealed by the theory and found in the earlier periods.

In the Persian Gulf War, the United States faced substantial joint production economies, making some form of cooperation very likely (Hypothesis 1). Although benefiting from large investments in strategic reach during the Cold War, existing military technologies and capabilities still required forward bases in the Gulf.[6] Without such bases, the kind of land war preferred by American military planners could not be fought. Even if they were smaller than those created by deterring an expansionist Soviet Union, substantial positive externalities were also produced by defending the principle of territorial integrity, blocking the emergence of a radical price maker in the international oil market, and preventing Iraq from developing an advanced weapons capability. Both for reasons of technological scale and burden sharing, cooperation promised substantial benefits for the United States.

In the Gulf, the United States had large specific assets at risk, and the expected costs of opportunism, at least under anarchy, were high (Hypothesis 2). This was especially true in relations between the United States and

---

[5] Finnemore 1996 correctly notes that humanitarian interventions occurred as early as the nineteenth century. The Cold War, however, largely blocked such possibilities. Until recently, Finnemore also notes, states did not offer humanitarian justifications for intervention even when they might have been appropriate.

[6] Doughty and Gruber 1996, 980.

Saudi Arabia. For the United States to fight a major land war in the region, there was no alternative to forward bases in the kingdom. This opened the United States to large risks if Saudi Arabia defected from the coalition or attempted to extract a greater share of the gains from cooperation.

To control its partners, the United States seized a leadership role within the coalition and made disproportionate contributions to the joint effort. This had the effect of transforming Saudi Arabia and other Gulf states into de facto American protectorates and reducing the risk that these states would act opportunistically (Hypothesis 4). Once the massive American forces were invited into Saudi Arabia, the Gulf states no longer had the ability to decide whether there would be a war and how it would be conducted; such decisions would be made in Washington, not Riyadh. Although other states could always leave the coalition and "go home," the Gulf states could not, effectively transferring control over their foreign policies to the United States for the duration of the crisis. By forming protectorates over its partners in the Gulf, the United States safeguarded its specific assets and allowed cooperation to go forward with a lower risk of opportunism. On the other hand, the United States also faced rapidly declining marginal gains from greater hierarchy, providing little incentive for it to pursue even more imperial relationships (Hypothesis 3).

In relations with its other partners, fewer specific assets were at risk and the expected costs of opportunism varied from moderate to low (Hypothesis 4). Some partners did play specialized and important roles. Britain and France provided NATO-quality troops that were clear substitutes for American forces; their divisions could not be easily replaced, except by an equivalent number of American troops. Their role within the coalition was critical. Although they did not participate directly in the war, the Soviet Union and China occupied key decision nodes within the international community, especially through their veto at the United Nations. Their opposition to American policy, to varying degrees, might have blocked the war. An active participant in the coalition, Syria occupied a similar position within the Arab world. For most non-Gulf states, however, the absence of any specific assets or roles and the ad hoc, voluntary nature of the coalition meant that the expected costs of opportunism were relatively small; most could have been replaced easily, or their absence would have been scarcely noted.

The governance costs imposed on the United States were high and rose substantially with hierarchy, making cooperation less attractive and limiting the United States to relatively anarchic security relationships (Hypotheses 6 and 7). By leading the coalition, and creating de facto protectorates in the Gulf, the United States expanded its decision-making authority and, in turn, its ability to act opportunistically toward others. Although the United States and Saudi Arabia agreed on general war aims prior to the initial deployment of troops, for instance, once American forces were on the ground there was little to prevent the former from adopting a more expansive mission (whereas Saudi Arabia, without an adequate military force, lacked this ability).

To safeguard against the potential for American opportunism, the United States and its partners agreed to work through existing international institutions, such as the United Nations, thereby giving countries like the Soviet Union an opportunity to obstruct American policy. They also created a coalition to constrain the United States in the actual conduct of the war. Both the inner coalition of states participating in Desert Shield/Storm and the outer coalition of states occupying key decision nodes in the international community served, in essence, as a "fire alarm," which if pulled would signal to all that the United States had breached its initial agreements and violated the international consensus on the goals or means of policy.[7] The constraints exerted on the United States both in the international community at large and in the coalition were substantial, and constituted the primary governance costs of cooperation. Had the United States sought to exercise even broader control over its partners, the constraints they would have extracted, in turn, would have been even greater, suggesting that governance costs rose rapidly with hierarchy.

Large joint economies, varying expected costs of opportunism that did not decline significantly with hierarchy, and high governance costs that rose with hierarchy placed competing pressures on the United States. Although the gains from joint production were potentially large and attractive, the risks and costs of cooperation promised to be substantial as well. In this case, the predictions of the theory on the choice between unilateralism and cooperation are not especially clear, although the primordial necessity of forward bases in the Gulf suggests that cooperation was somewhat more likely to be chosen. Unlike the situation during the Cold War, cooperation was not "obvious" in the Gulf case, perhaps accounting for the substantial reservations policy makers possessed at the time and the sense now, long after the war, that it was less of a success than it first appeared.[8] On the other hand, the specific assets at risk in the Gulf and the rapidly rising governance costs clearly suggest that the United States would seek some intermediate relationship, like a protectorate, with its partners in this region, and more anarchic relationships elsewhere. The pattern of observed relationships bears out this expectation.

In Somalia, by contrast, the joint production economies were very small (Hypothesis 1). The forces deployed to the strife-torn country were sufficiently limited and, at least initially, politically welcome that the mission could be staged and reinforced, when necessary, from "offshore"; forward bases were not required. The positive externalities generated by the human-

---

[7] On fire alarms as oversight mechanisms, see McCubbins and Schwartz 1984.
[8] On the possibility of unilateralism in the Gulf, see Baker 1995, 278.

itarian mission were not trivial, particularly to voters back home troubled by televised images of starving children, but they were not large. The withdrawal of the United States from Somalia after the deaths of eighteen servicemen highlights the limited benefits to the average voter: Americans, at least, were not willing to pay any substantial cost to end a humanitarian crisis far from their own neighborhoods.[9]

At the same time, the mission in Somalia incurred no specific assets. Although some partners were more important than others, especially NATO partners like France and Belgium, for reasons similar to those in the Gulf, none provided resources that could not be obtained elsewhere. And though some states occupied key institutional roles that could have blocked United States efforts, especially at the United Nations, it would have been difficult for others to oppose the delivery of humanitarian aid. Nonetheless, to safeguard against possible opportunism by its partners, the United States again chose to carry a disproportionate share of the burden and lead the coalition. Because no specific assets were at risk, however, the expected costs of opportunism were nil and no substantial hierarchy was necessary (Hypothesis 2).

Finally, the governance costs of cooperation were also quite small (Hypothesis 6). There were no significant constraints on the United States. The coalition did not check American ambition in the region, but rather served to signal only the country's humanitarian intent; since others could have vetoed the American proposal to send troops if they feared a more political agenda in Washington, their support confirmed the limited goals of the United States. In this case, the coalition tied America's hands only to objectives it had already set for itself.

Again, with competing pressures on the United States, the theory can predict the choice between unilateralism and cooperation only with difficulty. With small joint economies, low expected costs of opportunism, and low governance costs, it is not clear that cooperation will be chosen. Depending on which is actually smaller—the joint economies or the expected costs of opportunism and governance costs—the choice could go either way. As in the Gulf War, the lingering ambivalence in the United States over the intervention into Somalia may reflect the closeness of the alternatives: the "failure" in Somalia has done much to turn public opinion against future operations under the auspices of the United Nations and to support those who advocate a more unilateral role for the United States in world affairs. More important, low expected costs of opportunism and low governance costs that nonetheless rise with hierarchy predict that the United States would favor relatively anarchic security relationships. This prediction is confirmed by the evidence.

[9] This cost is different from the expected costs of opportunism or governance costs. It refers to the absolute cost to the United States from the mission in Somalia, not the costs of alternative security relationships. It does suggest, however, that the perceived benefits to the public from stabilizing Somalia were worth less than the lives of eighteen Americans.

## CREATING COALITIONS

The international flux produced by the end of the Cold War created the opportunity for the United States to construct a "new world order." The American design for this new era, embodying its preferred security relationships, emerged gradually over the course of the Persian Gulf crisis rather than as a well-articulated vision. Indeed, although the phrase was seized upon early in the crisis to describe the unfolding cooperation, the concept was only elaborated later.[10]

In a speech before a joint session of Congress on September 11, 1990, President George Bush set forth his vision of this new world. Declaring a "new partnership of nations," Bush described "a world where the rule of law supplants the rule of the jungle, a world where nations recognize the shared responsibility for freedom and justice, a world where the strong respect the rights of the weak."[11] The vision outlined in this speech served much the same purpose as Woodrow Wilson's Fourteen Points (see Chapter 4) and Harry S. Truman's speech in March 1947, which laid forth the so-called Truman Doctrine (Chapter 5). While dealing with the immediate issues of the conflicts at hand, each call contained within it a vision of order and articulated, with varying degrees of eloquence, a strategy for obtaining it.[12] Moreover, like Wilson's proposed League of Nations, Bush's new order was universalistic, based on the principles of sovereignty, territorial integrity, and the rule of law, formed around a community of power rather than a balance of power, and premised on a predominant role for the United States.[13] Many elements of the new world order also existed in microcosm within the Atlantic Community formed after 1945.[14] In this way, Bush's vision was consistent with the political traditions and past policies of the United States. What is new about the new world order, however, is the unprecedented willingness of the United States to work within the limits imposed by the international community.[15]

### The Persian Gulf War

The causes of the Gulf conflict are many and complex.[16] At its root was a growing political division in the Arab world. On one side stood the moderate Arab states, centered around Egypt, that worked with the United States and were ready to compromise on regional issues, including the conflict with

[10] Hayward 1994, 237–38; Hill 1994, 184; Crabb and Mulcahy 1995, 257.

[11] Bush 1990, 91.

[12] Tucker and Hendrickson 1992, 29–31.

[13] Ibid., 56–57; Russett and Sutterlin 1991; Schroeder 1994, 1.

[14] Schroeder 1994, 4; Hill 1994, 188

[15] Porat 1994, 348.

[16] For a critique of American policy leading up to the war, see Jentleson 1994, esp. 139–78.

Israel. On the other side were the more radical regimes that continued to exploit symbols of Arab nationalism, anti-Zionism, and anti-Americanism. Following its war with Iran, Iraq emerged as the leader of these states.

The collapse of the Soviet Union as a global competitor to the United States worsened this central cleavage. The moderate states believed it best to work with rather than against the United States; in a one-superpower world, they believed it bad policy to be on the wrong side of the one country that really counted. Conversely, the radical states sought to counter the increased power and presence of the United States and, in turn, what they saw as a new potential for Israeli regional hegemony.[17]

Saddam Hussein of Iraq most clearly articulated and championed this radical stance. Emphasizing the collective political and military strength of the Arabs if they worked together, as well as their economic power based on oil and financial instruments, he rallied many Arabs, even within otherwise "moderate" states, to his cause. Over the first half of 1990, Saddam became increasingly strident and belligerent in his public pronouncements on the United States and Israel, and by implication in his relations with the moderate Arab states.[18] As Saddam claimed in December 1990, it is "exactly because the balance is disrupted, because the USSR is out of the game, this is an opportunity to start establishing a new counterbalance to the United States."[19] As Secretary of State James Baker, paraphrasing Thucydides, concludes, "what made the invasion of Kuwait inevitable—and the war to redress it—was the decline of Soviet power, the ascension of American power, and the fear this caused in Saddam."[20]

The proximate cause of the conflict was the increasingly desperate financial status of Iraq.[21] During its war with Iran, Iraq borrowed large sums of money abroad, and plunging oil prices—in part because Kuwait and other Gulf states were regularly exceeding their OPEC production quotas—made repayment difficult. Moreover, maintaining a vanguard position in the Arab movement to balance against the United States precluded reductions in defense expenditures or other forms of fiscal retrenchment. Several times in the spring of 1990, Saddam insisted to Saudi Arabia and Kuwait that they write off Iraq's existing debt and advance his country a further $30 billion.[22] In the prelude to war, Iraq accused Kuwait and the United Arab Emirates at the Arab League meeting on July 17 of "an intentional scheme to glut the oil market." Calling this "part of the imperialist-Zionist plan against Iraq and the Arab nation," the memorandum circulated at the meeting went on to declare

[17] Telhami 1993, 187
[18] Dannreuther 1991/92, 14–16.
[19] US News and World Report 1992, 195.
[20] Baker 1995, 365.
[21] On Iraq's motivations for invading Kuwait, see Halliday 1991.
[22] Dannreuther 1991/92, 14–15.

this "an aggression that is not less effective than military aggression."[23] These demands resonated widely throughout the Arab world, especially in the "have not" states who commonly resented the small, wealthy, oil-producing states in the Gulf. Iraq's claims against Kuwait were not without support in the Arab world, even within states that eventually warred against it.[24]

The reaction of the international community to Iraq's invasion of Kuwait on August 1, 1990, was swift and negative. The United States, France, and Britain immediately froze all Kuwaiti and Iraqi assets in their countries, the Soviet Union halted the supply of arms to Iraq, and the United Nations Security Council passed Resolution 660 condemning the invasion and calling for the unconditional withdrawal of all Iraqi troops from Kuwait. In the following days, the economic embargo and halt in arms shipments were picked up by other countries. The embargo was formally mandated by the Security Council on August 6. On August 12, under the right of self-defense in Article 51 of the United Nations Charter, the United States began a de facto blockade of Iraq.[25] It was soon joined by Britain, Australia, the Netherlands, Belgium, and additional states. Others, however, refused to participate in the blockade unless the United Nations voted for joint action under Article 42 of the Charter. Resolution 665, authorizing countries to enforce the embargo against Iraq, was passed on August 25. This was the first of several times the United States went back to the United Nations for additional authority to carry out operations it originally justified under Article 51 in order to build a broader base of international support. Eventually, twelve nations besides the United States contributed sixty-six ships to the naval blockade.[26] By the end of August, Iraq was economically isolated.

In tandem with the economic sanctions and the blockade, the Bush administration set to work developing a military presence in the region ostensibly to deter further Iraqi aggression against Saudi Arabia and, later, to expel Iraq from Kuwait. Immediately after the invasion, President Bush—with his penchant for personalized diplomacy—and other high-ranking officials began consulting Arab leaders.[27] Saudi Arabia was critical for any military presence in the region; after several exchanges, Secretary of Defense Richard Cheney and others traveled to Saudi Arabia to brief King Fahd on Iraq's invasion—especially the buildup of Iraqi armor on Kuwait's southern border with Saudi Arabia—and to consult on possible coordinated efforts. There is

---

[23] Quoted ibid., 15

[24] Khalidi 1991, 167–71.

[25] Throughout, the United States referred to the blockade as "naval interdiction"; a formal blockade is an act of war and would have required congressional approval.

[26] U.S. Department of Defense, 1992, Appendix I, I 22–25. See also Table 6.1 below. In addition, Germany deployed ships to the Eastern Mediterranean, releasing other coalition ships for relocation to the Gulf; and Kuwait, Oman, and Saudi Arabia provided coastal defense.

[27] On Bush's personal diplomacy, see Crabb and Mulcahy 1995, 260.

considerable debate in the secondary literature over the purpose and effect of this meeting. For some analysts, Cheney appears to have exaggerated the Iraqi threat to Saudi Arabia and misled the King into an alliance that the United States alone wanted.[28] For others, the intelligence reports revealed an ominous buildup of armor, troops, and supplies and—although intent cannot be discerned from aerial photographs—the Iraqi threat was sufficient to draw the United States and Saudi Arabia into a mutually beneficial relationship.[29] There is no hard evidence—even in captured Iraqi documents subsequently released to the public—that Iraq was planning to invade Saudi Arabia. Nonetheless, both the United States and Saudi Arabia feared future Iraqi intimidation of the sort to which Kuwait had recently been subjected.[30] In retrospect, this supposedly fateful meeting between the American briefing team and Saudi rulers may have been epiphenomenal. Despite its consistent rebuffs of a formal alliance throughout the 1980s, Saudi Arabia had long planned to cooperate with the United States in the event of a significant threat to its security. The decision to invite Cheney and, in turn, the larger American forces was not capricious. In the view of Paul Wolfowitz, then undersecretary of defense for policy and a member of the American team that visited the kingdom, the Saudis knew what Cheney was coming to ask for and were diplomatic enough not to invite him if they were likely to turn him down.[31] According to the Saudis themselves and Secretary of State Baker, King Fahd had already decided upon his essential course of action prior to the secretary of defense's visit.[32]

With President Bush's personal support and intervention, Morocco, Egypt, and the states of the Gulf Cooperation Council quickly committed troops directly to Saudi Arabia—with Morocco's commitment occurring before the meeting with Cheney.[33] These moves by the Arab states were approved, and expanded, at the Arab League summit of August 10. Syria also announced that it was sending troops on August 11 (they arrived August 15). Eventually, twenty-six countries in addition to the United States contributed military forces to Operation Desert Shield (later Desert Storm). Including those that provided naval forces, the coalition comprised thirty-seven countries (see Table 6.1)

On October 30, the United States decided to double its troop strength in Saudi Arabia to develop an offensive capability (this decision was not announced until November 8, after the midterm elections). This had, of course,

---

[28] Smith 1992, 78–79.

[29] McCausland 1993, 6.

[30] Freedman and Karsh 1993, 92; Khaled bin Sultan 1995, 19.

[31] Interview with Paul Wolfowitz, then undersecretary of defense for policy, June 28, 1995. On the negotiations over Cheney's visit, see Woodward 1991, 243–46 and 254–59.

[32] Khaled bin Sultan 1995, 24–26; Baker 1995, 289.

[33] US News and World Report 1992, 85–86; Brune 1993, 57; Freedman and Karsh 1993, 93.

TABLE 6.1
Participation in the Persian Gulf Coalition

| Country | Personnel | Navy | Army | Air Force | Other |
|---|---|---|---|---|---|
| Argentina | 300 | X | | | |
| Australia | 1,230 | X | | | |
| Bahrain | 700 | | X | X | |
| Bangladesh | 2,330 | | X | | |
| Belgium | 550 | X | | | |
| Canada | 1,370 | X | | X | |
| Czechoslovakia | 140 | | | | S |
| Denmark | 90 | X | | | |
| Egypt | 39,160 | | X | | L |
| France | 19,330 | X | X | X | S |
| Germany[a] | 700 | X | | | |
| Greece[a] | 210 | X | | | |
| Hungary | 40 | | | | M |
| Italy | 1,310 | X | | X | |
| Korea (Rep. of) | 160 | | | | M |
| Kuwait | 7,800 | X | X | X | |
| Morocco | 1,880 | | X | | |
| Netherlands | 1,000 | X | | | |
| New Zealand | 50 | | | X | M |
| Niger | 480 | | X | | |
| Norway | 60 | X | | | |
| Oman | 940 | X | X | X | |
| Pakistan | 8,700 | | X | | |
| Philippines | 300 | | | | M |
| Poland | 200 | | | | M |
| Portugal | n/a | | | | M |
| Qutar | 1,580 | | X | X | |
| Romania | n/a | | | | M |

TABLE 6.1 *cont.*

| Country | Personnel | Navy | Army | Air Force | Other |
|---|---|---|---|---|---|
| Saudi Arabia | 137,160 | X | X | X | |
| Senegal | 500 | | X | | |
| Sierra Leone | 30 | | | | M |
| Spain | 770 | X | | | |
| Syria | 14,800 | | X | | |
| Turkey[b] | 100,000 | | | | |
| United Arab Emirates | 1,450 | | X | X | |
| United Kingdom | 31,930 | X | X | X | |

*Source:* U.S. General Accounting Office, 1991. Appendix II, 16–7.
*Notes:* Other category: S = special unit; L = logistics; M = Medical
[a]Assigned to Eastern Mediterranean
[b]Stationed on the Turkey-Iraq border

been contemplated for some time. As the administration became increasingly pessimistic during the fall and tensions within the coalition grew, the belief that Iraq needed to be driven out of Kuwait by force—or at least the threat of force—acquired greater credence and urgency.

The administration, however, failed to cultivate congressional, public, or foreign support for the troop expansion, and the decision to augment the troops in the region reignited previous fears of war.[34] In part to quell these fears, but also to ratchet up pressure on Iraq, the United States returned to the United Nations for authorization to use force to expel Iraq from Kuwait. After considerable wrangling, especially between the United States and the Soviet Union and France, the Security Council on November 29 approved Resolution 678, authorizing the use of "all necessary means" to expel Iraq from Kuwait.

After a seven-week "pause for peace" imposed by Russia and France as a condition of their support for Resolution 678 and intended to allow for a diplomatic solution, President Bush ordered the military operation to begin on January 16, 1991. A large and well-coordinated air campaign ensued, designed to weaken both Iraq and Iraqi forces in Kuwait. The ground war

[34] Freedman and Karsh 1993, 209; Dannreuther 1991/92, 39–40. On Bush's failure to cultivate public opinion, see Nacos 1994, 52. On the failure to consult with other coalition members, see Freedman and Karsh 1993, 209. Cheney's first hints that the administration was considering an augmentation of forces in October apparently caught the Saudis completely by surprise. Woodward 1991, 313.

began on February 23. After one hundred hours and the rout of the Iraqi army, President Bush called a cease-fire.[35]

## Operation Restore Hope

Following the overthrow of President Mohamed Siad Barre in January 1991, Somalia was thrown into political chaos. Drought, competition for land, and the struggle for political authority by competing groups combined to produce internal anarchy, widespread violence, and large-scale famine.[36] The conflict was primarily limited to the southern half of the country, where three main coalitions eventually vied for power.[37] In the southernmost areas, along the border with Kenya, troops and political leaders loyal to Siad Barre fought to remain a viable political force (the Somali National Front). The remainder of the region was controlled by the United Somali Congress (USC). The area north of Mogadishu, including the northern half of the city itself, was dominated by groups loyal to Mohamed Ali Mahdi, who was proclaimed interim president by his supporters after the fall of Siad Barre at a United Nations-sponsored conference in Djibouti. The area south of Mogadishu was controlled by Mohamed Farah Aidid and his allies. The director of the USC's military operations, Aidid was regarded by many, himself included, as a national hero for leading the victorious fight against Siad Barre. As chair of the USC (elected in 1990) and the strongest military leader in Somalia, Aidid believed himself to be the rightful heir to the presidency.

By late 1991, developments in Somalia were already a source of concern to the international community. In April 1992, after months of negotiations with the warring factions in Somalia, the United Nations Security Council agreed to provide unarmed cease-fire monitors for Mogadishu and associated security forces. Dubbed the United Nations Operation in Somalia, or UNOSOM, the mission was expanded in August 1992 to 4,219 personnel.[38] The United States began relief shipments in February 1991. In August 1992, President Bush announced an expanded effort called "Operation Provide Relief." Nonetheless, the situation in Somalia continued to deteriorate.[39] In 1992 alone, over 400,000 people died from starvation.

[35] For a concise summary of the military strategies employed in the war, see Freedman and Karsh 1991.

[36] On the struggle for land, see Cassanelli 1997; on the origins of the famine, see Natsios 1997.

[37] Northern Somalia largely avoided widespread violence and starvation. The northeast was dominated by the Somali Salvation Democratic Front, the northwest by the Somali National Movement. Under the SNM, the northwest declared itself an independent state—a move not yet recognized by any other country. United Nations 1996, 11–12.

[38] Ibid., 27.

[39] There is, to be sure, some debate on this point. Several analysts believe that the famine had already been essentially overcome and the country was thrown back into chaos by the intervention later in December. See Bryden 1995. Others argue that the first United Nations envoy,

By mid-November 1992, a consensus emerged within the United States government that UNOSOM was failing, with most supplies falling into the wrong hands and reinforcing the political power of the various "warlords." During Thanksgiving week, the Deputies Committee of the National Security Council developed a set of options for the president: 1. augment the current UNOSOM peacekeepers; 2. sponsor a United Nations "peacemaking" force to carry out the mission and provide an American quick reaction force for armed support; or 3. lead a large-scale military effort to fix the problem aggressively.[40] To the surprise of many, the lame-duck president opted for the third and most forceful option. On November 24, 1992, the secretary general of the United Nations issued a pessimistic report to the Council; one day later, President Bush offered the United Nations an American force to stabilize Somalia sufficiently for stalled food and relief deliveries to resume. On December 3, the Security Council passed Resolution 794 approving "all necessary means to establish as soon as possible a secure environment for humanitarian relief operations."[41]

The first elements of the Unified Task Force (UNITAF) were deployed in Somalia on December 9.[42] UNITAF eventually fielded 37,000 troops from twenty-one nations, including a peak total of 28,000 from the United States. This was the largest external military operation in Africa since 1945.[43]

UNITAF was designed as a strictly humanitarian and short-term operation. The mission statement of the United States forces, and by implication the rest of the coalition as well, was "to secure the major air and sea ports, key installations and food distribution points, to provide open and free passage of relief supplies, to provide security for convoys and relief organization operations and assist UN/NGOs [non-governmental organizations] in providing humanitarian relief under UN auspices."[44] Intentionally omitted from the mission statement were a general disarming of the militias, the reviving or training of police and other local security forces, mine clearing, or the rebuilding of the country's fractured physical infrastructure. Most important, UNITAF eschewed any mandate to reconstruct Somalia's political or social systems.

Originally intended to last only six weeks, UNITAF was to stabilize the

Mohamed Sahnoun, had made significant progress and that, if he had not been forced to resign, continuing negotiations might have rendered Operation Restore Hope unnecessary. See Stevenson, 1993, 151. On Sahnoun's early efforts, see Sahnoun 1994.

[40] Woods 1997, 157.

[41] Reprinted in United Nations 1996, 214–16.

[42] Ibid., 34.

[43] Freeman, Lambert, and Mims 1993, 61.

[44] Quoted ibid., 64. See also Kennedy 1997, 100; and Woods 1997, 159. Moreover, the Bush administration adopted rules of engagement that were little more than those provided for in United Nations peacekeeping (Chapter VI) operations, rather than exercising the "all necessary means" of a peace making (Chapter VII) operation. Clarke 1997, 10.

humanitarian situation and build the foundation for a follow-on United Nations force that would seek to restore political and social order. In short, the American-led rescue was to be followed by a United Nations-led rehabilitation. Although the United Nations always wished for a more extensive UNITAF operation—one that would cover the entire country and include disarmament—this two-phased plan was clear from the beginning and confirmed in an exchange of letters between Secretary General Boutros Boutros-Ghali and President Bush in early December.[45]

The limited objectives of UNITAF were rapidly and successfully met.[46] Within ninety days, according to James Woods, deputy assistant secretary of state for African affairs during Operation Restore Hope, "UNITAF had accomplished its mandate and was ready to withdraw . . . the famine in Somalia had been brought under control, a measure of tranquillity restored, and some important first steps taken to start the process of reconciliation."[47] On April 29, 1993, the United States officially notified the United Nations that it had accomplished its mission and was ready to transfer control of the operation to the international organization.[48]

On March 3, 1993, with the active support of the new administration of President Bill Clinton, the Security Council adopted Resolution 814, which called upon the United Nations, as before, "to assume responsibility for the consolidation, expansion, and maintenance of a secure environment throughout Somalia" and requested the secretary general to provide "assistance to the people of Somalia in rehabilitating their political institutions and economy and promoting political settlement and national reconciliation." This resolution is sometimes misunderstood as the beginning of a new mission of "nation building" in the strife-torn country, but in fact it merely codified the second step in the original two-phased plan outlined in December 1992. With the passage of Resolution 814, the transition from UNITAF to UNOSOM II officially began, and was completed on May 4, 1993.[49]

With the creation of UNOSOM II, the American force in Somalia was greatly scaled back to fewer than 5,000 troops. UNOSOM II was headed by United States Admiral Jonathan T. Howe (Ret.), the United Nations special envoy to Somalia.[50] The overall military commander of the United Nations

---

[45] On the differing views of the United States and United Nations over the mission of UNITAF, see Drysdale 1997, 128.

[46] Clarke and Herbst 1996, 76, argue instead that UNITAF should be regarded as a failure; having made the short-term nature of their intervention clear, the United States-led forces did not deter the warlords and their violence but merely created an incentive for them to lay low pending the arrival of the weaker United Nations forces.

[47] Woods 1997, 160.

[48] Freeman, Lambert, and Mims 1993, 71.

[49] United Nations 1996, 262–63.

[50] The appointment of a retired American admiral as the United Nations special envoy is now seen, at least by some in the American diplomatic community, as a mistake. Although the United

forces in Somalia was a former NATO commander, Lt. General Cevik Bir from Turkey (replaced in January 1994 by General Aboo Samah Bin-Aboo Bakar, from Malaysia). The deputy commander was United States General Thomas Montgomery, who simultaneously served as commander of all American forces in Somalia. Of the American troops in Somalia, approximately 3,000 served in logistics, communications, and intelligence positions and reported directly to Montgomery in his capacity as United Nations deputy commander. None of these "logistics" forces was deployed for combat. Another 1,100 troops were stationed on ships off the Somalia coast in a quick reaction force (QRF) intended to support United Nations troops in emergency situations. The QRF reported not to the United Nations command but to the United States Central Command (CENTCOM) in Tampa, Florida. Tactical control over the quick reaction force was delegated in specific instances to Montgomery in his capacity as commander of all United States forces in Somalia.[51] Finally, in August 1993, a unit of United States Army Rangers was added to the American contingent. This unit reported not to Montgomery, but directly to CENTCOM.[52] In both UNITAF and UNOSOM II, all American combat forces remained entirely under United States command.

With the withdrawal of the American forces, UNOSOM II was greatly weakened, with only 17,000 troops (excluding the American QRF) in Somalia in early May 1993.[53] This was far less than the authorized troop strength of 28,000, and nearly 20,000 less than the peak deployment in UNITAF. Moreover, many of the replacement forces were just arriving, often unprepared, and UNOSOM II was just beginning the difficult task of forging a unified command.[54] Rather than being the hoped for "seamless" web, the transition from UNITAF to UNOSOM II left the United Nations in a precarious position and the forces themselves in a situation of maximum vulnerability.

---

Nations wanted an American to head the operation to keep the United States involved and reassure other countries of this fact, Howe's military background introduced an unfortunate degree of ambiguity into the lines of authority. Given his background, Howe felt competent to get involved in military operations and planning and exercised his ties to the Pentagon directly rather than going through more traditional diplomatic channels. His presence also served to make UNOSOM II more of an American operation than was intended. Interviews with Herman J. Cohen, then assistant secretary of state for African affairs, November 13, 1996; Robert Houdek, then deputy assistant secretary of state for African affairs, November 13, 1996; and an anonymous Department of Defense official, November 12, 1996.

[51] U.S. Congress, Senate 1993a, 70–75 and 94–104.

[52] Clarke and Herbst 1996, 73.

[53] As of July 31, 1993, countries participating in UNOSOM II were: Australia, Bangladesh, Belgium, Botswana, Canada, Egypt, France, Germany, Greece, India, Italy, Kuwait, Malaysia, Morocco, New Zealand, Nigeria, Norway, Pakistan, Republic of Korea, Romania, Saudi Arabia, Sweden, Tunisia, Turkey, United Arab Emirates, United States (logistics forces), and Zimbabwe. Later Ireland and Nepal were added. United Nations 1996, 279–80 and 328.

[54] Ibid., 50.

Over the spring of 1993, relations between Aidid and the United Nations deteriorated. Aidid had originally welcomed the American forces under UNITAF. Based on conversations with Robert Oakley, ambassador at large, Aidid believed that at a minimum the United States would not change the internal balance of power to his detriment and that, at a maximum, he had been anointed by Washington as the new national leader of Somalia.[55] Aidid never held similar views about the United Nations, however, fearing that the organization really backed Mahdi.[56] During the transition from UNITAF, which believed itself to be apolitical by design, to UNOSOM II, which was given the self-consciously political task of rebuilding Somalia's social and governmental infrastructure, Aidid's suspicions of the United Nations and its expanded mandate combined to convince the militia leader that he would be denied the presidency he was seeking. As the strongest military leader, Aidid correctly recognized that any attempt to build order on principles other than force would leave him at a political disadvantage. This necessarily brought him into conflict with the United Nation's "bottom-up" state-building efforts. Rather than accept defeat, Aidid decided to challenge the United Nations, launching a major assault against a contingent of Pakistani peacekeepers on June 5 and provoking all-out war between himself and the UNOSOM II forces.[57]

As the violence escalated, the United States joined in the "hunt" for Aidid.[58] Whether it was a result of efforts by Howe, who coordinated his forceful response to the massacre of the Pakistani peacekeepers directly with the Pentagon,[59] or simply that having turned authority over to the United Nations

---

[55] Drysdale 1997, 129; interview with Cohen, November 13, 1996.

[56] Drysdale 1997, 123 and 125; Clarke 1997, 5.

[57] According to Woods 1997, 169, "from Aidid's perspective, the UN had invaded Somalia, had sought by innumerable actions to diminish his stature and power, and in June had declared war on him."

[58] At the time, and in many postmortems since, there was much emphasis placed on "mission creep" or the expansion of the mission under the Clinton administration. As the above makes clear, I believe, the UNOSOM II mandate was carefully crafted and adhered to by all parties. The expanded mission of the United Nations, and in turn the United States in its supporting role, was laid out at the beginning. In this sense, there was no mission creep. Where policy did "go off the rails" was in the ill-fated hunt for Aidid. This was, in part, structural, a response to Aidid's understandable if unfortunate attempt to block the United Nation's state-building effort. It was also a matter of policy and vision, however. Sahnoun, from the United Nations, and Oakley, the American intermediary, both viewed Aidid as central to the peace process, and sought to ensure that he was involved and respected. The United Nations and Howe, in turn, tended to regard Aidid as a "troublemaker" who could and should be politically marginalized. The latter view eventually took hold in the American government as well. Interviews with anonymous Department of Defense official, November 12, 1996, and Cohen, November 13, 1996.

[59] Interview with Cohen, November 13, 1996.

the mission no longer received the high level of attention it required,[60] the United States willingly joined in the war with Aidid's forces—indeed, it even sent the Rangers as reinforcements. The conflict culminated in an ill-fated raid on Aidid's headquarters in southern Mogadishu on October 3, 1993. This raid was planned, approved, and executed entirely by CENTCOM. Howe, Montgomery, and UNOSOM were notified of the operation only as it was beginning.[61] In a heavy battle, two American helicopters were shot down, eighteen Rangers were killed, seventy-five were wounded, and one was taken hostage. The body of an American serviceman was dragged through the streets past a jeering crowd of Aidid's supporters. In the view of one former advisor to UNOSOM, "October 3 was a major UN–U.S. military disaster, but in Somali eyes it was an unprecedented triumph over a perceived tyranny."[62] Aidid had won the war.[63]

Although the American public pulled back in horror from a humanitarian mission gone awry, the actual loss of life in Somalia was roughly equivalent to that in the earlier and "successful" interventions in Grenada and Panama.[64] Nonetheless, public support quickly evaporated—and the deaths crystallized growing doubts within the administration about the current policy. The United States soon reversed course and began to withdraw from Somalia. While announcing that additional reinforcements would be sent to Somalia, President Clinton pledged on October 7 that all American troops would be out of the country by March 31, 1994.[65] Many other countries, and especially the Europeans who had opposed the hunt for Aidid all along, quickly followed suit, pulling their forces out in tandem with the United States.[66] A limited number of United States forces were reintroduced into Somalia to facilitate the evacuation of the last UNOSOM II forces in March 1995—a difficult and risky operation that was an unrecognized success. With this evacuation, the involvement of both the United States and United Nations in Somalia was terminated, leaving a bitter legacy at home and abroad and growing disillusionment with United Nations "policing."[67]

The experience in Somalia left many in the United States disappointed with the United Nations. Following the October 3 clash, Senator Robert Byrd (D-WV) launched an attack on the organization, charging that "Americans by

[60] Curtis 1994, 315; interview with Houdek, November 13, 1996.

[61] United Nations 1996, 55 and 331.

[62] Drysdale 1997, 133.

[63] Woods 1997, 169.

[64] In eighteen months in Somalia, an estimated 30 Americans were killed. In Grenada, 19 were killed in a few days and, in Panama, 23 were killed in the attempt to arrest General Noriega on drug charges. Johnston and Dagne 1997, 202.

[65] Clinton 1993.

[66] On European opposition to the war on Aidid, see Prunier 1997, 143.

[67] Kirschten 1995.

the dozens are paying with their lives and limbs for a misplaced policy on the alter of some fuzzy multilateralism."[68] Given the central role of the United States in defining UNOSOM's mandate at each stage, this final result is most ironic.

## COALITIONS AND THE NEW WORLD ORDER

In the Persian Gulf War, Somalia, and all of its other post-Cold War interventions, the United States has built ad hoc coalitions of states. It has also requested and received authority from regional and international organizations to lead the military operations conducted in their names. Although many analysts have attempted to discern the nature of international politics after the Cold War and to identify likely threats to America's interests, there have been relatively few attempts to explain the particular response of the United States to this altered environment, especially its emphasis on coalitional politics. Two lines of explanation can be found in the existing literature. One explanation focuses on the principle of multilateralism, with some analysts emphasizing the role of norms and others taking a more functionalist approach. The second highlights problems of burden sharing.

John Ruggie has defined multilateralism as "an institutional form that coordinates relations among three or more states on the basis of generalized principles of conduct." This implies, he goes on to note, that multilateralism entails an "indivisibility among the members of a collectivity" and generates expectations of "diffuse reciprocity."[69] The coalitions found in both the Persian Gulf War and Somalia generally fit these conditions: they were premised on the collective definition of the security issues at stake, the broad expectation that countries would cooperate in problem solving, and the actual coordination of policy among more than two states. At the same time, their ad hoc nature limited expectations of diffuse reciprocity.

In his perceptive study of the new world order, Ruggie argues that multilateralism is a projection of America's distinct political culture. In his view, "a multilateral vision of world order is singularly compatible with America's collective self-concept as a nation. Indeed, the vision taps into the very *idea* of America."[70] Similarly, Inis Claude argues that multilateralism is now the legitimate form of international action. "Gradually, unilateralism—action taken without reference to the United Nations—has become widely regarded as improper conduct, whereas resort and deference to the United Nations are taken as evidence of international virtue. . . . Unilateralism . . . is far from

[68] Quoted in Johnston and Dagne 1997, 200.
[69] Ruggie 1993, 11. See also Keohane 1990.
[70] Ruggie 1996, 25.

dead," Claude concludes, "but the United States, among others, has shifted notably toward acceptance of the multilateralist position."[71]

Along similar lines, Martha Finnemore develops a norms-based analysis of humanitarian intervention, concluding that today "humanitarian intervention must be multilateral if states are to accept it as legitimate and genuinely humanitarian. Further, it must be organized under UN auspices or with explicit UN consent." She further argues that "nineteenth-century multilateralism was strategic. States intervened together to keep an eye on each other and discourage adventurism or exploitation of the situation for non-humanitarian gains. . . . Contemporary multilateralism [on the other hand] is political and normative."[72]

The episodes studied in this chapter cannot disconfirm this norms-based argument, as both are multilateral and led by the United States; indeed, all interventions since 1989 fit this description, more or less, and therefore support a norms-based account of American policy. A longer time frame and broader horizon, however, do raise several questions about the causal role of norms. First, norms and ideals should be most clearly reflected in foreign policy when a country is least constrained by the international system.[73] Yet the unfettered ability of the United States to intervene in Latin America over the last century has not produced a consistent pattern of multilateralism in the region. In the early 1900s, in fact, the United States often intervened unilaterally in the internal affairs of Caribbean and Central American countries to preempt European incursions into its informal empire. As late as the intervention in Panama in 1989, the United States acted unilaterally rather than multilaterally, even though it was free to pursue its ideals in any way it chose.

Second, even though multilateralism characterized relations between the United States and its European partners during the Cold War, this principle was not extended to the Pacific; relations between the United States, Japan, the Philippines, and the Trust Territory of the Pacific were all conducted on a bilateral basis. These two observations suggest that if the United States does project its norms onto the global scene, it does so in a highly selective fashion that itself needs to be explained.

Third, the current debate between unilateralists and internationalists suggests that the norm of multilateralism is contested. Whether to act alone or in concert with others is a key issue, and both sides make equal claims to American tradition and ideals and humanitarian motives. Whereas domestic debate is understood in the theory here as reflecting conditions of costly and

---

[71] Claude 1995, 50. For a more skeptical view of collective security in the current age by the same author see Claude 1993.

[72] Finnemore 1996, 181–82.

[73] Krasner 1978, 340.

incomplete information and as a process of interpolation and decision making, deep divisions in society pose a challenge for norms-based accounts.

Finally, with specific reference to Finnemore, multilateralism is, as Ruggie notes, a general form of organization that is not limited today to humanitarian interventions. We should avoid issue-specific explanations of generalized patterns of behavior whenever possible. Moreover, as I discuss below, contemporary coalitions are still quite strategic—more so in the Persian Gulf War, but even in the case of Somalia—and for precisely the same reasons Finnemore points to in the nineteenth-century cases. To ignore this dimension is to misread seriously the international politics of contemporary American foreign policy.

A second approach to multilateralism emphasizes its efficiency in solving problems of collective action among a large group of actors. In this view, even though the total transactions costs of negotiating an agreement increase with the number of actors, the marginal costs of adding yet another participant may decline, indicating that there are often economies of scale in negotiating cooperation.[74] If dyadic relations are generally the same, and broad cooperation would entail negotiating essentially the same agreement dyad by dyad, grouping the individual negotiations and agreements into a single multilateral relationship may reduce the total costs. Lisa Martin suggests that such economies of scale and, thus, multilateralism are most likely to be found in strategic situations characterized by the need for coordination and assurance and less likely to be found in conditions of collaboration and suasion.[75] Focusing on the benefit rather than the cost side of the equation, Miles Kahler, in turn, suggests that the gains from cooperation may often increase with the number of actors, offsetting the potentially rising transactions costs of negotiations. He also explores how states design international institutions to limit the rate at which transactions costs increase with larger numbers of actors.[76] To the extent that multilateralism is an efficient solution to coordinating a large number of states, then, we can more readily understand why it is adopted.

One problem with this approach is raised by Ruggie, namely, that although multilateralism has been around for centuries it is nonetheless primarily an American-led phenomenon that has become increasingly prevalent over the twentieth century. Why it is more efficient today than in the past thus requires explanation. More specifically, however, it is not clear whether the military interventions discussed in this chapter are coordination and assurance problems, where we would expect multilateralism, or collaboration and suasion problems, where we would not. One the one hand, in both the

---

[74] Keohane 1984, 90. See also Caporaso 1993, 62.

[75] Martin 1993, especially 108; and Ruggie 1993, 16–22.

[76] Kahler 1993. See also Hampson 1995, on how "multilateral" negotiations quickly collapse into "coalitional" negotiations to solve the large–n problem.

Persian Gulf War and Somalia, the United States and its partners needed to coordinate on a single policy—whether and how to fight the Iraqi forces in Kuwait, for instance—and to assure one another that they would not defect from the negotiated agreement. On the other hand, as in all collaborative situations where there are large positive externalities produced, distributional questions loomed large. In providing the collective good of liberating Kuwait or stabilizing Somalia, the question of who would bear the burden was central. Nor is it apparent that the transactions costs of the agreement declined at the margin with additional participants; in both cases, the United States eventually turned away otherwise willing participants (see below). Finally, it is not clear that the benefits of cooperation increased with the number of participants: the value to the world community of expelling Iraq from Kuwait and feeding the starving in Somalia was fixed, and the division of labor was small in the former and nil in the latter case (see below). In the end, multilateralism can be explained better not because it solves problems of cooperation at lower cost but because it is an effective safeguard against opportunism.[77] This suggests that the mechanism is less one of coordination and more one of control.

A second set of explanations for contemporary international coalitions focuses on burden sharing. For the American public, we are often told, burden sharing has been the watchword for the 1990s. The American people will no longer countenance their country playing the role of lone sheriff, but they are willing to be part of a global police force when costs are distributed evenly. In June 1995, only 19 percent of Americans believed the United States should be "the policeman of the world," whereas 74 percent thought the United Nations should take on this role. In April 1995, an overwhelming 89 percent of survey respondents agreed that "when there is a problem in the world that requires the use of military force, it is generally best for the U.S. to address the problem together with other nations working through the U.N. rather than going it alone." Likewise, when possible interventions are presented as United Nations operations, they usually get majority support, but when simply described as an American operation they are generally opposed. Americans also believe that multilateralism will be cheaper than unilateralism, at least in the long run.[78] There is little doubt that the American public "prefers" cooperation over unilateralism. It is easy to conclude from

[77] Although it is slightly outside her major thesis, Martin 1993, 110, notes that multilateralism can be used by others as a safeguard against hegemonic power.

[78] Kull 1995/96, 104–5. Rosner 1995/96 argues that there may be a substantial disjuncture between individual support for multilateralism and multilateralism as a cue in evaluating candidates. Although Americans support multilateralism in general, Rosner finds that when it is used as a description of candidates it tends to evoke unpopular images of liberal internationalism and antimilitarism.

this observation, in turn, that the president and Congress use international coalitions to pander to public sentiment and shield themselves from public opposition. Yet this emphasis on public attitudes and domestic political necessities begs the question of why the American public believes coalitions are today cheaper, more effective, or more legitimate than the alternatives. Since public opinion is not formed in a vacuum, the question arises of why a majority of people holds this particular set of beliefs at this moment in history.

In a carefully designed study of cooperation in the Persian Gulf War, Andrew Bennett, Joseph Lepgold, Danny Unger, and their collaborators examine five hypotheses to explain burden sharing: collective action, balance of threat, alliance dependence, historical learning, and domestic institutions and politics.[79] Including most of the countries that contributed directly to Operation Desert Shield/Storm, the editors find some evidence in nearly every case for each of their hypotheses. As a whole, the willingness of countries to contribute to the coalition is overdetermined. More specifically, the editors find that the contribution of the United States is best explained by collective action theory, which posits that large countries will bear a disproportionate responsibility for supplying public goods. They also find that this same theory cannot explain why others did not free ride.[80] To account for this, the editors point primarily to alliance dependence, finding that the countries most reliant upon the United States contributed the most.

Looking at the same case, I cannot disconfirm these hypotheses and findings. Nonetheless, I offer in this chapter a substantially different explanation of the coalition, one rooted in the politics of governing security cooperation. The coalition, in my view, was rooted less in the dependence of others upon the United States, and the influence that gave Washington, and more in the dependence of the United States on forward bases in the Gulf and the need to safeguard itself and others from the risks of costly opportunism.

### JOINT PRODUCTION ECONOMIES

American policy in the Persian Gulf was strongly influenced by the large joint production economies obtainable only through cooperation, including a technological need for land bases in the region, large positive externalities, and a limited division of labor. In the end, the large benefits made cooperation appealing. In Somalia, on the other hand, the joint economies were smaller and cooperation less attractive. In this second case, internalizing

---

[79] Bennett, Lepgold, and Unger 1997.

[80] There is a subtle contradiction in these two findings: if others contributed more than the theory would expect, then the American contribution was less disproportionate than suggested.

some of the positive externalities provided by the United States was a central motivation of policy, but even this was limited.

## Technology

The Gulf coalition was motivated first and foremost by a technological given.[81] For the United States to deploy sufficient military strength to deter Iraq's continuing aggression or intimidation and to compel it to withdraw from Kuwait required forward land bases in Saudi Arabia or, less attractively, some other Gulf state.[82] As the eventual conflict demonstrated, a scaled-backed air campaign could have been waged from aircraft carriers in the Gulf and long-range bombers deployed from around the globe. This option would have been punitive and retaliatory, but probably could not have driven Iraq out of Kuwait.[83] An assault on Iraqi forces in Kuwait was also possible from the sea, and was considered as part of Operation Desert Storm, but ultimately rejected as too dangerous for the Marines who would have to land on the heavily defended coast and too costly, as much of Kuwait City would have to be destroyed to "save" it. Neither a more limited air campaign nor an amphibious assault was considered—from the start—a viable response to the crisis. In addition, neither option conformed to the new military doctrine, developed and implemented in response to the debacle in Vietnam, which called for the use of massive force to crush opponents. Indeed, the only plan available from CENTCOM at the outset of the crisis—1002–90, a draft—was premised upon the large-scale deployment of American forces on Saudi territory.[84] Within hours of the Iraqi invasion of Kuwait, the National Security Council was already inquiring whether Saudi Arabia was prepared to offer bases to the United States.[85] Deciding to do more than punish Iraq through air power required significant numbers of troops on the ground and new security relationships with the Gulf states.

The technological limits on the deployment of large-scale American forces led the United States and Saudi Arabia to a mutually profitable trade: American troops for Saudi land. The United States benefited enormously from the strategic depth provided by the open desert. Forces could train extensively upon their arrival in the kingdom, stockpile weapons and supplies, and mass

---

[81] I do not address here the role of technology on the battlefield in the war against Iraq. I am concerned here with how technology shaped the formation of the coalition. On the technology of the war itself, see Biddle 1996 and the follow-up symposium on "The Gulf War and the Revolution in Military Affairs" in *International Security* 22, 2 (1997).

[82] Turkey was also important for its air bases.

[83] Interview with Wolfowitz, June 28, 1995. See also Woodward's 1991, 228, account of Schwarzkopf's briefing to President Bush on August 2.

[84] Woodward 1991, 228.

[85] Heikal 1992, 199; Freedman and Karsh 1993, 85.

safely behind the front lines.[86] This trade was facilitated by a decade of planning and preparation, including the construction of Saudi Arabia's military
infrastructure in the 1980s to United States military specifications.[87]

Although this basic technological fact accounts for the American overture
to Saudi Arabia, it cannot account for why Saudi Arabia took up the offer.
Nor can it account for the creation of the broader coalition. Only the dyads
of the United States and the Gulf states depended upon this technological
necessity.

In addition, technological limitations cannot account for the creation of
the coalition in Somalia. In this case, offshore deployments were used, with
American and other forces making prenegotiated air and amphibious land-
ings. Some troops, like the QRF in UNOSOM II, were permanently stationed
offshore. Although some air transports refueled in Kenya, military air support was also conducted largely from aircraft carriers and bases within
Somalia. In this case, the United States possessed the technological capability
to go it alone.[88] The similarity in security relationships created by the United
States in the Persian Gulf and Somalia despite different physical requirements
suggests that technology alone cannot account for the coalitions.

## The Division of Labor

There was a small but nonetheless important division of labor in the Gulf
coalition. The United States provided a disproportionate number of the
forces in Operation Desert Shield/Storm. The absolute contribution, of
course, does not determine the extent of the division of labor. Across the
various services, only the American contribution of aircraft was exceptionally
large: in the neighborhood of 75 percent of all combat aircraft, over 80
percent of all sorties flown, and over 90 percent of all ordinance delivered by
coalition forces. This suggests that, while contributing absolutely across the
board, the United States did specialize at the margin in aircraft (see Table
6.2).

In turn, several coalition members supplied important weapons or infrastructure items that were unavailable or available only in insufficient quantities in the United States. Great Britain, for instance, provided the majority
of the minesweeping vessels deployed in the Gulf—a holdover from the
Cold War when Britain had assumed primary responsibility for this task
within NATO. More generally, Britain tailored its deployments to the Gulf to
fill important niches in the coalition force structure, thereby magnifying the
real effect of its contribution.[89] Even Israel provided important land-mine-

[86] Record 1993, 73.

[87] Ibid.; Khaled bin Sultan 1995, 8.

[88] Interview with Martin Cheshes, then director of East African affairs in the Department of
State, November 4, 1996.

[89] Keohane 1994, 162–63.

TABLE 6.2
United States Contributions to the Persian
Gulf War as a Percent of Coalition Total

|                                      | Percent |
| ------------------------------------ | ------- |
| Combat troops (1)                    | 63      |
| Ground forces (2)                    | 69      |
| Tanks (1)                            | 47      |
| Aircraft (1)                         | 80      |
| Combat aircraft (2)                  | 76      |
| Fighter aircraft (3)                 | 72      |
| Strike sorties (4)                   | 88      |
| Non-strike sorties (4)               | 82      |
| Aerial ordinance delivered (4)       | 92      |
| Ships (2)                            | 60      |
| Killed in action (5)                 | 62      |
| Wounded in action (5)                | 59      |

*Sources:*
(1) Taylor and Blackwell 1991, 237.
(2) Matthews 1993, 313–16.
(3) U.S. Congress, Senate 1991, 236.
(4) Luttwak 1994, 228 and 232.
(5) Freedman and Karsh 1993, 409.

clearing equipment—a fact that appeared to worry the United States more than the Arab states.[90]

The United States was also dependent upon support from others both in getting to the Gulf and operating within it. It had only one-third of the heavy equipment transports necessary to execute the successful deception and "left hook" assault on Iraqi forces, and it borrowed transports from a wide variety of sources, including Czechoslovakia.[91] More important, perhaps, the Seventh Corps stationed in Germany could not have redeployed to the Gulf without foreign assistance; moving the corps required 465 trains, 312 barges, and 119 convoys of ships, nearly all of which came from America's European partners.[92] Within the theater, United States forces were also dependent upon

[90] Interview with Wolfowitz, June 28, 1995.
[91] Record 1993, 143.
[92] Blackwell, Mazarr, and Snider 1991, 7; Doughty and Gruber 1996, 983.

local trucks and Arab oil (which greatly reduced the shipping requirements from military stocks in the United States). Without some of these seemingly minor forms of assistance, the buildup of United States forces in the Gulf would have been slowed considerably.

These advantages from broad participation, however, must be discounted by the diseconomies introduced by additional members of the coalition. Although forces from each new country added to the total capability of the coalition, additional contributions—especially from non-NATO countries—degraded the per capita fighting effectiveness of the existing forces.[93] There was little interest in the United States in forces from countries that could not provide for themselves in the Gulf; in some cases, the necessary logistical support that would have been required was greater than the aid to be given.[94] The smaller force contributions were eventually assigned to guard "strongpoints" well to the rear in Saudi Arabia,[95] thereby enabling all units at the front to operate at division size or better and significantly reducing potential problems of command and control.[96] In the end, some countries wishing to contribute forces to the coalition, including Bulgaria and Honduras, were politely turned away because they could not be accommodated logistically.[97]

Within the coalition, the individual militaries possessed varying degrees of combat effectiveness. The Americans, for example, regarded the Saudi soldiers "as indolent, barefoot tea drinkers relying upon the Marines for protection."[98] More seriously, incompatibilities between forces, equipment, and strategies led to potentially disastrous battlefield decisions. Told that the United States Marines could not distinguish their Soviet T–62 tanks from Iraqi ones, Syrian forces refused to carry out their assigned role of guarding the left flank of the Second Marine Division on its thrust into Kuwait; moving to the West to follow the Egyptians and Kuwaitis, the Syrians left the Marine units open to attack from the Iraqi First Armored Division.[99] The Egyptians also deviated from the plan; once through the Iraqi trenches, they established blocking positions against an Iraqi counterattack that never came instead of proceeding ahead as intended.[100] In both cases, the Marines kept going forward, but with the important political consequence of getting to

[93] On the problems of coalition warfare in the Gulf, see Dunnigan and Bay 1992.

[94] Interviews with Wolfowitz, June 28, 1995, and Richard Haass, then Special Assistant to the President for Near East and South Asian Affairs on the National Security Council and the lead staff person for the "Deputies Committee" which met intensively over the course of the crisis, June 28, 1995.

[95] Khaled bin Sultan 1995, 252–60.

[96] Thompson 1993, 147 and 151.

[97] Record 1993, 73.

[98] Atkinson 1993, 206.

[99] US News and World Report 1992, 308; McCausland 1993, 55; Freedman and Karsh 1993, 395.

[100] Freedman and Karsh 1993, 395.

Kuwait City long before the Arab forces that were designated to liberate the area.

Many potential difficulties of this sort, of course, were averted by careful planning before the war and by force redundancies—further limitations on the division of labor. Within the American command pillar, the United States and European forces used NATO procedures and benefited tremendously from years of joint training. Past exercises with Egypt, which possessed one of the few capable armies in the region, and other Middle Eastern states also paid great dividends. During the buildup to the war, most of the Arab forces trained with Marine liaison officers, who later stayed with these units during combat. Even so, the Arab units, deployed on the dangerous southern border of Kuwait so that they would not violate the territory of Iraq, were supported by two divisions of Marines to ensure the successful liberation of Kuwait City. Although these plans and redundancies safeguarded the United States against possible opportunism within the coalition, they nonetheless diverted some American forces from other roles and responsibilities.[101]

To what extent the effectiveness of United States forces were degraded by their participation in the coalition is difficult to discern precisely. There was only one Persian Gulf War, fought only one way. Although certain important niches were filled by coalition forces, and the infrastructure was critical to the conduct of the war, more similar forces with extensive joint training, comparable equipment, and unified command and control structures would certainly have been more efficient. On balance, the benefits of the division of labor were modest—there were few synergies or "force multipliers" between United States and coalition forces—and effectiveness declined. The net benefits of the division of labor, although important, were small and cannot account for the preferred multilateral strategy.

The division of labor in Somalia was even more limited. Again, the United States provided the vast majority of forces. In UNITAF, the United States—along with others—deployed a wide range of troops, but mostly lightly armed infantry; in UNOSOM II, American forces were limited to crucial logistics roles and the more heavily armed QRF, suggesting a small division of labor. The clearest division of labor within Operation Restore Hope, however, indicates how limited the benefits actually were. In a holdover from restrictions on its aid to military dictatorships in Latin America, the United States was prohibited by law from providing police and police training to foreign countries. At the same time, Germany—participating in its first "out-of-area" peacekeeping mission—and other states were only too happy to contribute police and trainers in lieu of combat troops, and they stepped in

---

[101] The command and control system was the minimum necessary to defeat the more unified Iraqi system; a stronger and more capable enemy would have severely stressed the cooperative system adopted by the coalition. See McCausland 1993, 56.

to fill the gap left by the American restrictions.[102] This coincidence of interest solved several domestic political problems, but it provided few joint economies in the military arena.

The UNITAF forces were, at best, substitutes rather than complements for American forces.[103] Even here, however, the benefits were highly qualified. Although the United States did receive assistance from some NATO countries and countries with NATO-quality troops, many coalition members had never before worked or trained with American forces.[104] Some troops even arrived without adequate field support and had to be stationed near American supply lines, limiting the areas to which they could be deployed. In the eyes of one defense analyst, the coalition received far more "airport security" than it needed.[105] Some national contingents even demanded that the Americans protect them, lest any casualties create unpleasant political repercussions back home.[106] As in the Persian Gulf, the United States eventually turned away otherwise willing participants for lack of logistics capability and for fear of degrading coordination within the coalition. Before the end of December 1992, the United States was encouraging states to delay their participation and contribute to the follow-on United Nations force.[107]

Even assistance from America's NATO partners proved to be of limited value. Admiral Jacques Lanxade, commander of the French forces in Somalia, requested that his troops be assigned an area where "nothing was likely to happen." According to Gerard Prunier, "the feeling was that this was an American show and that as long as the French were going to have to watch from the sidelines, they might as well pick safe watching points."[108] On the other hand, Italy insisted on participating in UNITAF and UNOSOM II and wanted to be at the center of the action, despite the diplomatic problems posed for the coalition by the country's imperial history and past interventions in Somalia.[109] Reflecting strong disagreements over the proper mission of UNOSOM II, both Italy and France declined to participate in the hunt for Aidid, making a weak United Nations command and control structure even weaker and launching a minor political crisis within the coalition.[110] In the end, even America's most capable partners added less than "full value" to the joint effort.

[102] Interview with Cohen, November 13, 1996.

[103] Interview with Cheshes, November 4, 1996; and Houdek, November 13, 1996.

[104] Freemen, Lambert, and Mims 1993, 62.

[105] Interview with anonymous Department of Defense official, November 12, 1996.

[106] Interview with Cheshes, November 4, 1996.

[107] Freeman, Lambert, and Mims 1993, 69; interview with Cohen, November 13, 1996.

[108] Prunier 1997, 139. On the other hand, former deputy assistant secretary of state for African affairs Robert Houdek praised the French as very effective, and noted that their section was quiet because of their early and forceful stand against the militias.

[109] Prunier 1997, 137. Interview with Houdek, November 13, 1996.

[110] Prunier 1997, 143; Oakley n.d., 15.

## Positive Externalities

Burden sharing was perhaps the most important material benefit to the United States in both Operation Desert Shield/Storm and Operation Restore Hope. In the former, the Gulf states and other Arab members of the coalition benefited from the deterrence of further aggrandizement, the destruction of Iraq's ability to engage in regional intimidation, and the diminution Iraq's leadership role in the Islamic world. The Western members of the coalition, including Japan, benefited from the defense of the principle of territorial integrity—most likely a minor consideration in the calculations of most national capitals—and the breakup of a new and more radical price maker within OPEC.[111] Through cooperation, the United States sought to capture at least some of the positive externalities generated by expelling Iraq from Kuwait, deterring future regional aggression, defending the principle of territorial integrity, and ensuring the continued fragmentation of the world oil market. These benefits help explain why the United States would try to assemble a broad coalition; indeed, in a speech on September 17, 1990, President Bush emphasized just one theme in justifying the coalition: burden sharing.[112] By building the broadest possible coalition, the beneficiaries of the United States action in the Gulf could be made to contribute to the undertaking.

By themselves, however, the benefits of burden sharing do not explain the alacrity with which some (but not all) members of the coalition chose to contribute, especially once the United States made clear its intent to dominate the coalition. The major donors, and especially Germany and Japan, contributed only under substantial American pressure.[113] Others voluntarily came forward, including several who might have escaped America's ire completely if they had chosen to sit out the conflict.

Many states contributed to the coalition for private reasons, thereby offsetting the otherwise dominant tendency to free ride.[114] For most states, the actual costs of participation were minimal. Agreement between the United

---

[111] On the positive externalities created by deterring the Iraqi threat, see Terasawa and Gates 1993. Based on an attempt to balance subjectively defined interests in the Persian Gulf War with actual contributions, Terasawa and Gates 1993, 186, conclude that the Gulf states, "with the exception of Kuwait, appear to have borne a disproportionately small share of the Operation Desert Storm burden; and Japan and Germany appear to have borne a disproportionately large share of the burden." Brenner 1991, 665–66 captures the predominant feeling, however, noting that public opinion was "united in the conviction that Americans were undertaking a sacrifice for the sake of partners who were unwilling to contribute to the common cause on a scale commensurate with their stake."

[112] Bush 1990, 93. On the political importance attached to burden sharing, see Baker 1995, 288.

[113] On Germany and Japan, see Hellman 1997 and Unger 1997, respectively.

[114] On private interests and free riding in alliances, see Olson and Zeckhauser 1966.

States and Soviet Union no longer threatened to place them on the "wrong side" of any regional conflict, the various United Nations resolutions legitimated their participation, and their contributions were, for the most part, largely token, but welcomed and acknowledged by the United States anyway. In return for their participation in the American-led effort, even minor partners hoped to gain influence over the emerging new world order and to ensure that the Americans alone would not decide the crucial shape of the post-Cold War international system.[115] The motivations of Canada and Australia, who might have easily rebuffed American pressure to participate, are particularly revealing. In the minds of Prime Ministers Brian Mulroney and Bob Hawke, Ronnie Miller writes, their "commitment to Bush's diplomacy [in the Gulf crisis] would secure Canada and Australia's place in the new world order," or at least give them a seat at the diplomatic table.[116] For states in the region, moreover, participation in the coalition promised not only a role in setting the new world order but also in designing the new Middle East order that, although it was never officially linked to the resolution of the crisis, was nonetheless expected to follow the defeat of Iraq. Thus for states inside and outside of the region, the political openness created by the disintegration of the Cold War created private incentives to participate in the joint effort.

In the end, and under considerable American pressure in some cases, thirty-six other countries contributed ships to the blockade or ground or air forces to Operations Desert Shield/Storm (see Table 6.1 above). Many of these forces substituted for United States troops but, as suggested above, at a less than one-to-one ratio. Nonetheless, the contributions of others—especially the NATO-compatible forces from Europe—allowed the United States to reduce its overall contribution from what might have been required in a unilateral or smaller multilateral undertaking.

Seeking to balance the diseconomies inherent in diverse forces with a desire to capture some of the benefits provided to others, the United States preferred money over token forces that would otherwise have complicated military planning. Thanks to aggressive American fundraising expeditions, dubbed Tincup I and Tincup II, the United States collected nearly $54 billion in cash and in-kind contributions (see Table 6.3). With Saudi Arabia paying all in-theater costs of the American troops, these contributions covered almost 90 percent of the incremental cost of the campaign.[117] These fund-raising efforts emerged over the fall of 1990 and relied upon a mix of moral suasion and pragmatism: not only was it right for the foreign governments to contribute, they were told, it was smart, for the American people

---

[115] Keohane 1994, 163.

[116] Miller 1994, 74–79, quote on 79. For an analysis of "middle powers" in the Gulf conflict, see Cooper and Nossal 1997.

[117] Freedman and Karsh 1993, 358–61; Atkinson 1993, 493.

TABLE 6.3

Foreign Government Contributions to the United States for the Persian
Gulf War (as of April 10, 1992)

| | Contributions (in millions of U.S. dollars) | | |
|---|---|---|---|
| Contributors | Cash | In-Kind | Total |
| Saudi Arabia | $12,809 | $4,030 | $16,839 |
| Kuwait | 16,015 | 43 | 16,058 |
| United Arab Emirates | 3,870 | 218 | 4,088 |
| Japan | 9,441 | 571 | 10,012 |
| Gemany | 5,772 | 683 | 6,455 |
| Korea | 150 | 101 | 251 |
| Other | 7 | 22 | 29 |
| Total | $48,064 | $5,668 | $53,732 |

Source: U.S. General Accounting Office 1992.

would not look favorably upon countries that attempted to free ride.[118] Table
6.3 breaks down the major contributions by country, cash, and in-kind contributions. Although the United States did not turn a profit, as some early
critics suggested, it successfully induced others to contribute to an extent
seldom witnessed in international relations.

In Somalia, the positive externalities captured by the United States were
more limited but also quite important. In UNITAF, the United States paid
more than 75 percent of the total cost, for an estimated total of $800
million.[119] The remainder was borne by the participating countries that could
afford this expense themselves, or was paid from a special United Nations
fund largely contributed by the Japanese (and to a lesser extent by Saudi
Arabia).[120] Once UNOSOM II was established in May 1994, operating costs
were picked up by the United Nations under its peacekeeping budget, and
the incremental costs to the United States fell to approximately $6 million.
Nonetheless, the United States is the single largest contributor to the United
Nations peacekeeping account, providing slightly more than 30 percent of
the total. As a result, the burden sharing in UNOSOM II is less significant
than it first appears.[121]

Most important, in the views of several observers, was that the coalition

[118] Interview with Haass, June 28, 1996.
[119] Hirsch and Oakley 1995, 109; U.S. Congress, Senate 1993b, 26.
[120] Cohen 1992, 898.
[121] Hirsch and Oakley 1995, 109.

allowed for a quicker phase-out of American forces. Indeed, the majority of the American troops left in May 1993, long before those of other participating countries. Under a purely unilateral operation, American forces would have had to remain in Somalia far longer. The resources saved by the United States are best measured not by the number of troops deployed, at least in the early stages of the operation, but in the total number of troop days in Somalia.[122] By this indicator, the savings were not insignificant.

In summary, technological necessities were an important determinant of cooperation in the Persian Gulf, but were insignificant in Somalia. In both cases, the division of labor was quite small, and hardly an important force behind cooperation. In the Gulf, the positive externalities were large, and the United States could gain by internalizing these benefits within the coalition, but in Somalia the positive externalities were more modest. As in the other cases in this book, however, joint production economies are a necessary but insufficient condition for cooperation. This also depends upon the expected costs of opportunism and governance costs.

## Governing Cooperation in the Persian Gulf

Once the United States and the Gulf states recognized the potential gains from pooling their resources in the fight against Iraq, the diplomatic focus shifted not to ensuring the largest possible joint economies but to building a workable security relationship at an acceptable cost. As HRH General Khaled bin Sultan, head of the Joint Forces (Saudi) Command, notes, "If the truth be told, the task we faced during the crisis was not winning the war against Saddam. . . . That was the easiest part of it. . . . The greatest challenge we faced . . . was to make sure that the members of the Coalition worked together without friction or dispute."[123] Although the coalition did create important joint economies for the United States, the key questions are still whether it was worth the price and whether a better alternative existed.

### Expected Costs of Opportunism

The United States, the Gulf states, and other coalition members were drawn together by overlapping interests. To a greater or lesser extent, all wanted the Iraqi threat to the region reduced, the monarchy restored in Kuwait, and a stable Iraq in existence to contain the Shiite regime in Iran. States outside the Gulf also wanted to prevent the rise of a radical price maker within OPEC.

These shared and mutually reinforcing interests limited the probability of

---

[122] Interview with James Dobbins, National Security Council, November 13, 1996. Although not involved in Operation Restore Hope, Ambassador Dobbins conducted one of several internal "postmortems" on Somalia for the Clinton administration.

[123] Khaled bin Sultan 1995, 264–65.

opportunism by the partners of the United States. As one of the states most inclined to punish Iraq, moreover, the United States was not significantly threatened by entrapment from its partners. Having set out to deter further Iraqi aggression and, ultimately, to expel Iraq from Kuwait, the United States nonetheless feared throughout the crisis that its partners might abandon the coalition and thereby undermine its ability to respond in what was deemed an appropriate fashion. This was especially the case as the coalition moved closer to war through the fall of 1990.

Although united at the broadest level, the coalition was a diverse group of states. It is useful to distinguish, first, the "outer" coalition of states, such as Russia or China, that did not contribute to Operation Desert Shield/Storm but occupied key leadership roles within the international community because of their power and status or their veto at the United Nations; second, the "inner" coalition of countries that actually contributed forces; and third, within the latter, between the NATO allies, the "Arab coalition," and the Persian Gulf states.[124] Each of these groups possessed a special role within the coalition.

The security relationships constructed by the United States during the Persian Gulf crisis unfold like the layers of an onion, with the Gulf states at the center. Dependent upon highly specific bases in Saudi Arabia and other local states, the United States feared that it would be abandoned by these necessary partners. To control the potential for opportunism and reduce the expected costs, the United States seized the leadership position in the coalition against Iraq and transformed the Gulf states into protectorates. To gain their voluntary compliance with their own subordination, in turn, the United States needed to safeguard the Gulf states against the potential for opportunism inherent in its control over their foreign policies. The inner and outer coalitions were designed, at least in part, to permit the United States to exercise the leadership it believed necessary while at the same time demonstrating its commitment to act within the bounds of the prevailing international consensus. These safeguards worked because they included within them states that did not necessarily share America's interests and that could be counted on to criticize its leadership if it strayed too far from their views.

### THE GULF PROTECTORATES

Although the United States had made substantial investments in its ability to project force over distance during the Cold War, it was still dependent upon forward bases in the Gulf to fight a major land war. The highly specific nature of these bases was a basic fact of the Gulf War, and significantly

---

[124] Some minor contributors, such as Argentina and Australia, do not fit into these three categories.

colored the American response to the crisis, the security relationships it formed in the Gulf, and its broader strategy of building the coalition.

Throughout the fall, the United States was concerned that the Gulf states, and Saudi Arabia in particular, would abandon the coalition and reach an independent deal with Iraq. As President Bush expressed early in the deliberations on how to respond to the Iraqi invasion, "my worry about the Saudis is that they're going to be the ones who are going to bug out at the last minute and accept a puppet regime in Kuwait. We should be asking them how committed they are."[125] Early intelligence reports suggested that the Saudis were considering buying their way out of the crisis by paying billions of dollars from their oil revenue to Saddam.[126] Even after the initial agreement on August 6 to deploy troops to Saudi Arabia, Secretary of Defense Cheney continued to fret that the agreement might be "soft."[127] Had Saudi Arabia defected and reached a separate deal with Iraq, the entire foundation for America's response to the Iraqi invasion would have been undermined.

The Saudis, in turn, were initially skeptical of the American commitment to protect their kingdom and drive Iraq from Kuwait.[128] For the Saudis, the decision to invite the Americans into their country was critical. Saudi Arabia and the other Gulf states faced two unattractive options during the crisis—as the twist on an old saw went at the time, they were "between Iraq and a hard place." On the one hand, they could appease Iraq, reach some compromise over Kuwait, and leave themselves vulnerable to future threats and intimidation. Alternatively, they could seek to diminish, in one form or another, Iraq's regional dominance. Doing this unilaterally required a costly domestic mobilization that most likely could not be accomplished quickly enough to succeed (if at all). Choosing to confront Iraq, therefore, meant inviting in the Americans and becoming dependent upon them for their current and future security.[129] This dependence would severely constrain their sovereignty, a price the Saudis were willing to pay only if it was sure to remove future threats from Iraq. Not unreasonably, Saudi Arabia feared that the United States still suffered from a lingering "Vietnam syndrome" that would produce a tentative and gradualist response. They also worried that, although Bush administration officials had spoken out vigorously against Iraq, broader public opinion was more divided and might not sustain a commitment over the longer term. As King Fahd insisted to Prince Bandar bin Sultan, the Saudi

---

[125] Quoted in Woodward 1991, 251. Woodward uses direct quotes from private meetings only when at least one participant specifically recalls or took notes on what was said and is confident about the exact wording. Given the controversy over Woodward's reporting methods, however, these remarks should be treated cautiously.

[126] Ibid., 253; Von Vorys 1997, 65.

[127] Woodward 1991, 275.

[128] Heikal 1992, 200, 205; Von Vorys 1997, 63–65.

[129] Khaled bin Sultan 1995, 22, 26, and 306.

ambassador to the United States, "The most important thing is that they [the Americans] should be sure of what they want to do before they ask us about anything."[130] Bandar, in turn, made the same point more forcefully to Bush's national security advisor, Brent Scowcroft: "Do you guys have the guts or don't you? 'We don't want you to put out a hand and then pull it back,' the ambassador said, 'and leave us with this guy [Saddam] on our border twice as mad as he is now.'"[131]

The solution to this mutual suspicion emerged early on in the negotiations, and was the principal contribution of Secretary of Defense Cheney's visit to Saudi Arabia on August 6. The United States demonstrated its commitment by offering to send an initial force of 250,000 troops to Saudi Arabia; this signaled that President Bush was serious and deeply committed to resolving the Gulf crisis. The Saudis immediately recognized that this was not an incremental or half-hearted step. Appropriately reassured, King Fahd agreed to receive the American troops.

Saudi Arabia's acceptance of the large troop deployment, in turn, provided two critical forms of reassurance to the United States. First, by inviting the American troops, Saudi Arabia decisively broke with the radical Arab states, dramatically restricting its political and diplomatic alternatives for the future. As Lawrence Freedman and Efraim Karsh write, "once committed to the deployment of US troops in Saudi Arabia, there was no way back for King Fahd. His position could never be safe again unless Saddam was shamefully expelled from Kuwait or—even better—overthrown."[132] Locked into a confrontation with Iraq, Saudi Arabia could not back down or abandon the United States without substantial costs to itself.

Second, by committing so many troops—more than three and one-half times the number of existing Saudi forces[133]—the United States seized the leadership position in the budding coalition. Although the Gulf states had many more direct and immediate interests in the outcome of the struggle, the United States gained the decisive voice in the coalition. Negotiations with Iraq, the timing and conduct of the war, and the nature of the postwar regional order would be decided not in the capitals of the Gulf states but in Washington.

From the Saudi view, the Americans were guests in their country and, as such, were subordinate to their formal authority. As but one of the many symbolic demands made by the Saudis, Khaled insisted that his daily meetings with General Norman Schwarzkopf should always be held in his office,

---

[130] Quoted in Heikal 1992, 211–12.

[131] Quoted in Woodward 1991, 240. See also Freedman and Karsh 1993, 91; Khaled bin Sultan 1995, 26; Yetiv 1992, 203; and Guzzini 1994, 174–75.

[132] Freedman and Karsh 1993, 95.

[133] Ibid., 88.

forcing the American commander to come to him rather than vice versa.[134] Once invited in as "guests," however, the Americans quickly dominated and, in fact, came to control the household. As Khaled notes, one of his most important "symbolic but nonetheless crucial" tasks during Desert Shield/ Storm was "making sure our all-powerful American allies did not swallow us up."[135] By seizing the leadership role, the United States ensured that the Gulf states forfeited their ability to conduct independent foreign policies. This protected the United States against possible opportunism by Saudi Arabia and others. Real authority now lay with the United States.

Having established this important degree of control over their foreign policies, there was little to be gained by exerting even greater hierarchy over Saudi Arabia and its neighbors—especially given the skepticism and hostility toward the American role in the region. The Gulf states were largely embracing the United States to escape from possible Iraqi intimidation; had the United States pressed for even more authority over the internal political arrangements of its partners, rather than just their foreign policies, the invitation might never have been extended nor the coalition formed. In light of the highly specific assets at risk by the United States in the Gulf, and the rapidly rising governance costs of hierarchy (see below), transforming previously sovereign states into American protectorates was both necessary and, equally important, sufficient for cooperation to proceed.

### SAFEGUARDING COOPERATION

Establishing protectorates in the Gulf was central to American ambitions in the region. The Gulf states, in turn, were politically vulnerable at home and abroad for subordinating themselves to the United States, in general, and to an ally of Israel, in particular. As Mohamed Heikal, an Arab journalist, succinctly notes, "the first responsibility of a Saudi monarch is to keep intimate relations with Washington, and the second is to do all he can to hide it."[136] The predominance of the Western powers in the response to Iraq's invasion of Kuwait caused public opinion in the Arab states, initially opposed to Saddam, to begin to waver.[137] Most important, by transferring decision-making authority to Washington, the Gulf states opened themselves to the risk that the United States might act opportunistically, perhaps by expanding the war against Iraq into a crusade against all nondemocratic regimes in the region, which would necessarily implicate the Gulf kingdoms as well, or by forcing them to moderate their opposition to Israel in a postwar regional peace agreement. This potential for opportunism by the dominant state is inherent in any protectorate. Whether or not the United States intended to

---

[134] Khaled bin Sultan 1995, 192.
[135] Ibid., 32.
[136] Heikal 1992, 213.
[137] Ibid., 225.

act opportunistically is almost irrelevant. Its de facto control over the foreign policies of the Gulf states produced the possibility that it might act opportunistically, and this was sufficient to cause concern in the now vulnerable Gulf states.

To induce the Gulf states to subordinate themselves voluntarily, the United States had to make a credible commitment to Saudi Arabia and its other regional partners that it would not exploit its expanded decision-making authority.[138] The United States quickly created two institutions that allowed it to use its great strength to accomplish its objectives in the region but that also tied its hands and restrained it from exploiting its partners in the process. Within the Bush administration, this was less of a conscious strategy and more a feeling that it was the right thing to do. Nonetheless, it was a brilliant diplomatic maneuver that solved the problem of credible commitment and set an important precedent for future foreign policy initiatives by the United States.

The first safeguard was the inner coalition itself, indicating that the diverse alliance of states was rooted not only in the joint economies made possible from broader participation but also in the need to protect others from American dominance. Important to the functioning of the coalition was its largely anarchic structure, at least on the surface and for most non-Gulf partners. This allowed the coalition to serve as a check on American opportunism. If the United States dominated others in the same way it controlled the Gulf states, its other partners would lack the freedom to criticize Washington or call attention to its violations of the international consensus. The coalition could serve as an effective safeguard only to the extent that at least some important members were "free agents." At the same time, America's leading role gave it a decisive voice and allowed it to use others to meet its objectives despite the appearance of political equality.

This safeguard emerged in tandem with the overture to Saudi Arabia.[139] Sensing King Fahd's reluctance to invite in American troops, it was apparently President Bush's chief of staff, John Sununu, who first recognized that "By God, the man needs a cover, an Arab or Islamic cover." Soon thereafter, President Bush phoned King Fahd, asking whether the presence of American troops in Saudi Arabia might be more palatable if they were part of a more broadly based force. This offer appears to have resolved the political dilemma facing Fahd and his advisors.[140] President Bush and Secretary of State Baker

[138] On the early recognition of this point, see Cheney's remarks to King Fahd, where he noted explicitly that "The President asked me to assure you that we will stay as long as you want us. We will leave when you no longer need us. We will stay until justice is done but not stay a minute longer." Quoted in Woodward 1991, 269.

[139] Baker noted the need for an international coalition in his discussions with Soviet Foreign Minister Shevardnadze on August 3; Baker 1995, 278.

[140] Heikal 1992, 217–18.

quickly began consulting possible partners, especially in the Arab world. Morocco immediately extended an offer to Saudi Arabia to send troops to the Gulf. It was precisely to offset the view espoused so forcefully by Saddam on the consequences of a one-superpower world that a broad Arab and, more generally, international coalition was necessary.[141] In short, the coalition was put together not to balance against Iraq—a task for which it was helpful but not necessary—but to balance against the overweening power of the United States within the joint effort.[142] Indeed, emphasizing their political rather than military importance, Saudi Arabia wanted only token troops from its Arab partners, and accepted the large Egyptian force only at the insistence of General Schwarzkopf.[143] The individual countries in the coalition and how they constrained American policy is discussed below.

The coalition, in fact, was quite anarchic in structure. In the naval interdiction operation, coordination between the national forces was loose. The Gulf area was simply divided into segments and allocated to different countries for patrol. With the exception of the United States and Britain in the northern Gulf, the area closest to Iraq and Kuwait, there was no attempt to pool or coordinate operations; each country acted independently. Indeed, the separate forces did not even attempt to standardize rules of engagement, creating some unnecessary confusion.[144]

Similarly, although technically serving at the invitation of Saudi Arabia, each of the major contributors to Desert Shield/Storm—the United States, Britain, France, and Saudi Arabia—remained under national command. All other participants agreed prior to their deployment to subordinate themselves to the Joint Forces (Saudi) Command, led by Khaled. British forces served under the operational control of the United States. French forces coordinated with the Joint Forces Command during Desert Shield, but transferred to the tactical command of the United States in Desert Storm.[145] These complicated lines of authority resulted in two pillars of command: one headed by Khaled, with primary responsibility for coordinating the defense of the kingdom, and another led by Schwarzkopf, charged with offensive operations against Iraq.

Largely at the insistence of Saudi Arabia, which did not want its troops to serve on its own territory under any foreign command, there was no Su-

---

[141] See Fahd's remarks at the conclusion of Cheney's briefing in Woodward 1991, 271, where he explicitly pairs American deployment with Arab assistance, and Cheney's visit to King Hassan of Morocco on his return from Saudi Arabia, in Woodward 1991, 276.

[142] According to Haass, "The United States could have won the war militarily so long as it had adequate access to local facilities; the real value of the coalition was political." Interview, June 28, 1995. See also Brenner 1991, 670, and Tucker and Hendrickson 1992, 127.

[143] Heikal 1992, 25.

[144] On the naval deployments to the Gulf, see Neves 1995. On naval command and control, see McCausland 1993, 15–17.

[145] On difficulties with the French, see Baker 1995, 371.

preme Allied Commander within the coalition.[146] The American and Saudi forces worked on a collaborative or "parallel" basis. The United States commander, Schwarzkopf, and his Saudi counterpart, Khaled, conducted strategic-level planning through an informal but coequal relationship. Actual coordination and integration of the two command pillars occurred in $C^3IC$, which was staffed, in turn, by representatives of the United States, Saudi Arabia, and other national forces. This was the "workhorse" of the coalition, but even here one analyst describes the results as a "unity of effort, not a unity of command."[147] Field-level coordination between the forces was accomplished by NATO procedures in the American pillar and by attaching United States liaison teams to the Saudi-led forces. The liaison teams also acted as "shadow staff," assisting the Saudi and other Arab-Islamic commanders in translating the campaign plan into operational orders. Nonetheless, there remained considerable diversity in tactical doctrines.[148]

For most coalition members, form resembled substance, and they cooperated with the United States in relatively anarchic relationships. For the Gulf states, however, where the risk of opportunism really mattered, appearances and reality were quite different. Despite the trappings of equality, once they threw their support behind the United States and against Iraq, Saudi Arabia and the other Gulf states lost considerable decision-making authority, especially in the area of foreign policy. The timing of the air and ground campaigns, for instance, were each set by the United States and formally communicated to the heads of state in the coalition only hours before each began.[149] Although the operation was extensively planned in advance in consultation with the coalition partners, and the actual declaration of military hostilities was a surprise to no one, that it fell to President Bush to start the war—from Saudi territory—is symbolically important and provides clear evidence of who in the coalition was "calling the shots."[150]

The second safeguard was the "outer coalition" in the United Nations, which from the outset of the crisis played an important role in American policy toward the Gulf. The idea of using the United Nations as a source of

[146] Khaled bin Sultan 1995, 37. There is no evidence that the United States asked or pushed for the creation of a supreme commander. Yet this was a Saudi concern from the start and, indeed, a high diplomatic priority. Lt. Gen. Khaled's title as Commander of Joint Forces and Theater of Operations was self-consciously designed to preempt any attempt by the United States to obtain supreme commander status for Schwarzkopf.

[147] Yates 1993, 48.

[148] Ibid., 50. On the lack of operational coordination, see Gordon and Trainor 1995.

[149] Atkinson 1993, 23–24. Nonetheless, under a secret agreement with the United States, King Fahd had to authorize any offensive military operations that might be launched from his territory. Secretary of State Baker visited Saudi Arabia and received this authorization after his failed meeting in Geneva with Iraq's foreign minister, Tariq Aziz. Woodward 1991, 361.

[150] On the propensity of the United States to decide first and consult second, see Brenner 1991, 666.

legitimacy for United States efforts in the Gulf largely originated with Secretary of State Baker, but was received lukewarmly by the Pentagon and White House, who feared that it would overly constrain America's freedom of action.[151] Yet, it was exactly the chance that the United Nations might not approve American actions in the Gulf that made its support so influential. If the United States was exploiting its partners, their dissent would undermine support in the Security Council, possibly provoking a veto from one of the other permanent members, limiting the authority received by the United States, or forcing an alteration in policy. It was the possibility that the United Nations could block American policy that, in fact, conferred international legitimacy.[152]

This is seen most clearly in the approval of Resolution 678. In October and November, the coalition had begun to weaken, a fact that was apparent to administration insiders if not the general public.[153] The lack of diplomatic progress ignited new fears of war within the United States and other coalition partners. The doubling of American troop strength in the Gulf, without prior consultation with its partners or public discussion at home, magnified these fears. Iraq also slowly ate away at the coalition's unity by shrewdly manipulating the release of hostages in exchange for high-level diplomatic contacts, thereby easing its isolation within the world community.[154] As the coalition came under stress, Bush and Baker turned once again to the United Nations, reasoning that international approval would relegitimate American actions and reconsolidate the coalition, while at the same time signaling Iraq that it must get out of Kuwait.[155] Interestingly, Britain argued that United Nations approval was unnecessary and that the coalition already possessed sufficient authority under the right of self-defense in Article 51 of the United Nations Charter. Nonetheless, although at least partly sharing this view, the United States returned to the United Nations for explicit approval.[156] In seeking this support, the president and secretary of state undertook another diplomatic

[151] US News and World Report 1992, 36; Crabb and Mulcahy 1995, 259; interview with Wolfowitz, June 28, 1995. US News and World Report 1992, 82, and Baker 1995, 304, cite Bush as supportive of the United Nations from the beginning, although Woodward 1991, 284, suggests that he was skeptical that it could act effectively. Haass (interview, June 28, 1995) identifies three problems with relying upon the United Nations: 1. delay; 2. the risk that the United States might not get what it wanted; and 3. the danger of a precedent for future operations.

[152] Blackwell, Mazarr, and Snider 1991, 7.

[153] Woodward 1991, 319.

[154] Dannreuther 1991/92, 38.

[155] They also sought to strengthen domestic and congressional support. See Smith 1992, 207, 212. A senior aide to Secretary of State Baker also reasoned that United Nations backing would "box the Democrats in very nicely"; US News and World Report 1992, 155. See also Baker 1995, 322.

[156] Freedman and Karsh 1993, 228.

marathon, contacting heads of state and holding over two hundred meetings seeking foreign support.[157] In the end, the United States agreed to soften the language of the resolution, substituting "all necessary means" for "force," and giving into demands by the Soviet Union and France for a final try at diplomacy before initiating hostilities.[158] After making these concessions, support for expelling Iraq from Kuwait quickly firmed up. The diplomatic ploy worked.

In a March 1991 speech, President Bush stated that he probably would have gone to war against Iraq even without United Nations approval, suggesting that the legitimacy created by Resolution 678 was facilitative rather than decisive. Surely most of the inner coalition would have fought with the United States. The larger unknown is whether the United States would have gone ahead—or at least fought the war as it did—without the acquiescence of the Soviet Union.[159] In the end, the constraints exerted by the United Nations were reciprocal: because the legitimacy conferred by the world body was important to the United States, the latter was willing to compromise to obtain the former's approval; but as other countries valued their ability to constrain the United States and wanted to keep it working within the United Nations framework, the Americans were able to tug the organization in the direction they wanted it to go.[160] Nonetheless, the United Nations was an important safeguard against American opportunism.

While appealing to the United Nations for legitimacy, and accepting that some constraints on its policy were necessary to obtain support, the United States also worked hard to limit the authority exercised by the world body. Curiously, in the Korean War the United States was formally "mandated" by the United Nations to control the operation. In the Gulf War, the United States itself claimed de facto control and did not receive any formal authorization to lead the coalition forces—and leadership was de jure shared with Saudi Arabia.[161] Correspondingly, critics have charged that the United Nations abdicated its oversight responsibilities and weakened the organization in its failure to exert greater control over the United States.

The option of ceding greater authority to the United Nations was, in fact, under discussion at various moments during the conflict. Several attempts were made to activate the United Nations Military Staff Committee, charged under Article 41 of the United Nations Charter with overseeing military operations under the organization, composed of the military chiefs of staff of the permanent five members of the Security Council (and others, as appro-

---

[157] Brune 1993, 67; Woodward 1991, 333.

[158] Freedman and Karsh 1993, 230–32. On the wrangle over the wording of Resolution 678, see Woodward 1991, 334.

[159] Friedman 1991, 56; Springborg 1994, 50.

[160] Interview with Wolfowitz, June 28, 1995.

[161] Thompson 1993, 139.

priate), and responsible for the strategic direction of the armed forces.[162] These attempts did not amount to much, however, largely because of internal divisions within the Soviet Union. In discussing the naval blockade, for instance, the Soviet Union raised the question of activating the Military Staff Committee, but did not push hard for fear that it would be obligated to contribute ships to the operation. In September, Foreign Minister Eduard Shevardnadze raised the possibility of Soviet troops serving in the Gulf under the auspices of the Committee, and Baker went so far as to clear the participation of Soviet troops with King Fahd; again, however, the possibility was dropped under domestic criticism in the Soviet Union.[163]

Although open to a possibly greater role for the United Nations, the United States resisted any attempt to subordinate its own authority to that of the international organization. Most importantly, the United States feared micromanagement from an international body that might not share its military doctrines and war plans.[164] If it was activated, the United States made clear that the Military Staff Committee would have to function in a purely symbolic mode.[165] Even then, the United States was willing to consider this possibility if and only if the Soviet Union could be brought into the inner coalition, thereby limiting the latter's ability to act independently and potentially threaten American aims. Given the internal problems during what we now recognize as the death throes of the Soviet Union, integrating the collapsing superpower into the inner coalition was not possible. In the end, the United States agreed to lead the coalition only if it was bound by its partners but not by a formal international organization.

### OTHER PARTNERS

Outside of the Persian Gulf states, the United States relied on anarchic security relationships with its partners. Although some variation existed, fewer specific assets were at risk in the remainder of the inner coalition, thus lowering the expected costs of opportunism. In cases where specific assets did exist, the costs of establishing greater hierarchy over these parties were prohibitive. In addition, both safeguards discussed above depended for their effectiveness on the states in the inner and outer coalitions retaining a wide measure of foreign policy independence. If they too were controlled by the United States, they could not serve as a check on American opportunism.

---

[162] Arend and Beck 1993.

[163] Freedman and Karsh 1993, 126, 149–50; Dannreuther 1991/92, 29. This was an important case of the diplomats getting out ahead of the military in both the Soviet Union and the United States. American military officers would have been extremely concerned about sharing intelligence with the Soviet forces and, given Iraq's Soviet-supplied equipment, there would have been enormous problems in distinguishing friends from foes with Soviet forces on the American side of the line. Interview with Paul Wolfowitz, June 28, 1995. See also Baker 1995, 283.

[164] Interview with Wolfowitz, June 28, 1995.

[165] Interview with Haass, June 28, 1995.

The low level of asset specificity permitted anarchic security relationships, and the safeguards required them.

Britain and France were critical members of the inner coalition because of the resources they brought to the effort and their status as permanent members of the United Nations Security Council.[166] Of its coalition partners, only Britain and France contributed troops and equipment that could have been replaced only at significant cost to the United States.[167] Past investments in common NATO standards and procedures paid real dividends and made these troops virtual substitutes for American forces. The expected costs of opportunism were higher for these partners than others in the inner coalition. At the same time, if Britain or France left the coalition to protest American policy, this would have imposed substantial costs on the United States, giving them greater influence over American conduct than most others in the coalition. For these reasons, combined with their seats on the Security Council, Britain and France occupied key decision nodes in the coalition and served as important checks on American power.

Britain strongly backed the United States from the start of the crisis. Indeed, Margaret Thatcher's meeting with President Bush the day after the invasion of Kuwait is widely credited with stiffening the latter's resolve to stand up to Iraq. Despite the potential for disruption that arose from its contributions to the coalition and its veto at the United Nations, Britain was an important supporter behind America's leadership within the coalition.

France was a troublesome partner, but therefore a more effective restraint on the United States.[168] Although it offered qualified support for the United States in public, and promised its full support should conflict erupt, France nonetheless resisted the integration of its forces into the American command structure, adopted an independent course in the conflict, and made a series of diplomatic overtures to Iraq that were strongly opposed by the United States. With the largest Arab population of any European country and close ties to the Maghreb, where support for Saddam was high, France had long maintained a special relationship with Iraq based largely on the exchange of arms for oil. Iraq, in turn, had many supporters within the French government, including Defense Minister Jean-Pierre Chevènement, a founding member of the Iraqi-French Friendship Association. Throughout the crisis,

---

[166] For good overviews of Britain, see Lepgold 1997; of France, see Grunberg 1997.

[167] The contributions of other NATO members were sufficiently small that they could have been replaced more easily. See Table 6.1.

[168] On the political positions of the various European states during the Persian Gulf War, see Salmon 1992. Brenner 1991, 672 and 674, locates the source of Europe's differences with the United States in the failure of the former to recognize that a compromise solution might be unreachable and that war was necessary. France's "singularity," in turn, was premised on the United States continuing to take a firm stand against Iraq, thereby saving the government in Paris from the consequences of its appeasement policy.

France was willing to link the resolution of Iraq's position in Kuwait with a broader Middle East peace settlement, a move first publicly made by President François Mitterrand in a speech at the United Nations on September 24. The United States forcefully opposed the policy of linkage, and Secretary of State Baker apparently accused Mitterrand of making "an appeasement speech, like those heard in Europe in the 1930s."[169] A big question mark in the coalition from the beginning, France became increasingly vociferous over the fall.[170] Until the very end, long after the United States had positioned itself to expel Iraq from Kuwait by force, France continued to push for a compromise solution that might end the conflict short of war.[171]

There were few safeguards erected to control French opportunism during the crisis, despite a constant fear that initiatives arising in Paris might fracture the coalition. Not only would establishing greater control over France be extremely costly but to force it from the coalition or attempt to control it too tightly would vitiate its important role as a check on American opportunism. Rather, the United States simply accepted the risks from its most difficult partner in the inner coalition. France's role as a check on American power was clearly understood, and was no less effective for it. As French President Mitterrand noted in a meeting with King Hussein of Jordan, "We joined the coalition because we wanted to put the brakes on from the inside."[172]

The Arab coalition also occupied a key role within the inner coalition, and as a result possessed leverage over American policy. With the exception of Egypt, the Arab states of the inner coalition provided few forces to Operation Desert Shield/Storm. Operationally deficient, they provided little value-added to the coalition. Nonetheless, they were an important political counterweight to Iraq and inoculated the Gulf states against a potentially virulent anti-Americanism in the Islamic world.[173]

Syria, in particular, was a central target of American and Arab diplomacy.[174] As a center of Arab radicalism, Syria's participation in the coalition prevented Saddam—despite his best efforts—from successfully portraying the conflict as one of Western imperialism against Arab nationalism. Equally important, because Syrian and American interests clashed on so many dimensions, Syria was a critical fire alarm in the coalition. Given its differences with the United States, Syria could be expected to quit the coalition at the first sign of American opportunism, thereby sending a signal to other states—and especially

[169] Freedman and Karsh 1993, 167; Howorth 1994, 175–79.

[170] US News and World Report 1992, 314.

[171] On France's last-minute efforts, see Freedman and Karsh 1993, 264–74.

[172] Quoted in Heikal 1992, 252.

[173] Interview with Haass, June 28, 1995. This inoculation appears to have worked. Predictions that the presence of Western forces in the Gulf would set the "Arab street" ablaze largely fizzled. Interview with Wolfowitz, June 28, 1995.

[174] For an overview of Syria's role in the coalition, see Hinnebusch 1997.

other Arab states—that the United States was stepping outside the agreed-upon goals of the coalition. Other states, therefore, did not need to monitor American policy; they only needed to watch whether Syria was willing to participate in the American-led effort. This helps to explain why the United States exerted an extraordinary effort to bring Syria into the coalition and ensure that its troops actively participated in the fighting.[175] Like France, it was the anti-Americanism so manifest in other areas of Syrian foreign policy that made it critical to the coalition and a real check on American policy.

The members of the outer coalition also exerted significant influence over the United States. The immediate interests of the United States and the members of the outer coalition diverged sharply. These were, after all, countries that chose not to join the war effort but that nonetheless occupied key positions within the global community and whose support or acquiescence were deemed central to American policy. Of these, the Soviet Union was the most important.[176] Secretary of State James Baker, in reflecting on the Gulf crisis, notes that "from the start, I had viewed the Soviets as key. In every strategy calculation, I considered their support a prerequisite to a credible coalition. They had to be courted, nurtured, and included to a degree once unthinkable."[177] This critical role gave the Soviet Union considerable leverage over United States policy, and threatened at times to obstruct American goals and break apart the coalition.[178]

During the Cold War, Iraq had been a client of the Soviet Union, and President Mikhail Gorbachev was under strong pressure from military and political conservatives—as well as the so-called Arabists in the Foreign Ministry—not to abandon a long-time friend. Having already watched their empire in Eastern Europe dissolve, many did not now want to concede their remaining ties in the Middle East.[179] Although largely absorbed by the momentous events unfolding at home, Gorbachev nonetheless sought to reach a compromise solution to the Iraqi crisis, sending Yevgeny Primakov, one of the Soviet Union's leading experts on the Middle East, to Iraq as his personal intermediary in October and, with France, engineering the seven-week delay in Resolution 678.[180] On the eve of the land war, Gorbachev even undertook to bring about a last-minute compromise, much to the consternation of the United States, which worried that new negotiations at this stage would throw off its timetable or, worse, put it in the uncomfortable position of rejecting a superficially appealing agreement just as it was poised to destroy the Iraqi

---

[175] Baker 1995, 295–98, 373–74, and 376–77.

[176] See Hannah 1997.

[177] Baker 1995, 281–83, 287; quote on 281.

[178] Ibid., 396–410.

[179] On internal developments in the Soviet Union and their relationship to the Gulf War, see Ticktin 1991, 32–33.

[180] On Primakov's mission, see Freedman and Karsh 1993, 175–79.

army.[181] In the end, the Soviet Union did not prevent the United States from realizing its objectives, which it could have easily done by exercising its veto in the United Nations or giving Iraq satellite photos of the troops massing for the "left hook."[182] But its support came only at an uncomfortably high price (see below).

Central to the coalition because of the resources they brought to the Gulf or the key political roles they occupied, France with its "singularity" throughout the crisis, Syria with its long history of opposition to the United States, and the Soviet Union as the decaying but still opposed superpower were critical checks upon American policy. These constraints, in turn, were the primary governance costs of cooperation imposed on the United States, and they were sufficiently severe to cause many, especially in retrospect, to question the wisdom of security cooperation.

### Governance Costs

The United States bore three types of governance costs in constructing and maintaining cooperation during the Persian Gulf War. The first and most direct set of costs were incurred in leading the coalition, and especially in sending a large force to the Gulf. Although many have pointed to the military rationale behind the massive American forces sent to the Gulf in Operation Desert Shield/Storm, safeguarding itself against the risk of opportunism by others provides equally compelling political rationale, and helps explain why the United States did not push others even harder to send yet more forces to the Gulf. Of course, the massive deployment in the Gulf fit easily into the Pentagon's doctrine of using only overwhelming force. As a result, it is not clear how great a cost this was to the United States: if this was something the country would have wanted to do anyway, it bears no real cost for having done so. The direct costs of leadership were most likely quite small.

The second set of governance costs were incurred in inducing others to participate in the coalition. The list of favors, gifts, and political compromises made in assembling the coalition is lengthy. Egypt joined the coalition when the United States Treasury forgave $6.7 billion in previous loans.[183] In exchange for Syria's participation, the United States lifted sanctions previously imposed for its support of terrorism and turned a blind eye toward its final assault on Lebanon.[184] Syria also received $500 million in indirect aid from the United States, as well as $2 billion from Saudi Arabia and Kuwait, $500

---

[181] On the last-minute Soviet effort, see ibid., 374–85.

[182] Easterbrook 1991, 38.

[183] Yant 1991, 93; Atkinson 1993, 54. According to Woodward 1991, 287, Saddam tried to bribe Egypt to stay out of the anti-Iraq coalition. On Egypt's contributions, see Brumberg 1997.

[184] Atkinson 1993, 54; Pimlott 1992, 52.

million from Japan, and $200 million from Europe.[185] Turkey, a willing part-
ner in the coalition seeking to secure its position as linchpin between Europe
and the Middle East in the post-Cold War world, nonetheless received concessions on textile imports into the United States, trade credits, and approval
to resell American military equipment abroad.[186] Even members of the outer
coalition received concessions. Colombia, then a member of the Security
Council, was allowed to renounce its extradition treaty with the United
States.[187] Malaysia, another member, received a break on textile exports to the
United States.[188] China was pardoned by the Bush administration for
the crackdown on Tienanmen Square; by receiving Peking's foreign minister,
the first-high level visit since the assault on prodemocracy demonstrators,
the president was able to avoid a Chinese veto in the Security Council.[189] The
Soviet Union, the most critical member of the outer coalition, was particularly privileged, receiving at America's request a $4 billion line of credit
from Saudi Arabia.[190] The United States also chose, in exchange for Moscow's
support on Resolution 678, to avoid any harsh condemnation of the Soviet
crackdown on the Baltic states.[191] As *US News and World Report* concluded,
albeit in slightly exaggerated language, "in terms of actual dollars and compromised principles" the costs to the United States of building the coalition
against Iraq was "staggeringly high."[192]

In the end, only Yemen consistently rejected American overtures for support. As the only Arab state on the Security Council, and the poorest of the
Gulf states, Yemen was an important player in the drama at the United Na-
tions and deeply sympathetic to Saddam's political program in the Middle
East. It consistently refused to go along with the majority on most United
Nations resolutions on Iraq. Right up until the vote on Resolution 678, it
appeared undecided, and the United States exerted considerable pressure for,
at least, an abstention. When Yemen finally voted "no," Secretary of State
Baker, sitting in for the United States at the meeting, quickly penned the
Yemeni ambassador a note, informing him "that is the most expensive vote
you have ever cast." Three days later, the United States canceled $70 million
of previously allocated foreign aid.[193]

[185] Yant 1991, 93; US News and World Report 1992, 86.
[186] Bahcheli 1994, 437; Yant 1991, 93; US News and World Report 1992, 94–95; Atkinson
1993, 54. On Turkey's contributions to the Gulf War, see Sayari 1997.
[187] US News and World Report 1992, 94.
[188] Ibid., 94.
[189] Atkinson 1993, 54; Nacos 1994, 545. This linkage was explicit. See Baker 1995, 322–24.
[190] Baker 1995, 294–95.
[191] Smith 1992, 210; Atkinson 1993, 54.
[192] US News and World Report 1992, 94.
[193] Ibid., 181. See also Brune 1993, 68; Freedman and Karsh 1993, 233. Baker's account does
not contradict this explicit warning to Yemen, but it does differ slightly. Baker 1995, 325.
Although punishing Yemen was not a priority for the Bush administration, where it had discre-

The third, more indirect, but ultimately most important set of costs were the constraints imposed by the coalition on America's freedom of action. The magnitude of these governance cost depends, of course, upon an estimate of what the United States would have done in the Persian Gulf if it had fought unilaterally.[194] Although the United States never self-consciously gave up any important objectives under pressure from the coalition, its objectives and those of the coalition evolved simultaneously over the fall of 1990. In this sense, the self-conscious aims of the United States were endogenous to the politics of assembling and managing the coalition.[195] This makes discerning its autonomous goals—what it would have done on its own—particularly difficult, but not impossible.

The constraints imposed by the coalition are, perhaps, most clearly manifest in the limited objectives of the war. The early deployment of American forces to the Gulf was for the ostensible purpose of deterring further Iraqi aggression against Saudi Arabia. Clear from the outset, however, was a larger United States desire to compel Iraq's withdrawal from Kuwait, a desire made most evident in President Bush's famous remark only days after the invasion that Iraq's conquest of Kuwait "will not stand."[196] By the start of the war, the stated objectives had expanded to include expelling Iraq from Kuwait and destroying its nuclear, biological, and chemical warfare capability, its ballistic missile program, and its mechanized military units.[197] By the end of the war, American aims had expanded again to include the sound defeat and, thereby, delegitimation of Iraq and the replacement of Saddam Hussein by another leader drawn from the Sunni minority in Iraq. As evidence of the maximum possible objectives of the United States, an expanded war was envisioned in plans to continue the ground offensive to Baghdad, surround the city with American forces, and "liberate" it with Islamic forces.

The limited objectives of the war sat poorly with the American public, at least once the military imbalance between the coalition and Iraqi forces be-

---

tion it nonetheless choose to "lean on" the recalcitrant state. Interview with Haass, June 28, 1995.

[194] Note that the appropriate counterfactual is fighting unilaterally, not choosing to maintain sanctions longer or giving in to Iraq. These alternatives change the goal of American policy, not just the way in which its goal of expelling Iraq from Kuwait was pursued.

[195] At the same time, the war aims of the other coalition members were endogenous and also evolved over time. Nonetheless, they did not perfectly coincide with American objectives, Khaled bin Sultan 1995, 188 and 315. Paul Wolfowitz (interview, June 28, 1995) describes the process of building consensus within the coalition as one that reinforced internal brakes and strengthened the self-discipline of the United States.

[196] This was an apparently spontaneous comment that was cleared with neither his diplomatic and military officials nor the members of the emerging coalition, but that nonetheless reflected the building consensus in the National Security Council. Smith 1992, 90; US News and World Report 1992, 48, 79; Freedman and Karsh 1993, 76; Woodward 1991, 260.

[197] Dannreuther 1991/92, 46.

came evident. Clearly, America's crusading spirit would have been more satisfied with the maximum rather than minimum objectives. Reflecting this desire, the war has spawned a minor literature with titles such as "triumph without victory" and "hollow victory," reflecting the collective unease.[198] Even the limited objectives honed by the Bush administration over the fall were only partially fulfilled. Although Iraq was expelled from Kuwait, its military capability was not destroyed, as the repression of the Shiites in southern Iraq and the Kurds in northern Iraq immediately after the war attest. When the United States declared a cease-fire, leaving open an escape route back into Iraq, many of the best-equipped Republican Guard units avoided destruction. Reflecting both intelligence failures and the limits of air power, the coalition destroyed far less of Iraq's nuclear, biological, and chemical capability than expected, necessitating a subsequent United Nations-sponsored program to dismantle these facilities and continuing tension with Iraq over compliance. Finally, Saddam remained in power, having succeeded in putting down the internal resurrections and forestalling possible coups. As early as September 1991, Gregg Easterbrook could write that "it is not even clear that we won the war, though we certainly won the parade."[199]

In each case, the failure to fulfill these limited objectives can be placed, at least in part, on the coalition, which led to a lowest-common-denominator politics. Although Britain and Saudi Arabia apparently hoped to continue the war in order to defeat the Republican Guard units, there was at least implicit pressure from others in the coalition to keep the war more limited.[200] There was apparently little communication between senior United States officials and foreign governments in the closing hours of the war. Nonetheless, the views of the Soviet Union and France, in particular, were well known in advance and anticipated by the president and his inner circle in deciding upon the cease-fire.[201] Secretary of State Baker, at least, was genuinely fearful that the Soviet Union "might fracture the coalition by calling on the U.N. Security Council to halt the continuing slaughter."[202] Already shocked by the level of force used against Iraq, the Arabs were generally opposed to any further attacks on the retreating Iraqi forces, and continuing the war would have severely damaged relations with Arab governments in the coalition.[203] The United States certainly did not face an ultimatum from its partners, but according to Richard Haass, then special assistant to the president for Near East and South Asia affairs on the National Security Council staff, "it was

---

[198] US News and World Report 1992; Record 1993.

[199] Easterbrook 1991, 33.

[200] Freedman and Karsh 1993, 405 and 412.

[201] Interview with Wolfowitz, June 28, 1995.

[202] Baker 1995, 436.

[203] Heikal 1992, 316; Friedman 1991, 58. With more extensive war aims than most other Arab states, Saudi Arabia is the exception to this generalization.

more the administration's sense that we didn't have very long before the coalition began to come apart over this issue."[204] Bush later justified the decision to stop the war at one hundred hours because "the coalition was agreed on driving the Iraqis from Kuwait, not on carrying the conflict into Iraq or destroying Iraqi forces."[205] Reflecting on the war, Secretary of State Baker put it more pointedly: "pressing on to Baghdad would have caused not just a rift but an earthquake within the coalition . . . [and a] war to liberate Kuwait from a universally condemned invasion would have been transformed into a war of U.S. imperialism."[206] In the end, we do not know whether the United States, left completely to its own devices, would have given in to its crusading spirit and transformed the limited objectives formulated by the coalition into the unconditional defeat of Iraq.[207] Nonetheless, we can see clearly that the possibility of transforming the limited war into a crusade was blocked by the coalition.

The constraints of the coalition are also evident in the period before the war. As shown above, the United States deployed massive forces to the Gulf in part to assure the Saudis of its commitment and to establish control over the coalition. The massive deployment, however, also committed the United States to a combative stance against Iraq and, because of the difficulties of fielding a large force in a hostile climate, imposed a strict timetable on the resolution of the conflict. Most importantly, this limited the time in which sanctions could be allowed to have an effect.

To maintain the credibility of its commitment, and to deter others from defecting and cutting a separate deal with Baghdad, the United States had to insist upon no negotiations and no linkage with other issues. Again, the coalitional constraints overlapped with the internal desire of the Bush administration, which believed deeply that aggression should not be rewarded. Nonetheless, the hard diplomatic line followed throughout the conflict was a tremendous impediment to other avenues for potentially resolving the disposition of Kuwait and inhibited the United States from pursuing peace feelers from Iraq. As it was, the last-minute discussions with Iraq and especially the offer of a trip by Secretary of State Baker to Baghdad had the Saudis in a "cold sweat."[208] It is unlikely that negotiations would have produced a mutually acceptable outcome, given Iraq's insistence that Kuwait was an integral

---

[204] Interview with Haass, June 28, 1995.

[205] Gordon and Trainer 1994, 10.

[206] Baker 1996, M6.

[207] Gordon and Trainor 1995 place considerable responsibility on the United States military leadership, primarily concerned with the image of the armed forces rather than the diplomatic objectives of the president, for stopping the war "prematurely" at one hundred hours.

[208] On the secretary of state's proposed visit and actual meeting with Tariq Aziz in Geneva, see Baker 1995, 46–65, and Freedman and Karsh 1993, 240–45 and 253–60. The Saudi reaction was described by Wolfowitz; interview, June 28, 1995.

part of its territory and America's insistence on Iraq's unconditional withdrawal. But the need to hold the coalition together ensured that negotiations would never really begin.[209]

The coalition also restrained the actual conduct of the war. Not only could Saddam not be personally targeted, at least publicly,[210] but incursions into Iraq had to be limited. None of the Arab states joined in the left hook through Iraq, and none could countenance the violation of sovereignty of a fellow Islamic state. Also crucial was the question of Israel—a "silent" member of the outer coalition. Israel's role in the coalition was not to be drawn into the war and, thereby, potentially disrupt the inner coalition (in this case, opportunistic behavior by this partner would have been the opposite of "abandonment": rather, joining in). Even though the United States extracted secret commitments from Egypt, Saudi Arabia, Kuwait, and even Syria to remain in the war if Iraq brought Israel in,[211] the outcome was sufficiently in doubt that the United States nonetheless exerted considerable pressure on Israel to prevent it from responding even to direct Scud missile attacks on its territory. Deputy Secretary of State Lawrence Eagleburger was dispatched to Tel Aviv with a "blank check" to cover whatever Israel demanded to stay out of the war.[212] Israel, in turn, pressed the United States to make sure that the blow to Iraq's regional pretensions was decisive and to eliminate the only weapons that could pose an immediate threat to itself, the Scuds.[213] Poorly constructed and wildly inaccurate, the missiles were, for the inner coalition, militarily insignificant. Nonetheless, to buy Israel's "silence," the United States devoted a substantial fraction of its air power to destroying the Scuds; during the first phase of the air campaign, 15 percent of all sorties focused on surface-to-surface missiles.[214]

Already high, the governance costs confronting the United States appear to have risen rapidly with greater hierarchy. Unfortunately, in contrast to the occupations of Germany and Japan in Chapter 5, there is no direct counterfactual to probe the structure of governance costs. Nonetheless, considering alternative scenarios suggests that governance costs would have escalated rapidly with hierarchy. To safeguard Saudi Arabia from American exploitation, the United States paid a high cost in constraints on its own behavior. Given the widespread skepticism about America's role in the Middle East, any effort by the United States to exert even greater control over the king-

---

[209] Baker 1995, 352.

[210] Freedman and Karsh 1993, 434.

[211] Atkinson 1993, 83; Baker 1995, 306–8.

[212] Baker 1995, 388.

[213] Freedman and Karsh 1993, 336.

[214] Ibid., 264 and 309. Dannreuther 1991/92, 50, suggests that despite the magnitude of this effort, the resources devoted to the "Scud hunt" did not materially affect the success of the air campaign.

dom was likely to meet stiff resistance. Rather than simply tying its hands, the United States might have had to coerce Saudi Arabia into a more subordinate role—at great expense to itself both directly, in resources expended to persuade the Saudis to accept this more vulnerable position, and indirectly, in the political repercussions likely to occur in the region and elsewhere. What stands in the case of Saudi Arabia would seem to be magnified for other states in or out of the coalition. With fewer direct interests at stake in the Gulf, other partners would have resisted American domination even more strongly. Nothing was—or remains—more likely to generate a global balance of power against the United States than coercive attempts to subordinate partners to its will.

The United States willingly bore substantial costs in direct concessions and compromised principles to build the coalition, and accepted the constraints imposed upon it. With the exception of the United States-Saudi Arabia dyad, and perhaps ties with other regional states, the broader coalition was not a military necessity. Rather, the roots of the coalition were in the need to gain access to the necessary territory and infrastructure in Saudi Arabia and other Gulf states, the desire to safeguard these relationships against possible American opportunism, and—more generally—the need to mask America's influence and capabilities in a one-superpower world. The external constraints that confronted Washington were imposed not by the enemy but by America's partners.

### GOVERNING COOPERATION IN SOMALIA

In Somalia, the United States did not require significant cooperation with others in the region to mount the military intervention. Unlike Operation Desert Shield/Storm, the United States could have undertaken Operation Restore Hope unilaterally if it had so desired. Yet the United States, once again, chose to construct a coalition of states and to abide by the constraints of the United Nations.

Again, the "inner" coalition of states that contributed forces to Operation Restore Hope and the "outer" coalition of states embodied in the United Nations, especially the Security Council, were constructed to check American intentions and capabilities, lest the intervention spark fears of American imperialism. The constraints of the coalition, in turn, were deemed acceptable because they entailed few real governance costs: its partners did not actually prevent the United States from doing anything it wanted to do. In this case, creating a diverse coalition made clear to others that the United States was motivated only by humanitarian concerns and did not possess any larger foreign policy goals in the region. The coalition merely reinforced America's self-defined humanitarian objectives.

The eventual "failure" in Somalia was in part a product of the safeguards the United States imposed upon itself. More important, however, the mission finally collapsed because of the difficulties of nation building and the absence of political support for achieving this aim. The failure to restore stability in Somalia has generated considerable disappointment with the United Nations, and security cooperation more broadly, when the blame, such as it is, might be better directed toward home.

## Expected Costs of Opportunism

The expected costs of opportunism to the United States in Operation Restore Hope were relatively small. Although the United States did spread some of the burden of the humanitarian rescue of Somalia onto its partners and, later, the United Nations, it actually incurred few (if any) specific assets in undertaking the mission. No forward bases were required, and the troops and equipment deployed were not highly specialized.

In addition, the discretionary nature of the inner coalition meant that the interests of the countries that chose to participate were generally aligned. A broad call for international assistance was made and the coalition was simply assembled from the countries that responded. Most contributors shared America's desire to end the starvation, like Belgium, or felt it important to be seen assisting the United States, like Saudi Arabia. Unlike the Gulf War, where some countries were pressed to join the coalition, no specific targets were singled out or subjected to diplomatic pressure.[215]

Some countries, of course, did come to Somalia with their own political agendas, like Egypt, which had regional aspirations, or Italy, the former colonial power. Despite the low probability of opportunism and the absence of specific assets, the United States nonetheless adopted several safeguards against possible perfidy by such partners. As in the Persian Gulf War, the United States seized a controlling position within the coalition by contributing a majority of the forces—over 75 percent of the total at UNITAF's peak. Although all troops remained under national command, the United States insisted upon operational control over all UNITAF forces in Somalia and adopted rules of engagement written in the Pentagon, thereby keeping tight military control over most participants.[216] Indeed, the United States was willing to undertake a forceful intervention into Somalia only if there was no interference by others with its command and control of the entire coalition force.[217] For the smaller participants, this operational leverage was reinforced

---

[215] Interview with Dobbins, November 13, 1996, and Cohen, November 13, 1996.

[216] Hirsch and Oatley 1995, 75–76; Freeman, Lambert, and Mims 1993, 65.

[217] Oakley n.d., 3. It should be noted that the United States routinely places its troops under foreign operational command in NATO and elsewhere. Nonetheless, in the views of one Defense Department analyst, the United States will not place its troops under the operational command of those in whom it does not have great confidence. Interview with anonymous Department of Defense official, November 12, 1996.

by their dependence upon the American military infrastructure in Somalia. The larger and more self-sufficient contingents were assigned to their own geographic commands, which helped in these cases to limit possible political spillovers onto American forces or claims on additional resources. In these ways, the potential for opportunism was reduced even further. Given the low expected costs of opportunism, there was little need to consider greater hierarchy. More formal control by the United States over its partners in Somalia was largely unnecessary.

Conversely, the potential for the United States to act opportunistically both toward Somalia and the other countries in the region was substantial. Assuming the role of peacemaker gave the United States substantial residual rights of control and risked turning the once-sovereign state into a "neocolonial dependency." Somalis, and Aidid in particular, worried that a United Nations trusteeship might be imposed on the country,[218] a move that was actually discussed within both the United Nations and the State Department and reported in the news media.[219] Somalis also feared that the United States would reestablish order only to create a new political system that reflected Western values and interests rather than indigenous cultures and practices.[220] Thus, even apart from the warring factions that would be the immediate victims of peace, Somalis at large were apprehensive about their occupation by the forces of an external power.

Neighboring states also worried that a weak Somalia dependent upon the United States would allow the country to be used as a staging area for intervention elsewhere in the region.[221] Some feared that the intervention in Somalia might be a preemptive strike against Islamic fundamentalism.[222] The Islamic military government in Khartoum, described by one State Department official as "apoplectic" about the intervention, feared that Somalia might be used as a site to support an American move into the southern Sudan.[223] Less directly, others were concerned about precedent; causing a minor diplomatic row, the Kenyan government described Operation Restore Hope as an "invasion" of Somalia.[224]

---

[218] Drysdale 1997, 126.

[219] Muravchik 1993, 19. Also interviews with Cohen, November 13, 1996, and Cheshes, November 4, 1996. These discussions, however, were never advanced to the political level, and the idea of a trusteeship was quickly abandoned as "too expensive."

[220] Lefebvre 1993, 60; Stevenson 1993, 149.

[221] Lefebvre 1993, 58; Howe 1995, 50.

[222] Lefebvre 1993, 59–60.

[223] Ibid., 59. Interview with anonymous State Department official, November 7, 1996. This view was not shared by those State Department officials who were interviewed "on the record."

[224] Clark 1993, 120. Analysts describe relations between Kenya and the United States as particularly tense around this time, but attribute this to the American ambassador, Smith Hempstone, whom the regime hated for his prodding on human rights issues. Despite these tensions, however, Kenya did not oppose Operation Restore Hope. Interviews with Cheshes, November 4, 1996, and Houdek, November 13, 1996.

That these fears were exaggerated or, from the American point of view, wholly unjustified is, as in the Gulf case, both true and somewhat beside the point. A successful intervention in Somalia gave the United States de facto if not de jure control over the country and the ability to accomplish these goals if it so chose. Even if the Americans did not consciously possess such imperial designs, the countries of the region could not be confident that the United States might not exploit its new opportunities once the initial mission was accomplished. Just as in the Persian Gulf, where the United States might have given in to its crusading spirit and transformed a limited into an unlimited war, in Somalia the United States might have given in to a modern-day "manifest destiny" designed to rescue weak African regimes from themselves or from an encroaching Islamic fundamentalism.

Aware of these concerns, the United States, once again, self-consciously constructed both an inner and outer coalition to signal the Somalis and others of its limited, humanitarian ambitions.[225] To avoid charges of neo-colonialism in Somalia, the United States safeguarded its intervention to protect others against itself. In this case, with minor exceptions noted below, the safeguards were not imposed by others as a condition of cooperation but were clearly self-imposed. Surprisingly, despite the differences between the Gulf and Somalia, the safeguards took a remarkably similar form. Three specific safeguards were central.

First, as Jeffrey Lefebvre notes, "in order to avoid creating the wrong impression, the United States agreed to lead, but insisted that other states participate in the United Task Force."[226] The United States recognized clearly that it alone had the capacity to carry out the mission. As President Bush stated in his national address on the initial deployment, "Only the United States has the global reach to place a large security force on the ground in such a distant place quickly and efficiently." Yet, he continued, "We will not . . . be acting alone. I expect forces from about a dozen countries to join us in this mission."[227] In fact, this was not an expectation, but a prerequisite for American action. In deciding whether to go into Somalia, President Bush imposed two preconditions: that there must be a United Nations Security Council resolution under Chapter VII authorizing "all necessary means," and that other countries participate and contribute troops. Drawing upon his experience in Africa, the president did not want to reignite old fears of American imperialism, and wanted a multinational coalition to ensure that the nature of the mission was not misconstrued.[228] Only after other contributors

---

[225] The United Nations was itself not entirely immune from such concerns. See United Nations 1996, 52 and 270–72.

[226] Lefebvre 1993, 61; see also Howe 1995, 51.

[227] Bush 1992, 865.

[228] Interview with Cohen, November 13, 1996.

were lined up did the United States open discussions with the United Nations.[229]

Although the United States did not have a "shopping list" of countries it wanted in UNITAF, this concern with signaling the limited intent of the operation was reflected in the states eventually invited to join the coalition. The inclusion of three or four NATO countries was desired to help ease the burden. But once NATO members were involved, the United States needed other states, particularly from Africa and Asia, with interests similar to Somalia's and that could, therefore, play the role of fire alarm. In the words of one State Department official, this could not be a "white man's war."[230] To counter charges that the intervention might be directed against Islam, there was also an emphasis on recruiting at least a handful of Muslim countries; eventually Egypt, Morocco, Malaysia, Pakistan, and Saudi Arabia sent troops. Even so, the coalition was not as heavily Islamic as some in the State Department would have liked.[231] In short, in the words of Robert Houdek, then deputy assistant secretary of state for African affairs, "in putting together the coalition, we were primarily looking for diplomatic cover."[232] For this same reason, the United States needed to lead the coalition with a light hand lest it prevent its partners from playing their assigned roles as fire alarms.

Second, the nature of the mission was strictly limited in public pronouncements and in its planning and execution. As President Bush again stated in his address, "To the people of Somalia I promise this: We do not plan to dictate political outcomes. We respect your sovereignty and independence. Based on my conversations with other coalition leaders, I can state with confidence: We come to your country for one reason only, to enable the starving to be fed."[233] Accordingly, disarming the warlords and rebuilding the institutions of government in Somalia were explicitly ruled out. As noted, this conflicted with the desires of the United Nations, and especially Secretary General Boutros-Ghali, who hoped that the United States would make some progress on this score before turning the mission over to the United Nations. Nonetheless, to demonstrate its limited intent, the United States publicly and effectively tied its hands by ruling out this larger role and by refusing to plan for it.

Third, the United States insisted on working through the United Nations and, later, replacing UNITAF with a regular United Nations peacekeeping force as soon as possible, at most within several months. Given the prior United Nations mission in Somalia, had the United States chosen to act unilaterally or outside the organization it would have signaled to others that it

[229] Hirsch and Oakley 1995, 43, 45; Lefebvre 1993, 56; Howe 1995, 51.
[230] Interview with Houdek, November 13, 1996.
[231] Interview with anonymous State Department official, November 7, 1996.
[232] Interview with Houdek, November 13, 1996.
[233] Bush 1992, 866.

had possibly more expansive objectives. Acting within the United Nations, then, was not only effective burden sharing, but was also a non-negotiable self-imposed limitation on America's own freedom of action.[234] Setting the wheels of the United Nations operation in motion raised the costs to the United States of changing its mind and deciding to prolong its occupation of Somalia. This insistence on a quick hand-off, of course, was a source of considerable rancor between the United States, which wanted a rapid transition, and the United Nations, which sought to delay the transition. In an attempt to broaden American policy to include a greater nation-building role, the United Nations postponed planning for the transition, thereby hampering its abilities once the United States insisted on a May deadline.[235] Other states also failed to deploy their troop contributions on time, thereby leaving UNOSOM II dangerously under strength during the transition.[236] Nonetheless, the United States pushed for the earliest possible withdrawal of its combat forces and transition to UNOSOM II, at least in part to indicate that its objectives were purely humanitarian.

### Governance Costs

The governance costs of cooperation in Somalia were very low. The primary governance cost incurred in Operation Restore Hope was the disproportionate contribution of United States, necessary to secure its leadership of the coalition. The deployment of massive force to Somalia was undoubtedly something the United States, having decided to undertake the mission, would have wanted to do in any event, given its prevailing military doctrines. As in the Gulf War, "leadership" can only be partly counted as a governance cost of the coalition.

The United Nations did insist upon institutional checks on the American-led mission, but these were minor and exerted no significant constraints on the United States. As part of its initial authorizing resolution, the United Nations mandated that UNITAF provide regular reports. Accepting that all United States forces would serve only under national command, the United Nations also specified that the secretary general would assist in designing the command structure of UNITAF. Finally, the United Nations gave the Security

[234] Hirsch and Oakley 1995, 43. There was, of course, a parallel domestic issue that reinforced the need for a quick handoff to the United Nations. As a lame duck administration, the Bush team worked hard to convince itself and the electorate that it had not saddled the incoming Clinton administration with a major military conflict. Some in the Bush administration even pretended that if Clinton did not approve the mission, American forces, which began deployment on December 12, 1992, could be home by January 19, 1993, the day before the inauguration; in fact, 1,500 troops were brought home at that time in a symbolic gesture. In the end, of course, Clinton did support UNITAF.

[235] Ibid., 102–14.

[236] Howe 1995, 52–53.

Council the ability to terminate the UNITAF operation (albeit under the United States veto). Together, these provisions gave the United Nations greater formal authority over UNITAF and America's leadership position than over the Gulf coalition.[237]

Most importantly, the coalition exerted few constraints on American policy. This differs dramatically from the case of the Gulf War, where such constraints were the principal governance costs of cooperation. In view of the widespread impression that the United States was drawn into an expanded mission in Somalia by the coalition, and the United Nations in particular, this controversial point requires elaboration.

As noted above, the United States and United Nations differed on the appropriate mandate for UNITAF, but not on the long-term goals for the United Nations mission in Somalia. The United States, or at least its political leadership, immediately and consistently recognized that the ultimate goal in Somalia was the restoration of political stability, and that this would require a substantial state-building effort. Nonetheless, the United States maintained that these tasks appropriately belonged to the United Nations.[238] The United States did not oppose state building per se in Somalia, but it refused to take responsibility for that task upon itself. In drawing this firm distinction between the humanitarian mission of UNITAF, designed to protect and reopen relief operations, and the state-building mission of UNOSOM II, the United States sought to ensure that it would not be entrapped into a deep and prolonged intervention.

From the outset, UNOSOM II was charged with the more difficult task of rebuilding Somalia. UNOSOM II was to be an entirely multinational, United Nations operation. At the insistence of its partners, American troops did become associated with the United Nations command in UNOSOM II, but only in a limited capacity: logistics troops were under direct United Nations authority, but all combat troops were entirely under American command. Where UNITAF was "over-subscribed," with more countries than necessary willing to participate, few volunteered for UNOSOM II. Lacking faith in the international organization, others were not willing to participate in the operation unless the Americans remained involved in some capacity, however limited.[239] Thus, despite its original intent to wind down its involvement within six months, the United States ended up maintaining a relationship with UNOSOM II, with the separation of command between the logistics and combat troops and a continuing role for the QRF being the unhappy result of this international pressure. This was the only point at which the coalition constrained American policy in a significant way. Confirming the

---

[237] Towell 1992, 3,762; Pine 1992.

[238] Woods 1997, 161.

[239] Interview with Cohen, November 13, 1996.

importance of its role in UNOSOM II, when the United States decided in October 1993 to withdraw its troops from Somalia, other countries—and particularly the Europeans—quickly followed suit.[240]

Through this continuing relationship with UNOSOM II, the United States came to participate in the state-building effort of the United Nations. Nonetheless, although its ties with UNOSOM II were pressed upon it by others, the participation of the United States in this expanded mission was entirely by choice. Over the spring and early summer of 1993, the goals of the United States gradually evolved to resemble more closely the views of the United Nations. Despite its fear of entrapment and the careful design of the relationship to avoid this possibility, the United States and United Nations eventually came to see both the problem and solution in Somalia in similar terms. Aidid was identified as the principal impediment to peace, and once he attacked the United Nations forces he became the object of a sizable manhunt. If the United Nations did, in the end, entrap the United States into a larger mission in Somalia, it was only because it had a willing partner. As Joshua Muravchik pithily describes it, "there is no doubt that Boutros-Ghali and company pulled America deeper into Somalia than it likely would have gone on its own. But Boutros-Ghali got his way because the Clinton administration had a weakness for what he was seeking to do."[241] Similarly, a State Department official comments that "the UN did push us, but we're big boys, we knew what we were getting into, and we could have stopped it at any point."[242]

Not all members of the coalition agreed with the more coercive role gradually adopted by UNOSOM II, especially the hunt for Aidid. Indeed, the Europeans tended to view "the whole scheme as politically inept and militarily unsound," and several countries just quietly opted out.[243] Nonetheless, even opponents could hardly object to the larger ambition in Somalia, which had been part of the plan from the very first days of the intervention. Although some disagreed with the hunt for Aidid, all accepted the need to rebuild Somalia.

In the end, the coalition, despite the objections of some, could not constrain the United States from singling out Aidid and targeting its efforts at his capture. This suggests that coalitions cannot check great powers unless there are large gains from cooperation that are put at risk by opposition from

---

[240] Interviews with Dobbins and Houdek, both November 13, 1996. Many developing countries stayed on for the final year of UNOSOM II even after America's departure. They tended to regard peacekeeping in Somalia as no more dangerous or onerous than elsewhere, and were more drawn to the financial incentives of participating in United Nations peacekeeping activities.

[241] Muravchik 1993, 20.

[242] Interview with Houdek, November 13, 1996.

[243] Prunier 1997, 143; Oakley n.d., 15.

others, the partners are united in opposition to the dominant state's desires, or the opposing states are willing to expend the necessary resources and political capital to make their dissents widely known. In this case, America's partners simply stepped aside. In Somalia, the United States did not need its partners sufficiently to take heed of their views; indeed, when the Europeans dropped out of the hunt for Aidid, the Americans raced ahead alone. Nor was the coalition sufficiently unified and motivated to restrain the United States as it joined with the United Nations as partisans in the internal war. However, it is important to note that the United States was not entrapped into the expanded mission, but readily picked up the obligation. In no instance was the United States constrained from doing anything that it wanted to do, or forced to do anything it would have preferred to avoid. The coalition served not as a check on American policy, as it did in the Gulf, but more as a signal of the strictly humanitarian nature of its intentions.

Paradoxically, the ultimate failure to restore order in Somalia followed, in part, from the safeguards the United States imposed upon itself. The reasons for the collapse of the United Nations mission in Somalia are many and complex, of course, and are not all related to the issue of safeguards.[244] Nonetheless, two frequently cited "mistakes" follow directly from the safeguards employed to check American power. First, by restricting UNITAF to humanitarian missions, the United States failed to use the only window of opportunity in which the warlords might have been disarmed effectively.[245] An impartial disarmament of all clans might have succeeded early on, given the initial legitimacy of UNITAF, the political "shock" to the warlords provided by the arrival of outside forces, and the overwhelming superiority of the UNITAF forces.[246] Once the United Nations began its nation-building program, inevitably becoming a partisan in the internal conflict, and once American troops were replaced by the smaller and far less capable United Nations forces, the task of disarmament became far more difficult.[247]

Second, by insisting upon a quick hand-off, the United States transferred

---

[244] Two critical firsthand accounts are now available: Sahnoun 1994 and Hirsch and Oakley 1995. See also Clarke and Herbst 1997; Menkhaus 1994; Bryden 1995; Howe 1995; Stevenson 1993; and Clark 1993. James L. Woods offers a particularly succinct summary: "looking backward . . . there was no way the operation could have succeeded . . . because it was built on false premises . . . that the operation could be politically neutral, that the major Somali political actors and warlords could be persuaded or forced into a process of reconciliation, and that a UN-led international operation could restore the basic structures of Somali society in a time frame adequate to capture and sustain the momentum of the initial UNITAF phase and then to consolidate those gains to prevent backsliding into renewed strife and anarchy." Woods 1997, 168.

[245] Menkhaus 1994, 154–55; Clarke 1997, 13; Ganzglass 1997, 34.

[246] Howe 1995, 51.

[247] On the UN as partisan, see Menkhaus 1994, 156; on the difficulty of disarmament under UNOSOM II, see Howe 1995, 52–53; Stevenson 1993, 141.

responsibility to the United Nations before the latter was, in many respects, prepared to assume it. Thus, the warlords were able to challenge the United Nations at its moment of maximum vulnerability.[248] As the Somali factions racked up initial successes, UNOSOM II lost both credibility and legitimacy.[249] In safeguarding its own role in Somalia, the United States sowed several of the seeds of UNOSOM's ultimate demise.

Although these safeguards impeded the long-term success of the political efforts in Somalia, ultimately the mission failed because publics everywhere, but especially in the United States, were unwilling to pay the price necessary to end the suffering in Somalia. The collapse of domestic political order does not occur by accident. Political systems fragment because powerful groups and individuals desire ends that cannot be met within existing rules and institutions. Outside intervention, of whatever sort, does not by itself change these political ends or the political frustrations that give rise to internal conflict in the first place. Although UNITAF allowed food to be delivered where it was needed, it did not—and did not seek to—resolve the underlying clash of interests. As the United Nations dug in for the long haul and began the process of rebuilding the Somalian state, it inevitably became partisan. Establishing political competition on any foundation other than brute force disadvantaged the militarily stronger groups, in this case Aidid. He resisted, as any such leader would. To impose a solution in Somalia, or anywhere, requires the use of even greater force, which necessarily puts the "peacekeepers" at risk and is likely to produce some loss of life. This is an inevitable part of any effort to rebuild wartorn societies. This fact was hidden from publics in participating countries, and especially the United States, by treating the Somalian intervention as a purely "humanitarian mission," which it was in intent but could never be in practice. By masking its long-term purpose, publics were not led to see that humanitarian interventions do not stand on their own but must be complemented by efforts to rebuild societies. Perhaps had the Bush or Clinton administrations cultivated domestic support for forceful intervention in Somalia, the outcome might have been different. But in the end, the public made clear it was not willing to pay the necessary price to restore political order in Somalia. This led to failure, not entrapment by the United Nations or the constraints of the coalition.

## CONCLUSION

The coalitions the United States has formed since the end of the Cold War depend upon the joint production economies available through international cooperation. In cases of large-scale uses of force, as in the Persian Gulf War,

---

[248] Howe 1995, 53; Bryden 1995, 149.
[249] Menkhaus 1994, 157.

technological limitations demand that the United States have available to it forward land bases; this requires local partners. In nearly all interventions against either "backlash" or "failed" states, as in Iraq or Somalia, respectively, the United States produces positive externalities that benefit other states and thereby creates the opportunity for effective burden sharing. Generally missing from the new American coalitions, however, is a division of labor between partners, even of the limited form that sustained NATO for nearly fifty years.

Today, the risk that its partners will act opportunistically toward the United States is relatively low, even in anarchic security relationships. Nonetheless, the degree of asset specificity plays an important role in determining the security relationships the United States forms with its partners. Where assets are specific, as in the Persian Gulf case, the expected costs of opportunism are high and, as predicted, the United States seeks to exert substantial control over its partners. Where assets are less specific, as in Somalia, the expected costs of opportunism are smaller and less control is necessary. In both cases, however, its dominance and self-conscious strategy of international leadership creates the potential for the United States to act opportunistically toward its partners. Creating ad hoc coalitions and appealing to international support through the United Nations or other regional organizations have been the primary safeguards used to protect others from the side-effects of America's hegemony.

The governance costs of international cooperation are, today, comparatively high. In binding its hands, limiting its ability to act opportunistically, and constraining its autonomous objectives, the United States incurs substantial costs. Moreover, these governance costs escalate with greater relational hierarchy. Already concerned with the possibility of American opportunism, other states are likely to resist giving even more authority over their policies to the sole remaining superpower. To achieve greater control over its partners than at present, in turn, the United States would have to bind itself even more tightly or begin to coerce states into subordinate positions. Combined with the only marginal benefits from greater hierarchy, these rapidly escalating governance costs limit the United States to relatively anarchic security relationships.

America's "unipolar moment," Charles Krauthammer asserted soon after the Berlin Wall fell, would quickly and inevitably be followed by a return of multipolarity.[250] This pessimistic prognosis was soon followed by others. Neo-realist Cassandras predicted that Japan and Germany (within or without the European Union) would emerge as new poles in the international system, countries fearful of American power would balance against the United States, and driven by the "sameness effect" Japan, Germany, and other great powers

---

[250] Krauthammer 1990/91.

would soon acquire nuclear weapons.[251] A decade after the end of the Cold War, this dark vision of the future has not come to pass.[252] Whether neorealists got the Cold War "right," they have most certainly gotten the peace "wrong."[253]

States are not driven by international structures to respond in ineluctable ways. They shape their environments through their purposive choices.[254] The great wisdom of American foreign policy since the end of the Cold War has been to recognize that the United States must bind itself to earn the cooperation of others. By shaping but then working within the international consensus on the means and ends of policy and constraining itself through ad hoc coalitions, it limits its potential for opportunism and safeguards others against its overweening power. It signals to others its benign intent, and provides others with a means of monitoring its actions and checking its policies should they stray outside acceptable boundaries. By binding itself, the United States lessens the threat that its disproportionate capabilities might pose to other states and short-circuits the balancing processes expected by neorealist pessimists. This use of ad hoc coalitions is an effective contractual solution to a difficult political problem. Choices and security relationships matter in international politics.

[251] See Mearsheimer 1990; Layne 1993; Waltz 1993.

[252] Mearsheimer 1990 carefully premised his analysis on what would happen if the United States withdrew from Western Europe, which of course it has not yet done. Layne 1993 speculated over both a twenty- and a fifty-year time period; the latter has more to do with the implications of the "law of uneven growth" than with balancing. Despite these qualifications, none of the major trends they identified has become evident a decade after the end of the Cold War. For an insightful review of neorealism and contemporary policy, see Mastanduno 1997.

[253] Gaddis 1992/93.

[254] On a strategic choice approach to international relations, see Lake and Powell forthcoming; and Stein 1990.

*Chapter 7*

---

# RELATIONAL CONTRACTING AND
# INTERNATIONAL RELATIONS

THE CHAPTERS ABOVE have outlined a theory of relational contracting tailored to international security affairs. In this chapter, I explore the implications of the theory for the study of international relations. I also probe several extensions of the theory, posing two additional hypotheses and identifying four promising directions for future research.

## THE RELATIONAL CONTRACTING APPROACH

This is a study of contracting in international security relations. I have generally avoided use of this term to avoid prejudicing readers who rebel at the idea that there can be such things as "contracts" in the anarchic world of international politics. For many, a contract requires an enforcer, a third party that adjudicates disputes and mandates prescribed actions. Yet international anarchy neither vitiates the need to enforce agreements nor renders enforcement impossible; it only implies that contracts between polities must be self-enforcing—that is, it must be in the interests of the parties to carry out their terms. Focusing on contracting in international politics calls our attention not to the absence of a judicial authority but rather to the creative and important ways that polities design relationships and modify incentives to limit opportunism.

All international relationships are based on a bargain, which divides the available costs and benefits between the polities, and a contract or agreement, which enforces the bargain reached. Bargains and contracts are obviously related.[1] Some feasible bargains may lack any effective contract, and thus are impossible to reach in practice; knowing that the bargain cannot be enforced, the polities will not agree to that division in the first place. Likewise, the initial and ongoing costs of the contract may be greater than the joint gains, again rendering any bargain impractical. Although distinct, the bargain and contract must ultimately complement and reinforce one another. Nonetheless, contracting is concerned less with the substance of agreements and more with their enforcement.

Both bargains and contracts can be implicit and informal or explicit and formal. In some instances, the mutual interests of the polities may be so

[1] See Fearon 1998.

strong that they do not even recognize that they are bargaining. In others, one polity may be sufficiently powerful that it alone sets the terms of the deal, perhaps making an offer the second cannot refuse. In all cases, however, there is still a division of costs and benefits—in short, a bargain. In the same way, the incentives of the polities to abide by the terms of the bargain may be so strong and clear that enforcement is not an issue: each side is confident that the other will live up to the terms of the agreement and the contract between them is unproblematic. Or, like one-sided bargains, the terms of a contract may be imposed by the stronger party, most likely to its own advantage. Yet even in such circumstances there is some enforcement mechanism—be it the self-interest or power of the polities—and, thus, a contract.

International relationists often treat contracting as a secondary matter, implicitly assuming that enforcement mechanisms are epiphenomenal.[2] This does not follow axiomatically from the major theories of international relations, but contracting nonetheless tends to get short shrift. In focusing on the role of power in international bargaining, for example, realists typically overlook the question of enforcement. Presumably, if one polity is strong enough to set a bargain to its advantage, it is also strong enough to enforce that bargain. Similarly, for neoliberal institutionalists, the value of the cooperation permitted or facilitated by international regimes is the primary mechanism of enforcement. Since cooperation is beneficial, the expulsion of a state from the regime or the collapse of cooperation itself is understood as sufficient punishment to enforce the initial bargain.[3] Withdrawing or threatening to withdraw the benefits of cooperation thus sustains cooperation among a group of interacting polities. Looked at through these traditional lenses, it is easy to minimize the problem of enforcement and, indeed, the role of power itself in this process.

The art of politics is understanding the costs and benefits of alternatives and finding innovative ways of bridging gaps between competing interests. We often recognize the creative spark in bargaining—the outcome that allows parties to reach an accommodation. President John F. Kennedy's decision during the missile crisis to erect a formal blockade of Cuba while simultaneously reaching an informal agreement with the Soviet Union to remove the American missiles already in Turkey is a widely cited and highly creative bargain. Contracting is an equally creative process that also depends upon an understanding of the possible and the search for effective alternatives that will satisfy the competing parties. The use of ad hoc coalitions in the post-Cold War world to protect others from the potential for

---

[2] The literature on iterated games is the exception to this rule; see Axelrod 1984 and Oye 1986.

[3] Keohane 1984.

American opportunism is an imaginative contractual solution to a difficult political problem. For any bargain to go forward, there is an equally important contract behind it. Structuring contracts to protect the interests of the parties is a necessary part of the art of politics. As the cases above reveal, the absence of a viable contract doomed the League of Nations, as then construed, but the creative use of ad hoc coalitions has allowed cooperation to proceed in the current era. In all three of the periods examined in this book, the domestic debate in the United States turned more on the contracts with its partners than on the threats posed by third parties. By focusing on contracting we gain a new appreciation of the issues at stake in the domestic debates and insights into why some bargains succeeded while others failed or why the bargains took the peculiar forms they did. Contracting is important and deserves more explicit and focused attention by international relationists.

Both bargaining and contracting are central to international relations. As a corrective to the traditional emphasis, however, I have focused in this volume on problems of contracting. As we have seen, even very large gains from cooperation may be vitiated by high expected costs of opportunism or high governance costs. What appears to be a bargain that creates large benefits for one or both parties, and therefore should be feasible, may simply not be enforceable at a price at least one of the parties is willing to pay. Conversely, small gains from cooperation limit the expected costs of opportunism and governance costs polities are willing to bear; a bargain that appears "easy" to enforce may still not generate sufficient benefits to make it worthwhile for at least one party. Contracting is integral to all bargains and, as I hope the chapters above have shown clearly, central to the security of the United States.

## ALTERNATIVE APPROACHES

Relational contracting is not a new "paradigm" or approach to international politics, nor is it intended as such. My intent is not to pose a new "ism" in a field already crowded by theoretical "product differentiation." In my view, knowledge comes not from driving wedges between theoretical perspectives but from building on existing approaches in theoretically interesting and empirically useful ways. Accordingly, the approach here is more synthetic than antithetic.

In the field of international relations today, there are three major systemic approaches: neorealism, neoliberal institutionalism, and constructivism. Like the theory here, each is premised on unitary actors in a world without any political authority higher than the state. Each self-consciously excludes domestic politics from its theoretical structure.

Of these approaches, the theory developed here is most closely related to neoliberal institutionalism. Nonetheless, it differs in important ways. First, the theory posits that opportunism is a central problem inhibiting cooperation. Closely related to neoliberal institutionalist concerns with cheating, opportunism is nonetheless analytically narrower. Opportunism matters only when terminating the relationship or defecting from its terms is costly, and thus is a function of the extent to which assets are specific to that relationship. Contrary to some neoliberal accounts, not all defection or cheating matters. In addition, opportunism is but one factor that inhibits cooperation, and cannot be analyzed independently of the joint economies and governance costs of alternative relationships. Low expected costs of opportunism may still thwart cooperation if the joint economies are also small or governance costs are high, and high expected costs of opportunism may still permit cooperation if the joint economies are large or governance costs are small. Opportunism cannot be studied in isolation.

Second, the theory here views security relationships—equivalent to institutions, broadly defined—as instruments of control. In neoliberal institutionalism, regimes facilitate cooperation by providing information and reducing transactions costs.[4] In dilemmas of coordination, institutions merely allow states to select among multiple equilibria. In dilemmas of collaboration, where the socially optimal outcome is not an equilibrium, institutions modify behavior by raising the expected costs of defection: not only does the institution increase the probability that cheating will be detected, but cheating places the valuable institution itself at risk, thereby increasing the penalty for defection.[5] In the theory here, security relationships are designed to modify directly the incentives of the various actors; in this way, relationships become self-enforcing not simply because they themselves are valuable but because they are consciously crafted to alter the behavior of the parties. To cooperate, it is often necessary to exert some degree of control over others. Contracting is not only an art but also a form of power.

Finally, since coercion is always a possibility, cooperation may not be Pareto-improving. Contrary to neoliberal institutionalism, which relies on voluntary agreements between polities, cooperation is understood here to occur "in the shadow of power," as Robert Powell has recently termed it.[6] When coercion is possible and a substitute for voluntary negotiations, bargains and contracts need not benefit both parties—indeed, the benefits may be highly asymmetrical and may even leave one party worse off than before. We should not assume that cooperation is always beneficial, even to all of the parties directly involved.[7]

---

[4] Keohane 1984, 180, acknowledges that regimes can be used to control the behavior of others, but this theme is not developed in his work.

[5] Stein 1983; Martin 1992.

[6] Powell forthcoming.

[7] Keohane 1984, 70–71 and 73 acknowledges that cooperation may not improve *world* wel-

The theory is somewhat more distinct from neorealism. Although many of its predictions are consistent with neorealism, perhaps indicating the malleability of that approach, it does not assume that states merely seek survival or power or that they are "defensive positionalists."[8] Rather, polities are assumed to be utility maximizers, with security as but one necessary element of subjectively defined welfare. The theory also takes contracting as a central problem in international relations, and posits that polities can and do intentionally manipulate their environment and construct formal and informal mechanisms designed to modify their own behavior and enhance the prospects for cooperation. Finally, rather than defining international relations as the realm of fully and equally sovereign great powers, the theory here sees a more variegated landscape populated by polities lodged within more or less hierarchical relationships.[9] Seen through the lens of relational contracting theory, the international system is far more heterogeneous and politically nuanced than neorealists commonly recognize.

The theory of relational contracting posed here also differs from constructivist approaches to international relations. Constructivists begin from sociological foundations. I have rooted my variant of relational contracting theory firmly in economics.[10] International relations is, of course, a social realm. Many of the interactions described in the theory and case studies are premised on shared understandings. Especially in informal security relationships, the agreement between two polities is entirely implicit and depends upon each party recognizing and largely accepting its terms, whether these be based on equal rights of residual control (anarchy) or unequal rights (hierarchy). Indeed, since all agreements are necessarily incomplete (see Chapter 2), even formal, written, and duly ratified treaties depend on some shared understanding of their terms. The difference between a sociological and an economic understanding of international relations is less substantive and more methodological.

As I understand it, constructivism has two major tenets.[11] First, agents and structures are mutually constitutive. That is, actors create social structures—like the anarchic international system—through their actions. Social structures, in turn, constrain actors and shape their behaviors. Actors cannot be studied independently from their structures, and vice versa.

Second, shared understandings—or "norms" at the level of the system and

---

fare, but holds that voluntary agreements will be entered into, presumably, only if they provide net benefits to the contracting parties themselves.

[8] On alternative realist assumptions, see Grieco 1997.

[9] See the discussion of functional differentiation below.

[10] There is a broad range of scholars who are working at the intersection of these two traditions. See the diverse essays in Smelser and Swedberg 1994. On the more sociological side, see the essays in Swedberg 1993.

[11] See Katzenstein 1996a; Wendt 1987 and 1992; Adler 1997.

"identities" at the level of the actors—are central determinants of international relations and key to understanding social interactions. Norms and identities are the primary components of social structures and strongly shape behavior: it is not environmental conditions that drive actors but their socially constructed understandings of these conditions. Although they posit that norms and identities are produced by the interaction of actors and existing structures, constructivists have yet to articulate a clear theory explaining where norms or identities come from or how they come to be accepted by actors. In any given empirical application, norms and identities are largely taken as "given" or exogenous.[12] Nonetheless, constructivists assume that, as the product of mutually constituted agents and structures, norms and identities are at least partly autonomous from environmental conditions.

The theory here recognizes the importance of shared understandings. These understandings, however, are interpreted as a set of prior beliefs held by the actors about the nature of the strategic environment they face and the preferences and past actions of other actors. These prior beliefs are the foundation upon which actors estimate the probability distributions of each independent variable (see Chapter 3). These beliefs, in turn, are assumed to be updated (through Bayes's rule) as new information becomes available, and thus to reflect the historical knowledge and experience of the actors. Through this mechanism of updating, beliefs are presumed to conform over time to the actual state of the world or, if the environment is changing, to track the path through which the world is evolving. Beliefs are understood to be endogenous, over the long run, to the social interaction being explained and, contrary to constructivism, largely consistent with the conditions facing those actors.

In this formulation, the debate over the League of Nations (see Chapter 4) was a process through which *domestic* actors updated their beliefs by interpolating between the conflicting pieces of information held by distinct individuals. Political leaders struggled to reach some understanding of the environment in which the United States was embedded and the likely consequences of alternative courses of action. Similarly, the early diplomatic maneuverings between the United States and Saudi Arabia in 1990 allowed each state to probe the intentions of the other and to clarify the terms and consequences of the protectorate that would be eventually created. At both home and abroad, political debate was important to creating shared understandings of the security relationships the United States was on the verge of entering. Yet to acknowledge that shared understandings are important to security relationships is not necessarily to accept the presumption of constructivists

---

[12] Kowert and Legro 1996, 469.

that norms and identities are autonomous from environmental conditions. Nor does it diminish the importance of joint economies, expected costs of opportunism, and governance costs in structuring the choices of polities.

## IMPLICATIONS FOR INTERNATIONAL RELATIONS

In the nineteenth century, while eschewing alliances and maintaining a strictly unilateral foreign policy toward Europe, the United States built a continental empire. Despite his opposition to "entangling alliances," for instance, President Thomas Jefferson was a vigorous advocate of this early expansion.[13] At the end of the century, the United States contemplated building an overseas empire. Although they were later prominent unilateralists, President Theodore Roosevelt and Senator Henry Cabot Lodge were vocal supporters of this overseas effort. For these statesmen, foreign entanglements and empires were entirely different things.

Scholars of international relations wear the same blinders, and take an overly narrow view of foreign entanglements. Scholars accept too readily a "Westphalian model" of interstate relations—an acceptance demonstrated most clearly, perhaps, in the very name of the discipline.[14] This is true for constructivist and even postmodern theorists who challenge the deterministic nature of this model.[15] Looking through a lens of interactions between states, scholars generally ignore the wide range of possible relationships between polities. Alliances are but one form of foreign entanglement. Numerous more hierarchical alternatives also exist, both in theory and practice. Failing to examine these hierarchical relationships stunts inquiry.

As a discipline, international relations is highly restricted in the types of relationships it examines. Anarchic relations are assumed to characterize international politics, or at least relations between its "important" actors.[16] This is a truism at the level of the international system, but it is a gross distortion of the variety of relations between polities. When different relationships are considered, scholars treat the alternatives separately and as autonomous topics of investigation. As noted in Chapter 2, the existing literatures on alliances and empires remain separate "islands of theory," with very few analysts apparently aware that they are surrounded by the same body of water. This restricted inquiry limits our theoretical and empirical reach and introduces serious distortions into our understanding of international politics.

[13] Tucker and Hendrickson 1990.

[14] For a discussion of the Westphalian model, see Krasner 1993 and 1995/96; Lyons and Mastanduno 1995.

[15] These theorists tend not to offer a conceptualization of the relational alternatives but to focus on the meaning and consequences of "anarchy." See Wendt 1992; Biersteker and Weber 1996.

[16] Waltz 1979, 94.

*International Institutions*

The debate over the question "Do international institutions matter?" illustrates clearly the problems of not considering relevant alternatives.[17] Critics of neoliberal institutionalism typically make two arguments, both of which imply that institutions do not constrain states significantly: they suggest that most institutions merely codify what states would have wanted to do anyway, or that institutions do not constrain behavior because there can be substantial cheating.[18] The debate surrounding this question has implicitly limited the alternatives to unilateralism and cooperation within anarchic relationships. Hierarchic alternatives are not included. As a result, the dependent variable is artificially truncated and the analyses, both pro and con, are plagued by problems of selection bias.[19] Once this bias is corrected, or its implications understood, international institutions and the forces that create and sustain them appear more important and robust.

With its emphasis on alternative relationships, the theory here implies that we are most likely to observe anarchic institutions under two sets of conditions. First, when joint production economies are small, a state will enter into a relationship only if it expects that its partner will live up to their agreement, as a high risk of opportunism is likely to negate the limited benefits of cooperation, and the agreement does not greatly constrain its own behavior, implying that the governance costs of cooperation are also low. In other words, when joint economies are small, we should expect anarchic relationships only when it is in the interests of the parties to abide by agreements and the accords themselves do not impose significant costs. Anarchic institutions are chosen, in other words, when the need to alter the behavior of the contracting parties is smallest. That such institutions fail to modify the behavior of states significantly should hardly be surprising.

Second, we can also expect anarchic relationships to arise when joint economies are large but governance costs rise rapidly with hierarchy. In these cases, the potential gains make cooperation attractive but hierarchy is not a feasible solution for problems of opportunism. States will then choose to "cooperate under anarchy" as long as the expected costs of opportunism and governance costs do not exceed the benefits created by the joint economies.[20] Despite a high probability or cost of opportunistic behavior by partners,

---

[17] Another possible example is the debate over whether empire "pays." The consensus here is that although empire may not improve the welfare of the country as a whole, it does serve the interests of politically important domestic groups. See Davis and Huttenback 1986; Lebergott 1980. This literature does not, however, compare empires to their relevant alternatives.

[18] See Mearsheimer 1994/95. For a response, see Keohane and Martin 1995.

[19] On selection bias, see King, Keohane, and Verba 1994, 128–39. For a similar analysis of selection bias in international cooperation, see Downs, Rocke, and Barsoom 1996.

[20] The phrase is from Oye 1986.

states may still enjoy net gains from cooperation, but they will appear small as the large gains from joint economies are dissipated by frequent opportunism. Under these circumstances, we will also typically observe numerous defections, states largely ignoring or accepting these defections, and—surprisingly—continuing cooperation.

Critics of the role and importance of international institutions correctly identify the limits of anarchic relationships, but fail to recognize that the observed "weakness" of extant institutions is the product of selection bias. Anarchic institutions are most likely to be constructed by states precisely when they matter least: when they provide little value added, reflect rather than influence preferred behaviors, or permit substantial opportunism. Hierarchical relationships will tend to arise when more is at stake.[21]

Selection bias always under-estimates causal relationships, suggesting that those factors which produce international institutions are more significant and, in turn, that international governance broadly defined is a more important source of cooperation than past studies have revealed. To assess fully the factors supporting international institutions or observe institutions that "matter," we must include more hierarchic alternatives in our studies. Rather than focusing simply on international organizations or regimes as sources of cooperation, we should turn our attention to protectorates, informal empires, and empires.

### Functional Differentiation in the International System

In his classic theory of the international system, Kenneth Waltz maintained that states are not differentiated by the functions they perform. Since under anarchy all states are required to provide for their own security, he maintained, states are "like units."[22] John Ruggie strongly criticized this notion of functional undifferentiation, claiming that Waltz's (and Durkheim's) second dimension of structure really refers to the principles upon which the constituent units are separated and, as the feudal period demonstrates, sovereignty is not the only principle consistent with anarchy.[23] The theory here sheds light on this debate.

---

[21] To assess properly the importance of international institutions we must also examine non-agreements, which by nature are unobservable. There is an enormous range of potential cooperation that is never realized because the joint economies are too small, the expected costs of opportunism are too large, or governance costs are too high. In these cases, it is not (only) the absence of a feasible bargain but, rather, the inability to create an effective contract that thwarts cooperation. In this sense, the failure of cooperation can nearly always be linked directly to the absence of the conditions that allow effective international institutions to arise. As a "close call" for cooperation, the League of Nations (Chapter 4) provides a good opportunity to probe the politics of a "nonagreement."

[22] Waltz 1979, 93–97.

[23] Ruggie 1983. For a response, see Waltz 1986.

The functional differentiation of polities will typically be lower in uni-lateral and anarchic relationships than in hierarchic relationships, but contingent upon the degree of asset specificity. This partly confirms Waltz's contention that his second dimension of structure, the differentiation of the units, drops out in anarchic systems. Yet a division of labor or reliance upon others for certain positive externalities—both of which introduce some func-tional differentiation in a dyad—is not precluded in anarchy when the rele-vant assets are "generic" or do not produce significant quasi rents. Functional similarity may be associated with anarchy, as maintained by Waltz, but it does not follow axiomatically from the absence of authority higher than the state. Empirical confirmation of Waltz's position, which is accepted by Ruggie for the modern period, is again dependent upon the selection bias introduced by focusing only on relations between fully sovereign states.

Conversely, some degree of asset specificity, and thus some expected costs of opportunism, may be accepted by states when joint economies are large or governance costs small, as in the security relationships formed between the United States and its European partners after World War II. As we have seen, an anarchic international system does not preclude cooperation in largely anarchic relationships even when assets are specific—or, in Waltz's terms, when the units are functionally differentiated.

More broadly, recognizing the wide variety of hierarchical relation-ships present in the international system suggests that there is an important degree of functional differentiation in international relations. Hierarchical relationships in international politics can only be ignored through a defini-tional sleight of hand, which limits the analysis to "major" members of the system—that is, states.[24] Doing so, however, excludes nearly four centuries of European imperialism, arguably one of the most important series of events in human history, as well as numerous other cases of relational hierarchy. Even today, in a world of supposedly sovereign states, hierarchies continue to exist around the world. The United States itself maintains imperial relationships with varying degrees of local autonomy over several Caribbean islands, most notably Puerto Rico, and in Micronesia, especially Guam; infor-mal empires over many states in Central America, who although sovereign are not free to determine their own forms of domestic rule, as repeatedly demonstrated in the 1980s; and protectorates in the Persian Gulf. It is true that the subordinate members of these dyads are only "minor" polities. Such hierarchies are nonetheless important analytically because they render problematic some of what is often taken for granted in existing theories of international relations. They are also important politically. As shown in Chapter 6, the transformation of Saudi Arabia and other regional states into American protectorates was central to the Persian Gulf War. Had the United

[24] See Waltz 1979, 93.

States not been able to establish effective control over these critical partners, a land war to expel Iraq from Kuwait would have been more far more costly and, perhaps, not worth the expense.[25]

### Armaments-Alliance Tradeoffs

Several significant attempts have been made to model armaments-alliance tradeoffs in international politics. These models are closely related to the theory developed here, particularly in their ambition to think across the range of strategies available to states. The logic of armaments-alliance tradeoffs seems intuitively plausible. If alliances are more efficient, they should produce lower levels of defense spending. Unfortunately, few statistically significant and robust results have been found. Benjamin Most and Randolph Siverson find little support for the hypothesis, whereas Michael Altfeld and James Morrow find that armaments and alliances are often positively related, taking the form of complements rather than substitutes. The strongest evidence for the tradeoff is found by Morrow.[25]

The theory developed here suggests that the armaments-alliance research program is incorrectly structured. The tradeoff is not between arms and alliances, but between unilateralism and cooperation, with the latter taking a range of relational forms. When the expected costs of opportunism are comparatively high or governance costs low, for instance, the relevant choice may be between unilateralism and empire, not unilateralism and alliances. If polities hedge against the higher risks of opportunism in anarchic relationships by preserving redundant military capabilities, as might be expected, the tradeoff between unilateralism and empire will be even more stark than that between unilateralism and alliances. Even though the tradeoff posited in the literature may exist in principle, measures of defense spending and alliance formation may fail to capture the relevant forms or may grossly underestimate the real tradeoff. As in the other examples above, incorporating the hierarchic options available to states is necessary for adequate tests. The failure to include such options, in turn, may account for the disappointing results in current studies.

### Alliance Performance and Imperial Overextension

Thomas Christensen and Jack Snyder have posed a theory of alliance performance to explain what they describe as two "errors" or "pathologies," namely, chain ganging and buck passing.[26] Their approach combines Waltz's structural theory of international politics with a set of propositions on motivated

---

[25] Altfeld 1984; Most and Siverson 1987; Altfeld and Morrow, n.d.; and Morrow 1993.
[26] Christensen and Snyder 1990, 138 and 141.

biases and military technology.[27] Snyder and others, in turn, have recently suggested that countries, for domestic reasons, are prone to imperial pathologies: they tend to expand beyond the point where marginal gain equals marginal cost, producing "imperial overextension."[28] The theory here differs on the interpretation and implications of these pathologies.

First, we should typically see less chain ganging, buck passing, and other forms of opportunism than a neorealist (Waltz) or modified neorealist (Christensen and Snyder) would predict. States expend resources and create hierarchies, in general, and safeguards, in particular, to control opportunism. The theory suggests that we should observe high levels of opportunism only when the joint economies are large and governance costs are high or escalate rapidly with hierarchy. Under these circumstances, anarchic cooperation may still be the optimal choice for polities. Similarly, the key question in imperial overextension is whether the marginal increase in governance costs is greater than the marginal reduction in the expected costs of opportunism from greater hierarchy—a tradeoff on which the existing literature is largely silent.

Second, and equally important, we cannot necessarily infer from observations of chain ganging, buck passing, or overextension that an alliance or empire was dysfunctional or pathological. As discussed in Chapter 3, states do not know the precise costs and benefits of alternative relationships at any given time and for every dyad. Rather, they estimate a probability distribution of expected behaviors; to say that chain ganging is more likely, for instance, is actually to describe a shift in the probability distribution toward greater opportunism. With any choice in a probabilistic world, states create for themselves a wide variety of possible real world outcomes—some better than expected, some worse—despite their best intentions. Sometimes partners will be less opportunistic than expected, leaving the state better off than anticipated, sometimes partners will be more opportunistic, making the state worse off. Sometimes the governance costs of empire will be smaller than projected, creating a situation in which empire "pays"; sometimes the governance costs will be larger than expected. States can—indeed, some portion of the time, must—find themselves in the "tails" of the probability distribution on one or more variables. Sometimes states are lucky, sometimes unlucky, as the case may be. But to infer states are prescient, in the first instance, or pathological, in the second, is to misunderstand the consequences of choice in a probabilistic world.

Concluding that states act pathologically is especially problematic when based on a small number of prominent cases. World wars and other catastrophes attract our attention because they are atypical policy failures—instances in which actual events significantly underperform expectations. Prominent

---

[27] Ibid., 145.
[28] Snyder 1991; Kennedy 1987; Kupchan 1994.

cases are likely to possess extreme values on one or more variables and be drawn from the "unlucky" tails of the probability distributions. Focusing only on prominent cases creates a severe problem of selection bias that potentially invalidates the analysis.

The literatures on alliance performance and imperial overextension have spawned a progressive research agenda on the domestic sources of grand strategy. The implication of the theory here is not that these analyses are necessarily wrong or that the new agenda is misplaced. Domestic politics can distort grand strategy in consequential ways.[29] But we should not jump to conclusions nor presume that states are acting pathologically simply from observing costly outcomes. The full explication of the costs and benefits of alliances, empires, and other security relationships is a necessary prior step that is too often overlooked.

## Two Further Hypotheses

In this section, I examine two additional hypotheses deduced from the theory. These hypotheses are intended to suggest how the theory may be generalized beyond the subject of American foreign policy. They also open the way to future tests based on a larger number of observations.

### Voluntary Unifications

Hypothesis: As it is difficult and costly to safeguard against the risk of exploitation by dominant states, voluntary unifications of polities into relational hierarchies will be rare. Those that do occur will produce federal states with central governments that are relatively constrained in their powers and constituent members that retain significant residual rights of control.

A full test of this hypothesis would require 1. the identification of all relevant polities; 2. a classification scheme that codes all dyads as unilateral or arrayed along a continuum from anarchy to hierarchy; and 3. a measure of the force employed by members in forging relationships. Although the data required for a decisive test of this proposition do not exist, the prediction does appear to be broadly consistent with the historical record.

Voluntary unifications of territories are, indeed, unusual. Although their categories do not quite capture the concepts outlined here, Gary Goertz and Paul Diehl find that unification accounts for only about 4.8 percent of all territorial changes in the period 1816–1980.[30] As they define it, unification

---

[29] In other work, I have argued that state rent seeking can lead to rational empire building where the social costs exceed the social gain. See Lake 1992 and 1997.

[30] Goertz and Diehl 1992, esp. 54, 139, and Appendix.

can involve the use of armed force as long as a treaty is concluded that formally transfers the territory. The unifications of Italy and Germany in the late nineteenth century, which both occurred under the shadow of force, alone account for approximately twenty-eight of the thirty-seven observed unifications. Excluding these cases reduces the number of unifications to 1.2 percent of all territorial changes.[31]

As these findings suggest, it is difficult to identify unifications in which force within dyads—actual or threatened—does not appear to have played a central role. This itself is telling. Yet there are at least three relatively clear-cut cases in which the use or threat of force between the constituent states was very limited: the foundings of the United States, Switzerland, and Australia.[32] In all three, residual rights of control were clearly and self-consciously retained by the contracting parties rather than ceded to the newly created central government.

The tenth amendment to the Constitution of the United States explicitly reserves all powers not expressly granted to the federal government to the states and the people; that Congress, the executive, and the judiciary have gradually chipped away at these residual rights of control does not negate the intent of the framers but merely demonstrates how difficult it is to safeguard against future exploitation from the center and how a deepening division of labor creates incentives for greater hierarchy.

In Switzerland, Article 3 of the constitution creates what has been referred to as a system of "double sovereignty." It specifies that "the Cantons are sovereign so far as their sovereignty is not limited by the Federal Constitution and as such they exercise all rights which are not delegated to the Federal Power." The cantons are allowed to enter into international treaties so long as they are not detrimental to the interests of the federation and other cantons. They may also maintain their own permanent military forces as long as the number does not exceed three hundred—a number perhaps more significant in 1874 when the constitution was enacted than today.[33] Nonetheless, the constitutional provisions suggest that large residual rights of control are retained by the cantons, even some rights over traditional "foreign policy" instruments.

The Commonwealth of Australia, created as a federation at the initiative of

[31] Including the three south German states as voluntary unifications (see below), increases unifications to 1.6 percent of all territorial changes.

[32] None of these cases is included in the territorial change dataset. Canada provides an interesting contrast. Where Australia initiated its change in status, and the individual states succeeded in obtaining residual rights of control, Canada was created through the initiative and actions of Britain; in seeking to establish an effective but independent agent in North America, Britain centralized power in Canada—despite the wide differences in the provinces that might have made federalism and local autonomy a more effective form of rule. See Bhagwan and Bhushan 1985, 81 and 193.

[33] See ibid., esp. 10; and Adams and Cunningham 1889; Luck 1985; Baker 1993, 19–41. For a discussion of the Swiss case in similar terms, see Weber 1997b.

the contracting parties, also specifies the powers of the central government and reserves residual rights to the states.[34] The individual colonies received "responsible government" from Britain between 1855 and 1860 (except Western Australia, which received such powers in 1890). Under this system of rule, the colonies developed individually most of the powers of sovereign states: colonial borders served as customs barriers and each colony had separate defense forces, postal systems, and so on. A first attempt at federation failed in 1891, but the second, between 1897 and 1898, eventually succeeded in establishing a federal government. Federal authorities are enumerated in Article 51 of the constitution; all other powers are reserved to the individual states. As in the United States, power has shifted to the federal government over time through both the High Court and constraints on taxation in the states. Nonetheless, residual rights remain firmly vested in the individual states.

These voluntary federations contrast in both process and outcome with Italy's more coercive unification. Formed through war with Austria in the north and, later, the conquest of the Kingdom of the Two Sicilies in the south, the constitutional monarchy of Piedmont merely annexed the territories and imposed its own centralized rule of law on the unified land.[35]

Interestingly, Germany may be the exception that proves the rule. The North German Confederation was forged in the war of 1866, yet the imperial constitution specified a list of areas in which the empire was dominant and reserved residual rights to the individual states. Despite the "hegemonic" role of Prussia within the empire, this reservation of residual rights for the states nonetheless poses something of an anomaly for the hypothesis. The answer lies in expectations of the future. Despite the role of coercion, the initial constitution was crafted with an eye toward the eventual *voluntary* expansion of the empire. Chancellor Otto von Bismarck, the imperial architect, resisted demands for complete centralization and insisted upon a weak federal construct in order to induce the southern German states to join the empire, which they did in 1871 after being abandoned by their Austrian and French allies.[36] Even in shadow of force, voluntary unifications appear to demand the retention of at least some residual rights of control by the contracting parties.

## Technology and Cooperation

Hypothesis: As technological scale economies expand and reduce the
    costs of projecting force over distance, polities will be more likely
    to cooperate and enter into more security relationships.

[34] See McMinn 1979; La Nauze 1972; and Aitkin and Jinks 1985.

[35] See Whyte 1965; Beales 1971; Holt 1971. For the period following unification, see Smith 1989.

[36] See Koch 1984 and Hucko 1987. On the imperial constitution itself, see Willoughby and Fenwick 1974.

As above, a full test of this proposition would require the identification of all relevant polities and a classification of all dyads as cooperating or not cooperating. Although we do not have all the necessary data, reasonable proxies are nonetheless available that permit a preliminary assessment. Although they must be interpreted cautiously, the results appear to support the proposition.

Security cooperation can, of course, take a wide variety of forms, but we only have systematic data available for interstate alliances. The number of alliances in the international system can be used as a proxy for the number of anarchic security relationships between polities. Although this does not include implicit or de facto alliances, there is no particular reason in the theory above to expect formal and informal security relationships to differ systematically in frequency.

Focusing only on the anarchic end of the continuum of security relationships, however, significantly undercounts the amount of cooperation between polities and introduces an important selection bias. If a systematic relationship between technological scale economies and alliances is found, we can infer that the effect would be more robust and significant if the full range of relationships could be included in the analysis. Thus, by anticipating the effect of truncating the dependent variable, we can partially correct for the selection bias and adjust our conclusions appropriately.

Data on alliances are drawn from the dataset on Annual Alliance Membership, 1815–1965.[37] The number of alliances in the international system is derived by summing the defense alliances possessed by each state in each year.[38] The absolute number of alliances in the system is, strictly speaking, an event count variable. In a cross-sectional environment, the Poisson distribution is well suited for modeling event count data, but it is inappropriate in a time series analysis. Nonetheless, because the minimum number of alliances is bounded at zero, standard OLS estimation is inappropriate. To address this issue, the first difference of the number of alliances (that is, the annual net change in alliances) is used instead, and is calculated as the total number of alliances in a given year minus the previous year's total.

Measures of technological innovation and scale economies are necessarily more indirect. As proxies for the costs of projecting force over distance, I use four different indicators of transportation costs. Although based on civilian transportation, it seems reasonable to assume that the costs of moving goods or people generally parallel the costs of moving equipment and troops. As

---

[37] Singer and Small n.d. Neutrality alliances and ententes are also included in this dataset, but neither of these relationships appears to involve active cooperation as defined in Chapter 2.

[38] Alternatively, the absolute number of defense alliances could be divided by two for a "dyadic" measure, but this would have no substantive effects on the results below.

transportation costs decline, the change in the number of alliances should increase (that is, the sign on transportation costs should be negative). The variables are defined as follows.

- British grain (1815–1872): a price series based on freight factors to London from, variously, the Baltic, Black Sea, east coast of North America, South America, and Australia, in constant shillings[39]
- Tramp shipping (1869–1919): an index of tramp shipping rates (1869 = 100)[40]
- Chicago to Liverpool (1880–1935): a price series of freight rates on grain (per 100 pounds) from Chicago to Liverpool via rail to seaboard and then by ship, in constant 1996 dollars[41]
- Rail costs (1852–1938): a price series based on receipts per passenger mile traveled on all railways in Great Britain, in constant pounds (average of 1867–1877)[42]

These rate series cover varying periods, origins and destinations, and forms of transportation. They are not directly comparable. Using multiple measures of the same basic variable, however, provides greater confidence in the results. The series on grain shipments from Chicago to Liverpool is particularly interesting as it combines rail and ocean freight rates, thereby reflecting competition within and between competing transportation technologies. All of these freight rate series end prior to World War II. As a result, the analysis is confined to the period of "classic" or multipolar diplomacy.[43]

I also include three control variables all based on a more "realist" interpretation of international politics. First, I control for the level of threat within the core of the international system. *Threat* is measured by the sum of military personnel per capita for Germany, France, and the United Kingdom, the three main antagonists during the period examined here. The intuition behind this measure is that as the major powers mobilize greater proportions of their populations, the overall level of tension or threat in the system is likely to rise (whether military personnel per capita rises in response to increased threats or itself causes increased threats is unimportant for this test). *Threat* should be positively related to changes in the number of alliances. Second, I control for power disparities between the major states. *Power* is defined by

[39] From Harley 1988, 873–75; based on reestimate of earlier series in North 1958.

[40] From Mitchell 1962, 224. "Tramp" refers to unscheduled ships.

[41] *Statistical Abstract of the United States*, various years.

[42] Mitchell 1962, 225–27, 474–75. The "overall" Sauerbeck-Statist Price Index (average of 1867–1877 = 100) is used to convert current into constant prices for the entire period.

[43] After World War II, air transportation emerges as a significant rival to ship and rail transportation. No attempt was made to duplicate these results for air transport rates in more recent periods. See Chapter 5.

British iron and steel production minus German iron and steel production, tapping into differences in economic capacity between the industrial leader for this period and the primary industrial challenger to the status quo. As British output falls relative to German output—that is, as *power* declines—changes in the number of alliances should increase.[44] Third, I control for the level of *industrialization*, defined by energy usage per capita in the United Kingdom. *Industrialization* should be positively related to changes in the number of alliances. Data for all three variables are from the National Capabilities Dataset.[45]

Since this is a time series analysis, I also include *year* to control for any secular trends and the dependent variable lagged one year. Three changes in the annual number of alliances are of particular note. In 1849, the wide array of defense pacts among the German princely states was terminated, only to be renewed in 1850. These alliances appear to have been dissolved and re-formed for reasons unrelated to the hypothesis being tested here. In 1867, the unification of Germany caused the average number of alliances in the system to plummet from 78.2 per year (1816–1866) to 14.3 (1867–1935), as these formerly anarchic relationships were transformed into hierarchic relationships. As strong outliers, these years are excluded from the analysis as appropriate. Transportation costs and the control variables may affect changes in alliances only with some time lag, and a range of alternative models was estimated. Each model below is the "best fit." In most cases, the sign on the transportation cost variable was not sensitive to alternative specifications.[46]

The results are presented in Table 7.1.[47] Transportation costs, as expected, are negatively and significantly related to changes in the number of alliances. As transportation costs decline, indicating that it is cheaper and easier to project force over distance, the number of alliances significantly increases. This relationship is found across all four indicators of transportation costs, suggesting that the results, although tentative, are relatively robust. Given the

[44] For the period covered by British grain (1815–1872), I also tested a threat variable defined as the sum of the military personnel per capita for Britain and France only, but it had no substantive effect on the results reported below. I also tested a second power variable, defined as British iron and steel production minus French iron and steel production. This variable did not effect the results, either.

[45] Singer and Small 1993.

[46] Only in the case of tramp shipping did a positive and significant relationship emerge (with a one-year lag on tramp shipping and a two-year lag on threat, power, and industrialization). This model might be considered a better fit based on the F-test and $R^2$, but it exists only in this one specification, whereas the negative relationship holds across different lags, and is inconsistent with the results of the other transportation indicators. Only the negative relationship is reported here.

[47] Standard tests do not indicate the presence of heteroscedasticity, and the LaGrange Multiplier test does not indicate the presence of serial auto-correlation.

TABLE 7.1
Transportation Costs and Annual Changes in Alliances, 1816–1938

| | Alliance Change (standard errors in parentheses) | | | |
|---|---|---|---|---|
| | British Grain (1815–1872)[a] | Tramp Shipping (1869–1919)[b] | Chicago to Liverpool (1880–1935)[b] | Rail Costs (1852–1938)[a] |
| Transportation Costs | −1.766* (0.795) | −0.015* (0.006) | −1.238** (0.368) | −4.942* (1.886) |
| Threat | −96.123 (170.366) | 33.644** (12.553) | 19.601* (7.369) | −2.819 (36.170) |
| Power | 0.001 (0.003) | 0.000 (0.000) | 0.000* (0.000) | 0.000 (0.000) |
| Industrialization | −0.966 (1.019) | −2.094 (1.242) | −2.516 (1.418) | −1.080** (0.393) |
| Lagged dependent Variable (1 yr.) | −0.024 (0.042) | −0.274* (0.122) | −0.396 (0.124)** | −0.250* (0.105) |
| Year | −0.134 (0.237) | 0.095** (0.033) | 0.003 (0.041) | 0.087** (0.029) |
| Constant | 263.990 (437.423) | −172.513** (61.976) | 11.005 (79.455) | −159.566** (54.955) |
| N | 53 | 68 | 56 | 80 |
| R-squared | 0.154 | 0.254 | 0.345 | 0.240 |

*Note:* Two-tailed test: $p<.05$ *; $p<.01$ **

[a] No lag on transportation costs, threat, power, or industrialization.

[b] No lag on transportation costs; one year lag on threat, power, and industrialization.

problem of selection bias noted above, which underestimates the causal effect of transportation costs, these results can be taken as generally supportive of the theory.

Surprisingly, the control variables do not perform well. *Threat* has the predicted sign and is significantly related only when tramp shipping and Chicago to Liverpool are used to measure transportation costs. *Power* has a small effect and carries the wrong sign in all models, but is significant in only one (Chicago to Liverpool).[48] *Industrialization* also has the inverse effect and is significant only when rail costs are used.[49] Dropping these control variables

[48] Power is significant at the .10 level for tramp shipping.

[49] Industrialization is significant at the .10 level for tramp shipping and Chicago to Liverpool.

from the equations does not significantly alter the results for transportation costs.[50] This suggests that the cost of projecting force over distance matters more than some of the more traditional realpolitik concerns.

These results are preliminary, rather than definitive. The proxies are crude. The analysis focuses on only one of three possible sources of joint production economies—technological scale economies—and does not include the expected costs of opportunism or governance costs. These latter variables are, as the theory above suggests, more relevant to the choice of alternative security relationships, but they are also related to the overall level of cooperation of concern here. Indeed, given the interaction between the variables in the theory above, it is somewhat surprising that the effect of one source of joint production economies is significant at all. The findings should be interpreted cautiously. Nonetheless, the results are suggestive, and indicate that the theory is pointing to at least one important determinant of security cooperation.

## FUTURE DIRECTIONS

As discussed in Chapter 3, the case studies above do not purport to be a conclusive test of the theory. Nonetheless, the predictions of the theory are broadly consistent with the empirical record and are plausible given the available historical knowledge (see Chapter 8). It is hoped that readers have been sufficiently provoked that they will take up the challenge of refining, extending, and ultimately revising the theory and case studies outlined here.

Looking forward, I see four main avenues for further work on relational contracting in international relations. First, the theory laid out in Chapter 3 needs to be reformulated along fully strategic lines. As noted there, the present theory is decision rather than game theoretic in construction. Attention has also been overly focused on the choices and actions of the dominant polity—not inappropriately I would argue, given the position of the United States throughout much of the twentieth century—but more explicit attention needs to be devoted to the choices and strategies of other polities. Although I am confident in the hypotheses and implications of the current version, these need to be confirmed in a game theoretic model and, I anticipate, pushed in new directions.

Second, the variables central to the theory need to be operationalized more fully and data need to be developed on appropriate indicators for a larger number of cases. For reasons discussed at the end of Chapter 3, joint economies, expected costs of opportunism, and governance costs are all difficult to measure, especially over the full range of alternative relationships.

[50] Only in the case of tramp shipping do transportation costs become statistically insignificant at standard levels. In all other models, transportation costs remain the same or become more significant.

Proxies for these variables are necessary. In a related fashion, hypotheses with more direct and readily observable implications need to be derived. I attempted to illustrate how this might be carried out in the previous section, but much more needs to be done.

Third, domestic-level variables need to be integrated into the theory of relational contracting. Like neoliberal institutionalism, neorealism, and constructivism, the theory here abstracts from domestic politics and focuses on the interactions of polities. Although a useful first step in theory construction, this unduly limits the range of important causal variables considered. The contrast between the security relationships formed by the United States and Soviet Union after 1945, for instance, was related to their differing circumstances and contractual opportunities. Most importantly, the Soviet Union faced higher expected costs of opportunism and lower governance costs, and correspondingly pursued more hierarchic security relationships in Eastern Europe.[51] Yet the alternative relationships pursued by the two superpowers may also have been related to differences in their political intentions and desires. I have shown elsewhere that nondemocratic states, like the Soviet Union, are likely to have a larger optimal size and, thus, an imperialist bias in their foreign policies.[52] Not all states are equally threatening and, for domestic reasons, some are better partners than others.

In addition, substantial research now suggests that alternative sets of domestic institutions may influence the ability of states to make credible commitments in international relations.[53] In particular, scholars have argued that open political regimes with multiple internal checks and balances are able to make more credible commitments to current policy. An alliance commitment by a democratic state, it follows, is inherently more credible than a similar commitment by an autocratic state—in other words, the democratic state is less likely to act opportunistically. In turn, states with democratic institutions may be able build greater joint economies, have a lower risk of opportunism, or require fewer externally imposed safeguards, suggesting that they may cooperate more frequently in anarchic relationships than other states.[54] During the Cold War, again, the United States was far more transparent than the Soviet Union, and the multiple vetoes over policy reinforced its ability to commit credibly to its current policies. In but one example, the Great Debate allowed Europeans to be more confident that the United States would come through on its security promises. Domestic institutions do not, of course, provide an ironclad guarantee of commitment, as widespread dissatisfaction with the limited aims of the Persian Gulf War suggests. Popular control over

[51] Lake 1996 and 1997.
[52] Lake 1992 and 1997.
[53] See Cowhey 1993; Fearon 1994; Simmons 1994.
[54] This may explain the tendency of democracies to ally with one another. See Siverson and Emmons 1991.

the instruments of foreign policy, in this instance, might well have expanded America's war aims beyond those of its coalition partners. Nonetheless, domestic institutions do reinforce the ability of democracies to cooperate in general and to cooperate within anarchic institutions in particular.

Finally, the theory here can be extended beyond security to other issue areas. Although the labels change, for instance, the same continuum laid out in Chapter 2 exists in economic relationships as well, ranging from anarchic agreements (each state retains full rights of residual control), to customs unions (polities give up tariff autonomy), economic unions (polities give up autonomy over external economic relations and some autonomy over fiscal and monetary policy), and finally hierarchies (all residual rights are wholly transferred to another polity).[55] It follows that the same factors—joint economies, expected costs of opportunism, and governance costs—will feature in determining the optimal economic relationship. Problems of contracting are ubiquitous in international relations.

---

[55] For an analysis of the economic and security relationships between the newly independent states of the former Soviet Union, see Hancock 1998.

## Chapter 8

## CONCLUSION

SINCE THE NATION'S FOUNDING, but most acutely over the last century, American foreign policy has been torn between unilateralism and security cooperation, and within the latter between more anarchic and more hierarchic security relationships. At the end of World War I, the United States had to decide between its historic unilateralism and the promise of cooperation. The League of Nations fell victim to the risks of opportunism and the costs of governance in a world where the benefits from pooling resources and efforts with others were distinctly limited. After World War II, the United States had to decide how to utilize the new technologies it controlled, where to establish its defense perimeter, and how best to manage relations with its partners. With large gains from jointly producing security, moderate expected costs of opportunism that did not decline with hierarchy, and low governance costs that rose rapidly with hierarchy, the United States choose relatively anarchic security relationships with almost all of its partners, although significant variations existed. Today, the United States stands poised between a return to unilateralism and continued cooperation. To date, cooperation has triumphed. In the Persian Gulf War, the gains from pooling resources and efforts with others were large, the risks of opportunism were high in the Gulf states—leading to the establishment of protectorates in the region—but moderate to low elsewhere, and the constraints imposed upon the United States by its partners were substantial. In Somalia, the gains were small, but so were the expected costs of opportunism and governance. Future American policy remains up for grabs.

The available historical evidence is largely consistent with the theory. The foreign policy choices of the United States fit with plausible readings of the independent variables. In addition, the policy debates in each era reveal a process of deliberation over precisely the kinds of tradeoffs expected by the theory. The great debates over American foreign policy have focused on identifying and constructing optimal security relationships for the United States and have been driven by differing assessments of the gains from cooperation, the risks posed by perfidious partners, and challenges of governing relationships with others—especially the likely constraints on America's own freedom of action.

In this final chapter I survey the hypotheses laid out in Chapter 3 in light of events during the American century. I conclude with a brief examina-

tion of current debates within the United States and the contradictions in
current policy.

## THE AMERICAN CENTURY RECONSIDERED

In summarizing the theory in Chapter 3, I posed seven general hypotheses.
Not every hypothesis pertains to every episode of American foreign policy
examined above, and definite readings of each variable were not always possible. Nonetheless, the evidence generally supports the expectations of the
theory. For each hypothesis, I summarize the logic, illustrate the proposition
with brief references to the cases, and highlight implications for our current
understandings of international cooperation and security.

$H_1$:  The greater the joint production economies, the more likely
polities are to cooperate.

Joint production economies provide the foundation for all international cooperation. Without at least some gains from pooling resources and efforts
with others, the expected costs of opportunism and governance costs, inherent in all joint undertakings, will inevitably thwart cooperation. The larger
the technological scale economies, positive externalities that are internalized
in a relationship, and the division of labor, the more polities gain from cooperation. The greater the gains, in turn, the higher the costs of opportunism
and governance that can be sustained in cooperation.

The interwar and Cold War cases illustrate well the effects of joint production economies on the prospects for cooperation. After World War I, the
joint economies anticipated by the United States were too small to offset the
expected costs of opportunism and governance costs of security cooperation,
both in the progressive internationalist's modestly hierarchical vision of the
League of Nations and the conservative internationalist's strictly anarchic
alternative. After World War II, the substantially expanded joint production
economies permitted the United States to absorb with ease expected costs of
opportunism that were not dissimilar to those found in the earlier period
and lower governance costs of cooperation. Where politicians and analysts
alike were divided over the merits of alternative proposals in the first case,
they were far more unified behind the "obvious" benefits of cooperation in
the second. Although joint production economies alone are insufficient to
explain the change in policy, the substantial increase was central in the
choice of cooperation after World War II.

Large joint production economies were also important in stimulating cooperation in the Persian Gulf case. Indeed, given the high expected costs of
opportunism and high governance costs in this instance, the joint production
economies were arguably decisive in permitting cooperation between the
United States and its Gulf and, less directly, other coalition partners. The

small joint production economies in Somalia, however, remind us that it is the gains from pooling resources and efforts with others relative to the expected costs of opportunism and governance costs that ultimately determines policy.

In the current literature on international cooperation, joint production economies are too often assumed, rather than investigated, and taken as fixed, rather than treated as a variable.[1] To cite a simple but common example, when the prisoner's dilemma is taken as the quintessential problem of international relations, analysts are implicitly, at least, assuming that joint production economies exist (mutual cooperation is preferred to mutual defection). In the repeated version of this game, moreover, the joint production economies are assumed to remain constant over time.[2] The theory and cases here suggest that such assumptions may often be inappropriate. Rather, we should treat the "gains from cooperation" as a variable—in fact, a very important variable.

$H_2$:  The greater the expected costs of opportunism, the less likely
        polities are to cooperate.

Along with governance costs, opportunism is the principal impediment to cooperation. The higher the probability of opportunistic behavior by partners, the greater the specific assets at risk, or both, the less attractive cooperation in any form is to polities. The expected costs of opportunism are a primal force in either permitting or inhibiting cooperation.

Expected costs of opportunism played a central role in every case discussed above, but their overall effect is best seen, perhaps, in Somalia. In this instance, there were relatively few joint production economies, and governance costs escalated rapidly with hierarchy—thereby limiting the United States to largely anarchic security relationships that could not significantly reduce the risk of opportunism. In a situation that might otherwise preclude cooperation, the expected costs of opportunism were sufficiently low that the joint effort could proceed. No specific assets were at risk and the interests of its partners did not diverge significantly from those of the United States. Although analysts often point to America's humanitarian motives to explain this case, the negligible expected costs of opportunism were an equally important permissive condition for cooperation. The case of Somalia contrasts with the interwar period. In a similar situation of small joint economies and

---

[1] Keohane 1984, 6, writes that his theory "takes the existence of mutual interests as given and examines the conditions under which they will lead to cooperation." A focus on joint production economies transforms these mutual interests into a variable.

[2] The prisoner's dilemma is evoked by both realists and neoliberals. See Oye 1986; Grieco 1990; Yarbrough and Yarbrough 1992; and Gowa 1994. Although these authors are aware that the cardinal value of the payoffs matter, no attempt is made to measure or trace the implications of changes in these values in a systematic fashion.

escalating governance costs, the expected costs of opportunism blocked
security cooperation between the wars. For the United States, fears of
opportunism were the decisive barrier to pooling resources and efforts with
Europe.

Although the expected costs of opportunism are clearly recognized as important in current theories of international cooperation, they are, like joint
production economies, too often treated as fixed and invariant. To continue
the same example as above, the expected costs of opportunism are reflected
in the prisoner's dilemma by the "sucker's payoff" (one polity cooperates
while the other defects). But in the single-shot and repeated versions of this
game, these costs are usually not specified clearly and are assumed to remain
constant. As above, this study suggests that such assumptions are unwar-
ranted, and perhaps actually misleading. The expected costs of opportunism
vary widely across potential partners and over time.

H₃:   The more rapidly the expected costs of opportunism decline with
       hierarchy, the more likely polities are to choose hierarchical
       security relationships.

Security relationships differ in their ability to reduce the probability of opportunistic behavior by partners. Anarchic relationships are always less effective than hierarchic relationships, according to the logic of the theory, but the
difference between the alternatives may not be constant over time or across
dyads. The more efficacious hierarchy is, the more often polities should form
such relationships.

Evaluating this hypothesis requires, even more than the others examined
here, probing counterfactual relationships. Given the clustering of America's
security relationships during the past century toward the anarchic end of the
continuum of possible relationships (see Figures 2.1 and 5.1), estimating
these counterfactuals is especially difficult. The American occupations of
Germany and Japan provide the most direct evidence of the efficacy of hierarchy in relations between important partners during the modern era. As
discussed in Chapter 5, the United States clearly estimated, at the time, that
hierarchy was likely to be ineffective in controlling these partners over the
long run. Expecting that little would be gained from hierarchy, the United
States moved rapidly to restore sovereignty and embed both states into loose
American protectorates. In Micronesia, by contrast, the source of the likely
opportunism was very different—not resentment of American dominance,
but internal political collapse. In this case, hierarchy could be efficacious,
helping to explain why it was chosen in this anomalous instance.

Although the theory clearly suggests the general form that the expected
costs of opportunism should take—highest in anarchy, lowest in hierarchy—
how and why security relationships differ in their effectiveness remains an
open question. By ignoring international hierarchy, the current literature on

cooperation is largely silent on this question, and offers little guidance on estimating the efficacy of alternative relationships. This is a suggestive area for further research.

$H_4$:  The more specific the assets at risk in cooperation, the more likely
        polities are to form hierarchical security relationships.

Opportunism is not necessarily costly. In the absence of relationally specific assets, abandonment, entrapment, or exploitation by partners—however frequent and perhaps irritating—imposes few costs. In turn, polities create hierarchies to control partners precisely when opportunism, if it were to occur, is detrimental. Polities form hierarchies to cope with the risks of opportunism in the presence of specific assets.

The protectorates created by the United States in the Persian Gulf provide clear evidence for this hypothesis. Dependent upon forward bases in the region, the United States faced enormous costs if Saudi Arabia or other regional partners acted opportunistically. To cooperate with the Gulf states, the United States seized the decisive voice in the coalition by sending a disproportionately large number of troops to the Gulf and transformed the regional states into protectorates. By leading the coalition, the United States managed relations with Iraq and determined the nature, timing, and conduct of the war.

A similar pattern emerged in the early Cold War period. In Europe, the United States enjoyed multiple base sites and had fewer specific assets at risk; outside Germany, a sphere of influence prevailed. In the Pacific, on the other hand, forward bases, a perimeter defense that could be vitiated by possible gaps, and a limited number of first-class ports created the need for more hierarchical security relationships. The United States, in turn, established protectorates with Japan and the Philippines, extracted as a condition for independence, and an empire in Micronesia. Where the assets were more specific, the United States imposed more hierarchical relationships even on its Cold War partners.

Specific assets have important implications for theories of cooperation and international relations, more generally. For many theorists, the risk of defection is the primary impediment to cooperation. This has led to a robust research agenda on transparency, reciprocity, regimes, and other mechanisms for revealing and punishing defection.[3] All this is helpful and necessary, but defection is too often treated in an undifferentiated manner. Not all defection is equally costly. It varies with the specific assets at risk. Moreover, the focus on anarchic relationships in cooperation theory ignores the potentially more important and robust response of hierarchy. When opportunism is very costly, polities will choose either not to cooperate or to cooperate only within

---

[3] Krasner 1983; Keohane 1984; and Martin 1992.

some hierarchical relationship. Anarchic relationships are expected precisely in those instances where few specific assets are at risk.

$H_5$: The greater the probability of opportunism by partners, the less likely polities are to invest in relationally specific assets.

When the probability of opportunism is high, polities are less likely to expose themselves to additional costs by investing in specific assets. If cooperation is nonetheless attractive, they may try to counteract their exposure by creating relational hierarchies. If the joint economies are small, and can only be expanded by investing in more specific assets, or if hierarchy can only be built at a high governance cost, polities may choose not to cooperate rather than make themselves vulnerable to opportunism by others.

Cooperation between the world wars was plagued by exactly this problem. Given the high probability of opportunism, and high governance costs that limited it to generally anarchic relationships, the United States (and possibly other states) could not contemplate investments in specific assets. Fearful of opportunism, the United States choose not to make itself vulnerable to European actions. By eschewing specific assets, however, the United States also gave up significant opportunities to increase its joint production economies. Even though further technological maturation was necessary to sustain cooperation in any event, no division of labor was entertained and forward bases were not considered. The failure to expand the joint production economies where possible after the war doomed the League, in particular, and security cooperation, more generally. Facing a lower risk of opportunism after 1945, the United States reversed course, invested in specific assets, and built a strong and enduring foundation for cooperation.

Joint production economies and the expected costs of opportunism are interrelated, and partly endogenous to the choice of security relationships. To build large joint economies often requires some specific assets, but a high probability of opportunism deters such investments and makes unilateralism comparatively more attractive. This problem of endogenity complicates the choices of real decision makers, and poses problems of inference for analysts.

This hypothesis parallels the predictions of many neorealists that states will avoid becoming dependent upon or vulnerable to others, and that this quest for autonomy inhibits cooperation.[4] It differs in several important ways, however. To avoid costly opportunism by others, polities may fail to cooperate but they may also create hierarchical security relationships to govern their joint efforts. The range of choice is broader than neorealists suggest. In addition, fears of costly opportunism need not preclude cooperation, even in anarchy, depending upon the other factors at play in the theory. If the joint production economies are sufficiently large, and governance costs in

---

[4] Waltz 1979; Grieco 1990; and the discussion of functional differentiation in Chapter 7.

anarchy sufficiently small, polities may still choose to cooperate even knowing that their partners may act opportunistically.

H$_6$:  The larger the governance costs, the less likely polities are to
        cooperate.

Governance costs are the second major impediment to cooperation. The greater the governance costs, the less likely polities are to pool their resources and efforts with others. Whether they arise from sidepayments to subordinate polities, constraints on the dominant state, or coercion, governance costs deter polities from cooperating.

Governance costs were a primary constraint on America's entry into the League of Nations. Although the fetters likely to be imposed on the United States by the League were tolerable to the progressive internationalists, a majority in the Senate judged these governance costs too high, and preferred a less hierarchical alternative or unilateralism. Joined together in this way, the conservative internationalists and irreconcilables defeated cooperation. As repeated throughout this volume, however, governance costs by themselves do not determine the choice of relationship. In the Persian Gulf case, the constraints imposed by the international community on the United States were at least equal to those of the proposed League, but they were offset by substantial joint production economies.

Although governance costs have been central to decision makers and popular debates over security policy, they have been largely absent from theories of international cooperation and security. As noted in Chapter 3, joint production economies and expected costs of opportunism have long been at the core of international relations theory. Governance costs, however, have typically been overlooked. In part, this stems from a concentration on anarchic relationships, where governance costs are least likely to be important. But even studies of imperialism have largely ignored their effects. The theory and case studies here demonstrate, I hope, the importance of including governance costs in our analyses. As discussed in Chapter 6 and below, to cite but one example, the debate over American foreign policy today is driven, in part, by conflicting estimates of the governance costs of cooperation—how tightly must the United States bind itself to gain the voluntary cooperation of others? To ignore such costs is to misunderstand one of the central issues separating contemporary unilateralists and internationalists.

H$_7$:  The less rapidly governance costs increase with hierarchy, the more
        likely polities are to choose hierarchical security relationships.

Governance costs increase with hierarchy, inhibiting polities from forming more hierarchical relationships. Although the theory expects that governance costs will vary systematically across alternative relationships—smaller in anarchy, larger in hierarchy—it does not define particular levels for particular relationships. Like the expected costs of opportunism ($H_3$), how governance costs vary across alternative security relationships is an empirical question.

Estimating governance costs requires, once again, counterfactual analysis, and the postwar American occupations are again revealing. In the cases of Germany and Japan under the occupation, the costs of direct rule and side-payments to gain their voluntary compliance clearly pushed the costs of hierarchy to almost prohibitive levels, despite the status of these countries as defeated and despised wartime enemies. Although generalizing from these exceptional cases may be problematic, it would appear that the costs to the United States of acquiring and maintaining hierarchy could only be larger for other great power partners. This implies that governance costs generally rose sharply with hierarchy during the American century, and that the United States was frequently limited by this factor to relatively anarchic security relationships. This remains true today. Even in the Persian Gulf, the United States paid dearly in constraints on its own behavior in exchange for a limited hierarchy over its regional partners.

By largely ignoring governance costs, scholars overlook important limits and sources of change in world politics. At the systemic level, governance costs that rise with hierarchy help explain why we continue to live in a world of many sovereign states. Without some countervailing pressure, polities would push inexorably toward greater hierarchy and, eventually, world empire. It is not necessarily the system that prevents consolidation of hierarchical world government, or that the balancing mechanism prevents any state from achieving world hegemony.[5] Rather, there are limits to hierarchical authority created by escalating governance costs.

Likewise, escalating governance costs help explain the evolution from a world of global empires in the nineteenth century into a world of sovereign states today—arguably one of the greatest political transformations in human history.[6] Through the "success" of European imperialism, acephalous political communities—or communities that at least appeared acephalous to the Europeans when they first engaged these polities—were remade into compliant "quasi states" that generally live up to their international obligations, despite the shift toward greater anarchy in their relationships with countries of the "core."[7] The benefits of direct rule have declined greatly. Equally important,

---

[5] Waltz 1959.

[6] Outside of his critique of Lenin's theory of imperialism, Waltz 1979 mentions imperialism only once, in an aside on imperialism as a form of system management (205). In a recent volume edited by Katzenstein 1996a, constructivists also pay scant attention to imperialism, even though the approach is explicitly intended to challenge our "taken-for-granted" categories and concepts of international politics; imperialism is mentioned once in a discussion of Snyder's work (27), and twice as a subject in its own right, each time receiving no more than one sentence of attention (36 and 59).

[7] Jackson 1990.

any attempt to impose or reimpose empire would meet considerable—and costly—resistance. Although there would be no doubt who would win in any contest of coercion between states of the core and the periphery if they were equally committed to the object in question, the governance costs facing prospective imperialists today are proportionately greater than in the past. Barring any unforeseen increases in the joint production economies of cooperation or in the assets specific to current relationships with peripheral states, escalating governance costs suggest that imperialism, so common at the beginning of the American century, is now largely obsolete.[8]

This survey reinforces two themes of this volume. First, security relationships must be understood as varying along a continuum from anarchy to hierarchy. The failure to specify and consider alternative security relationships places intellectual blinders on analysts of international politics, biases our estimates of the causes and consequences of world politics, and renders us mute on many of the most important events and transformations in international history. Any complete theory of international politics needs to consider explicitly the full range of possible relationships between polities.

Second, to explain why polities sometimes act unilaterally and sometimes cooperate, and how they choose between alternative security relationships, we must examine all three of the principal causal variables in the theory. Joint production economies, the expected costs of opportunism, and governance costs are all necessary, but none alone is sufficient, to explain foreign policy choices. The theory generates useful comparative static predictions. But in any particular case, all else is not constant and we must explicitly examine all of the variables. Knowing that, say, the joint production economies between the United States and Saudi Arabia are large does not, by itself, tell us whether cooperation was likely in the Gulf War. In the end, it is how the joint production economies, expected costs of opportunism, and governance costs stand in relation to one another that ultimately determines whether and in what form polities choose to cooperate.

## TOWARD A NEW AMERICAN CENTURY

The end of the Cold War has kicked off a soul-searching debate over foreign policy within the United States. As in the past, the central cleavage is between unilateralists, who in the grand tradition of Washington and the founding fathers eschew entangling relationships, and internationalists, who

---

[8] The one exception to this rule might be the problem of "failing states." In most cases, however, those states most at risk of internal chaos are not in security relationships with the great powers and do not possess significant relationally specific assets. Only in the area of the former Soviet Union do failing states and large relationally specific assets coincide. See Hancock 1998.

advocate cooperation and see security relationships as effective instruments for controlling the behavior of partners.

As the analysis posed above leads us to expect, and as outlined in Chapter 6, current practitioners already have a sense of the political tradeoffs suggested by the theory and are deeply engaged in a process of interpolating between the incompletely informed views of many different individuals. Even though contemporary events help validate the theory, it can also be used to sharpen the domestic political debate, highlight issues that separate alternative perspectives, and emphasize points for sustained discussion. Just as the theory led us to see the episodes in Chapters 4 through 6 in a different light, so too can it lead us to see different issues and variations in the debate over the future of American foreign policy.

Contemporary unilateralists are divided into two major schools of opinion.[9] Their differences often overwhelm their apparent similarities, but they are united in their advocacy of foreign policy independence for the United States. Neo-isolationists, as they are often called, advocate a fundamental retrenchment in American foreign policy and a withdrawal into an "offshore balancing" role for the United States.[10] Primacists, on the other hand, seek to preserve America's current political hegemony and prevent potential challengers from arising.[11] Both schools see relatively few gains from security cooperation and a high risk of opportunism in the international environment. Although they differ in the level of activism they recommend, both call for the United States to act unilaterally in foreign affairs.

In a world largely devoid of threats to American security, neo-isolationists call for the United States to "come home" and adopt a policy of strategic "restraint" in foreign policy.[12] They see few gains from pooling resources and efforts with other. Seeking only a continental defense, neo-isolationists believe that it is difficult for both the United States and others to project force over distance. Only nuclear weapons provide significant strategic reach, and a secure second strike capability vitiates the ability of others to threaten the United States and obviates any need by Americans to reach beyond their current borders.[13] Pulling back within "fortress America," the United States should not provide assistance to others, and should expect none in return. In terms of the theory above, neo-isolationists estimate that contemporary joint production economies are very small and provide little basis for international cooperation.

---

[9] On the following schools of thought, see Posen and Ross 1996/97.

[10] Layne 1993 and 1997; Gholz, Press, and Sapolsky 1997. For the most developed and original statement of this position, see Nordlinger 1995.

[11] Huntington is probably the leading academic proponent of primacy; see Huntington 1993. Primacists draw upon Gilpin 1981 and Kennedy 1987. For a critique, see Jervis 1993.

[12] Gholz, Press, and Sapolsky 1997.

[13] Ibid., 7–13, 29; Layne 1997, 97–112; see also Posen and Ross 1996/97, 12.

Neo-isolationists are also profoundly skeptical of the ability of the United States to control the behavior of others through security institutions. Without recognizing the apparent contradiction, they also fear that these same institutions will constrain the United States to act against its interests.[14] "Foreign entanglements" will necessarily entrap the country into conflicts that it could and should otherwise avoid. Security cooperation in any form, in this view, is not only of limited value, it is dangerous.[15]

Emphasizing the unprecedented power of the United States, and the desire to preserve this position against all challengers real and imagined, primacists tend to discount the joint gains from international cooperation. They typically do not ask how pooling resources and efforts with others can enhance the security of the United States or reduce its defense burden. This is unfortunate, for their own logic implies that the United States should be able to control its partners easily, even within relatively anarchic security relationships; the expected costs of opportunism should be relatively low, favoring a policy of cooperation. Primacists should be pressed hard to articulate why cooperation produces few benefits for the United States, and whether opportunism by others is or is not a significant risk.

Both neo-isolationists and primacists, in turn, emphasize the constraints exerted on the United States by security cooperation. Both see the United States straining under fetters imposed by partners in the Persian Gulf, Bosnia, and around the globe, and call for a more independent policy in order to break these ties. For neo-isolationists, all security relationships are necessarily "entangling," and should be avoided. For primacists, existing security institutions dominated by the Untied States are acceptable instruments, but multilateral institutions should be shunned and used only when necessary for "diplomatic cover."[16] As with the conservative internationalists in the interwar period and unilateralists in the Cold War, primacists worry about the creation of organic institutions that may take on an independent existence and possibly constrain the United States at some future time. Just as states that might potentially challenge the United States must be stopped, so too must international institutions that might limit the nation's foreign policy independence. Primacists should also be pushed on the question of how the United States can unilaterally and aggressively pursue its own interests against those of others without generating a counter-balance in response.[17]

Contemporary internationalists are also organized into two basic schools. Advocates of selective engagement call for a restricted but positive role for the United States in world affairs, focused on containing great power threats.[18]

[14] Gholz, Press, and Sapolsky 1997, 15–17.
[15] Posen and Ross 1996/97, 13–14.
[16] Ibid., 39–40.
[17] Gholz, Press, and Sapolsky 1997, 37.
[18] Van Evera 1990, and Art 1991.

Supporters of cooperative security, a modern-day form of collective security, maintain that peace is indivisible, and back an aggressive American policy to prevent conflicts abroad.[19] Despite the very different goals they advocate for American policy, both schools see international cooperation as the appropriate means.

Internationalists emphasize the gains to the United States from cooperation, highlighting the positive externalities provided by others as well as opportunities for burden sharing. They also recognize that projecting American power around the globe, and especially in areas like the Persian Gulf, often requires local partners. For both schools, substantial joint production economies provide a strong foundation for cooperation.[20] For advocates of cooperative security, moreover, the expansion of the existing division of labor within NATO and, perhaps, the creation of a similar infrastructure within other international organizations promises to increase the benefits of cooperation and further wed the United States to a policy of engagement.[21] As noted in Chapter 5, this is an important impetus behind the movement to enlarge NATO.

Internationalists, in turn, tend to minimize the risks of opportunism and the constraints on the United States imposed by its partners. If neo-isolationists are unduly skeptical of foreign entanglements, internationalists have perhaps an exaggerated faith in the ability of international institutions to allow the United States to control others at an acceptable cost.[22] Internationalists certainly have the record of the last decade to sustain their position, and this provides no small measure of support. But just as the primacists should be expected to explain why the gains from cooperation are small and the risks of opportunism high, advocates of cooperation should be called upon to explain how and why international institutions can effectively regulate international affairs without unduly limiting America's freedom of action.

Proponents of different policies ultimately rest their views on different estimates of an uncertain future. As in the past, it is difficult to know which estimates are correct, and which are not. Partisans provoke debate, which is useful, but they often decide first and analyze second. This book identifies a set of questions on relational contracting that, as history confirms, are central in foreign policy debates. Nonetheless, the questions are often left implicit or answered only incompletely by partisans of competing policies. With the aid of the theory, the historical chapters above have attempted to draw the questions and their answers together in a coherent fashion. Contemporary advo-

---

[19] Carter, Perry, and Steinbruner 1992, and Nolan 1994.

[20] Art 1991; Posen and Ross 1996/97, 24–26.

[21] Posen and Ross 1996/97, 24–25.

[22] There are, of course, diverse opinions on this issue. Advocates of selective engagement are somewhat more skeptical of international institutions than proponents of cooperative security, but the former still support NATO and other existing institutions; see ibid., 20.

cates of alternative foreign policies could improve the quality of the current debate, and the answers that will eventually be reached, by addressing clearly the following issues.

- How large are the benefits from pooling resources and efforts with others? Can these benefits be expanded without incurring more relationally specific assets?
- What are the risks entailed in cooperation? How can the expected costs of opportunism be best managed?
- What are the costs of monitoring, safeguarding, and enforcing agreements between partners? How do these costs vary over alternative relationships?

By asking and answering questions clearly, perhaps Americans can more quickly and ably reason their way to the future.

### Contracting Contradictions

The current debate remains vigorous because, as in the interwar period, the United States is caught in a world of almost equally attractive alternatives. There are no "obvious" answers to the questions posed above. Even though the policies ultimately chosen were similar, conditions in the Persian Gulf and Somalia were quite different. Small changes in any of the variables in the theory might have led to a different outcome, especially in the latter case. Had the risks of opportunism been greater, or the constraints on the United States even tighter, unilateralism might well have been the optimal policy, and the post-Cold War world might look very different today. In a world of many challenges, each response must be decided on its own terms. There are, however, two general tensions in current policy. Our choices today will be judged tomorrow by how well these contradictions are managed.

First, American leadership facilitates cooperation by reducing the probability of opportunism by partners, but it also limits the gains from cooperation. By providing a disproportionate share of the forces in joint military operations in order to establish control over its partners, as in the Persian Gulf War and Somalia, the United States precludes an effective international division of labor and foregoes opportunities to share its defense burdens with others. By operating within ad hoc coalitions of similar and more "trustworthy" states, it further limits the division of labor. By leading, the United States constrains the joint production economies it enjoys and thereby limits the expected costs of opportunism and governance it is willing to bear. As with the League, where the high risk of opportunism prevented it from considering ways of expanding the possible benefits of cooperation, the United States today is limiting the gains from cooperation and, in turn, the expected costs of opportunism and governance costs it can pay.

In seeking to reduce the risks of opportunism, the United States threatens to undermine its own incentives for cooperation. In an era of unprecedented American power, it is easy to believe that the United States can or should seek to control all risks, including those from potential partners. Leadership does control opportunism, but it also weakens the roots of cooperation.

Second, by leading, the United States subordinates other states. This further limits the burdens it can expect others to shoulder, for the United States must buy their compliance with new sidepayments or, equivalently, less burden sharing. More importantly, establishing international hierarchies, as in the Gulf War, requires great constraints on the United States and raises the governance costs of cooperation. America cannot lead unless others follow, and its partners will not follow unless the United States takes them where they are willing to go. The United States has considerable influence over the international consensus, but leading within this consensus binds it to a significant degree. These governance costs are increasingly unpopular with American voters, and may be the primary impediment to cooperation in the future.

In an era of seemingly unlimited American power, constraints on the use of that power are hard to endure. Americans must shield themselves against an exaggerated desire to control the risks of cooperation and guard against an undue demand for foreign policy autonomy. If the United States chooses to act alone in foreign policy, Americans should be careful that the independence gained outweighs the cooperation lost.

# REFERENCES

Aceves, William J. 1996. The Economic Analysis of International Law: Transaction Cost Economics and the Concept of State Practice. *University of Pennsylvania Journal of International Law* 17:995–1,068.

Achen, Christopher H. 1988. A State with Bureaucratic Politics is Representable as a Unitary Rational Actor. Paper presented at the annual meeting of the American Political Science Association, Washington, D.C.

Acheson, Dean. 1969. *Present at the Creation: My Years in the State Department.* New York: Norton.

Adams, Francis Ottiwell, and C. D. Cunningham. 1889. *The Swiss Confederation.* London: Macmillan.

Adams, Gordon, and Eric Munz. 1988. *Fair Shares: Bearing the Burden of the NATO Alliance.* Washington, D.C.: Center on Budget and Policy Priorities.

Adler, Emanuel. 1992. Europe's New Security Order: A Pluralistic Security Community. In *The Future of European Security*, edited by Beverly Crawford. Berkeley: Center for German and European Studies, University of California, Berkeley.

———. 1997. Seizing the Middle Ground: Constructivism in World Politics. *European Journal of International Relations* 3:319–63.

Adler, Selig. 1966 [1957]. *The Isolationist Impulse: Its Twentieth-Century Reaction.* New York: Free Press.

Aitkin, Don, and Brian Jinks. 1985. *Australian Political Institutions.* 3rd ed. Carlton, Aust.: Pitman.

Allison, Graham. 1971. *Essence of Decision: Explaining the Cuban Missile Crisis.* Boston: Little, Brown.

Alston, Lee J., Thráinn Eggertsson, and Douglass C. North, eds. 1996. *Empirical Studies in Institutional Change.* New York: Cambridge University Press.

Altfeld, Michael F. 1984. The Decision to Ally: A Theory and Test. *Western Political Quarterly* 37:523–44.

Altfeld, Michael F., and James D. Morrow. n.d. Sources of Security: Measuring the Relationship Between Alliances and Armaments. Photocopy.

Ambrosius, Lloyd E. 1987. *Woodrow Wilson and the American Diplomatic Tradition: The Treaty Fight in Perspective.* New York: Cambridge University Press.

———. 1991. *Wilsonian Statecraft: Theory and Practice of Liberal Internationalism during World War I.* Wilmington, DE: Scholarly Resources.

Arend, Anthony Clark, and Robert J. Beck. 1993. *International Law and the Use of Force: Beyond the UN Charter Paradigm.* New York: Routledge.

Art, Robert. 1991. A Defensible Defense: America's Grand Strategy after the Cold War. *International Security* 15, 4:5–53.

Ashley, Richard K. 1984. The Poverty of Neorealism. *International Organization* 38: 225–61.

Atkinson, Rick. 1993. *Crusade: The Untold Story of the Persian Gulf War.* Boston: Houghton Mifflin.

Axelrod, Robert. 1984. *The Evolution of Cooperation*. New York: Basic Books.

Bahcheli, Tozun. 1994. Turkey, the Gulf Crisis, and the New World Order. In *The Gulf War and the New World Order: International Relations of the Middle East*, edited by Tareq Y. Ismael and Jacqueline S. Ismael. Gainesville: University Press of Florida.

Baker, J. Wayne. 1993. The Covenantal Basis for the Development of Swiss Political Federalism: 1291–1848. *Publius* 23:19–41.

Baker, James A. 1996. Why the U.S. Didn't March to Bagdhad. *Los Angeles Times*, September 8:M1 and 6.

Baker, James A., III, with Thomas M. DeFrank. 1995. *The Politics of Diplomacy: Revolution, War and Peace, 1989–1992*. New York: G. P. Putnam's Sons.

Baldwin, David A. 1985. *Economic Statecraft*. Princeton: Princeton University Press.

———, ed. 1993. *Neorealism and Neoliberalism: The Contemporary Debate*. New York: Columbia University Press.

———. 1997. The Concept of Security. *Review of International Studies* 23:5–26.

Balfour, Michael. 1982. *West Germany: A Contemporary History*. London: Croom Helm.

Barnet, Richard J. 1983. *The Alliance: America, Europe, Japan--Makers of the Postwar World*. New York: Simon and Schuster.

———. 1990. *The Rocket's Red Glare: War, Politics and the American Presidency*. New York: Simon and Schuster.

Barnett, Michael N., and Jack S. Levy. 1991. Domestic Sources of Alliances and Alignments: The Case of Egypt, 1962–1973. *International Organization* 45:369–95.

Beales, Derek. 1971. *The Risorgimento and the Unification of Italy*. New York: Barnes and Noble.

Bean, Richard. 1973. War and the Birth of the Nation State. *Journal of Economic History* 33:203–21.

Becker, Gary J. 1968. Crime and Punishment: An Economic Approach. *Journal of Political Economy* 76:169–217.

Bendor, Jonathan, and Thomas H. Hammond. 1992. Rethinking Allison's Models. *American Political Science Review* 86:301–22.

Bennett, Andrew, Joseph Lepgold, and Danny Unger, eds. 1997. *Friends in Need: Burden Sharing in the Persian Gulf War*. New York: St. Martin's Press.

Berger, Thomas U. 1996. Norms, Identity, and National Security in Germany and Japan. In *The Culture of National Security: Norms and Identity in World Politics*, edited by Peter J. Katzenstein. New York: Columbia University Press.

Betts, Richard K. 1992. Systems for Peace or Causes of War? Collective Security, Arms Control, and the New Europe. *International Security* 17, 1:5–43.

Bhagwan, Vishnoo, and Vidya Bhushan. 1985. *The Constitutions of Switzerland, Canada, Japan, and Australia*. New Delhi: Sterling Publishers.

Bhagwati, Jagdish. 1982. Directly-Unproductive, Profit-Seeking (DUP) Activities. *Journal of Political Economy* 90:988–1,002.

———. 1983. DUP Activity and Rent Seeking. *Kyklos* 36:634–37.

Biddle, Stephen. 1996. Victory Misunderstood: What the Gulf War Tells Us about the Future of Conflict. *International Security* 21, 2:139–79.

Biersteker, Thomas J., and Cynthia Weber, eds. 1996. *State Sovereignty as Social Construct*. New York: Cambridge University Press.

Blackwell, James, Michael J. Mazarr, and Don M. Snider. 1991. *The Gulf War: Military Lessons Learned*. Washington, D.C.: Center for International Strategic Studies.

Botting, Douglas. 1985. *In the Ruins of the Reich*. London: George Allen & Unwin.

Boyer, Mark A. 1993. *International Cooperation and Public Goods: Opportunities for the Western Alliance*. Baltimore: Johns Hopkins University Press.

Brands, H. W. 1992. *Bound to Empire: The United States and the Philippines*. New York: Oxford University Press.

Brenner, Michael. 1991. The Alliance: A Gulf Post-Mortem. *International Affairs* 67: 665–78.

Brumberg, Daniel. 1997. From Strategic Surprise to Strategic Gain: Egypt's Role in the Gulf Coalition. In *Friends in Need: Burden Sharing in the Persian Gulf War*, edited by Andrew Bennett, Joseph Lepgold, and Danny Unger. New York: St. Martin's Press.

Brune, Lester H. 1993. *America and the Iraqi Crisis, 1990–1992: Origins and Aftermath*. Claremont, CA: Regina Books.

Bryden, Matthew. 1995. Somalia: The Wages of Failure. *Current History* 94, 591:145–51.

Brzezinski, Zbigniew K. 1967. *The Soviet Bloc: Unity and Conflict*. Revised and enlarged ed. Cambridge: Harvard University Press.

Buckley, Roger. 1982. *Occupation Diplomacy: Britain, the United States and Japan, 1945–1952*. New York: Cambridge University Press.

Buehrig, Edward H. 1955. *Woodrow Wilson and the Balance of Power*. Bloomington: Indiana University Press.

Bueno de Mesquita, Bruce. 1981. *The War Trap*. New Haven: Yale University Press.

———. 1993. The Game of Conflict Interactions: A Research Program. In *Theoretical Research Programs: Studies in the Growth of Theory*, edited by Joseph Berger and Morris Zelditch, Jr. Stanford: Stanford University Press.

Bueno de Mesquita, Bruce, and David Lalman. 1992. *War and Reason: A Confrontation between Domestic and International Imperatives*. New Haven: Yale University Press.

Bull, Hedley. 1977. *The Anarchical Society: A Study of Order in World Politics*. New York: Columbia University Press.

Bull, Hedley, and Adam Watson, eds. 1984. *The Expansion of International Society*. New York: Oxford University Press.

Bunce, Valerie. 1985. The Empire Strikes Back: The Transformation of the Eastern Bloc from a Soviet Asset to a Soviet Liability. *International Organization* 39:1–46.

Burk, Kathleen. 1981. Economic Diplomacy between the Wars. *Historical Journal* 24:1,003–15.

Bush, George (President). 1990. Toward a New World Order. *Dispatch* (U.S. Department of State) 1, 3:91–94.

———. 1992. Humanitarian Mission to Somalia. *Dispatch* (U.S. Department of State) 3, 49:865–66.

Buzan, Barry. 1991. *People, States, and Fear: An Agenda for International Security Studies in the Post-Cold War Era*. 2d ed. Boulder, CO: Lynne Rienner.

Cain, P. J., and A. G. Hopkins. 1993. *British Imperialism*. 2 vols. New York: Longman.

Calhoun, Frederick S. 1986. *Power and Principle: Armed Intervention in Wilsonian Foreign Policy*. Kent, OH: Kent State University Press.

———. 1993. *Uses of Force and Wilsonian Foreign Policy*. Kent, OH: Kent State University Press.

Calleo, David P. 1987. *Beyond American Hegemony: The Future of the Western Alliance*. New York: Basic Books.

——. 1989. The American Role in NATO. *Journal of International Affairs* 43:19–28.

Calleo, David P., and Benjamin M. Rowland. 1973. *America and the World Political Economy: Atlantic Dreams and National Realities.* Bloomington: Indiana University Press.

Caporaso, James A. 1993. International Relations Theory and Multilateralism: The Search for Foundations. In *Multilateralism Matters: The Theory and Praxis of an Institutional Form,* edited by John Gerard Ruggie. New York: Columbia University Press.

Carlton, James R. 1981. NATO Standardization: An Organizational Analysis. In *NATO after Thirty Years,* edited by Lawrence S. Kaplan and Robert W. Clawson. Wilmington, DE: Scholarly Resources.

Carr, E. H. 1939. *The Twenty-Year's Crisis.* London: Macmillan.

Carter, Ashton B., William J. Perry, and John D. Steinbruner. 1992. *A New Concept of Cooperative Security.* Washington, D.C.: Brookings Institution.

Cassanelli, Lee V. 1997. Somali Land Resource Issues in Historical Perspective. In *Learning from Somalia: The Lessons of Armed Humanitarian Intervention,* edited by Walter Clarke and Jeffrey Herbst. Boulder, CO.: Westview Press.

Christensen, Thomas J. 1996. *Useful Adversaries: Grand Strategy, Domestic Mobilization, and Sino-American Conflict, 1947–1958.* Princeton: Princeton University Press.

Christensen, Thomas J., and Jack Snyder. 1990. Chain Gangs and Passed Bucks: Predicting Alliance Patterns in Multipolarity. *International Organization* 44:137–68.

Clark, Jeffrey. 1993. Debacle in Somalia. *Foreign Affairs* 72, 1:109–23.

Clarke, Walter. 1997. Failed Visions and Uncertain Mandates in Somalia. In *Learning from Somalia: The Lessons of Armed Humanitarian Intervention,* edited by Walter Clarke and Jeffrey Herbst. Boulder, CO.: Westview Press.

Clarke, Walter, and Jeffrey Herbst. 1996. Somalia and the Future of Humanitarian Intervention. *Foreign Affairs* 75, 2:70–85.

——, eds. 1997. *Learning from Somalia: The Lessons of Armed Humanitarian Intervention.* Boulder, CO.: Westview Press.

Claude, Inis L., Jr. 1993. The Gulf War and Prospects for World Order by Collective Security. In *The Persian Gulf Crisis: Power in the Post-Cold War World,* edited by Robert F. Helms II and Robert H. Dorff. Westport, CT: Praeger.

——. 1995. The United States and Changing Approaches to National Security and World Order. *Naval War College Review* 48, 3:46–61.

Clay, Lucius D. 1950. *Decision in Germany.* Garden City, NY: Doubleday.

Clinton, Bill (President). 1993. U.S. Military Involvement in Somalia. *Dispatch* (U.S. Department of State) 4, 42: 713–14.

Coase, Ronald H. 1937. The Nature of the Firm. *Economica* 4:386–405.

——. 1960. The Problem of Social Cost. *Journal of Law and Economics* 3:1–44.

Cohen, Herman J. 1992. Update on Operation Restore Hope. *Dispatch* (U.S. Department of State) 3, 51:896–98.

Cohen, Warren I. 1993. *America in the Age of Soviet Power, 1945–1991.* Volume 4 in *The Cambridge History of American Foreign Relations.* New York: Cambridge University Press.

Cook, Don. 1989. *Forging the Alliance: NATO, 1945–1950.* New York: Arbor House.

Cooper, Andrew, and Kim Richard Nossal. 1997. The Middle Powers in the Gulf Coalition: Australia, Canada, and the Nordics Compared. In *Friends in Need: Burden*

*Sharing in the Persian Gulf War*, edited by Andrew Bennett, Joseph Lepgold, and Danny Unger. New York: St. Martin's Press.

Cooper, John Milton, Jr. 1983. *The Warrior and the Priest: Woodrow Wilson and Theodore Roosevelt.* Cambridge: Harvard University Press.

Costigliola, Frank. 1984. *Awkward Dominion: American Political, Economic, and Cultural Relations with Europe, 1919–1933.* Ithaca: Cornell University Press.

Cowhey, Peter F. 1993. Domestic Institutions and the Credibility of International Commitments: Japan and the United States. *International Organization* 47:299–326.

Crabb, Cecil V., and Kevin V. Mulcahy. 1995. George Bush's Management Style and Operation Desert Storm. *Presidential Studies Quarterly* 25:251–65.

Craig, Gordon A. 1955. *NATO and the New German Army.* Princeton: Center for International Studies, Princeton University.

Curtis, Willie. 1994. The Inevitable Slide into Coercive Peacemaking: The US Role in the New World Order. *Defense Analysis* 10:305–21.

Dahlman, Carl J. 1979. The Problem of Externality. *Journal of Legal Studies* 22:141–62.

Dallek, Robert. 1983. *The American Style of Foreign Policy: Cultural Politics and Foreign Affairs.* New York: Alfred A. Knopf.

Dannreuther, Roland. 1991/92. *The Gulf Conflict: A Political and Strategic Analysis* (Adelphi Paper 264). London: International Institute for Strategic Studies.

David, Steven R. 1991. Explaining Third World Alignment. *World Politics* 43:233–56.

Davidson, Eugene. 1961. *The Death and Life of Germany: An Account of the American Occupation.* New York: Alfred A. Knopf.

Davis, Franklin M., Jr. 1967. *Come as a Conqueror: The United States Army's Occupation of Germany, 1945–1949.* New York: Macmillan.

Davis, Lance E., and Robert A. Huttenback. 1986. *Mammon and the Pursuit of Empire: The Political Economy of British Imperialism, 1860–1912.* New York: Cambridge University Press.

DeConde, Alexander, ed. 1957. *Isolation and Security: Ideas and Interests in Twentieth-Century American Foreign Policy.* Durham: Duke University Press.

Deutsch, Karl, et al. 1957. *Political Community and the North Atlantic Area: International Organization in the Light of Historical Experience.* Princeton: Princeton University Press.

Divine, Robert A. 1967. *Second Chance: The Triumph of Internationalism in America during World War II.* New York: Atheneum.

Doughty, Robert A., and Ira D. Gruber. 1996. *Warfare in the Western World, Volume II: Military Operations since 1871.* Lexington, MA: D. C. Heath.

Dow, Gregory K. 1987. The Function of Authority in Transaction Cost Economics. *Journal of Economic Behavior and Organization* 8:13–38.

Dower, John W. 1979. *Empire and Aftermath: Yoshida Shigeru and the Japanese Experience, 1878–1954.* Cambridge: Harvard University Press.

Downs, George W., David M. Rocke, and Peter N. Barsoom. 1996. Is the Good News about Compliance Good News about Cooperation? *International Organization* 50:379–406.

Doyle, Michael W. 1986. *Empires.* Ithaca: Cornell University Press.

Drysdale, John. 1997. Foreign Military Intervention in Somalia: The Root Cause of the Shift from UN Peacekeeping to Peacemaking and Its Consequences. In *Learning from Somalia: The Lessons of Armed Humanitarian Intervention*, edited by Walter Clarke and Jeffrey Herbst. Boulder, CO.: Westview Press.

Dudley, Leonard. 1990. Structural Change in Interdependent Bureaucracies: Was Rome's Failure Economic or Military? *Explorations in Economic History* 27:232–48.

———. 1992. Punishment, Reward and the Fortunes of States. *Public Choice* 74:293–315.

Duffield, John S. 1995. *Power Rules: The Evolution of NATO's Conventional Force Posture*. Stanford: Stanford University Press.

Duke, Simon W. 1993. *The Burdensharing Debate: A Reassessment*. New York: St. Martin's.

Dulles, Foster Rhea. 1963 [1954]. *America's Rise to World Power, 1898–1954*. New York: Harper and Row.

Dunn, Frederick S. 1963. *Peace-Making and the Settlement with Japan*. Princeton: Princeton University Press.

Dunnigan, James F., and Austin Bay. 1992. *From Shield to Storm: High-Tech Weapons, Military Strategy, and Coalition Warfare in the Persian Gulf*. New York: William Morrow.

Duroselle, Jean-Baptiste. 1963. *From Wilson to Roosevelt: Foreign Policy of the United States, 1913–1945*. Cambridge: Harvard University Press.

Easterbrook, Gregg. 1991. Operation Desert Shill. *New Republic*, September 30, 1991: 32–42.

Eggertsson, Thráinn. 1990. *Economic Behavior and Institutions*. New York: Cambridge University Press.

Evangelista. Matthew A. 1982/83. Stalin's Postwar Army Reappraised. *International Security* 7, 3:110–38.

Fearon, James D. 1991. Counterfactuals and Hypothesis Testing in Political Science. *World Politics* 43:169–95.

———. 1993. Ethnic War as a Commitment Problem. Photocopy.

———. 1994. Domestic Political Audiences and the Escalation of International Disputes. *American Political Science Review* 88:577–92.

———. 1995. Rationalist Explanations for War. *International Organization* 49:379–414.

———. 1998. Bargaining, Enforcement, and International Cooperation. *International Organization* 52:269–305.

Findlay, Ronald. 1994. Towards a Model of Territorial Expansion and the Limits of Empire. Unpublished paper.

Finnemore, Martha. 1996. Constructing Norms of Humanitarian Intervention. In *The Culture of National Security: Norms and Identity in World Politics*, edited by Peter J. Katzenstein. New York: Columbia University Press.

Fox, William T. R., and Annette Baker Fox. 1967. *NATO and the Range of American Choice*. New York: Columbia University Press.

Freedman, Lawrence, and Efraim Karsh. 1991. How Kuwait Was Won: Strategy in the Gulf War. *International Security* 16, 2:5–41.

———. 1993. *The Gulf Conflict, 1990–1991: Diplomacy and War in the New World Order*. Princeton: Princeton University Press.

Freeman, Waldo D., Robert B. Lambert, and Jason D. Mims. 1993. Operation Restore Hope: A US CENTCOM Perspective. *Military Review* 73, 9:61–72.

Friedberg, Aaron L. 1988. *The Weary Titan: Britain and the Experience of Relative Decline, 1895–1905.* Princeton: Princeton University Press.

Frieden, Jeffry A. 1988. Sectoral Conflict and U.S. Foreign Economic Policy, 1914–1940. *International Organization* 42:59–90.

———. 1994. International Investment and Colonial Control: A New Interpretation. *International Organization* 48:559–93.

———. forthcoming. Actors and Preferences in International Relations. In *Strategic Choice and International Relations*, edited by David A. Lake and Robert Powell. Princeton: Princeton University Press.

Friedman, David. 1977. A Theory of the Size and Shape of Nations. *Journal of Political Economy* 85:59–77.

Friedman, Julian R., Christopher Bladen, and Steven Rosen. 1970. *Alliance in International Politics.* Boston: Allyn and Bacon.

Friedman, Norman. 1991. *Desert Victory: The War for Kuwait.* Annapolis, MD: Naval Institute Press.

Friend, Theodore. 1965. *Between Two Empires: The Ordeal of the Philippines, 1929–1946.* New Haven: Yale University Press.

Furubotn, Eirik G., and Rudolf Richter, eds. 1991. *The New Institutional Economics: A Collection of Articles from the Journal of Institutional and Theoretical Economics.* College Station: Texas A&M University Press.

Gaddis, John Lewis. 1982. *Strategies of Containment: A Critical Appraisal of Postwar American National Security Policy.* New York: Oxford University Press.

———. 1987. *The Long Peace: Inquiries into the History of the Cold War.* New York: Oxford University Press.

———. 1992/93. International Relations Theory and the End of the Cold War. *International Security* 17, 3:5–58.

———. 1997. *We Now Know: Rethinking Cold War History.* New York: Oxford University Press.

Gaffaney, Timothy J. 1995. Linking Colonization and Decolonization: The Case of Micronesia. *Pacific Studies* 18, 2:23–59.

Gale, Roger W. 1979. *The Americanization of Micronesia: A Study of the Consolidation of U.S. Rule in the Pacific.* Washington, D.C.: University Press of America.

Gallagher, John, and Ronald Robinson. 1953. The Imperialism of Free Trade. *Economic History Review* 2nd. Ser., 6, 1:1–15.

Ganzglass, Martin R. 1997. The Restoration of the Somali Justice System. In *Learning from Somalia: The Lessons of Armed Humanitarian Intervention*, edited by Walter Clarke and Jeffrey Herbst. Boulder, CO.: Westview Press.

Gardner, Richard N. 1980. *Sterling-Dollar Diplomacy in Current Perspective: The Origins and Prospects of Our International Economic Order*, expanded ed. New York: Columbia University Press.

George, Alexander L., and Juliette L. George. 1964 [1956]. *Woodrow Wilson and Colonel House: A Personality Study.* New York: Dover.

George, Alexander L., and Timothy J. McKeown. 1985. Case Studies and Theories of Organizational Decision Making. *Advances in Information Processing in Organizations* 2:21–58.

Gholz, Eugene, Daryl G. Press, and Harvey M. Sapolsky. 1997. Come Home, America: The Strategy of Restraint in the Face of Temptation. *International Security* 21, 4:5–48.

Gilbert, Felix. 1961. *To the Farewell Address: Ideas of Early American Foreign Policy.* Princeton: Princeton University Press.

Gilpin, Robert. 1975. *U.S. Power and the Multinational Corporation: The Political Economy of Foreign Direct Investment.* New York: Basic Books.

———. 1981. *War and Change in the International System.* New York: Cambridge University Press.

———. 1987. *The Political Economy of International Relations.* Princeton: Princeton University Press.

Goertz, Gary, and Paul F. Diehl. 1992. *Territorial Changes and International Conflict.* New York: Routledge.

Goldgeier, James M. 1998. NATO Expansion: The Anatomy of a Decision. *Washington Quarterly* 21, 1:85–102.

Goldman, Emily O. 1994. *Sunken Treaties: Naval Arms Control between the Wars.* University Park: Pennsylvania State University Press.

Gombert, David, and Richard Kugler. 1995. Free Ride Redux: NATO Needs to Project Power (and Europe Can Help). *Foreign Affairs* 74, 1:7–12.

Gordon, Michael R., and Gen. Bernard E. Trainor. 1994. How Iraq Escaped to Threaten Kuwait Again. *New York Times International*, October 23:1 and 10.

———. 1995. *The General's War: The Inside Story of the Conflict in the Gulf.* Boston: Little, Brown.

Gowa, Joanne. 1994. *Allies, Adversaries, and International Trade.* Princeton: Princeton University Press.

Greenwood, David. 1977. Defense and National Priorities since 1945. In *British Defense: Policy in a Changing World*, edited by John Bayliss. London: Croom Helm.

Gregor, A. James, and Virgilio Aganon. 1987. *The Philippine Bases: U.S. Security at Risk.* Washington, D.C.: Ethics and Public Policy Center.

Grieco, Joseph M. 1990. *Cooperation among Nations: Europe, America, and Non-Tariff Barriers to Trade.* Ithaca: Cornell University Press.

———. 1997. Realist International Theory and the Study of World Politics. In *New Thinking in International Relations Theory*, edited by Michael W. Doyle and G. John Ikenberry. Boulder, CO.: Westview.

Griener, C. 1985. The Defense of Western Europe and the Rearmament of West Germany, 1947–1950. In *Western Security: The Formative Years: European and Atlantic Defense, 1947–1953*, edited by Olav Riste. New York: Columbia University Press.

Grosser, Alfred. 1955. *The Colossus Again: Western Germany from Defeat to Rearmament.* New York: Frederick A. Praeger.

———. 1971. *Germany in Our Time: A Political History of the Postwar Years.* New York: Praeger.

Grossman, Sanford J., and Oliver D. Hart. 1986. The Costs and Benefits of Ownership: A Theory of Vertical and Lateral Integration. *Journal of Political Economy* 94:691–719.

Grunberg, Isabelle. 1997. Still a Reluctant Ally? France's Participation in the Gulf War Coalition. In *Friends in Need: Burden Sharing in the Persian Gulf War*, edited by Andrew Bennett, Joseph Lepgold, and Danny Unger. New York: St. Martin's Press.

Guinsburg, Thomas N. 1982. *The Pursuit of Isolationism in the United States Senate from Versailles to Pearl Harbor.* New York: Garland.

Guzzini, Stefano. 1994. Power Analysis as a Critique of Power Politics: Understanding Power and Governance in the Second Gulf War. Ph.D. diss., European University Institute, Florence, Italy.

Hager, Robert P., and David A. Lake. Forthcoming. Balancing Empires: Competitive Decolonization in International Polities. *Security Studies* 8, 4.

Halliday, Fred. 1991. The Gulf War and Its Aftermath: First Reflections. *International Affairs* 67:223–34.

Hampson, Fen Osler. 1995. *Multilateral Negotiations: Lessons from Arms Control, Trade, and the Environment.* Baltimore: Johns Hopkins University Press.

Hancock, Kathleen. 1998. Economic Vulnerability in a Two-Level Bargaining Game: The Case of Relations between Russia and the Other Former Soviet States. Paper prepared for the annual meeting of the International Studies Association, Minneapolis.

Hannah, John B. 1997. Soviet Contributions to the Gulf War Coalition. In *Friends in Need: Burden Sharing in the Persian Gulf War,* edited by Andrew Bennett, Joseph Lepgold, and Danny Unger. New York: St. Martin's Press.

Harkavay, Robert E. 1993. The Changing Strategic and Technological Basis, 1945–1962. In *U.S. Military Forces in Europe: The Early Years, 1945–1970,* edited by Simon W. Duke and Wolfgang Krieger. Boulder, CO.: Westview Press.

Harley, C. Knick. 1988. Ocean Freight Rates and Productivity, 1740–1913: The Primacy of Mechanical Invention Reaffirmed. *Journal of Economic History* 48:851–76.

Harries, Meirion, and Susie Harries. 1987. *Sheathing the Sword: The Demilitarization of Japan.* London: Hamish Hamilton.

Hart, Oliver. 1990. An Economist's Perspective on the Theory of the Firm. In *Organization Theory: From Chester Barnard to the Present and Beyond,* edited by Oliver E. Williamson. New York: Oxford University Press.

Haynes, George H. 1938. *The Senate of the United States, Its History and Practice.* Boston: Houghton Mifflin.

Hayward, Malcolm. 1994. The Making of the New World Order: The Role of the Media. In *The Gulf War and the New World Order: International Relations of the Middle East,* edited by Tareq Y. Ismael and Jacqueline S. Ismael. Gainesville: University Press of Florida.

Heikal, Mohamed. 1992. *Illusions of Triumph: An Arab View of the Gulf War.* London: HarperCollins.

Heine, Carl. 1974. *Micronesia at the Crossroads: A Reappraisal of the Micronesia Political Dilemma.* Honolulu: University Press of Hawaii.

Hellman, Gunther. 1997. Absorbing Shocks and Mounting Checks: Germany and Alliance Burden Sharing in the Gulf War. In *Friends in Need: Burden Sharing in the Persian Gulf War,* edited by Andrew Bennett, Joseph Lepgold, and Danny Unger. New York: St. Martin's Press.

Herring, Richard J., and Robert E. Litan. 1995. *Financial Regulation in the Global Economy.* Washington, D.C.: Brookings Institution.

Hill, Enid. 1994. The New World Order and the Gulf War: Rhetoric, Policy, and Politics in the United States. In *The Gulf War and the New World Order: International Relations of the Middle East,* edited by Tareq Y. Ismael and Jacqueline S. Ismael. Gainesville: University Press of Florida.

Hinnebusch, Raymond A. 1997. Syria's Role in the Gulf War Coalition. In *Friends in*

*Need: Burden Sharing in the Persian Gulf War*, edited by Andrew Bennett, Joseph Lepgold, and Danny Unger. New York: St. Martin's Press.

Hirsch, John L., and Robert B. Oakley. 1995. *Somalia and Operation Restore Hope: Reflections on Peacemaking and Peacekeeping*. Washington, D.C.: United States Institute of Peace Press.

Hobbs, David. 1989. *NATO and the New Technologies*. New York: University Press of America.

Hoffman, Stanley. 1968. *Gulliver's Troubles, or the Setting of American Foreign Policy*. New York: McGraw-Hill.

Hogan, Michael J. 1977. *Informal Entente: The Private Structure of Cooperation in Anglo-American Economic Diplomacy, 1918–1928*. Columbia: University of Missouri Press.

Holden, Gerard. 1989. *The Warsaw Pact: Soviet Security and Bloc Politics*. New York: Basil Blackwell.

Holsti, Ole R., P. Terrence Hopmann, and John D. Sullivan. 1973. *Unity and Disintegration in International Alliances: Comparative Studies*. New York: Wiley.

Holt, Edgar. 1971. *The Making of Italy, 1815–1870*. New York: Atheneum.

Holt, W. Stull. 1933. *Treaties Defeated by the Senate*. Baltimore: Johns Hopkins Press.

Howe, Jonathan T. 1995. The United States and United Nations in Somalia: The Limits of Involvement. *Washington Quarterly* 18, 3:49–62.

Howorth, Jolyon. 1994. French Policy in the Conflict. In *International Perspectives on the Gulf Conflict, 1990–91*, edited by Alex Danchev and Dan Keohane. New York: St. Martins.

Hucko, Elmar M., ed. 1987. *The Democratic Tradition: Four German Constitutions*. New York: Berg.

Huntington, Samuel P. 1993. Why International Primacy Matters. *International Security* 17, 4:68–83.

Ireland, Timothy P. 1981. *Creating the Entangling Alliance: The Origins of the North Atlantic Treaty Organization*. Westport, CT: Greenwood Press.

Iriye, Akira. 1993. *The Globalizing of America, 1913–1945*. Volume 3 in *The Cambridge History of American Foreign Relations*. New York: Cambridge University Press.

Ismay, Lord. 1956. *NATO: The First Five Years, 1949–1954*. Utrecht: North Atlantic Treaty Organization.

Jackson, Robert H. 1990. *Quasi-States: Sovereignty, International Relations, and the Third World*. New York: Cambridge University Press.

James, Alan. 1986. *Sovereign Statehood: The Basis of International Society*. Boston: Unwin and Hyman.

Jensen, Michael C., and William H. Meckling, 1976. Theory of the Firm: Managerial Behavior, Agency Cost and Ownership Structure. *Journal of Financial Economics* 3:305–60.

Jentleson, Bruce W. 1994. *With Friends Like These: Reagan, Bush, and Saddam, 1982–1990*. New York: W.W. Norton.

Jervis, Robert. 1976. *Perception and Misperception in International Politics*. Princeton: Princeton University Press.

———. 1978. Cooperation under the Security Dilemma. *World Politics* 30:167–214.

———. 1983. Security Regimes. In *International Regimes*, edited by Stephen D. Krasner. Ithaca: Cornell University Press.

——. 1993. International Primacy: Is the Game Worth the Candle? *International Security* 17, 4:52–67.

Jodice, David A. 1980. Sources of Change in Third World Regimes for Foreign Direct Investment, 1968–1976. *International Organization* 34:177–206.

Johnston, Harry, and Ted Dagne. 1997. Congress and the Somalia Crisis. In *Learning from Somalia: The Lessons of Armed Humanitarian Intervention*, edited by Walter Clarke and Jeffrey Herbst. Boulder, CO.: Westview Press.

Jonas, Manfred. 1990 [1966]. *Isolationism in America, 1935–1941*. Chicago: Imprint Publications.

Jones, Robert A. 1990. *The Soviet Concept of "Limited Sovereignty" from Lenin to Gorbachev: The Brezhnev Doctrine*. London: Macmillan.

Kahler, Miles. 1993. Multilateralism with Small and Large Numbers. In *Multilateralism Matters: The Theory and Praxis of an Institutional Form*, edited by John Gerard Ruggie. New York: Columbia University Press.

Kaplan, Lawrence S., ed. 1968. *NATO and the Policy of Containment*. Lexington, MA.: D.C. Heath.

——. 1980. *A Community of Interests: NATO and the Military Assistance Program 1949–1951*. Washington, D.C.: Office of the Secretary of Defense, Historical Office.

——. 1984. *The United States and NATO: The Formative Years*. Lexington: The University Press of Kentucky.

——. 1988. *NATO and the United States: The Enduring Alliance*. Boston: Twayne.

Karber, Phillip A., and Jerald A. Combs. n.d. The United States, NATO, and the Soviet Threat to Western Europe: Military Estimates and Policy Options, 1945–1963. Unpublished paper.

Katzenstein, Peter J. 1985. *Small States in World Markets: Industrial Policy in Europe*. Ithaca: Cornell University Press.

——, ed. 1996a. *The Culture of National Security: Norms and Identity in World Politics*. New York: Columbia University Press.

——. 1996b. *Cultural Norms and National Security: Police and Military in Postwar Japan*. Ithaca: Cornell University Press.

Kennedy, David M. 1980. *Over Here: The First World War and American Society*. New York: Oxford University Press.

Kennedy, Kevin M. 1997. The Relationship between the Military and Humanitarian Organizations in Operation Restore Hope. In *Learning from Somalia: The Lessons of Armed Humanitarian Intervention*, edited by Walter Clarke and Jeffrey Herbst. Boulder, CO.: Westview Press.

Kennedy, Paul. 1983. *Strategy and Diplomacy, 1870–1945*. London: George Allen and Unwin.

——. 1987. *The Rise and Fall of Great Powers: Economic Change and Military Conflict from 1500–2000*. New York: Random House.

Keohane, Dan. 1994. British Policy in the Conflict. In *International Perspectives on the Gulf Conflict, 1990–91*, edited by Alex Danchev and Dan Keohane. New York: St. Martins.

Keohane, Robert O. 1983. The Demand for International Regimes. In *International Regimes*, edited by Stephen D. Krasner. Ithaca: Cornell University Press.

——. 1984. *After Hegemony: Cooperation and Discord in the World Political Economy*. Princeton: Princeton University Press.

———. 1990. Multilateralism: An Agenda for Research. *International Journal* 45:731–64.

Keohane, Robert O., and Lisa L. Martin. 1995. The Promise of Institutionalist Theory. *International Security* 20, 1:39–51.

Keohane, Robert O., and Joseph S. Nye, eds. 1972. *Transnational Relations and World Politics*. Cambridge: Harvard University Press.

———. 1977. *Power and Interdependence: World Politics in Transition*. Boston: Little, Brown.

Khaled bin Sultan, HRH General. 1995. *Desert Warrior: A Personal View of the Gulf War by the Joint Forces Commander*. New York: HarperCollins.

Khalidi, Walid. 1991. Why Some Arabs Support Saddam. In *The Gulf War Reader: History, Documents, Opinions*, edited by Micah L. Sifry and Christopher Cerf. New York: Random House.

Kiewiet, D. Roderick, and Mathew D. McCubbins. 1991. *The Logic of Delegation: Congressional Parties and the Appropriations Process*. Chicago: University of Chicago Press.

Kindleberger, Charles P. 1973. *The World in Depression, 1929–1939*. Berkeley and Los Angeles: University of California Press.

King, Gary, Robert O. Keohane, and Sidney Verba. 1994. *Designing Social Inquiry: Scientific Inference in Qualitative Research*. Princeton: Princeton University Press.

Kirschten, Dick. 1995. A Contract's out on U.N. Policing. *National Journal*, January 28:231–32.

Kissinger, Henry. 1994. *Diplomacy*. New York: Simon and Schuster.

Klein, Benjamin, Robert G. Crawford, and Armen A. Alchian. 1978. Vertical Integration, Appropriable Rents, and the Competitive Contracting Process. *Journal of Law and Economics* 21:297–326.

Knock, Thomas J. 1992. *To End All Wars: Woodrow Wilson and the Quest for a New World Order*. New York: Oxford University Press.

Kobrin, Stephen J. 1980. Foreign Enterprise and Forced Divestment in LDCs. *International Organization* 34:65–88.

Koch, H. W. 1984. *A Constitutional History of Germany in the Nineteenth and Twentieth Centuries*. New York: Longman.

Kowert, Paul, and Jeffrey Legro. 1996. Norms, Identity, and Their Limits: A Theoretical Reprise. In *The Culture of National Security: Norms and Identity in World Politics*, edited by Peter J. Katzenstein. New York: Columbia University Press.

Krasner, Stephen D. 1976. State Power and the Structure of International Trade. *World Politics* 28:317–47.

———. 1978. *Defending the National Interest: Raw Materials Investments and U.S. Foreign Policy*. Princeton: Princeton University Press.

———, ed. 1983. *International Regimes*. Ithaca: Cornell University Press.

———. 1989. Realist Praxis: Neo-Isolationism and Structural Change. *Journal of International Affairs* 43:143–60.

———. 1993. Westphalia and All That. In *Ideas and Foreign Policy: Beliefs, Institutions, and Political Change*, edited by Judith Goldstein and Robert O. Keohane. Ithaca: Cornell University Press.

———. 1995/96. Compromising Westphalia. *International Security* 20, 3:115–51.

Krauthammer, Charles. 1990/91. The Unipolar Moment. *Foreign Affairs* 70, 1:23–33.

Kugler, Richard L. 1991. *The Great Strategy Debate: NATO's Evolution in the 1960s* (A RAND Note: N-3252-FF/RC). Santa Monica: RAND Corporation.

Kull, Steven. 1995/96. What the Public Knows that Washington Doesn't. *Foreign Policy* 101:102–15.

Kuniholm, Bruce. 1993. Great Power Rivalry and the Persian Gulf. In *The Persian Gulf Crisis: Power in the Post-Cold War World*, edited by Robert F. Helms II and Robert H. Dorff. Westport, CT: Praeger.

Kunz, Diane B. 1991. *The Economic Diplomacy of the Suez Crisis*. Chapel Hill: University of North Carolina Press.

Kupchan, Charles A. 1994. *The Vulnerability of Empire*. Ithaca: Cornell University Press.

Kupchan, Charles A., and Clifford A. Kupchan. 1991. Concerts, Collective Security, and the Future of Europe. *International Security* 16, 1:114–61.

LaFeber, Walter. 1985. *America, Russia, and the Cold War, 1945–1984*. 5th ed. New York: Knopf.

———. 1993. *The American Search for Opportunity, 1865–1913*. Volume 2 in *The Cambridge History of American Foreign Relations*. New York: Cambridge University Press.

———. 1994. *The American Age: United States Foreign Policy at Home and Abroad since 1750*. 2d ed. New York: Norton.

———. 1997. *The Clash: A History of U.S.–Japanese Relations*. New York: Norton.

Lake, Anthony. 1993. From Containment to Enlargement. *Dispatch* (U.S. Department of State) 4, 39:658–64.

Lake, David A. 1987. The Expansion of Sovereignty: Imperialism, Decolonization, and the Constitutive Principle of International Relations. Paper presented at the Annual Meeting of the American Political Science Association, Chicago.

———. 1988. *Power, Protection, and Free Trade: International Sources of U.S. Commercial Strategy, 1887–1939*. Ithaca: Cornell University Press.

———. 1992. Powerful Pacifists: Democratic States and War. *American Political Science Review* 86:24–37.

———. 1993. Leadership, Hegemony, and the International Economy: Naked Emperor or Tattered Monarch with Potential? *International Studies Quarterly* 37:459–89.

———. 1996. Anarchy, Hierarchy and the Variety of International Relations. *International Organization* 50:1–33.

———. 1997. The Rise, Fall, and Future of the Russian Empire: A Theoretical Interpretation. In *The End of Empire? The Transformation of the USSR in Comparative Perspective*, edited by Karen Dawisha and Bruce Parrott. Armonk, NY: M.E. Sharpe.

Lake, David A., and Patrick M. Morgan, eds. 1997. *Regional Orders: Building Security in a New World*. University Park: Pennsylvania State University Press.

Lake, David A., and Robert Powell, eds. forthcoming. *Strategic Choice and International Relations*. Princeton: Princeton University Press.

La Nauze, J. A. 1972. *The Making of the Australian Constitution*. Carlton, Victoria: Melbourne University Press.

Lane, Frederic C. 1958. Economic Consequences of Organized Violence. *Journal of Economic History* 18:401–17.

———. 1979. *Profits from Power: Readings in Protection Rent and Violence-Controlling Enterprises*. Albany: State University of New York Press.

Langlois, Richard N., ed. 1986. *Economics as a Process: Essays in the New Institutional Economics*. New York: Cambridge University Press.

Laukhuff, Perry. 1956. The Price of Woodrow Wilson's Illness. *Virginia Quarterly Review* 32:598–610.

Layne, Christopher. 1993. The Unipolar Illusion: Why New Great Powers Will Rise. *International Security* 17, 4:5–51.

———. 1997. From Preponderance to Offshore Balancing: America's Future Grand Strategy. *International Security* 22, 1:86–124.

Lebergott, Stanley. 1980. The Returns to U.S. Imperialism, 1890–1919. *Journal of Economic History* 40:229–52.

Lefebvre, Jeffrey A. 1993. The U.S. Military Intervention in Somalia: A Hidden Agenda? *Middle East Policy* 3, 1:44–62.

Leffler, Melvyn P. 1979. *The Elusive Quest: America's Pursuit of European Stability and French Security, 1919–1933*. Chapel Hill: University of North Carolina Press.

———. 1984. The American Conception of National Security and the Beginnings of the Cold War, 1945–48. *American Historical Review* 89:346–81.

———. 1992. *A Preponderance of Power: National Security, the Truman Administration, and the Cold War*. Stanford: Stanford University Press.

Legro, Jeffrey. 1995. *Cooperation under Fire: Anglo-German Restraint during World War II*. Ithaca: Cornell University Press.

Lepgold, Joseph. 1997. Britain in Desert Storm: The Most Enthusiastic Junior Partner. In *Friends in Need: Burden Sharing in the Persian Gulf War*, edited by Andrew Bennett, Joseph Lepgold, and Danny Unger. New York: St. Martin's Press.

Levy, Jack S. 1994. Learning and Foreign Policy: Sweeping a Conceptual Minefield. *International Organization* 48:279–312.

Lewis, Kevin N. 1989. *U.S. Force Structure Trends: A Primer*. Santa Monica, CA: RAND Corp.

Lindsay, James M. 1994. *Congress and the Politics of U.S. Foreign Policy*. Baltimore: Johns Hopkins University Press.

Lipson, Charles. 1991. Why Are Some International Agreements Informal? *International Organization* 45:495–538.

———. 1994. Understanding International Contracts: Building Institutions and Sustaining Agreements in an Anarchic World. Paper prepared for the Annual Meeting of the American Political Science Association.

———. 1995. Techniques and Problems of International Contracting. Paper prepared for the Annual Meeting of the International Studies Association, Chicago.

Louis, Wm. Roger, ed. 1976. *Imperialism: The Robinson and Gallagher Controversy*. New York: New Viewpoints.

———. 1977. *Imperialism at Bay: The United States and the Decolonization of the British Empire, 1941–1945*. New York: Oxford University Press.

Lowi, Theodore. 1967. Making Democracy Safe for the World: National Politics and Foreign Policy. In *Domestic Sources of Foreign Policy*, edited by James N. Rosenau. New York: Free Press.

Luck, James Murray. 1985. *A History of Switzerland*. Palo Alto: Society for the Promotion of Science and Scholarship.

Lundestad, Geir. 1986. Empire by Invitation? The United States and Western Europe, 1945–1952. *Journal of Peace Research* 23:263–77.

———. 1992. *The American Empire*. New York: Oxford University Press.

Lunn, Simon. 1983. *Burden-sharing in NATO* (Chatham House Papers 18). London: Routledge & Kegan Paul.

Luttwak, Edward N. 1976. *The Grand Strategy of the Roman Empire: From the First Century A.D. to the Third*. Baltimore: Johns Hopkins University Press.

———. 1994. The Air War. In *International Perspectives on the Gulf Conflict, 1990–91*, edited by Alex Danchev and Dan Keohane. New York: St. Martin's.

Lyons, Gene M., and Michael Mastanduno, eds. 1995. *Beyond Westphalia? State Sovereignty and International Intervention*. Baltimore: Johns Hopkins University Press.

MacDonald, Douglas J. 1995/96. Communist Bloc Expansion in the Early Cold War. *International Security* 20, 3:152–88.

Maddison, Angus. 1982. *Phases of Capitalist Development*. New York: Oxford University Press.

Maoz, Zeev. 1996. *Domestic Sources of Global Change*. Ann Arbor: University of Michigan Press.

Martin, Lisa L. 1992. *Coercive Cooperation: Explaining Multilateral Economic Sanctions*. Princeton: Princeton University Press.

———. 1993. The Rational State Choice of Multilateralism. In *Multilateralism Matters: The Theory and Praxis of an Institutional Form*, edited by John Gerard Ruggie. New York: Columbia University Press.

Martin, Michael L. 1981. *Warriors to Managers: The French Military Establishment since 1945*. Chapel Hill: University of North Carolina Press.

Martínez, Rubén Berríos. 1997. Puerto Rico's Decolonization. *Foreign Affairs* 76, 6:100–14.

Mastanduno, Michael. 1988. Trade as a Strategic Weapon: American and Alliance Export Control Policy in the Early Postwar Period. *International Organization* 42: 121–50.

———. 1992. *Economic Containment: CoCom and the Politics of East-West Trade*. Ithaca: Cornell University Press.

———. 1997. Preserving the Unipolar Moment: Realist Theories and U.S. Grand Strategy after the Cold War. *International Security* 21 4:49–88.

Mastny, Vojtech. 1979. *Russia's Road to the Cold War: Diplomacy, Warfare, and the Politics of Communism, 1941–1945*. New York: Columbia University Press.

Matthews, Ken. 1993. *The Gulf Conflict and International Relations*. New York: Routledge.

Matthews, R.C.O. 1986. The Economics of Institutions and the Sources of Growth. *Economic Journal* 96:903–10.

May, Ernest R. 1973 [1961]. *Imperial Democracy: The Emergence of America as a Great Power*. New York: Harper and Row.

McCalla, Robert B. 1996. NATO's Persistence after the Cold War. *International Organization* 50:445–75.

McCausland, Lt. Col. Jeffrey. 1993. *The Gulf Conflict: A Military Analysis* (Adelphi Paper 292). London: International Institute for Strategic Studies.

McCoy, Alfred W. 1981. The Philippines: Independence without Decolonization. In *Asia: The Winning of Independence*, edited by Robin Jeffrey. New York: St. Martin's.

McCraw, Thomas K., ed. 1988. *The Essential Alfred Chandler: Essays toward a Historical Theory of Big Business*. Boston: Harvard Business School Press.

McCubbins, Mathew D., and Thomas Schwatz. 1984. Congressional Oversight Over-looked: Police Patrols versus Fire Alarms. *American Journal of Political Science* 2:165–79.

McDougall, Walter A. 1997. Back to Bedrock: The Eight Traditions of American State-craft. *Foreign Affairs* 76, 2:134–46.

McKeown, Timothy J. 1986. The Limitations of "Structural" Theories of Commercial Policy. *International Organization* 40:43–64.

McMinn, W. G. 1979. *A Constitutional History of Australia*. New York: Oxford University Press.

McNeil, William C. 1986. *American Money and the Weimar Republic: Economics and Politics on the Eve of the Great Depression*. New York: Columbia University Press.

McNeill, William H. 1982. *The Pursuit of Power*. Chicago: University of Chicago Press.

Mearsheimer, John J. 1990. Back to the Future: Instability in Europe after the Cold War. *International Security* 15, 1:5–56.

———. 1994/95. The False Promise of International Institutions. *International Security* 19, 3:5–49.

Menkhaus, Ken. 1994. Getting out vs. Getting through: U.S. and U.N. Policies in Somalia. *Middle East Policy* 3, 1:146–62.

Messer, Robert L. 1977. Paths Not Taken: The United States Department of State and Alternatives to Containment, 1945–1946. *Diplomatic History* 1:297–319.

Mill, John Stuart. 1978 [1859]. *On Liberty*, edited by Elizabeth Rapaport. Indianapolis: Hackett Publishing.

Miller, Gary J. 1992. *Managerial Dilemmas: The Political Economy of Hierarchy*. New York: Cambridge University Press.

Miller, Gary, and Kathleen Cook. 1994. Leveling and Leadership in States and Firms. Political Economy Working Paper, School of Business and Center in Political Economy, Washington University, St. Louis.

Miller, James Edward. 1986. *The United States and Italy, 1940–1950: The Politics and Diplomacy of Stabilization*. Chapel Hill: University of North Carolina Press.

Miller, Ronnie. 1994. *Following the Americans to the Persian Gulf: Canada, Australia, and the Development of the New World Order*. Rutherford, NJ: Fairleigh Dickinson University Press.

Millett, Allan R. 1996a. Assault from the Sea: The Development of Amphibious Warfare between the Wars: The American, British, and Japanese Experiences. In *Military Innovation in the Interwar Period*, edited by Williamson Murray and Allan R. Millett. New York: Cambridge University Press.

———. 1996b. Patterns of Military Innovation in the Interwar Period. In *Military Innovation in the Interwar Period*, edited by Williamson Murray and Allan R. Millett. New York: Cambridge University Press.

Milner, Helen. 1992. International Theories of Cooperation among Nations: Strengths and Weaknesses. *World Politics* 44:466–96.

Mitchell, B. R. 1962. *Abstract of British Historical Statistics*. New York: Cambridge University Press.

Morgenthau, Hans J. 1978. *Politics among Nations: The Struggle for Power and Peace*. 5th ed., rev. New York: Knopf.

Morrow, James D. 1991. Alliances and Asymmetry: An Alternative to the Capability Aggregation Model of Alliances. *American Journal of Political Science* 35:904–33.

———. 1993. Arms versus Allies: Trade-offs in the Search for Security. *International Organization* 47:207–33.

———. 1994. *Game Theory for Political Scientists*. Princeton: Princeton University Press.

———. Forthcoming. The Strategic Setting of Choices: Signaling, Commitment, and Negotiation in International Politics. In *Strategic Choice and International Relations*, edited by David A. Lake and Robert Powell. Princeton: Princeton University Press.

Most, Benjamin A., and Randolph M. Siverson. 1987. Substituting Arms and Alliances, 1870–1914: An Exploration in Comparative Foreign Policy. In *New Directions in the Study of Foreign Policy*, edited by Charles F. Hermann, Charles W. Kegley, Jr., and James N. Rosenau. Boston: Allen and Unwin.

Most, Benjamin A., and Harvey Starr. 1984. International Relations Theory, Foreign Policy Substitutability, and "Nice" Laws. *World Politics* 36:383–406.

Muravchik, Joshua. 1993. Beyond Self-Defense. *Commentary* 96, 6:19–24.

Murdock, James C., and Todd Sandler. 1984. Complementarity, Free Riding, and the Military Expenditures of NATO Allies. *Journal of Public Economics* 25:83–101.

Murray, Williamson. 1996a. Armored Warfare: The British, French and German Experiences. In *Military Innovation in the Interwar Period*, edited by Williamson Murray and Allan R. Millett. New York: Cambridge University Press.

———. 1996b. Strategic Bombing: The British, American, and German Experiences. In *Military Innovation in the Interwar Period*, edited by Williamson Murray and Allan R. Millett. New York: Cambridge University Press.

Murray, Williamson, and Allan R. Millett, eds. 1996. *Military Innovation in the Interwar Period*. New York: Cambridge University Press.

Nacos, Brigitte Lebens. 1994. Presidential Leadership during the Persian Gulf Conflict. *Presidential Studies Quarterly* 24:543–61.

Natsios, Andrew S. 1997. Humanitarian Relief Intervention in Somalia: The Economics of Chaos. In *Learning from Somalia: The Lessons of Armed Humanitarian Intervention*, edited by Walter Clarke and Jeffrey Herbst. Boulder, CO: Westview Press.

Neves, Juan Carlos. 1995. Interoperability in Multinational Coalitions: Lessons from the Persian Gulf War. *Naval War College Review* 48, 1:50–62.

Nevin, David. 1977. *The American Touch in Micronesia*. New York: W.W. Norton.

Niou, Emerson M. S., and Peter C. Ordeshook. 1994. Alliances versus Federations: An Analysis with Military and Economic Capabilities Distinguished. Photocopy.

Nolan, Janne E., ed. 1994. *Global Engagement: Cooperation and Security in the 21st Century*. Washington, D.C.: Brookings Institution.

Nordlinger, Eric A. 1995. *Isolationism Reconfigured: American Foreign Policy for a New Century*. Princeton: Princeton University Press.

North, Douglass C. 1958. Ocean Freight Rates and Economic Development, 1750–1913. *Journal of Economic History* 17:537–55.

———. 1981. *Structure and Change in Economic History*. New York: Norton.

———. 1990. *Institutions, Institutional Change and Economic Performance*. New York: Cambridge University Press.

Nye, Joseph S., and Sean M. Lynn-Jones. 1988. International Security Studies: A Report of a Conference on the State of the Field. *International Security* 12, 4:5–27.

Oakley, Robert B. n.d. Somalia Case Study. Patterson School Symposium. Photocopy.

O'Halloran, Sharyn. 1994. *Politics, Process, and American Trade Policy*. Ann Arbor: University of Michigan Press.

Olson, Mancur. 1982. *The Rise and Decline of Nations: Economic Growth, Stagflation, and Social Rigidities*. New Haven: Yale University Press.

Olson, Mancur, and Richard Zeckhauser. 1966. An Economic Theory of Alliances. *Review of Economics and Statistics* 48:266–79.

Oneal, John R., and Mark A. Elrod. 1989. Burden Sharing and the Forces of Change. *International Studies Quarterly* 33:435–56.

Osgood, Robert Endicott. 1953. *Ideals and Self-Interest in America's Foreign Relations: The Great Transformation of the Twentieth Century*. Chicago: University of Chicago Press.

Oye, Kenneth A., ed. 1986. *Cooperation under Anarchy*. Princeton: Princeton University Press.

Papayoanou, Paul A. 1995. The Process of Alliance Formation: A Signaling Game Approach. University of California, San Diego. Photocopy.

Parrini, Carl P. 1969. *Hier to Empire: United States Economic Diplomacy, 1916–1923*. Pittsburgh: University of Pittsburgh Press.

Parsons, Edward B. 1978. *Wilsonian Diplomacy: Allied-American Rivalries in War and Peace*. St. Louis: Forum Press.

———. 1989. Some International Implications of the 1918 Roosevelt-Lodge Campaign against Wilson and a Democratic Congress. *Presidential Studies Quarterly* 19:141–57.

Patterson, James T. 1996. *Grand Expectations: The United States, 1945–1974*. New York: Oxford University Press.

Pedlow, Gregory W. 1993. The Politics of NATO Command, 1950–1962. In *U.S. Military Forces in Europe: The Early Years, 1945–1970*, edited by Simon W. Duke and Wolfgang Krieger. Boulder, CO: Westview Press.

Perkins, Bradford. 1993. *The Creation of a Republican Empire, 1776–1865*. Volume 1 in *The Cambridge History of American Foreign Relations*. New York: Cambridge University Press.

Pimlott, John. 1992. The Gulf Crisis and World Politics. In *The Gulf War Assessed*, edited by John Pimlott and Stephen Badsey. London: Arms and Armour Press.

Pine, Art. 1992. U.S. Insists on Control of Its Troops. *Los Angeles Times*, December 25: A10 and 12.

Porat, Meir. 1994. Israel and the New World Order. In *The Gulf War and the New World Order: International Relations of the Middle East*, edited by Tareq Y. Ismael and Jacqueline S. Ismael. Gainesville: University Press of Florida.

Posen, Barry R. 1984. *The Sources of Military Doctrine: France, Britain, and Germany between the World Wars*. Ithaca: Cornell University Press.

Posen, Barry R., and Andrew L. Ross. 1996–97. Competing Visions for U.S. Grand Strategy. *International Security* 21, 3:5–53.

Powell, Robert. 1990. *Nuclear Deterrence Theory: The Search for Credibility*. New York: Cambridge University Press.

———. forthcoming. *In the Shadow of Power: States and Strategies in International Politics*. Princeton: Princeton University Press.

Prunier, Gerard. 1997. The Experience of European Armies in Operation Restore

Hope. In *Learning from Somalia: The Lessons of Armed Humanitarian Intervention*, edited by Walter Clarke and Jeffrey Herbst. Boulder, CO: Westview Press.

Quester, George H. 1966. *Deterrence before Hiroshima: The Airpower Background of Modern Strategy*. New York: John Wiley & Sons.

——. 1977. *Offense and Defense in the International System*. New York: John Wiley & Sons.

Rasmussen, Eric. 1989. *Games and Information: An Introduction to Game Theory*. Cambridge, MA: Basil Blackwell.

Record, Jeffrey. 1993. *Hollow Victory: A Contrary View of the Gulf War*. Washington, D.C.: Brassey's (US).

Ripley, Randall B., and James M. Lindsay, eds. 1993. *Congress Resurgent: Foreign and Defense Policy on Capitol Hill*. Ann Arbor: University of Michigan Press.

Risse-Kappen, Thomas, ed. 1995. *Bringing Transnational Relations Back In: Non-State Actors, Domestic Structures, and International Institutions*. New York: Cambridge University Press.

Roeder, Philip G. 1993. *Red Sunset: The Failure of Soviet Politics*. Princeton: Princeton University Press.

——. 1997. From Hierarchy to Hegemony: Patterns of Security among the Soviet Successor States. In *Regional Orders: Building Security in a New World*, edited by David A. Lake and Patrick M. Morgan. University Park: Pennsylvania State University Press.

Rosenau, James N. 1992. Governance, Order, and Change in World Politics. In *Governance without Government: Order and Change in World Politics*, edited by James N. Rosenau and Ernst-Otto Czempiel. New York: Cambridge University Press.

Rosenau, James N., and Ernst-Otto Czempiel. 1992. *Governance without Government: Order and Change in World Politics*. New York: Cambridge University Press.

Rosner, Jeremy D. 1995/96. The Know-Nothings Know Something. *Foreign Policy* 101:116–29.

Ruggie, John Gerard. 1983. Continuity and Transformation in the World Polity: Toward a Neorealist Synthesis. *World Politics* 35:261–85.

——, ed. 1993. *Multilateralism Matters: The Theory and Praxis of an Institutional Form*. New York: Columbia University Press.

——. 1996. *Winning the Peace: America and World Order in the New Era*. New York: Columbia University Press.

Russett, Bruce. 1985. "The Mysterious Case of Vanishing Hegemony: Or Is Mark Twain Really Dead?" *International Organization* 39:207–31.

Russett, Bruce, and James S. Sutterlin. 1991. The U.N. in a New World Order. *Foreign Affairs* 70, 2:69–83.

Sahnoun, Mohamed. 1994. *Somalia: The Missed Opportunities*. Washington, D.C.: United States Institute of Peace Press.

Salmon, Trevor C. 1992. Testing Times for European Political Cooperation: The Gulf and Yugoslavia, 1990–1992. *International Affairs* 68:233–53.

Sayari, Sabri. 1997. Between Allies and Neighbors: Turkey's Burden Sharing Policy in the Gulf Conflict. In *Friends in Need: Burden Sharing in the Persian Gulf War*, edited by Andrew Bennett, Joseph Lepgold, and Danny Unger. New York: St. Martin's Press.

Schaller, Michael. 1985. *The American Occupation of Japan: The Origins of the Cold War in Asia*. New York: Oxford University Press.

Schroeder, Paul W. 1976. Alliances, 1815–1945: Weapons of Power and Tools of Management. In *Historical Dimensions of National Security Problems*, edited by Klaus Knorr. Lawrence: University Press of Kansas.

———. 1994. The New World Order: A Historical Perspective. ACDIS (Program in Arms Control, Disarmament, and International Security) Occasional Paper, University of Illinois at Urbana-Champaign.

Schuker, Stephen A. 1976. *The End of French Predominance in Europe: The Financial Crises of 1924 and the Adoption of the Dawes Plan*. Chapel Hill: University of North Carolina Press.

Schulte Nordholt, Jan Willem. 1991. *Woodrow Wilson: A Life for World Peace*. Berkeley and Los Angeles: University of California Press.

Schwartz, Thomas. 1987. Votes, Strategies, and Institutions: An Introduction to the Theory of Collective Choice. In *Congress: Structure and Policy*, edited by Mathew D. McCubbins and Terry Sullivan. New York: Cambridge University Press.

Searle, John. 1995. *The Construction of Social Reality*. New York: Free Press.

Shelanski, Howard A., and Peter G. Klein. 1995. Empirical Research in Transactions Costs Economics: A Review and Assessment. *Journal of Law, Economics, and Organization* 11:335–61.

Shirk, Susan L. 1993. *The Political Logic of Economic Reform in China*. Berkeley and Los Angeles: University of California Press.

Silverman. Dan P. 1982. *Reconstructing Europe after the Great War*. Cambridge: Harvard University Press.

Simmons, Beth A. 1994. *Who Adjusts? Domestic Sources of Foreign Economic Policy during the Interwar Years*. Princeton: Princeton University Press.

Singer, J. David, and Melvin Small. n.d. *Annual Alliance Membership Data, 1815–1965* (computer file). Ann Arbor, MI: Inter-university Consortium for Political and Social Research, distributor.

———. 1993. *National Material Capabilities Data, 1816–1985* (computer file). Ann Arbor, MI: Inter-university Consortium for Political and Social Research, distributor.

Siverson, Randolph M., and Juliann Emmons. 1991. Birds of a Feather: Democratic Political Systems and Alliance Choices in the Twentieth Century. *Journal of Conflict Resolution* 35:285–306.

Siverson, Randolph M., and Harvey Starr. 1991. *The Diffusion of War: A Study of Opportunity and Willingness*. Ann Arbor: University of Michigan Press.

Smelser, Neil J., and Richard Swedberg, eds. 1994. *The Handbook of Economic Sociology*. Princeton: Princeton University Press.

Smith, Denis Mack. 1989. *Italy and Its Monarchy*. New Haven: Yale University Press.

Smith, Jean Edward, ed. 1974. *The Papers of General Lucius D. Clay, Germany 1945–1949*. 2 vols. Bloomington: Indiana University Press.

———. 1992. *George Bush's War*. New York: Henry Holt and Co.

Smith, Robert Aura. 1958. *Philippine Freedom, 1946–1958*. New York: Columbia University Press.

Smith, Tony. 1981. *The Pattern of Imperialism: The United States, Great Britain, and the Late-Industrializing World since 1815*. New York: Cambridge University Press.

Snidal, Duncan. 1985. The Limits of Hegemonic Stability Theory. *International Organization* 39:579–614.

Snyder, Glenn H. 1984. The Security Dilemma in Alliance Politics. *World Politics* 36:461–95.

———. 1990. Alliance Theory: A Neorealist First Cut. *Journal of International Affairs* 44:103–22.

Snyder, Jack L. 1984. *The Ideology of the Offensive: Military Decision Making and the Disasters of 1914.* Ithaca: Cornell University Press.

———. 1991. *Myths of Empire: Domestic Politics and International Ambition.* Ithaca: Cornell University Press.

Springborg, Robert. 1994. The United Nations in the Gulf War. In *The Gulf War and the New World Order: International Relations of the Middle East,* edited by Tareq Y. Ismael and Jacqueline S. Ismael. Gainesville: University Press of Florida.

Spruyt, Hendrik. 1994. *The Sovereign State and its Competitors: An Analysis of Systems Change.* Princeton: Princeton University Press.

Stares, Paul B. 1990. *Allied Rights and Legal Constraints on German Military Power.* Washington, D.C.: Brookings Institution.

Stein, Arthur A. 1983. Coordination and Collaboration: Regimes in an Anarchic World. In *International Regimes,* edited by Stephen D. Krasner. Ithaca: Cornell University Press.

———. 1990. *Why Nations Cooperate: Circumstance and Choice in International Relations.* Ithaca: Cornell University Press.

———. 1993. Domestic Constraints, Extended Deterrence, and the Incoherence of Grand Strategy: The United States, 1938–1950. In *The Domestic Bases of Grand Strategy,* edited by Richard Rosecrance and Arthur A. Stein. Ithaca: Cornell University Press.

Steinbruner, John. 1974. *The Cybernetic Theory of Decision: New Dimensions of Political Analysis.* Princeton: Princeton University Press.

Stevenson, Jonathan. 1993. Hope Restored in Somalia? *Foreign Policy* 91:138–54.

Stigler, George J. 1970. The Optimum Enforcement of Laws. *Journal of Political Economy* 78:526–36.

Stone, Randall W. 1996. *Satellites and Commissars: Strategy and Conflict in the Politics of Soviet-Bloc Trade.* Princeton: Princeton University Press.

Strang, David. 1991. Anomaly and Commonplace in European Political Expansion: Realist and Institutionalist Accounts. *International Organization* 45:143–62.

Strange, Susan. 1987. The Persistent Myth of Lost Hegemony. *International Organization* 41:51–74.

Stromberg, Roland N. 1963. *Collective Security and American Foreign Policy: From the League of Nations to NATO.* New York: Frederick A. Praeger.

Stromseth, Jane E. 1988. *The Origins of Flexible Response: NATO's Debate over Strategy in the 1960s.* New York: St. Martin's.

Stromseth, Jonathan. 1989. Unequal Allies: Negotiations over U.S. Bases in the Philippines. *Journal of International Affairs* 43:161–88.

Swedberg, Richard, ed. 1993. *Explorations in Economic Sociology.* New York: Russell Sage Foundation.

Taylor, William J., and James Blackwell. 1991. The Ground War in the Gulf. *Survival* 33:230–45.

Telhami, Shibley. 1993. Arab Public Opinion and the Gulf War. In *The Political Psychology of the Gulf War: Leaders, Publics, and the Process of Conflict*, edited by Stanley A. Renshon. Pittsburgh: University of Pittsburgh Press.

Terasawa, Katsuaki L., and William R. Gates. 1993. Burden-Sharing in the Persian Gulf: Lessons Learned and Implications for the Future. *Defense Analysis* 9:171–95.

Tetlock, Philip E., and Aaron Belkin. 1996. *Counterfactual Thought Experiments in World Politics: Logical, Methodological, and Psychological Perspectives*. Princeton: Princeton University Press.

Thompson, Julian. 1993. The Military Coalition. In *Iraq, the Gulf Conflict and the World Community*, edited by James Gow. New York: Brassey's (UK).

Ticktin, H. H. 1991. The Political Economy of Soviet-U.S. Relations over the Invasion of Kuwait in the Period August 1990 to March 1991. In *The Gulf War and the New World Order*, edited by Haim Bresheeth and Nira Yuval-Davis. London: Zed Books.

Till, Geoffrey. 1996. Adopting the Aircraft Carrier: The British, American, and Japanese Case Studies. In *Military Innovation in the Interwar Period*, edited by Williamson Murray and Allan R. Millett. New York: Cambridge University Press.

Tilly, Charles. 1985. War Making and State Making as Organized Crime. In *Bringing the State Back In*, edited by Peter B. Evans, Dietrich Rueschemeyer, and Theda Skocpol. New York: Cambridge University Press.

———. 1990. *Coercion, Capital, and European States, AD 990–1990*. Cambridge, MA: Basil Blackwell.

Towell, Pat. 1992. Suffering Spurs Unprecedented Step as U.N. Approves Deployment. *Congressional Quarterly* December 5:3,759–63.

Treverton, Gregory F. 1978. *The Dollar Drain and American Forces in Germany: Managing the Political Economics of Alliance*. Athens: Ohio University Press.

———. 1985. *Making the Alliance Work: The United States and Western Europe*. Ithaca: Cornell University Press.

Triska, Jan F., ed. 1986. *Dominant Powers and Subordinate States: The United States in Latin American and the Soviet Union in Eastern Europe*. Durham: Duke University Press.

Trubowitz, Peter. 1998. *Defining the National Interest: Conflict and Change in American Foreign Policy*. Chicago: University of Chicago Press.

Tucker, Robert W., and David C. Hendrickson. 1990. *Empire of Liberty: The Statecraft of Thomas Jefferson*. New York: Oxford University Press.

———. 1992. *The Imperial Temptation: The New World Order and America's Purpose*. New York: Council on Foreign Relations Press.

Ulam, Adam B. 1974. *Expansion and Coexistence: Soviet Foreign Policy, 1917–1973*. 2d ed. New York: Praeger.

Unger, Danny. 1997. Japan and the Gulf War: Making the World Safe for Japan-U.S. Relations. In *Friends in Need: Burden Sharing in the Persian Gulf War*, edited by Andrew Bennett, Joseph Lepgold, and Danny Unger. New York: St. Martin's.

United Nations. 1996. *The United Nations and Somalia, 1992–1996* (Blue Book Series, volume 8). New York: United Nations.

U.S. Arms Control and Disarmament Agency. 1975. *World Military Expenditures and Arms Trade, 1963–1973*. Washington, D.C.: GPO.

U.S. Congress. Senate. Committee on Armed Services. 1991. *Hearings on Operation Desert Shield/Storm*. 102nd Cong., 1st sess.

———. 1993a. *Hearings on Current Military Operations in Somalia*. 103rd Cong., 1st sess.

———. 1993b. *Hearings on Current Military Operations*. 103rd Cong., 1st sess.

U. S. Congress. Senate. Committee on Foreign Relations. 1961. *Documents on Germany, 1944–1961*. 87th Cong., 1st sess.

U.S. Department of Commerce. 1975. *Historical Statistics of the United States, Colonial Times to 1970*, Parts 1 and 2. Washington, D.C.: GPO.

U.S. Department of Defense. 1992. *Conduct of the Persian Gulf War: Final Report to Congress*, Appendices A-S. Washington, D.C.: GPO.

U.S. Department of State. 1952. Security Treaty between the United States of America and Japan, Signed September 8, 1951, Proclaimed April 28, 1952 (Document 2,491, pages 3,329–40). In *United States Treaties and Other International Agreements*, vol. 3. Washington, D.C.: GPO.

U.S. General Accounting Office. 1991. *Persian Gulf: Allied Burden Sharing Efforts*. GAO/NSIAD-92–71.

———. 1992. *Operation Desert Shield/Storm: Foreign Government and Individual Contributions to the Department of Defense*. GAO/NSIAD-92–144.

US News and World Report. 1992. *Triumph Without Victory: The Unreported History of the Persian Gulf War*. New York: Times Books.

Van Creveld, Martin. 1989. *Technology and War: From 2000 B.C. to the Present*. New York: Free Press.

Van Evera, Stephen. 1984. Cult of the Offensive and the Origins of the First World War. *International Security* 9:58–107.

———. 1986. Why Cooperation Failed in 1914. In *Cooperation under Anarchy*, edited by Kenneth A. Oye. Princeton: Princeton University Press.

———. 1990. Why Europe Matters, Why the Third World Doesn't: American Grand Strategy after the Cold War. *Journal of Strategic Studies* 13, 2:1–51.

Vernon, Raymond. 1971. *Sovereignty at Bay: The Multinational Spread of U.S. Enterprises*. New York: Basic Books.

Von Vorys, Karl. 1997. *American Foreign Policy: Consensus at Home, Leadership Abroad*. Westport, CT: Praeger.

Wall, Irwin M. 1991. *The United States and the Making of Postwar France, 1945–1954*. New York: Cambridge University Press.

Wallander, Celeste A., and Robert O. Keohane. 1995. An Institutional Approach to Alliance Theory (Working Paper 95–2). Cambridge: Center for International Affairs, Harvard University.

Walt, Stephen M. 1987. *The Origins of Alliances*. Ithaca: Cornell University Press.

———. 1991. The Renaissance of Security Studies. *International Studies Quarterly* 35:211–39.

Waltz, Kenneth N. 1959. *Man, the State, and War: A Theoretical Analysis*. New York: Columbia University Press.

———. 1967. *Foreign Policy and Domestic Politics: The American and British Experience*. Berkeley: Institute of Governmental Studies Press, University of California.

———. 1979. *Theory of International Politics*. Reading, MA: Addison-Wesley.

———. 1986. Reflections on Theory of International Politics: A Response to My Critics. In *Neorealism and Its Critics*, edited by Robert O. Keohane. New York: Columbia University Press.

———. 1993. The Emerging Structure of International Politics. *International Security* 18, 2:44–79.

Watts, Barry, and Williamson Murray. 1996. Military Innovation in Peacetime. In *Military Innovation in the Interwar Period*, edited by Williamson Murray and Allan R. Millett. New York: Cambridge University Press.

Weber, Katja. 1997a. Hierarchy amidst Anarchy: A Transaction Costs Approach to International Security Cooperation. *International Studies Quarterly* 41:321–40.

———. 1997b. Transaction Costs Revisited: Delving into Relative Causal Weights. Paper presented to the annual meeting of the American Political Science Association, Washington, D.C.

Weber, Steve. 1991. *Multilateralism in NATO: Shaping the Postwar Balance of Power, 1945–1961*. Research Series Number 79, University of California, Berkeley. International and Area Studies.

Weingast, Barry R., and William J. Marshall. 1988. The Industrial Organization of Congress: Or, Why Legislatures, Like Firms, are Not Organized as Markets. *Journal of Political Economy* 96:132–63.

Weinstein, Edwin A. 1981. *Woodrow Wilson: A Medical and Psychological Biography*. Princeton: Princeton University Press.

Wells, S. F., Jr. 1985. The First Cold War Buildup: Europe in United States Strategy and Policy, 1950–1953. In *Western Security: The Formative Years: European and Atlantic Defense, 1947–1953*, edited by Olav Riste. New York: Columbia University Press.

Wendt, Alex. 1987. The Agent-Structure Problem in International Relations Theory. *International Organization* 41:335–70.

———. 1992. Anarchy Is What States Make of It: The Social Construction of Power Politics. *International Organization* 46:391–425.

White, Donald W. 1996. *The American Century: The Rise and Decline of the United States as a World Power*. New Haven: Yale University Press.

Whyte, Arthur James. 1965. *The Evolution of Modern Italy*. New York: W.W. Norton.

Widenor, William C. 1980. *Henry Cabot Lodge and the Search for an American Foreign Policy*. Berkeley and Los Angeles: University of California Press.

Wiebes, Cees, and Bert Zeeman. 1983. The Pentagon Negotiations March 1948: The Launching of the North Atlantic Treaty. *International Affairs* 59:351–63.

Williams, Phil. 1985. *The Senate and US Troops in Europe*. London: Macmillan.

Williams, William Appleman. 1972. *The Tragedy of American Diplomacy*. 2nd and enlarged ed. New York: Dell.

Williamson, Oliver. 1975. *Markets and Hierarchies: Analysis and Antitrust Implications*. New York: Free Press.

———. 1985. *The Economic Institutions of Capitalism: Firms, Markets, and Relational Contracting*. New York: Free Press.

———, ed. 1990. *Organization Theory: From Chester Barnard to the Present and Beyond*. New York: Oxford University Press.

———. 1991. Strategizing, Economizing, and Economic Organization. *Strategic Management Journal* 23:75–94.

———. 1994. Transaction Cost Economics and Organization Theory. In *The Handbook of Economic Sociology*, edited by Neil J. Smelser and Richard Swedberg. Princeton: Princeton University Press.

Willoughby, W. W., and C. G. Fenwick. 1974 [1919]. *The Inquiry Handbooks*, vol. 16. Reprint, Wilmington, DE. Originally published as *Types of Restricted Sovereignty and of Colonial Autonomy*. Washington, D.C.: GPO.

Wilson, Joan Hoff. 1971. *American Business and Foreign Policy, 1920–1933*. Boston: Beacon.

Wittman, Donald. 1991. Nations and States: Mergers and Acquisitions; Dissolutions and Divorce. *American Economic Review* (Papers and Proceedings) 81:126–29.

Wolfers, Arnold. 1952. National Security as an Ambiguous Symbol. *Political Science Quarterly* 67:481–502.

Woods, James L. 1997. U.S. Government Decisionmaking Processes during Humanitarian Operations in Somalia. In *Learning from Somalia: The Lessons of Armed Humanitarian Intervention*, edited by Walter Clarke and Jeffrey Herbst. Boulder, CO: Westview.

Woodward, Bob. 1991. *The Commanders*. New York: Simon and Schuster.

Yant, Martin. 1991. *Desert Mirage: The True Story of the Gulf War*. Buffalo, NY: Prometheus Books.

Yarbrough, Beth V., and Robert M. Yarbrough. 1992. *Cooperation and Governance in International Trade: The Strategic Organizational Approach*. Princeton: Princeton University Press.

———. 1994. International Contracting and Territorial Control: The Boundary Question. *Journal of International and Theoretical Economics* 150:239–64.

Yates, Mark B. 1993. Coalition Warfare in Desert Storm. *Military Review* 73, 10:46–52.

Yetiv, Steve A. 1992. The Outcomes of Operations Desert Shield and Desert Storm: Some Antecedent Causes. *Political Science Quarterly* 107:195–212.

Young, Oran R. 1994. *International Governance: Protecting the Environment in a Stateless Society*. Ithaca: Cornell University Press.

Zink, Harold. 1957. *The United States in Germany, 1944–1955*. Princeton: D. Van Nostrand.